Financial Reporting Quality in Emerging Economies

MÜNSTERANER SCHRIFTEN ZUR INTERNATIONALEN UNTERNEHMENSRECHNUNG

Herausgegeben von Peter Kajüter

Band 14

Zu Qualitätssicherung und Peer Review der vorliegenden Publikation

Die Qualität der in dieser Reihe erscheinenden Arbeiten wird vor der Publikation durch den Herausgeber der Reihe geprüft.

Notes on the quality assurance and peer review of this publication

Prior to publication, the quality of the work published in this series is reviewed by the editor of the series.

Gregor Hagemann

Financial Reporting Quality in Emerging Economies

Empirical Evidence from Brazil and South Africa

PL ACADEMIC RESEARCH

Bibliographic Information published by the Deutsche Nationalbibliothek
The Deutsche Nationalbibliothek lists this publication in the Deutsche Nationalbibliografie; detailed bibliographic data is available in the internet at http://dnb.d-nb.de.

Zugl.: Münster (Westfalen), Univ., Diss., 2016

D 6
ISSN 1868-7687
ISBN 978-3-631-71543-7 (Print)
E-ISBN 978-3-631-71544-4 (E-PDF)
E-ISBN 978-3-631-71545-1 (EPUB)
E-ISBN 978-3-631-71546-8 (MOBI)
DOI 10.3726/b10689

PL Academic Research is an Imprint of Peter Lang GmbH.

Peter Lang – Frankfurt am Main · Bern · Bruxelles · New York · Oxford · Warszawa · Wien

This publication has been peer reviewed.

www.peterlang.com

Preface

Over the past years, emerging economies such as the BRICS countries have gained increasing attention by international investors and financial analysts due to their rapid economic growth and considerable market potential. However, the information environment in emerging economies is traditionally low which makes investment decisions in these countries particularly challenging. To improve corporate reporting practices, many emerging economies have implemented changes in their financial reporting regulation, in particular by adopting International Financial Reporting Standards (IFRS).

Compared to the vast amount of research about corporate reporting practices in developed countries, there is much less evidence in this respect about emerging economies. In particular, there is hardly any empirical research on the differences in corporate financial reporting quality between industrialized countries and emerging economies. Typically, companies in emerging economies face specific characteristics due to, for instance, the country's culture, historical development, accounting regulation, education system and capital market system.

In this study, Gregor Hagemann conducts a comprehensive empirical investigation to analyze the financial reporting practices of listed companies in the two emerging economies Brazil and South Africa. For this purpose, he measures the financial reporting quality of the sample companies and determines factors influencing the observed quality of financial reporting. Furthermore, capital market consequences of financial reporting are explored by examining whether companies providing a higher financial reporting quality benefit from reduced information asymmetries. The results for the companies from Brazil and South Africa are contrasted to those for a sample of companies from Germany representing an industrialized economy.

Financial reporting quality is an abstract construct and the existing literature lacks a uniform definition. Following a multidimensional understanding, Gregor Hagemann captures multiple facets of financial reporting quality by considering not only the content, but also the readability of the entities' annual reports as well as earnings management indicators. The operationalization of these dimensions of financial reporting quality for each sample company provides interesting results regarding the companies' reporting policies and identifies significant differences between the emerging economies (Brazil and South Africa) and the developed economy (Germany).

The findings further provide remarkable insights of differing determinants of financial reporting quality across the investigated countries, e.g. the role of company size, ownership concentration and analyst following. In the capital market study, Gregor Hagemann provides empirical evidence that an increased quality of financial reporting is significantly associated with lower information asymmetries for companies from Brazil, South Africa and Germany.

The findings of this study are useful for academics in conducting further research. In addition, the empirical results have several implications for practitioners. Preparers of corporate reports are able to take the descriptive results and the analysis of potential capital market consequences into account and reconsider their existing reporting policy to meet the information needs of important stakeholders. Furthermore, the results reveal determinants of financial reporting quality and, thereby, help users of corporate reports – particularly investors and financial analysts – to interpret and evaluate the provided information. Governmental authorities, regulators and standard setters in emerging economies can consider the findings for the further development of the financial reporting regulation in their jurisdiction.

With its comprehensive empirical investigation, this study sheds light on the practice, determinants and capital market consequences of the financial reporting quality of companies from the emerging economies Brazil and South Africa as well as from Germany. Thereby, the study provides a valuable contribution to the existing literature. Considering the increasing importance of emerging economies in the global economy, I am convinced that this thesis will be interesting and helpful to a large number of readers from both academia and practice.

Münster, August 2016 Prof. Dr. Peter Kajüter

Acknowledgement

I conducted this study during my time as a PhD-student and research assistant at the Chair of International Accounting at the University of Münster. The Münster School of Business and Economics accepted the thesis as a dissertation in May 2016.

In the following, I would like to thank everyone who supported me during the three years of this dissertation project as well as everyone who made my time in Münster unforgettable. First, I sincerely thank my academic teacher and supervisor Prof. Dr. Peter Kajüter who enabled me to write my dissertation in the field of financial reporting in an emerging economy setting and provided me with great support throughout the entire working process. His valuable guidance and professional feedback at different stages of the research project have greatly contributed to the success of this work. His considerable engagement in regular doctoral seminars helped me to make continuous progress of the study. I also seize the opportunity to warmly thank Prof. Dr. Dr. h.c. Jörg Baetge, who reviewed my thesis as a second referee as well as Prof. Dr. Ulrich van Suntum for being the third referee at my disputation.

Moreover, my colleagues, fellow PhD students and dear friends at the Chair of International Accounting made my time so unique and enjoyable. The last years with them are rich in unforgettable moments, such as our Ijsselmeer sailing cruises, WiWi-Cup soccer competitions, unexpected office parties, doctoral graduation celebrations and animated nightlife in Münster, Amsterdam and Cologne. In particular, I thank Dr. Martin Nienhaus and Florian Klassmann who selflessly provided me with great support in statistical questions at any time. I will miss the epic soccer matches and subsequent soccer-related disussions with Alex Schulz, Stefan Hannen and the most relaxed roommate Friedrich Kalden. I further dedicate special thanks to Stephanie Eckerth and Marcel Baki who are not only great friends you can talk to even during tough nights in the office, but also supported me during the final stages of my study through both moral assistance and proofreading of my thesis. I further want to thank Daniela Peters whose social attitude and engagement considerably contributed to the extraordinary collegial atmosphere at the Chair. I will also miss my "newer" colleagues Tobias Langehaneberg, Martin Vogelpohl, Matthias Nienaber, Max Meinhövel, Henrik Schirmacher and Kai Schaumann who were great and clever team players with a fantastic sense of humor.

With great joy, I further remember the "old times" I had spent with my former colleagues Julius Hannemann, Dr. Christina Voets, Dr. Daniel Blaesing, Dr. Thomas Blades, Dr. Moritz Schröder and Dr. Maximilian Saucke. They warmly welcomed me and introduced me to the challenges as a research assistant and PhD student. Daniel already supported me as a Bachelor student and eased my start at the Chair. Thomas was the perfect training partner for jogging, indoor cycling as well as pleasant evening swims in the Canal. I will never forget the great moments I spent with Max at various occasions including a number of tennis and soccer matches which we played, watched or analyzed.

I further would like to thank the student assistants Christian Sandmann, Nikolas Haas and Manuel Herkenhoff for their extraordinary commitment to support my research project.

Furthermore, I am thankful for my friends Christoph Picker and Dennis Haking whom I could always count on during the last years. I dedicate special thanks to Pascal Dillenseger who is the greatest friend you can wish for. Being a PhD student of Physics himself, he had great understanding for my situation and, thus, was able to support me in many ways.

I further would like to mention my former Indian colleagues and friends Mangesh Hirve and Akhil Arora, who boosted my interest and passion for both India in particular as well as emerging economies in general. Therefore, our time together in Pune somehow paved the way towards the decision for the topic of this thesis. I also would like to thank Professor Frederick Lindahl (George Washington University) who encouraged me to consider the field of international accounting as interesting focus for my future studies during a semester abroad in Turku, Finland. Thereby, he helped me to find the right track for my academic education.

After all, I have been able to finish my doctorate studies successfully due to the support of my family. Foremost, I cannot thank my wife Monika enough for all she has done for me over the past years. She strengthened my ambition to enter the PhD program in Münster being aware of the fact that this would also affect our relationship. She was always interested in my research and, with her unlimited joy and positive energy, she helped me to master any challenges. There are no words to express the way that I feel about you. My brother Gernot has not only been a wonderful brother to me, but is simultaneously an incredible friend of mine ever since I can think. I also thank my parents-in-law Erich and Emilie as well as my brothers-in-law Martin, Thomas and Andreas who lovingly welcomed me with open arms to their family.

My academic education culminating in the doctorate has only been possible through the loving and selfless support of my mother Regina and my father Werner who have encouraged me to pursue all my personal ambitions and have always been on my side, regardless whether I am in Frankfurt, Münster, Turku or Pune. I am deeply grateful for everything that they have done for me throughout my entire life. To them, my parents, I dedicate this thesis.

Münster, August 2016 Gregor Hagemann

Contents overview

Contents

Index of figures

Index of tables

Tables in Appendix

Index of abbreviations

ADHGB	Allgemeine Deutsche Handelsgesetzbuch (General German Commercial Code)
Adj.	Adjusted
ADR	American Depositary Receipt
AFAANZ	Accounting and Finance Association of Australia and New Zealand
AG	Aktiengesellschaft
AICPA	American Institute of Certified Public Accountants
AIM	*Amihud* Illiquidity Measure
AIMR	Association for Investment Management and Research
AktG	Aktiengesetz (German Stock Corporation Act)
ANOVA	Analysis of Variance
APB	South African Accounting Practices Board
ARC	Annual Report Competition
ASEAN	Association of Southeast Asian Nations
ASL	Average Sentence Length
ASW	Average Number of Syllables per Word
BaFin	Bundesanstalt für Finanzdienstleistungsaufsicht (German Financial Supervisory Authority)
BAR	Best Annual Report
BAS	Bid-Ask Spreads
B2B	Business-to-business
B-BBEE	Broad-Based Black Economic Empowerment
B2C	Business-to-customer
BFuP	Betriebswirtschaftliche Forschung und Praxis (Journal)
BM&F	Brazilian Mercantile & Futures Exchange
BM&FBOVESPA	Brazilian Securities, Commodities and Futures Exchange (Bolsa de Valores, Mercadorias & Futuros de São Paulo)
BRA	Brazil
BRIC	Brazil, Russia, India and China
BRICK	Brazil, Russia, India and South Korea
BRICS	Brazil, Russia, India, China and South Africa
BRL	Brazilian Real
CAPM	Capital Asset Pricing Model
CEO	Chief Executing Officer
CFaR	Cash Flow at Risk
Cf.	Confer
CFC	Brazilian Federal Council of Accounting
CFO	Chief Financial Officer
CFO	Cash Flow from Operations
CHN	China

CICR	Corporate Information Committee Report
CIFAR	Center of International Financial Analysis and Research
CIVETS	Colombia, Indonesia, Vietnam, Egypt, Turkey and South Africa
Cov	Covariance
CPA	Certified Public Accountant
CPC	Comitê de Pronunciamentos Contábeis (Brazilian Accounting Pronouncements Committee)
CSP	Corporate Social Responsibility
CVM	Comissão de Valores Mobiliários (Brazilian Securities and Exchange Commission)
Dax	Deutscher Aktienindex
DBW	Die Betriebswirtschaft (Journal)
DCGK	Deutscher Corporate Governance Kodex (German Corporate Governance Code)
DISC	Disclosure Measure by *Hail*
DRS	Deutsches Rechnungslegungs Standard
DSCORE	Disclosure Measure by *Botosan*
DVA	Statement of added value
EBEN	European Business Ethics Network
EBIT	Earnings Before Interest and Taxes
EBITDA	Earnings Before Interest, Taxes, Depreciation and Amortization
EBT	Earnings Before Taxes
EBXI	Earnings Before Extraordinary Items and Discontinued Operations
EC	European Commission
Ed(s).	Editor(s)
EE	Emerging Economy
EEC	European Economic Community
EFTA	European Free Trade Association
E.g.	Exempli gratia
EPS	Earnings per Share
Et al.	Et alii
Etc.	Et cetera
EU	European Union
EVA	Economic Value Added
EY	Ernst & Young
F	*IASB* Conceptual Framework
F-10	Frontier Strategy Group Top Ten Emerging Markets
FAF	Financial Analyst Federation
FASB	Financial Accounting Standards Board

FCW	Fraction of Complex Words
Fog	Gunning Fog Index
FRE	Flesch Reading Ease Index
FREP	German Financial Reporting Enforcement Panel
FRQ	Financial Reporting Quality
FS	Financial Statements
FTC	Federal Trade Commission
FTSE	Financial Times Stock Exchange
FWB	Frankfurter Wertpapier Börse (Frankfurt Stock Exchange)
FY	Financial Year
G5	Group of Five
G20	Group of Twenty
GAAP	Generally Accepted Accounting Principles
GAS	German Accounting Standards
GDP	Gross Domestic Product
GER	Germany
GNI	Gross National Income
GoB	Grundsätze ordnungsmäßiger Buchführung (Generally accepted principles on proper bookkeeping)
GRI	Global Reporting Initiative
HGB	Handelsgesetzbuch (German Commercial Code)
HR	Human Resources
http	Hypertext Transfer Protocol
IAS	International Accounting Standard(s)
IASB	International Accounting Standards Board
IASC	International Accounting Standards Committee
IBE	Institute of Business Ethics
IBER	International Business & Economics Research Journal
I/B/E/S	Institutional Brokers' Estimate System
IBM	International Business Machines Corporation
Ibovespa	Índice Bovespa
IBrX	Brazil 100 Index
IBSA	India, Brazil, South Africa
ICGSM	International Conference on Governance & Strategic Management
IDV	Individualism versus Collectivism
I.e.	Id est
IFC	International Finance Corporation
IFRIC	International Financial Reporting Interpretations Committee
IFRS	International Financial Reporting Standard(s)
IIRC	International Integrated Reporting Council

IMF	International Monetary Fund
IN	Introduction
IND	India
Intl.	International
IPO	Initial Public Offering
<IR>	Integrated Reporting
IRZ	Zeitschrift für Internationale Rechnungslegung (Journal)
IVR	Indulgence versus Restraint
JBER	Journal of Business & Economics Research (Journal)
JSE	Johannesburg Stock Exchange
King III	King Code of Governance for South Africa
KPI	Key Performance Indicator
KPMG	Klynfeld, Peat, Marwick, Goerdeler
LR	Listings Requirements
Ltd.	Limited
LTO	Long-Term Orientation versus Short-Term Orientation
M&A	Mergers & Acquisitions
MACCR	Magnitude of Accruals Proxy
MAS	Masculinity versus Femininity
Max	Maximum
MD&A	Management's Discussion and Analysis
MDax	Mid-Cap-DAX
Mgmt.	Management
Min	Minimum
MIST	Mexico, Indonesia, South Korea and Turkey
MIT	Massachusetts Institute of Technology
MSCI	Morgan Stanley Capital International
N-11	Next eleven
NAICS	North American Industry Classification System
NiCE	Nijmegen Center for Economics
No.	Number
NYSE	New York Stock Exchange
OB	Objective
OCI	Other Comprehensive Income
OECD	Organization for Economic Cooperation and Development
OLS	Ordinary Least Squares
OPEC	Organization of the Petroleum Exporting Countries
OTC	Over the Counter

P.	Page(s)
PASW	Predictive Analytics SoftWare
Pctl.	Percentile
PDF	Portable Document Format
PDI	Power Distance
PiR	Internationale Rechnungslegung (Journal)
P&L	Profit and Loss
PPE	Property, Plant and Equipment
PPICS	Peru, Philippines, Indonesia, Colombia and Sri Lanka
PPP	Purchasing Power Parity
PSM	Propensity Score Matching
PwC	PricewaterhouseCoopers
Q	Quarter
QC	Qualitative Characteristics
R&D	Research and Development
REV	Revenues
ROA	Return on Assets
ROE	Return on Equity
ROSC	Report on the Observance of Standards and Codes
RQ	Research Question
RUS	Russia
RSA	Republic of South Africa
SA	South Africa
SAS	Statement of Auditing Standards
SDax	Small-Cap-DAX
SEC	Securities and Exchange Commission
SIC	Standard Industrial Classification
SME	Small and Medium-Sized Enterprise
S&P	Standard & Poor's
SPSS	Statistical Package for the Social Sciences
SRI	Stanford Research Institute
SSRN	Social Science Research Network
Std. Dev.	Standard deviation
TACCR	Total Accruals
TecDax	Deutscher Technologieindex
TIMP	Turkey, Indonesia, Mexico and Philippines
UAI	Uncertainty Avoidance
UK	United Kingdom
UN	United Nations
U.S.	United States

USA	United States of America
VaR	Value at Risk
Var	Variance
VIF	Variance Inflation Factor
VRZ	Value Reporting by the University of Zurich (Index)
Vs.	Versus
WEO	World Economic Outlook
WTO	World Trade Organization
WWW	World Wide Web
ZAR	South African Rand
Zeros	Fraction of Zero-Return Days

Index of symbols

&	And
%	Percent
*	Indicator of Significance
<	Less than
Σ	Sum
α	Constant Regression Term
a	Fraction of Company Shares
β	Regression Coefficient
C	Number of Samples in Kruskal-Wallis Test
d	Achieved Score for Disclosure Index
$	U.S. Dollar
ε	Error Term
€	Euro
F	F-value of the F-Test
H	Hypothesis
i	Item in the Company/Sample/Shareholder Index
M	Maximum Score
n	Number of Companies/Items/Observations/Shareholders
p	Probability (Significance Level)
Q	Quarter
R^2	Regression Coefficient of Determination
r	Return
T	Number of Total Trading Days
t	Item in the Year Index

1 Introduction

1.1 Motivation and research questions

> *"High quality, transparent financial statements facilitate investing in the same way that maps facilitate sailing - by clarifying the environment and therefore reducing risk of the unknown."*[1]

This statement by *Lynn E. Turner*, Chief Accountant of the *U.S. Securities & Exchange Commission (SEC)*, illustrates the importance of **high quality information** in a company's financial statements. Capital market participants depend on high quality corporate information as a basis for capital allocation decisions.[2] However, it is questionable, as to what extent companies indeed *clarify the environment* for the users of financial statements through reporting activities.

In particular, the quality of corporate information provided in **emerging economies** is deemed to be lower than in developed countries, not only in financial statements, but also other financial reporting instruments, such as the companies' entire annual reports. Reporting differences between companies from emerging economies and developed countries are frequently explained by less favorable institutional and cultural environments in emerging economies.[3] *Fülbier/Klein* (2013) summarize reasons for such cross-country differences:

> *"Financial accounting is rooted in national thoughts, traditions and institutional settings. As a consequence, accounting has developed heterogeneously over time and fulfilled contracting purposes in divergent national environments."*[4]

In the emerging economy of Brazil, for example, the economic policy, corporate governance[5] and legal enforcement tend to be weaker than in developed countries,[6] which may lower the level of financial reporting quality of Brazilian companies. Also characteristics of the national culture are assumed to negatively affect the reporting quality of companies in Brazil.[7] Hence, the results of studies conducted in developed countries cannot always be transferred to emerging economies.

However, **research** on financial reporting in emerging economies is scarce. *Chen et al.* (2014) emphasize the importance of research on less developed economies: "*So far, there is little consensus on firms' motives for voluntary disclosure, even in developed economies.*"[8] This statement implies that there is an even greater need for additional research on corporate

---

1 *Turner* (2000).

2 Cf. *Chen et al.* (2011), p. 1259.

3 Cf. amongst others *Cooke/Wallace* (1990), p. 79; *Salter* (1998), p. 211; *Lopes et al.* (2007), p. 2; *Ball et al.* (2003), p. 235; *de Lima et al.* (2010), p. 257; *Iatridis* (2012), p. 103; *Nobes* (2014), p. 24-30.

4 *Fülbier/Klein* (2013), abstract.

5 For the role of corporate governance, cf. also *La Porta et al.* (2000).

6 Cf. *de Lima et al.* (2010), p. 255.

7 Cf. *Borker* (2012), p. 313-324; *Hofstede* (2001), p. 500.

8 *Chen et al.* (2014), p. 18.

disclosures in less developed economies than in developed economies. *Chen et al.* (2011) support this view and put particular focus on emerging economies:

> "*Compared with the large literature on developed countries' accounting systems and managers' reporting incentives, much less is known about the role of accounting in emerging markets.*"[9]

The lack of research on emerging economies seems surprising in the light of contemporary developments worldwide. In times of increasing globalization, international businesses and capital markets have grown rapidly in recent years and are still expanding at a high pace.[10] In particular, a considerable fraction of the global resources has been allocated to emerging economies. The total market capitalization of those countries' stock exchanges rose from $ 83 billion in 1983 to $ 3 trillion in 1999, an increase by 36 times.[11] In spite of recent drawbacks, it is widely agreed that the rapid economic growth will continue so that emerging markets will stay in the focus of investors.[12] Ever since the investment bank *Goldman Sachs* published "*Dreaming With BRICs: The Path to 2050*"[13] in 2003 particularly the BRIC (Brazil, Russia, India and China), and later the **BRICS** (including South Africa), countries have experienced both a rapid development and great attention.[14] For the future, *The World Bank's* Global Development Horizons report predicts that emerging economies will expand between 2011 and 2025 by an average of 4.7% each year, more than twice the developed countries' 2.3%.[15] Recent forecasts by the *International Monetary Fund (IMF)* support this prognosis, as it expects emerging economies to expand by 4.7% in 2016, whereas advanced economies will solely grow by 2.4%.[16] For the BRICS, *The World Bank* (2015a) even predicts economic growth above 5% between 2015 and 2017.[17] Moreover, the six major emerging economies, including Brazil, China, India, Indonesia, the Republic of Korea, and Russia, are assumed to collectively account for more than half of global growth by 2025.[18] This development comes along with a tremendous amount of resource allocation decisions made by capital providers all over the world. However, referring to the emerging economy of China, investment analyst *Aaron Levitt* points out that

> "*[...] investing in Asia's Dragon economy isn't as easy as buying stock in Germany.*"[19]

According to *Levitt* (2012) one of the reasons for occurring investment problems is a relatively **low level of corporate information.**[20] Moreover, investment in emerging econo-

9 *Chen et al.* (2011), p. 1256.
10 Cf. *Rodrigues et al.* (2012), p. 23.
11 Cf. *Gup* (2005), p. 62.
12 Cf. *IMF* (2015c), p. 4.
13 *Wilson/Purushothaman* (2003), p. 1.
14 Cf. *Bieling* (2014), p. 379.
15 Cf. *The World Bank* (2011), p. 3.
16 Cf. *IMF* (2015c), p. 2.
17 Cf. *The World Bank* (2015a), p. 4.
18 Cf. *The World Bank* (2011), p. 3.
19 *Levitt* (2012).
20 Cf. *Levitt* (2012).

mies is prone to increased volatility of returns.[21] This fact underpins the importance of corporate information to lower investment risks in line with the initial quotation by *Lynn E. Turner*. On the whole, investors face major obstacles to enter emerging markets, "*[...] in large part because information about these markets is scarce or, if available, of doubtful reliability.*"[22]

Hence, the impact of financial reporting on the behavior of investors is of particular interest. Economic theory suggests that increased financial reporting quality leads to an increased and more equal information basis among all investors, which reduces the investors' risks that other investors are better informed and, thus, lowers adverse selection concerns.[23] This decrease in **information asymmetries** is expected to increase the liquidity of a stock.[24] In line with theory, the majority of empirical research provides evidence that high-quality financial reporting results in reductions of information asymmetries.[25] However, other studies do not find such economic consequences.[26] Ultimately, there is still no general consensus on the relation between financial reporting quality and information asymmetries. Although most capital market studies have been conducted in developed countries (particularly in the U.S.),[27] capital market effects might be easier to detect in an **emerging economy setting** due to a lower financial reporting level.[28] Companies from such a low reporting environment have a better opportunity to differentiate themselves from competitors through the disclosure of information than companies from an increased disclosure environment, as *Lopes et al.* (2007) illustrate for the example of Brazil:

> *"The institutional environment in Brazil is characterized by poor investor protection and uninformative accounting numbers. In this environment firms with better prospects could try to opt out of the country's poor institutional environment [...].*"[29]

On the whole, the results of financial reporting studies in developed countries may not be transferable to emerging economies due to their specific financial reporting characteristics

With respect to financial reporting regulation worldwide, regulators in a number of countries have taken tremendous measures to improve the quality of financial information over the past decades.[30] Examples for these reforms are the Sarbanes-Oxley Act in the United States (U.S.) in 2002 as well as the **mandatory** introduction of International Financial Reporting Standards (IFRS) in numerous countries, e.g. Germany in 2005. From the perspective of an international investor, however, the harmonization by IFRS adoption does

21 Cf. *Harvey* (1995), p. 22.
22 *Errunza* (1983), p. 51.
23 Cf. *Verrecchia* (1983), p. 182-183; *Glosten/Milgrom* (1985), p. 71; *Nienhaus* (2015), p. 4.
24 Cf. *Leuz/Verrecchia* (2000), p. 92.
25 Cf. amongst others *Diamond/Verrecchia* (1991); *Botosan* (1997); *Leuz/Verrecchia* (2000); *Botosan* (1997); *Bhattacharya/Daouk* (2002); *Hail* (2002); *Frankel/Li* (2004); *Francis et al.* (2005b); *Daske et al.* (2008).
26 Cf. amongst others *Hughes et al.* (2007); *Core et al.* (2008); *de Lima et al.* (2010); *Eugster* (2014).
27 Cf. *Chen et al.* (2011), p. 1256.
28 Cf. *Hail* (2002), p. 766; *Lopes et al.* (2007), p. 1.
29 *Lopes et al.* (2007), p. 1.
30 Cf. *Tang* (2008), p. 1.

not inevitably guarantee that companies from different countries apply the same IFRS rules consistently. *Ioannou/Serafeim* (2014) show that local contexts and institutional differences influence the companies' application of mandatory reporting regulation on country level.[31] Moreover, *Ali et al.* (2004) provide evidence that the general level of compliance with financial reporting regulation varies considerably across countries.[32]

In addition to mandatory financial statements, companies frequently provide **voluntary** information in their **annual reports**, which are a major source of corporate information to multiple user groups.[33] Plenty of research finds that information in annual reports is associated with the decisions of capital market participants, such as investors and financial analysts.[34] However, as particularly annual reports do not only address investors and financial analysts, but also other stakeholders of a company, the preparers of annual reports may also consider the information needs of, for instance, customers, employees, authorities or the general public. Typical information in the reports is related to, for example, strategy, prospects, risks, products, employees, remuneration or sustainability issues (as recommended by the *Global Reporting Initiative (GRI)*[35]. In spite of extensive prior research, companies' voluntary reporting practices are still a *black box* regarding various facets. For instance, *Beyer et al.* (2010) state that

> "*[...] it is surprising how little we still know about fundamental issues, such as [...] the objective of managers in making voluntary disclosures [...]*"[36].

The above paragraphs have revealed the current importance of financial reporting quality in emerging economies which serves as a starting point for this study's **problem statement**. The study takes advantage of the particular environments in the emerging economies **Brazil** and **South Africa** to empirically investigate financial reporting quality. The results are compared to the corresponding findings for the developed country of **Germany**. There are several reasons for the selection of these three sample countries. First, Brazil and South Africa are part of the BRICS countries and, therefore, have gained particular investor attention and experienced massive economic growth over the past years. Second, the two emerging economies are comparable regarding their gross domestic product (GDP) per capita. Germany is regarded as a developed country with well-established mandatory and voluntary financial reporting activities (e.g., comprehensive management report disclosures). A comparison of the study's results among these countries provides evidence, as to what extent financial reporting practices indeed differ and whether the emerging economies provide a lower **quality of financial reporting**. Third, in all three countries, there are stock exchanges with regular trading. Thus, the study is able to both examine and compare the financial reporting quality of companies which are listed on the countries' major stock exchanges. Fourth, the fact that the three sample countries have adopted the IFRS enhances the **comparability** of the results and may raise the expectation

---

31 Cf. *Ioannou/Serafeim* (2014), p. 1.

32 Cf. *Ali et al.* (2004), p. 183.

33 Cf. *Baetge et al.* (2012), p. 59 and 62.

34 Cf. amongst others *Sengupta* (1998); *Francis et al.* (2005b); *de Lima et al.* (2010); *Fu et al.* (2012).

35 Cf. *Global Reporting Initiative* (2013).

36 *Beyer et al.* (2010), p. 336.

of harmonized financial reporting practices in these countries. Fifth, the selected companies in the three countries publish annual reports in English so that international investors can use and compare the annual reports as a basis for their decisions. The annual reports are used as research objects in this study's empirical analysis.

The **research objective** of this study is threefold in line with the three conducted sub studies (cf. Figure 1-1). (1) First, the study aims at measuring and describing financial reporting quality in Brazil, South Africa and Germany. However, measuring financial reporting quality is not trivial. The literature provides neither a consensus on the definition of *financial reporting quality* nor on a generally accepted measurement technique. Because of its context-specificity, a direct empirical assessment inevitably includes varying preferences among multiple user groups with dissimilar preferences.[37] Consequently, many researchers use indirect measures by focusing on attributes which are assumed to affect the quality of financial reporting, such as the applied accounting standards, earnings management, financial restatements or timeliness of earnings.[38] This study uses three measures to capture financial reporting quality. Besides the calculation of accruals-based **earnings management** proxies, the study conducts a **content analysis** of the sample companies' annual reports on the basis of a comprehensive disclosure index. Moreover, the **readability** of (textual passages of) these annual reports is assessed as an additional measure of financial reporting quality.

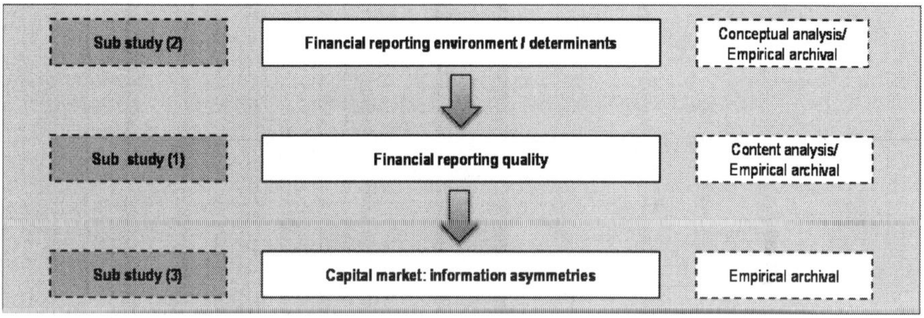

Figure 1-1: Research fields of the study

(2) As illustrated in Figure 1-1, the observed financial reporting quality is influenced by the financial reporting environment and, in particular, specific determinants. Thus, the second objective is to explore underlying **determinants** which influence the companies' decisions to report certain information. These determinants comprise country-specific effects, which may be responsible for a "*homogenous quality across firms within a country*"[39], as well as company-specific characteristics (e.g., company size).[40] (3) Third, the study investigates whether high financial reporting quality leads to capital market consequences

[37] Cf. *Botosan* (2004), p. 291; *Daske/Gebhardt* (2006), p. 466.

[38] Cf. amongst others *Schipper/Vincent* (2003); *Verdi* (2006); *Barth et al.* (2008); *Daske et al.* (2008); *Francis et al.* (2008); *Dechow et al.* (2010); *Stubben* (2010); *Kent et al.* (2010); *Chen et al.* (2011); *Kamarudin/Wan Ismail* (2014).

[39] *Lopes* (2011), p. 342.

[40] Cf. *Lopes/Walker* (2012), p. 54.

and indeed lowers **information asymmetries** among capital market participants. Furthermore, the thesis strives for cross-country comparisons regarding all three objectives. By contrast to single-country studies, this study's cross-country design guarantees an increased generalizability of its results.

Following the three research objectives, the study poses six **research questions (RQ)**. The first set of research questions is concerned with the observed financial reporting practices (analyzed on the basis of the measured financial reporting quality) both within each country and across the three countries:

RQ1a	Which financial reporting practices can be observed in Brazil, South Africa and Germany (within-country study)?
RQ1b	How do financial reporting practices differ across Brazil, South Africa and Germany (cross-country study)?

Moreover, the analysis of determinants of financial reporting quality is captured by the following research questions:

RQ2a	What determines financial reporting quality?
RQ2b	How do determinants of financial reporting quality differ across Brazil, South Africa and Germany?

In line with the third research objective, the third set of research questions emphasizes the general discussion on the relation between financial reporting quality and information asymmetries as well as the concrete effects in the study's sample countries:

RQ3a	Does financial reporting quality influence information asymmetries?
RQ3b	How do information asymmetries differ across Brazil, South Africa and Germany?

By examining the above research questions, the **contribution** of the study to the existing literature is multifold. First, the study provides a comprehensive analysis of the companies' financial reporting practices in two major emerging economies in comparison to a developed country. Although already *Marston* (1986) as well as *Salter* (1998) have described differences in corporate disclosures between companies from more and less developed countries, up-to-date research is scarce. Second, the determinants of financial reporting activities in an emerging economy setting are widely unexplored, as described above. Thus, this study investigates the determinants of financial reporting quality in the regarded emerging economies on company-level. The additional investigation of a developed country allows comparisons of both country-specific and company-specific factors influencing financial reporting quality in each of the sample countries. Third, the study contributes to the controversial discussion on the relation between financial reporting quality and information asymmetries (capital market effects) in general as well as in emerging economies in particular. The study's setting is appropriate for this purpose, as such economic consequences are assumed to be easier to detect in an emerging economy environment. In light of the importance of emerging economies and the unique setting of the investigation, the results of the study have implications for investors, financial analysts, regulators, preparers of financial reports, auditors as well as academics.

The following section 1.2 provides the study's scientific positioning which determines its research strategy. Section 1.3 presents the outline of the study.

1.2 Scientific positioning of the study

Science is the

> "*[...] knowledge of why things are the way they are, of the kinds of thing there are to be found in nature, and of the laws governing these things.*"[41]

The philosophy of science (also referred to as *science of science*)[42] does not regard science as an end in itself, but elaborates on different reasons of science. *Kosiol* (1964) distinguishes four **objectives of sciences:**[43] (1) On a *descriptive* basis, it is the goal to both define and describe phenomena observed in reality against the background of their empirical validity. (2) In a next step, the described phenomena and their characteristics (*explanandum*) shall be explained *theoretically* on the basis of propositions (*explanans*). (3) Picking up the thereby acquired knowledge on causal relationships and applying it to practical issues is the main idea of the *pragmatic* objective. (4) In addition, science may also intend to develop *normative* guidelines, according to which people are supposed to behave.

Examining the nature and contribution of science itself, the philosophy of science pursues a **meta-scientific** approach,[44] as it comprises the characteristics of the individual sciences, including the terms, categorizations, principles of cognition, languages, objectives as well as research methodologies of each scientific discipline.[45] Hence, the philosophy of science captures also the characteristics of business economics, which is the underlying discipline of this study. In line with the objectives of both modern business economics and positive accounting theory to explain and predict actual economic practices,[46] this study aims at investigating differences in international accounting practices and, thus, belongs to the category of applied sciences, rather than theoretical sciences.[47] As such, it generates knowledge inductively (the generalization of specific observations) and puts emphasis on *Kosiol's* pragmatic approach.

41 *Bird* (1998), p. 6.
42 Cf. e.g. *Mäki* (2008), p. 551.
43 Cf. *Kosiol* (1964), p. 745. For the following description of the scientific objectives, cf. also *Schweitzer* (1978), p. 2-5.
44 Cf. *Kornmeier* (2007), p. 6.
45 Cf. *Fülbier* (2004), p. 266.
46 Cf. *Fülbier* (2004), p. 267; *Watts/Zimmerman* (1986), p. 2.
47 However, also theoretical research might be conducted in the field of business economics, cf. *Kornmeier* (2007), p. 22-23.

Research projects select a **research strategy** in line with the research objectives, which they pursue. As illustrated in Figure 1-2, studies can adopt a conceptual, empirical or analytical research strategy.[48]

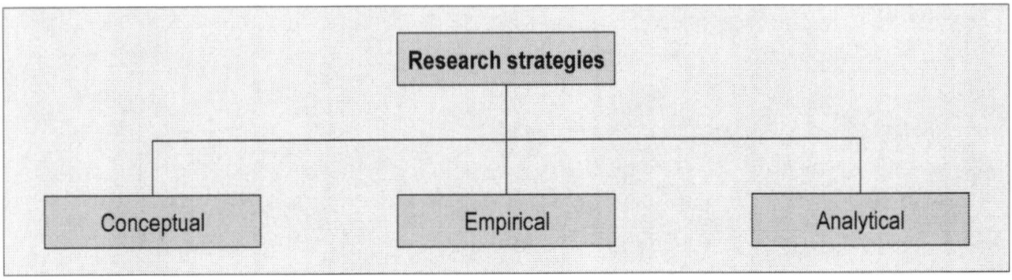

Figure 1-2: Research strategies according to *Grochla* (1978)

The **conceptual strategy** generally attempts to investigate complex causal relationships on the basis of plausibility considerations.[49] The approach resembles a mental simulation, which makes use of heuristic-functioning models, and strives for an immediate gain in knowledge. In the literature, hardly any results of such research are premised on quantified figures. Critics attach solely limited explanatory power to the conceptual strategy, as it regards subjectively assumed relationships as evident or existent on the basis of experience, rather than on systematic confrontation with reality. Claimed statements can be seen as interpretative, hypothetical or speculative, so that their accuracy largely depends on the expertise and analytical capabilities of the researcher.[50]

By contrast to the conceptual strategy, studies pursuing the **empirical strategy** gain knowledge systematically to validate developed hypotheses through empirical examination.[51] On the one hand, the empirical studies are able to describe the reality without the intention to provide a concurrent explanation of the observations, e.g. for official statistics or public opinion polling. On the other hand, empirical-cognitive evidence is supposed to provide, based on an empirically-reliable foundation, both explanations of cause-effect-relationships and a prognosis of prospective developments. A crucial element of an empirical study is its methodology, which can be manifold. Empirical data collection methods comprise, inter alia, case studies, field research and experiments. To analyze the collected data, researchers use various research techniques, such as regression analyses. However, the fact that the researcher has to choose a method may result in the problems of the empirical strategy. Errors can particularly occur regarding the definition of adequate terms to describe a situation, the operationalization of variables as well as the selection and application of appropriate techniques for analysis.

Unlike the above described research strategies, the **analytical strategy** does not strive for absolute understanding of the reality, but rather aims at abstract modelling of problems

---

48 Cf. *Grochla* (1978), p. 71.

49 Cf. here and in the following *Grochla* (1978), p. 72-75.

50 Cf. *Saucke* (2015), p. 10.

51 Cf. here and in the following *Grochla* (1978), p. 78-85.

which are based on generalized excerpts of reality.[52] The analytical strategy's objective is to find the best possible solution to a defined problem. For that purpose, researchers use complex and logical methods to generate decision-useful and mostly quantitative solutions.

This study investigates real financial reporting phenomena being observed amongst large listed companies in the two emerging economies Brazil and South Africa, on the one hand, in contrast to German entities, on the other. Since it is the objective to provide comprehensive descriptions and explanations of financial reporting practices and corresponding capital market effects, the study applies an **empirical research strategy**.

Referring to the differentiation between deductive and inductive approaches to gain knowledge, modern researchers have developed different theoretical methodologies stipulating how research should be conducted. Supporters of **conventionalism** argue that deduction-based research (from the general to the specific) is able to generate true scientific systems.[53] Particularly the observed natural laws determine the measuring standards on earth and are with absolute certainty regarded as irrefutable.[54] This assumption of irrefutability by conventionalists is the main reason why *Karl R. Popper* created the so-called **critical rationalism**, although he accepts conventionalism as scientific theory with a differing objective and definition of science.[55] *Popper*, however, posits

> *"[...] that falsifiability, or refutability, is a criterion of the scientific status of a theory."*[56]

According to critical rationalism, the human reason is fallible and, thus, all knowledge of mankind can never be seen as ultimately true, as it might be falsified at all times.[57] A verification of statements is, thus, not possible. To gain additional knowledge, researchers shall attempt to falsify existing theories which have not been falsified yet. The detection of mistakes is no reason for disappointment, but rather considered favorable, as correcting these mistakes contributes to advances in problem-solving abilities. The described interplay of gradual progress and (partly) elimination of hypotheses is based on **methodological rationalism** and brings researchers closer to an implied *objective reality*, about which they try to gain knowledge (**critical realism**).[58] Counterintuitively, critical rationalists prefer statements which fail easily in tests over those which hardly ever fail, since the latter can hardly be examined and, thus, are of no value at all.[59] According to *Popper*, only empirical research is appropriate for such testing and is, therefore, able to generate new knowledge, which then has to stand intersubjective testing.[60]

---

[52] Cf. here and in the following *Grochla* (1978), p. 85-86.

[53] Cf. *Popper* (2005), p. 56. As most important conventionalists *Popper* names *Poincaré, Duhem, Dingler* and *Eddington*, cf. *Popper* (2005), p. 54.

[54] Cf. *Popper* (1957), p. 55.

[55] Cf. *Popper* (1957), p. 56.

[56] *Popper* (1957), p. 160.

[57] Cf. here and in the following *Raffée/Abel* (1979), p. 3-5; *Popper* (1957), p. 180 and 185.

[58] Cf. *Fülbier* (2005), p. 22; *Raffée/Abel* (1979), p. 4-5.

[59] Cf. *Lingnau* (1995), p. 124-125.

[60] Cf. *Ulrich/Hill* (1976), p. 345.

Moreover, *Popper* (1957) criticizes inductively-generated knowledge, as he denies the inductive approach to use observations of the past as an indicator for future developments, stating:

> *"My reply is that it is reasonable to believe that the future will be very different from the past in many vitally important respects."*[61]

Although he knows that numerous tested and widely-accepted laws are likely to hold in the future, *Popper* uses this statement to underpin his fundamental conviction that it might be dangerous to put unconditional trust in inductively-derived laws, as some of them may prove unreliable.[62]

Besides critical rationalism, the second scientific approach which has shaped business economics is the **constructivism** of the so-called *Erlanger School*.[63] In line with critical rationalism also constructivism assumes that knowledge is generally fallible.[64] However, being less rigorous than critical rationalists, constructivists suspect that deductive research in combination with comprehensive argumentation can lead to results, which are regarded as *true*, if there is an intellectual consensus on it.[65] Hence, this pragmatic understanding of *truth* is a major difference to the critical rationalism with its objective reality as basis for empirical testing. Moreover the strict deductive methodology of constructivism, which reveals its rationalistic roots,[66] is not found in critical rationalism. As constructivists act on the assumption that human rationality is solely fallible to some extent, the literature distinguishes *consequent fallibilism* in critical rationalism and *limited fallibilism* as part of constructivism, which allows methodologically-reasonable decisions.[67]

In accordance with the above described research questions, this study's empirical research strategy is substantially in line with *Popper's* critical rationalism, as it encompasses his **three steps** of empirical research:[68] First, the study identifies causal relationships of interest, which have remained to be explained so far (**problem**). An example is the impact of certain influencing factors on a company's financial reporting quality, or the reaction of investors on the financial reporting activities of an entity. In a second step, the researcher develops hypotheses which provide an explanation (**solution**) to the raised problem. The theoretical foundation of this work is primarily based on institutionalism, yet, also considers additional theoretical approaches. In accordance with *Popper* (1957) this empirical investigation aims at (partly) eliminating the formulated hypotheses or the implicit null hypotheses, respectively.[69] Third, this ongoing interplay of hypotheses development and elimination generates additional knowledge in the sense of *reliable statements* (**nomologi-**

---

61 *Popper* (1957), p. 185.
62 Cf. *Popper* (1957), p. 185.
63 Cf. *Fülbier* (2005), p. 22. The leading representative of the *Erlanger School* is *Paul Lorenzen.*
64 Cf. *Raffée/Abel* (1979), p. 6.
65 Cf. *Fülbier* (2005), p. 23; *Raffée/Abel* (1979), p. 6.
66 Cf. *Fülbier* (2005), p. 23.
67 Cf. *Raffée/Abel* (1979), p. 4.
68 Cf. *Fülbier* (2005), p. 22.
69 For a detailed explanation of hypothesis testing, cf. section 4.2.1.

cal hypotheses). Meeting the premise of critical rationalism, all tested hypotheses in this study are falsifiable, so that their elimination is generally feasible.

1.3 Outline of the study

The study comprises seven chapters.

The **first chapter** points out the relevance of the research project and develops both the study's research objective and the research questions. Moreover, the selected research approach is explained to position the study as part of scientific research.

The **second chapter** provides the conceptual foundation of the study. After the description of the fundamental purpose and addressees of financial reporting, the chapter defines financial reporting quality (FRQ) and gives an overview on how to measure this abstract concept. Moreover, the particular role of emerging economies in the global economy is described and typical accounting characteristics of emerging economies are presented. Finally, the chapter characterizes the country-specific financial reporting environments in the sample countries Brazil, South Africa and Germany.

Based on this study's research objective, the **third chapter** provides a review of existing studies on the identified research objectives of financial reporting practice, determinants and capital market consequences. In line with this study, the literature review distinguishes between indirect and direct measures of FRQ. Based on the discussion of prior studies' results, implications and research gaps for this study are derived.

In the **fourth chapter**, the theoretical conceptual framework of the research project is illustrated. Besides institutionalism as theoretical basis, also both the culture approach and societal effects approach are taken into account to explain financial reporting practices. Moreover, the theoretical framework is the basis for the development of the study's research hypotheses.

The research design is shown in the **fifth chapter**. First, the empirical field of the study is described including the characteristics of the sample. Afterwards, the chapter explains the methodology of the applied FRQ measures as well as the analysis methods separately for each study.

The **sixth chapter** presents the empirical results of the study. In accordance to the three research fields, first, the results of the different FRQ measures are shown. Second, the chapter reports the findings of the FRQ determinants analysis, which distinguishes between isolated and simultaneous analyses of the identified determinants. Third, the results of the capital market study reveal, as to what extent FRQ is associated with information asymmetries.

The **seventh chapter** summarizes the study's main results, provides implications for multiple interest groups, discusses limitations and provides an outlook.

Figure 1-3 illustrates the outline of the study.

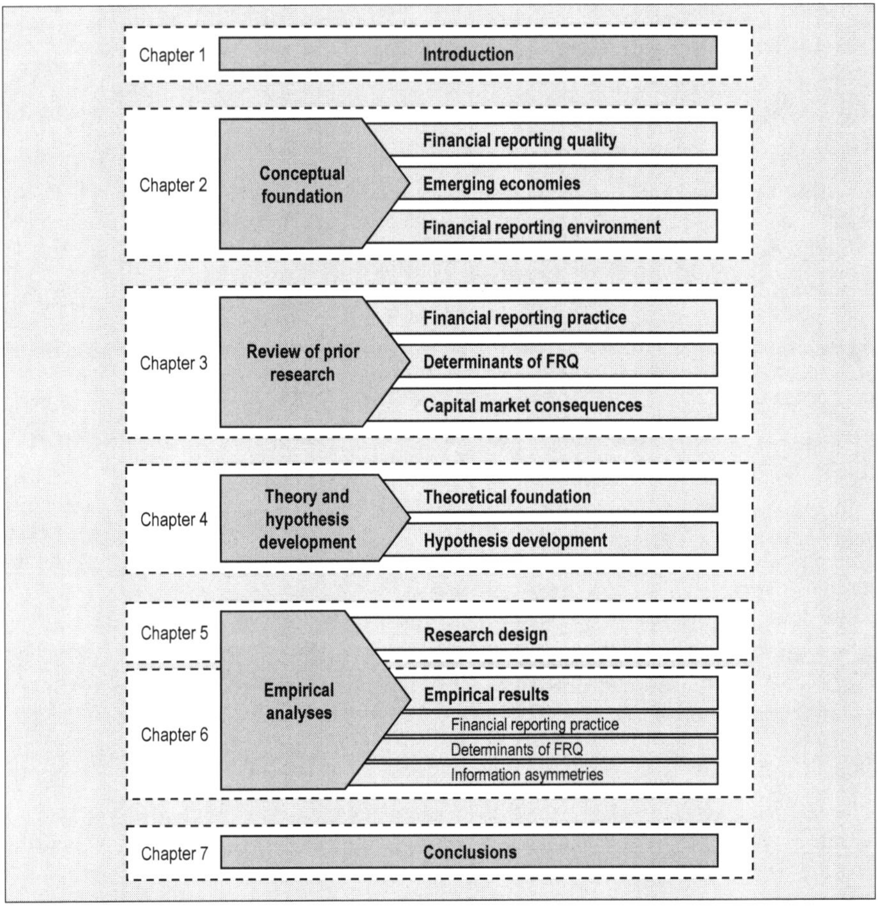

Figure 1-3: Outline of the study

2 Conceptual foundation

2.1 Basis of financial reporting quality

2.1.1 Purpose and addressees of financial reporting

A company's business activities are concerned with the **transformation of resources** involving several players, such as suppliers, customers and providers of financial resources.[70] Figure 2-1 illustrates typical flows of cash, resources, goods and services between the involved players. While **internal management accounting** is concerned with informing the company's managers on the basis of company-specific rules, **external financial accounting** is intended to inform external parties and mostly based on standardized rules.[71]

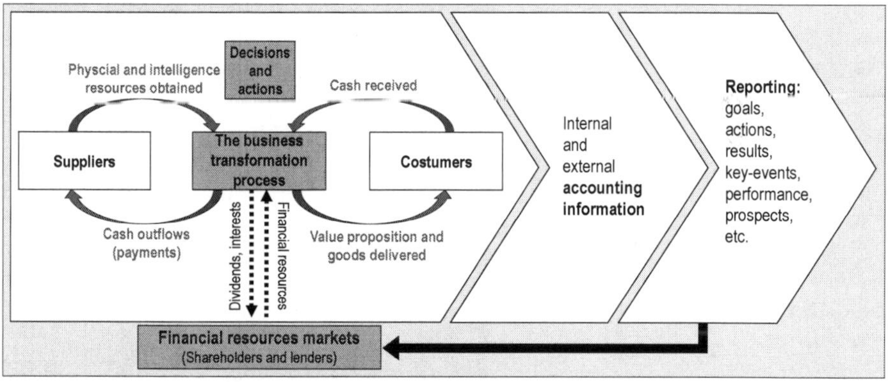

Figure 2-1: Business operations, accounting and reporting
Following *Stolowy et al.* (2013), p. 6.

As providers of shareholders and lenders only provide capital to earn a return (dividends and interests), they require information about the use of their funds and resulting outcomes.[72] As shown in Figure 2-1, the company selects a certain piece of information out of all accounting information and reports this to the capital providers. Hence, these disclosures can be regarded as the published result of accounting.[73] Corporate reports may include information on, inter alia, goals, actions, results and performance. However, the information can be reported via various **reporting vehicles**, on which *Healy/Palepu* (2001) give an overview distinguishing between regulated disclosures, voluntary disclosures as well as disclosures by information intermediaries:

> "*Firms provide disclosure through regulated financial reports, including the financial statements, footnotes, management discussion and analysis, and other regulatory filings. In addition, some firms engage in voluntary communication, such as*

70 Cf. here and in the following *Stolowy et al.* (2013), p. 3-7.
71 Cf. *Pellens et al.* (2014), p. 2.
72 Cf. here and in the following *Stolowy et al.* (2013), p. 5-7.
73 Cf. *Pellens et al.* (2014), p. 4.

management forecasts, analysts' presentations and conference calls, press releases, internet sites, and other corporate reports. Finally, there are disclosures about firms by information intermediaries, such as financial analysts, industry experts, and the financial press."[74]

In line with *Healy/Palepu* (2001), this study uses a wide **definition of financial reporting** which not only captures financial reporting through financial statements, but also reporting of information via other reporting instruments, such as specific parts of the annual report (e.g., CEO's letter to the shareholders, management report).

However, the literature has not found a consensus on who the **addressees** of financial reporting are. The *International Accounting Standards Board (IASB)* pursues the objective of financial reporting that companies provide information particularly to "*existing and potential investors, lenders and other creditors*"[75]. These addressees require information which helps them assessing the prospects of a company's future cash flows.[76] In addition, the *IASB* identifies other interest groups, "*[...] such as regulators and members of the public [...]*"[77], who might benefit from the information.[78]

Following *Moxter* (1976), *Fink et al.* (2013) argue that the addressees of management reporting (which is part of financial reporting according to the *IASB*)[79] are all groups of persons that have a **legitimate interest** to obtain corporate information.[80] Groups have such a legitimate interest, if they largely depend on a company's economic situation and on external corporate reporting as a source of information. For example, as the general public has developed an increasing interest in corporate activities over the past years, particularly concerning sustainable activities and corporate governance practices, *Fink et al.* (2013) regard, inter alia, the general public as a separate interest group of corporate reporting.[81] In contrast, competitors who also have a large interest in the corporate information, are no addressee of corporate reporting, since they do not have a legitimate interest which is worth protecting.[82]

According to the **stakeholder approach**, an entity's economic success depends on resources provided by multiple stakeholders (e.g., capital, production factors, supplied parts, infrastructure).[83] As the stakeholders are able to limit or even deny the access to resources, companies have an incentive to keep their business activities in line with requirements of stakeholders as well as to report information which meet their stakeholders' information needs.[84] However, as the requirements among stakeholders may differ and result in con-

---

[74] *Healy/Palepu* (2001), p. 405. *Management discussion and analysis* is the U.S. management report (the term differs across countries), cf. *Fink et al.* (2013), p. 37.

[75] Cf. *IASB* Conceptual Framework Objective 2 (F.OB2).

[76] F.OB3.

[77] F.OB10.

[78] Cf. F.OB10.

[79] Cf. *IASB* Practice Statement Management Commentary Introduction 4 (IN 4).

[80] Cf. here and in the following *Fink et al.* (2013), p. 11. This approach follows *Moxter* (1976), p. 94-99.

[81] Cf. *Fink et al.* (2013), p. 11.

[82] Cf. *Fink et al.* (2013), p. 12.

[83] For a detailed description of the stakeholder approch, cf. section 4.1.5.4.3.

[84] Cf. *Ullmann* (1985), p. 552; *Freeman et al.* (2010), p. 10-12.

flicts of interest, companies need to prioritize stakeholder groups.[85] As an advocate of the stakeholder approach, the King Code of Governance for South Africa (King III) by the *Institute of Directors in Southern Africa* posits the *stakeholder inclusive model*, according to which the legitimate interests of all stakeholders have to be considered when companies make decisions. In particular: "*The shareholder, on the premise of this approach, does not have a predetermined place of precedence over other stakeholders.*"[86]

The following section develops a definition of financial reporting quality on the basis of the above described wide understanding of financial reporting addressing multiple interest groups in line with *Fink et al.* (2013).

2.1.2 Definition of financial reporting quality

The FRQ concept is based on the idea that certain information is better in fulfilling a specific purpose than others.[87] For example, information of higher FRQ can allow investors a more profitable capital allocation. In spite of the vast literature concerned with FRQ, however, there is no consensus on a generally accepted definition of FRQ. Researchers view FRQ as an abstract concept. For instance, *Cohen et al.* (2004) point out that

> "*[...] the notion of financial reporting quality remains a vague concept.*"[88]

Similarly, *Jonas/Blanchet* (2000) who attempt assessing FRQ from an auditor's perspective underpin the problem:

> "*Auditors, audit committee members, and management are [...] struggling to define 'quality of financial reporting'.*"[89]

Nevertheless, a precise definition of FRQ in the sense of this study is crucial to comprehend and interpret its research results. When reviewing existing understandings of FRQ, *Jonas/Blanchet* (2000) distinguish two general categories: (1) *user needs* and (2) *shareholder/investor protection*.[90] Table 2-1 gives an overview of approaches for each category.

Focus	Recommended Approach
User Needs	IASB / FASB Conceptual Framework Jenkins Committee Recommendations Earnings Persistence Model
Shareholder / Investor Protection	Kirk Committee Recommendations SEC Panel's Recommendation No. 8 SAS No. 61 (as amended)

Table 2-1: Focus of financial reporting quality definitions
Following *Jonas/Blanchet* (2000), p. 355.

[85] Cf. *Freeman et al.* (2010), p. 27.
[86] King Code of Governance for South Africa 2009, p. 12.
[87] Cf. here and in the following *Pounder* (2013), p. 18.
[88] *Cohen et al.* (2004), p. 91.
[89] *Jonas/Blanchet* (2000), p. 353.
[90] Cf. here and in the following *Jonas/Blanchet* (2000), p. 354-356.

User needs approaches argue that the usefulness of financial information to its users determines FRQ. Both the *IASB* and U.S. *Financial Accounting Standards Board (FASB)* Conceptual Frameworks emphasize that financial reporting shall provide decision useful information (primarily for investment and credit decisions) and further define **qualitative characteristics** to achieve this objective, as illustrated in Figure 2-2 (*IASB* Conceptual Framework).[91] The qualitative characteristics of useful financial information[92] shall be taken into account, unless the benefits of reporting a certain piece of information does not justify the corresponding reporting costs (*cost constraint*).[93] The *IASB* distinguishes between fundamental and enhancing qualitative characteristics. According to the two **fundamental qualitative characteristics**, useful information has to be both relevant and faithfully represented. Information is relevant, if it can make a difference in the users' decisions.[94] To meet this criterion, the information either contributes to the users' forecasts (*predictive value*) or is able to confirm or change, respectively, earlier assessments (*confirmatory value*).[95] Besides relevance, the Conceptual Framework requires the faithful representation of information to be in fact useful.[96] According to the Conceptual Framework, a depiction is represented faithfully, if it is *complete*, *neutral* and *free from error*.[97] Although the Conceptual Framework seems to stipulate both fundamental characteristics equally, *Pellens et al.* (2014) find indication that *relevance* might dominate *faithful representation*.[98] The **enhancing qualitative characteristics** *comparability*, *verifiability*, *timeliness* and *understandability* are capable of increasing the usefulness of relevant and faithfully represented information.[99]

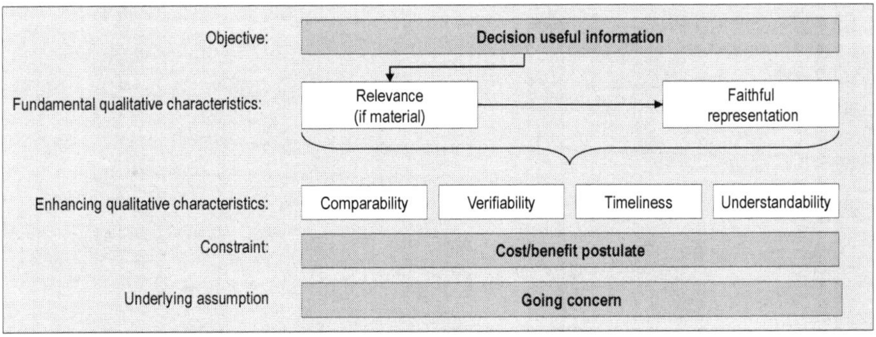

Figure 2-2: System of IASB's Conceptual Framework
Following *Pellens et al.* (2014), p. 97.

---

91 Cf. F.OB2.
92 Cf. *IASB* Conceptual Framework Qualitative Characteristics (F.QC).
93 Cf. F.QC35-39.
94 Cf. F.QC6.
95 Cf. F.QC7-F QC10.
96 Cf. here and in the following F.QC12.
97 Cf. F.QC12. For a description of *completeness*, *neutrality* and *freedom from error*, cf. F.QC13-15.
98 Cf. *Pellens et al.* (2014), p. 94.
99 Cf. F.QC19.

The second user needs approach (cf. Table 2-1), the reporting recommendations by the *Jenkins Committee*, detect concrete information needs of users, such as to obtain a forward-looking perspective;[100] however, the quality of such information is also evaluated on the basis of the standard setters' major qualitative characteristics.[101] According to the Earnings Persistence approach, financial information is of high quality, if it particularly helps investors to segregate the earnings and other financials of a company's core activities from those of its non-core activities.

The second category by *Jonas/Blanchet* (2000) (cf. Table 2-1) comprises **shareholder/investor protection** approaches, which demand that shareholders are provided with full and transparent financial information.[102] Although the criteria to reach this objective of high quality information may overlap with those under the *user needs* category, the main difference is that companies shall not only provide decision-useful information, but "*[...] as much information as possible[...]*"[103]. The approaches emphasize, inter alia, the following factors as determinants of FRQ: the clarity of disclosures (Recommendation No. 8 of the *Blue Ribbon Committee on Improving the Effectiveness of Corporate Audit Committees*); transparency and comparability (*SEC*); consistency and completeness of information and disclosures (*Auditing Standards Board's* Statement of Auditing Standards (SAS) No. 61) as well as the indication of conservative, moderate, or extreme choices of accounting principles (*Kirk Committee*, Advisory Panel on Auditor Independence).

While the Panel's Recommendation No. 8 and SAS No. 61 approaches refer to accounting principles and, thus, emphasize financial statements as basis for FRQ, *Jonas/Blanchet* (2000) argue that FRQ is not only related to financial statements, but also to information released through other instruments, such as press releases, analysts' briefings, presentations and web sites.[104] They further posit that financial reporting is not simply an end product, but it is a process including the steps illustrated in Figure 2-3.

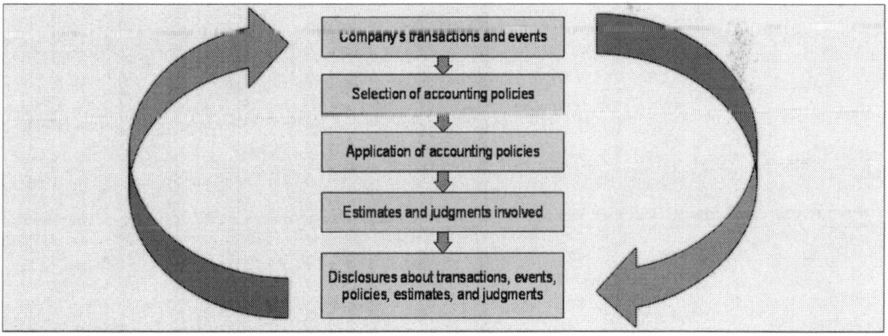

Figure 2-3: The financial reporting process
Following *Jonas/Blanchet* (2000), p. 355.

100 Cf. *AICPA* (1994), p. 4.

101 Cf. here and in the following *Jonas/Blanchet* (2000), p. 354-356.

102 Cf. here and in this paragraph *Jonas/Blanchet* (2000), p. 357-358.

103 *Jonas/Blanchet* (2000), p. 358.

104 Cf. here and in the following *Jonas/Blanchet* (2000), p. 354-355.

Finally, each step determines an entity's overall FRQ. Companies select and apply accounting policies for its corporate transactions and events. This involves estimates and judgments which, consequently, are included in the company's disclosed information.

Apart from the outlined approaches defining FRQ, other researchers provide concrete definitions of FRQ. A concise definition of FRQ is given by *Biddle et al.* (2009) who

> "*[...] define financial reporting quality as the precision with which financial reporting conveys information about the firm's operations, in particular its expected cash flows, that inform equity investors*"[105].

In line with the above *user needs* approaches, the *precision of information* provided to the important user group of *equity investors* is assumed to determine decision usefulness. The strong focus on cash flows by *Biddle et al.* (2009) can be explained by their U.S. perspective.[106] However, the definition falls short of covering the entire range of FRQ. In fact, it is not simply the precision of disclosed information, which contributes to its quality, but also more information may be useful to investors. Therefore, *Chen et al.* (2010) focus in their definition on

> "*[...] the extent to which the financial statement information reflects the underlying economic situation.*"[107]

As criticized by *Jonas/Blanchet* (2000), FRQ is not necessarily limited to information available in financial statements, but information can also be received from other reporting instruments, such as the entire annual report of a company. Therefore, this study uses a **multidimensional understanding** of FRQ considering different sources and types of information. Earnings quality is regarded as one of these dimensions of total FRQ. The following definition of earnings quality by *Dechow et al.* (2010) emphasizes the extent of provided information similar to the aforementioned definition by *Chen et al.* (2010):

> "*Higher quality earnings provide more information about the features of a firm's financial performance that are relevant to a specific decision made by a specific decision-maker.*"[108]

Following *Dechow et al.* (2010) as well as the *IASB* Conceptual Framework, this study's definition of FRQ shall focus on decision useful information. Also *Ball/Shivakumar* (2005) focus in their definition of earnings quality on the usefulness of information, however, specify potential users of the information:

> "*[...] the usefulness of financial statements to investors, creditors, managers and all parties contracting with the firm.*"[109]

In line with *Ball/Shivakumar* (2005), this study considers various **interest groups** (not solely investors), as it analyzes, inter alia, annual reports which address several interest groups. However, this study's research questions are raised in a capital market setting and

---

[105] *Biddle et al.* (2009), p. 113.
[106] For the strong U.S. focus on cash flows, cf. e.g. *Bodnar/Gebhardt* (1999), p. 164.
[107] *Chen et al.* (2010), p. 222.
[108] *Dechow et al.* (2010), p. 344.
[109] *Ball/Shivakumar* (2005), p. 126.

particularly the results of the information asymmetry study[110] depend on the behavior of capital market participants. Consistent with this setting of the study, the focus of the analysis is on investors and financial analysts as main users of financial reporting. In addition, other stakeholders are considered as legitimate users of financial reporting following the view by *Fink et al.* (2013).[111] Based on the above discussion, this study **defines FRQ** as follows:

> *"Financial reporting quality is the decision usefulness of the information which companies provide to existing or potential investors and financial analysts as well as other legitimate interest groups."*

2.1.3 Measures of financial reporting quality

On the basis of this study's definition of FRQ, this section reviews measures developed in accounting research to capture FRQ and selects FRQ measures for this study's empirical examination. *Van Beest et al.* (2009) distinguish between indirect and direct measures of FRQ. While **direct measures** focus on particular elements of disclosures and examine the content of information in detail,[112] **indirect measures** are proxies "*[...] focusing on attributes that are believed to influence quality of financial reports.*"[113] Figure 2-4 gives an overview of major indirect and direct measures of FRQ.

Financial reporting quality

Indirect measures	Direct measures
▪ Readability	▪ Disclosure index
▪ Earnings quality/earnings management: – Accruals – Earnings persistence – Earnings smoothness – Timeliness and loss recognition – Target beating	▪ Analyst evaluation

Figure 2-4: Indirect and direct measures of FRQ
Classification based on *van Beest et al.* (2009), p. 27; *Dechow et al.* (2010), p. 351-352.

Indirect measures:

Indirect measures of FRQ can be multifold. An early example for such an indirect measure are *Barry/Brown* (1985) who assess a company's reporting level on the basis of the number of observed returns for the company's security as well as the time period, for which the security has been listed on a major exchange.[114] Figure 2-4 shows that besides

---

[110] Cf. sections 5.3.4 and 6.3.

[111] Cf. section 2.1.1.

[112] Cf. *van Beest et al.* (2009), p. 27.

[113] *van Beest et al.* (2009), p. 3.

[114] Cf. *Barry/Brown* (1985), p. 419-420.

earnings quality/earnings management proxies also the **readability** of corporate reports can be determined indirectly. Readability proxies are based on obvious attributes of texts.[115] A widely used proxy is the so-called *Fog index* which takes into account the number of words per sentence and number of syllables per word in a textual passage to calculate a readability proxy.

As shown in the previous section, *Dechow et al.* (2010) state that **earnings quality** depends on the amount of decision-relevant information concerning a company's financial performance.[116] They identify the earnings quality categories presented in Figure 2-4.[117] Some of these earnings quality categories include proxies which are specifically used to measure **earnings management** (e.g., accruals-based proxies), whereas some also capture other aspects of earnings quality. Regarding the relation between earnings quality and earnings management *Dechow et al.* (2010) posit that "*[...] earnings management is assumed to erode earnings quality.*"[118] One reason for the popularity of earnings management models in the literature might be the following finding: *"CFOs state that earnings are the most important financial metric to external constituents [...]"*[119]. *Healy/Wahlen* (1999) posit:

> "*Earnings management occurs when managers use judgment in financial reporting and in structuring transactions to alter financial reports to either mislead some stakeholders about the underlying economic performance of the company or to influence contractual outcomes that depend on reported accounting numbers.*"[120]

The managers' objectives to use discretion are not obvious. On the one hand, they may aim at maximizing their expected utility and, therefore, engage in a "*[...] purposeful intervention in the financial reporting process, with the intent of obtaining some private gain [...]*"[121] *(opportunistic view)*.[122] On the other hand, preparers of financial statements may use discretion provided by reporting regulation to signal additional information to stakeholders, in particular, investors *(private information view)*.[123] An advantage of earnings management measures over other measures is that researchers are able to calculate the proxies on readily available information included in the companies' financial statements and databases, respectively.[124]

Concerning the first earnings quality measure in Figure 2-4, **accruals** generally refer to liabilities and non-cash accounts on a balance sheet (e.g., receivables or depreciation).[125]

---

[115] Cf. here and in the following *Li* (2008), p. 222.

[116] Cf. *Dechow et al.* (2010), p. 344.

[117] Figure 2-4 includes only earnings quality proxies from the category *properties of earnings*; in addition, *Dechow et al.* (2010) present earnings quality proxies from the categories *investor responsiveness to earnings* as well as *external indicators of earnings misstatements*, cf. *Dechow et al.* (2010), p. 345. For a tabulated characterization of commonly used earnings quality proxies, cf. *Dechow et al.* (2010), p. 351-352.

[118] *Dechow et al.* (2010), p. 345.

[119] *Graham et al.* (2005), p. 13.

[120] *Healy/Wahlen* (1999), p. 368.

[121] *Schipper* (1989), p. 92.

[122] Cf. *Elbannan* (2011), p. 211.

[123] For a similar argumentation, cf. *Dechow et al.* (2010), p. 362.

[124] Cf. *Dechow et al.* (1995), p. 201.

[125] Cf. *Goncharov* (2005), p. 9.

However, the accruals-based accounting system determines all balance sheet items, except for cash.[126] Their accounting entries are recognized in those periods in which they economically occur to measure a company's performance during a finite period.[127] This accruals-based performance measure can be divided into a normal (also non nondiscretionary or unmanaged) and abnormal (also discretionary or managed) part.[128] Normal accruals occur when preparers of financial statements apply accounting regulation neutrally. Abnormal accruals arise when decision-makers exert discretion. Thus, accruals models are based on "*[...] the idea that abnormal accruals [...] erode decision usefulness.*"[129] In most cross-country studies accruals-based proxies analyze the relationship between changes in accruals and changes in cash flows from operations.[130] *Dechow/Dichev* (2002), for instance, measure accruals quality as "*[...] the extent to which working capital accruals map into operating cash flow realizations, where a poor match signifies low accrual quality.*"[131] In more detail, the accruals model by *Dechow/Dichev* (2002) "*[...] separates accruals based on their association with cash flows by regressing working capital accruals on cash from operations in the current period, prior period, and future period, as well as the change in revenues and property, plant, and equipment (PP&E).*"[132] However, the literature suggests numerous concepts to measure accruals quality.[133]

The theoretical foundation of the **earnings persistence** concept is that the more persistent a company's earnings are, the higher the quality of the earnings/cash flow inputs used in DCF valuation models and, thus, the more useful the valuation model.[134] From an investor perspective, current earnings is a more useful summary indicator of future earnings for companies with more persistent earnings than for companies with less persistent earnings.[135] Thus, *Penman/Zhang* (2002) state that high-quality earnings are *sustainable* earnings, whereas earnings which are *unsustainable* due to accounting treatments would be of lower quality.[136]

According to *Copeland* (1968) **earnings smoothing** "*[...] moderates year-to-year fluctuations in income by shifting earnings from peak years to less successful periods*"[137]. Managers may engage in earnings smoothing to enhance both earnings persistence and earnings informativeness.[138] Nonetheless, the attempt to smooth permanent cash flow changes leads to a lower informativeness and, in particular, less timely information. Numerous, empirical studies using earnings smoothing measures do not focus on the question, whether the observed earnings smoothing is decision useful or not, but rather investigate which factors

[126] Cf. *Dechow et al.* (2010), p. 353.
[127] Cf. *Goncharov* (2005), p. 9.
[128] Cf. here and in the following *Goncharov* (2005), p. 10; *Dechow et al.* (2010), p. 358.
[129] *Dechow et al.* (2010), p. 348.
[130] Cf. *Dechow et al.* (2010), p. 362.
[131] *Dechow/Dichev* (2002), p. 36.
[132] *Francis et al.* (2008), p. 66.
[133] Cf. *Stubben* (2010), p. 698.
[134] Cf. *Dechow et al.* (2010), p. 350.
[135] Cf. *Dechow et al.* (2010), p. 352.
[136] Cf. *Penman/Zhang* (2002), p. 238.
[137] *Copeland* (1968), p. 101.
[138] Cf. here and in the following *Dechow et al.* (2010), p. 351.

(e.g., accounting choices) make managers engage in earnings smoothing.[139] Hence, although these studies use earnings smoothing measures, they do not necessarily directly provide evidence on earnings quality. Another stream of empirical research examines whether earnings smoothing indeed improves informativeness, as it better reflects a company's actual performance, or whether earnings smoothing is rather used opportunistically to manipulate earnings figures and, thus, does not enhance informativeness and earnings quality.[140] These *consequences* studies, however, struggle to find a consensus, whether decision usefulness and, thus, FRQ increases with earnings smoothness. While the cross-country study by *Leuz et al.* (2003) argues that earnings smoothing reduces earnings quality (and, thus, FRQ),[141] the U.S. study by *Tucker/Zarowin* (2006) finds that earnings smoothing increases earnings informativeness and, thus, earnings quality.[142] The problem of these investigations is to separate informative smoothness (e.g., due to fundamental accounting decisions) from artificial smoothness (e.g., due to opportunistic behavior).

Ball/Shivakumar (2005) posit that a **timely recognition** of economic gains and losses (income) in accounting earnings increases the usefulness of financial statements.[143] *Basu* (1997) refers to gains and losses as good and bad news, respectively, and argues that although both are incorporated in earnings quality, preparers of financial statements tend to recognize good news quicker than bad news representing **losses** (accounting conservatism).[144] Earnings measures for this conservatism (timely loss recognition) are based on the assumption that gains are more persistent than losses under conservative loss recognition. Hence, companies with negative earnings changes are expected to have recognized economic losses which are transitory and will not reoccur in the future.[145] *Ball/Shivakumar* (2005), for instance, use a proxy following *Basu* (1997), which regresses earnings changes on lagged earnings change to identify transitory components in income.[146] This approach is able to show that incorporated economic gains are less transitory than losses.[147]

Target beating approaches assume earnings management, if corporate earnings either exactly meet or are marginally above a certain benchmark value (*targets*).[148] *Burgstahler/Dichev* (1997) find that a relatively small number of companies report small losses compared to a relatively large number of companies which show small profits in

---

139 Cf. here and in the following *Dechow et al.* (2010), p. 361-362. For these *determinants* studies, cf. inter alia *White* (1970); *McNichols/Wilson* (1988); *Dharan* (1987); *Chaney et al.* (1988); *Kanagaretnam et al.* (2004).

140 Cf. here and in the following *Goncharov* (2005), p. 11-12; *Dechow et al.* (2010), p. 361-362. For these *consequences* studies, cf. inter alia *Schipper/Vincent* (2003); *Christie/Zimmerman* (1994); *Bowen et al.* (2008). For a discussion on the influence of earnings smoothing on earnings informativeness, cf. *Ewert/Wagenhofer* (2011).

141 Cf. *Leuz et al.* (2003), p. 509.

142 Cf. *Tucker/Zarowin* (2006), p. 267-268.

143 Cf. *Ball/Shivakumar* (2005), p. 84.

144 Cf. here and in the following *Basu* (1997), p. 7.

145 Cf. *Goncharov* (2005), p. 16.

146 Cf. *Ball/Shivakumar* (2005), p. 86.

147 Cf. *Goncharov* (2005), p. 16.

148 Cf. *Dechow et al.* (2010), p. 351.

their financial statements.[149] The interpretation of this phenomenon is that companies with small losses manage earnings to report a (small) profit.[150] Therefore, FRQ proxies such as *small profits* and *small loss avoidance* capture "*[...] one specific dimension of earnings quality.*"[151] However, the reasons for such observations are controversially discussed in the literature. *Beaver et al.* (2007), for instance, argue that the discontinuity in earnings distribution around zero is caused by asymmetric income tax effects,[152] rather than opportunistic earnings management. *Dechow et al.* (2003) reveal that discretionary accruals of companies with small losses are not different from discretionary accruals of small profit companies.[153] On the whole, *Dechow et al.* (2010) conclude "*[...] that there is no measure of earnings quality that is superior for all decision models.*"[154]

Direct measures:

Although a multitude of studies measure FRQ directly, the **operationalization** is not trivial. For example, the direct measurement of FRQ on the basis of the concrete qualitative characteristics of the *IASB* Conceptual Framework, which enhance the decision usefulness of information, seems difficult.[155] In particular, the *relevance* of a certain piece of information might differ considerably across different user groups, as the following example reveals:[156] "*Someone assessing the risk associated with an equity position in a firm may focus on risk disclosures that are irrelevant to someone assessing bankruptcy risk.*"[157] In analogy to *relevance*, also *understandability* depends on the users of the information, as (complex) information might not be equally understandable for every potential user. *Botosan* (2004) further questions whether external users of financial information are able to observe the economic activities underlying the information. However, this would be necessary to evaluate, whether the information is *faithfully represented.*

In accordance with Figure 2-4, common measures of FRQ are disclosure indices and analyst evaluations of disclosures.[158] While **analyst evaluations** use questionnaires or interviews to examine how financial analysts, investors or other users of corporate reporting perceive financial reporting practices,[159] **disclosure index** measures inspect the actual reporting medium (e.g., annual reports, company websites) on the basis of content analyses.[160] However, the literature discusses controversially, whether direct measures, particu-

149 Cf. *Burgstahler/Dichev* (1997), p. 100.
150 Cf. *Dechow et al.* (2010), p. 364.
151 *Dechow et al.* (2010), p. 364.
152 Cf. *Beaver et al.* (2007), p. 525.
153 Cf. *Dechow et al.* (2003), p. 381.
154 *Dechow et al.* (2010), p. 345.
155 Cf. *Botosan* (2004), p. 289-290.
156 Cf. here and in this paragraph *Botosan* (2004), p. 290-291.
157 *Botosan* (2004), p. 291.
158 Cf. among others *Sengupta* (1998); *Botosan/Plumlee* (2002); *Beretta/Bozzolan* (2004); *Cahan et al.* (2005); *Oberdörster* (2009); *Eugster* (2014).
159 Cf. *Hassan/Marston* (2010), p. 10.
160 Cf. *Hassan/Marston* (2010), p. 15. For a detailed description of disclosure index-based content analyses, cf. section 5.2.2.

larly disclosure indices, in fact measure **disclosure quality** or rather disclosure **quantity**.[161] *Hassan/Marston* (2010) argue that existing research tends to capture disclosure quantity, if studies simply count information items in a disclosure index. They further posit that as there is no generally agreed construct of disclosure quality, disclosure quantity measures are frequently used as measures of disclosure quality.[162] *Leuz/Verrecchia* (2000) point out "*[...] that theory is sufficiently broad as to allow the notion of 'increased levels of disclosure' to be interpreted as either an increase in the quantity of disclosure or an increase in the quality of disclosure (or both).*"[163]

In line with this study's multidimensional definition of FRQ, *Ecker et al.* (2006) conclude: "*It seems unlikely that any single measure would be best in all research settings [...]*"[164]. As not all potential measures of FRQ can be applied at once and also an aggregation of measures seems not appropriate due to the different dimensions of the measures, this study focuses on **three FRQ measures** which capture specific aspects of total FRQ. While the selected **accruals-based earnings management proxies** as well as **readability measures** (inter alia, the Fog index) can be adopted from the prevalent literature, this study's **disclosure index measure** is self-constructed to be suitable for the study's cross-country setting. Consistent with the aforementioned multidimensional understanding of FRQ, the illustration in Figure 2-5 shows that each measure is only able to capture a certain part, but not the total abstract construct of FRQ (represented by the whole box). In line with this concept, *Hribar et al.* (2014) criticize that existing accruals-based proxies solely measure a small part of FRQ and, thus, develop an own measure which shall provide "*[...] a more global assessment of financial statement quality than focusing exclusively on one facet of accounting quality, such as how well accruals map into cash flows.*"[165]

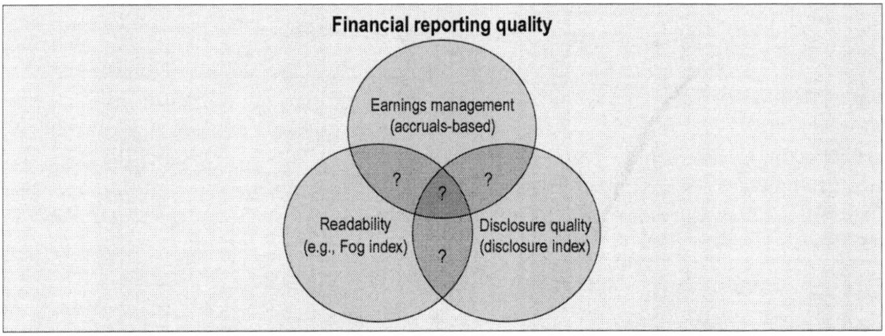

Figure 2-5: This study's FRQ measures

Further, the question marks in Figure 2-5 indicate that it is unclear, as to what extent the different measures overlap. For earnings management and disclosure quality measures, for

[161] Cf. here and in the following *Hassan/Marston* (2010), p. 32-33.
[162] For criticism of this approach, cf. *Beretta/Bozzolan* (2004), p. 266; *Botosan* (2004), p. 290-294.
[163] *Leuz/Verrecchia* (2000), p.92 (original text contains emphases).
[164] *Ecker et al.* (2006), p. 779.
[165] *Hribar et al.* (2014), p. 536.

instance, *Salewski et al.* (2014) expect consistent results, arguing "*[...] the greater the amount and the higher the quality of disclosures are, the smaller the room for earnings management [...].*"[166] In contrast, *van Beest et al.* (2009) point out that earnings management measures solely use information included in the companies' financial statements,[167] whereas "[...] *a comprehensive measurement tool of financial reporting quality would at least include the complete annual report, including both financial and nonfinancial information.*"[168] According to this argument, earnings management and disclosure quality measures could not provide consistent results, since only the latter is able to consider entire annual reports. Also readability measures may focus on entire annual reports.

The analysis has shown that prior research uses a large number of both indirect and direct measures for FRQ. It is debatable whether these proxies can be used interchangeably as substitutes, because they measure different facets of FRQ. Therefore, this study applies three different measures for FRQ and analyzes the results of each measure separately. In addition, the results are compared to investigate, as to what extent the three measures overlap and, thereby, shed light on the question marks in Figure 2-5.

2.2 Emerging economies and their accounting environment

2.2.1 Definition of emerging economies

Section 2.2 is concerned with emerging economies and their accounting environment. While this section provides a common understanding of the term *emerging economy*, in the following sections the role of emerging economies in the global economy is described (section 2.2.2) and their accounting characteristics (section 2.2.3) are discussed.

The literature does not provide a uniform definition of **emerging economies**. In general, however, an emerging economy is a **developing country** "*[...] that is on its way to becoming an industrialized nation [...]*"[169] and "*[...] that has achieved some industrial capacity [...]*"[170]. An important characteristic of emerging economies is rapid **economic growth**.[171] There are several reasons for the rapid development and enormous economic growth of such economies. Among others, liberalization and deregulation efforts (e.g., privatization) boosted particularly the economies in the former Eastern Bloc[172], but also e.g. India and

166 Cf. *Salewski et al.* (2014), p. 31.
167 Cf. *van Beest et al.* (2009), p. 7.
168 *van Beest et al.* (2009), p. 7.
169 *World Heritage Encyclopedia* (2014b).
170 *World Heritage Encyclopedia* (2014b).
171 Cf. *Nölke et al.* (2014), p. 9; *World Heritage Encyclopedia* (2014a).
172 Former Soviet-Bloc countries as well as China are examples of so-called *transitional economies*, cf. *Eggertsson* (1997), p. 74; *Polishchuk* (1997), p. 80. A transitional economy is developing from a centrally planned to a modern market economy, cf. *Eggertsson* (1997), p. 75. Critical issues in this process are typically concerned with, inter alia, privatization, stabilization, macroeconomic and monetary policies, liberalization and property rights, cf. *Benham/Benham* (1998), p. 51. However, it is difficult to determine when a transitional economy has reached the status of an advanced market economy; further, the actual difference between an emerging and a transitional economy is questionable, as both aim at catching up with advanced developed economies, cf. *Ezzamel/Xiao* (2011), p. 626.

Brazil.[173] Simultaneously, the economies opened up to international trade facilitating both the flow of goods and foreign direct investments.[174]

A multitude of constellations, acronyms and terms have been created for **groups of emerging economies**.[175] Specific examples are MIST, TIMP, CIVETS, G5, F-10 and PPICS, some of which have already disappeared from public view.[176] In the 1980s, South-East Asian economies, particularly Japan, South Korea, Singapore, Hong Kong and Taiwan managed to obtain the tag *Asian Tigers* due to their immense economic growth; however, the term began to perish during the Southeast Asian financial crisis of 1997/1998.[177] In 2001, the former Goldman Sachs economist *Jim O'Neill* identified four economies with particular potential for economic growth which he referred to by the acronym *BRIC* representing Brazil, Russia, India and China.[178] On this basis, the group of BRIC countries indeed intensified intra-BRIC collaboration (e.g., through annual summits) and the group was officially joined by South Africa (*BRICS*) on the first of the henceforth annual *BRICS summits* in 2011.[179] Instead of South Africa, another constellation adds South Korea to the BRIC forming the BRICK countries.[180] In 2005 *Jim O'Neill* reviewed the economic development of the BRIC countries and came up with an additional set of countries with considerable economic potential: the *next eleven* (also N-11) include Bangladesh, Egypt, Indonesia, Iran, Korea, Mexico, Nigeria, Pakistan, Philippines, Turkey and Vietnam. However, *O'Neill et al.* (2005) expect only Mexico and South Korea to possibly become as important as the BRIC countries.[181] Another powerful and already long-lasting regional group of countries is the Association of Southeast Asian nations (ASEAN).[182] Founded in 1967, the collaboration between Indonesia, Malaysia, Philippines, Singapore, Thailand, Brunei, Myanmar, Cambodia, Laos, and Vietnam contributed to the nations' social, cultural and economic development and, aggregating the GDP of all members, would represent the eighth largest economy in the world.[183]

The above mentioned as well as some other countries are frequently not only referred to as **emerging economies**, but also as **emerging markets**. The latter term *market* is primarily used in terms of *financial market* referring to the stock market in connection with investments into this market.[184] In the narrow sense, such a financial market comprises capi-

---

[173] Cf. *Rosefielde* (2007), p. 170-171; *Rajagopalan/Zhang* (2008), p. 56; *Schmalz/Ebenau* (2014), p. 45-46.

[174] Cf. *Hoskisson et al.* (2000), p. 252.

[175] Cf. *World Heritage Encyclopedia* (2014a).

[176] MIST (Mexico, Indonesia, South Korea and Turkey); TIMP (Turkey, Indonesia, Mexico, Philippines); CIVETS (Colombia, Indonesia, Vietnam, Egypt, Turkey, South Africa), Group of five (G5) (Brazil, China, India, Mexico, South Africa); F-10 (Frontier Strategy Group) (China, Brazil, India, Mexico, Russia, Indonesia, Colombia, Argentina, Chile, Turkey); PPICS (Peru, Philippines, Indonesia, Colombia, Sri Lanka), cf. *World Heritage Encyclopedia* (2014a).

[177] For a comprehensive description of the Southeast Asian crisis in 1997/1998, cf. *Corsetti et al.* (1999).

[178] Cf. *O'Neill* (2001), p. 1.

[179] Cf. *Fifth BRICS Summit* (2013).

[180] Cf. *Adams et al.* (2013), p. 4.

[181] Cf. *O'Neill et al.* (2005), p. 7.

[182] Cf. *Acharya* (2014).

[183] Cf. *World Heritage Encyclopedia* (2014b).

[184] Cf. *Füss* (2004).

tal markets, money markets, credit markets and foreign exchange (currency) markets.[185] To investors and financial analysts, however, emerging capital markets including equity markets are generally of most interest. In contrast, the term *emerging economy* rather encompasses all economic activities of a country.[186]

> "*The term 'emerging markets' should not be considered in the spirit of a parallel to emerging economies, even though there is an obvious relationship, in that the emergence of capital markets is considered by some as one of the indicators of a developing country's 'taking off' into industrial development.*"[187]

As multiple economic characteristics are related to the financial reporting practices in a country, this study generally uses the term *emerging economy.*

As mentioned before, "*[...] there remains no universally accepted operational definition [...]*"[188] of emerging economies. However, the following terminological delineations provide a **classification of emerging economy** groups.[189] With explicit regard to capital markets, *Errunza* (1983) distinguishes three general groups. First, antique markets which have lasted for centuries, however, are only recently developing major capital markets, such as India, Chile or Mexico.[190] Second, the development of some emerging markets benefited from particular conditions, e.g. the financial industry focus on Singapore and Hong Kong or the support of Jordan by the *Organization of the Petroleum Exporting Countries (OPEC).* Third, it is also feasible that entirely new markets have the structure and potential for economic growth, such as the example of South Korea has shown.

Moreover, major international organizations provide country classifications according to certain criteria. In the following, the classification models by the *World Bank*, the *United Nations (UN)*, the *International Monetary Fund (IMF)* and the *Organization for Economic Co-operation and Development (OECD)* are presented and applied to the BRICS countries as particularly large and typical emerging economies. These models help to characterize the BRICS countries, although not all of them explicitly distinguish between emerging and non-emerging economies.

The **World Bank** does not use the terms *emerging* or *developed economies* to avoid judgments, but rather classifies a country according to its gross national income (GNI)[191] per capita. The *World Bank* uses GNI, as it is relatively simple to calculate and associated with other non-monetary measures in a country, such as quality of life, life expectancy and enrollment rates in school.[192] In line with its classification criteria from 1 July 2014, it groups countries into the following categories: low income (below $ 1,046 per capita),

[185] Cf. *Bösch* (2013), p. 35.
[186] Cf. *Bösch* (2013), p. 464.
[187] *Errunza* (1983), p. 57.
[188] *Fifield et al.* (1998), p. 2.
[189] Cf. *Füss* (2004), p. 9.
[190] Cf. here and in the following *Errunza* (1983), p. 51-52. More precisely, this first group of antique markets would actually have to be called *re-emerging markets*, as these markets already used to have large and active equity markets, cf. *Goetzmann/Jorion* (1999), p. 2.
[191] The GNI generally captures the value added of all residents of a country, cf. *The World Bank* (2015b).
[192] Cf. *The World Bank* (2015b).

lower middle income ($ 1,046 to $ 4,125 per capita), upper middle income ($ 4,126 to $ 12,745 per capita) and high income (above $ 12,745 per capita).[193]

In its annual Human Development Report, the *Development Programme* of the **UN** publishes the Human Development Index which ranks countries according to the three key dimensions of human development *long and healthy life*, *knowledge* and *decent standard of living*.[194] To operationalize these dimensions, the Index comprises numerous measures including life expectancy at birth, mean years of schooling and estimated GNI per capita. The report identifies four groups of development levels: very high, high, medium and low. However, the *UN* underpins that there is no established definition of *developing*, *emerging* or *developed* economies and states that commonly the following regions are called *developed*: Japan, Canada, USA, Australia, New Zealand and Europe.[195]

The **IMF** classifies countries either as *advanced economies* or *emerging market and developing economies* according to certain criteria including e.g. per capita income level, export diversification (to lower the impact of massive oil exports in some countries) and global financial system integration.[196] However, neither does the *IMF* publish concrete criteria for the classification, nor are there strict thresholds which countries have to meet to be classified into a certain category; the *IMF* rather reclassifies a country, if there are overwhelming changes regarding relevant criteria.[197]

The members of the so-called *rich-man's club* **OECD** used to be only highly-developed and industrialized countries.[198] Over the past few years, however, also countries such as Mexico or Chile became members and the *OECD* engages in close partnerships with countries such as China, India and Brazil, which the *OECD* regards as major *emerging economies* besides Argentina, Indonesia, the Russian Federation and South Africa.[199] Although the international organization provides no precise definition of this term *emerging economy*, it considers the following features to determine emerging economies: *robust growth*, *integration into the world economy* and *income level*.[200] Deviating from the *OECD's* evaluation, the country of South Africa was classified as industrialized country by the *World Trade Organization (WTO)*, in which South Africa became a member state in 1995 and also the EU did not include South Africa in trade agreements with developing countries (e.g., the Lomé Convention).[201]

Table 2-2 reveals that the classifications of the BRICS countries according to the above organizations are not consistent. While the IMF and OECD classify all BRICS countries as emerging economies, the classifications of the World Bank (based on income) and the UN (based on human development) group the BRICS countries into different categories.

193 Cf. *The World Bank* (2014).
194 Cf. here and in the following *United Nations Development Programme* (2014), p. 160-163.
195 Cf. *United Nations* (2013a).
196 Cf. following *IMF* (2015a).
197 Cf. *IMF* (2015d), p. 147.
198 Cf. *The Economist* (2006), p. 3.
199 Cf. *OECD* (2015).
200 Cf. *OECD* (2011), p. 48.
201 Cf. *Claar* (2014), p. 198.

The relatively low income and development level of India, for instance, may suggest that the country does not belong to the group of emerging economies.[202] Thus, the understanding of emerging economy in this study focuses on the **economic growth** and growth potential of a country as well as the progress in its economic development towards an industrialized country.[203] This is in line with the more general understanding of *emerging* by *Bekaert/Harvey* (2002):

> "*Of course, the basic idea behind the term is that these countries 'emerge' from less-developed status and join the group of developed countries.*"[204]

In accordance with *Bekaert/Harvey* (2002), the classification scheme in Table 2-2 suggests that the BRICS economies are indeed in the process of *emerging*, as they are mostly in the process of development from countries with low human development and low income towards countries with high human development and high income. This understanding is consistent with this study's objective to investigate financial reporting practices in countries, which are of increasing global economic importance, however, do not already have the same characteristics as developed countries. The classification of the study's sample countries Brazil and South Africa into the group of *emerging* countries is further confirmed by the fact that in 2015 all BRICS countries are represented in the MSCI Emerging Markets Index, which captures equities in 23 emerging markets.[205]

Organization	Brazil	Russia	India	China	South Africa
IMF	Emerging/ developing	Emerging/ developing	Emerging/ developing	Emerging/ developing	Emerging/ developing
World Bank	Upper middle income	High income	Lower middle income	Upper middle income	Upper middle income
UN	High human development	High human development	Medium human development	High human development	Medium human development
OECD	Emerging economy	Emerging economy	Emerging economy	Emerging economy	Emerging economy

Table 2-2: BRICS country classifications
Following *Graser* (2011), p. 53. Sources: *IMF* (2015d); *The World Bank* (2015b); *United Nations Development Programme* (2014).

The following section 2.2.2 describes the role of emerging economies in the global economy to show the need for high-quality information and, thus, financial reporting as basis for capital allocation decisions. Furthermore, section 2.2.3 presents accounting characteristics which can affect financial reporting practices in emerging economies. In section 2.3 the specific financial reporting environments of this study's sample economies Brazil,

[202] Cf. *Becker* (2012), p. 2.
[203] This approach is in line with several definitions of *emerging economy* in the literature, cf. amongst others *Janovsky et al.* (2011), p. 27-30; *Hofbauer* (2011), p. 7.
[204] *Bekaert/Harvey* (2002), p. 429.
[205] Cf. *MSCI* (2015).

South Africa and Germany are analyzed. These descriptions help to interpret the empirical results of the study.

2.2.2 Role of emerging economies in the global economy

The rise of emerging economies is one of the global *megatrends* at least over the past ten years. To further deepen the understanding of emerging economies, this section explains their role in the global economy by the example of the BRICS countries. The group of BRICS economies has gained importance and moved from the status of a mere **investment target** for some global investors to **sales markets** which companies are keen to enter.[206] Moreover, the BRICS also fulfill global investing and lending functions. However, each of the five countries took a different path to make use of its individual potential, such as raw materials, skilled workforce or a considerable domestic market. Being aware of the fact that they will economically outpace Western Europe, Japan and the USA in less than one generation, rising countries have developed a new self-perception and self-confidence.[207] The countries are represented in global organizations (e.g., IMF, G20, WTO) and, in addition, organize emerging economy conferences, such as the aforementioned annual BRICS summits or the Shanghai Cooperation Organization.[208]

Moreover, emerging countries are involved in numerous **cooperation** projects partnering with other emerging countries.[209] Founded in 2003, the so-called *IBSA* alliance encompasses India as well as both of this study's sample countries Brazil and South Africa.[210] The collaboration aims at improving the living conditions in the three countries through increased intra-IBSA trade which is likely to exceed its initial target volume of $ 25 billion in 2015.[211] Collaboration with industrialized economies seems to be much more difficult, as the global power relations are changing so that the EU, for example, is struggling to reform its *strategic partnerships* with the BRICS.[212]

The pace of emerging economies' rise has even increased since the global **financial crisis** 2008/09, when traditional financial systems crashed throughout all major economies.[213] In comparison to numerous Western economies, the BRICS countries managed to successfully overcome the financial crisis.[214] For instance, the crisis barely affected the Brazilian banking system, as it had widely remained a part of the public sector and strict regulation restrained the national financial institutions' access to worldwide derivatives trading.[215] However, both the global financial crisis in 2008/09 and the second financial turmoil a few years later, which had its roots in the Eurozone in 2011, caused a massive decrease in foreign demand and economic growth in emerging economies (e.g., Brazil, India

[206] Cf. here and in the following *Bieling* (2014), p. 379-380.
[207] Cf. *Nölke et al.* (2014), p. 9.
[208] Cf. *Stuenkel* (2014), p. 89-92.
[209] For an overview of major collaborations, cf. *Keukeleire et al.* (2011), p. 9.
[210] Cf. *IBSA Dialogue Forum* (2015).
[211] Cf. *Stuenkel* (2014), p. 309; *IBSA Dialogue Forum* (2015).
[212] Cf. *Bieling* (2014), p. 388.
[213] Cf. *Nölke et al.* (2014), p. 10; *Schmalz/Ebenau* (2014), p. 43.
[214] Cf. *Schmalz/Ebenau* (2014), p. 44-45.
[215] Cf. here and in the following *Schmalz/Ebenau* (2014), p. 49-50 and 53.

and China). As a consequence, the BRICS countries called for more influence in global economic regulation on their summit in New Delhi in 2012, where they demanded, inter alia, stricter regulations of financing systems, commodity prices and an international reserve currency to strengthen their own positions as well as to lower the risk of negative impacts from an anticipated European recession.[216] Retrospectively, the BRICS countries, except for Russia, were barely affected by the financial crisis, but rather by the following recession; however, they managed to implement economic stimulus programs and intensified intra-BRIC trading.[217]

After years of rapid growth, most emerging economies have experienced **economic setbacks** and massive internal transformation processes concerning e.g. national identities and their new geopolitical strength.[218] South Africa, for instance, could not achieve its growth target of five percent over the past years.[219] Taking 1999 as base year, the relative development of the GDP in the BRICS countries is illustrated in Figure 2-6 and compared to the GDP development in Germany:

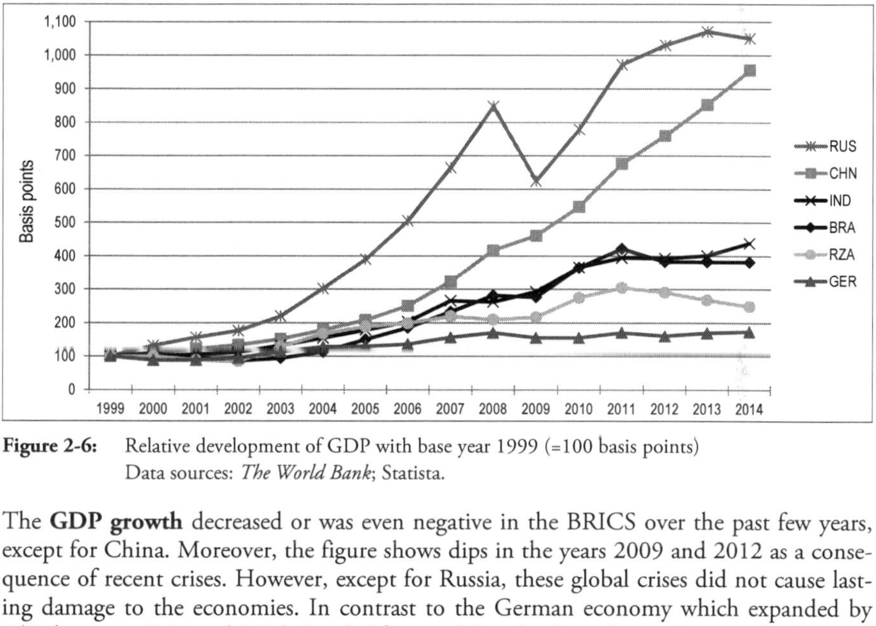

Figure 2-6: Relative development of GDP with base year 1999 (=100 basis points)
Data sources: *The World Bank*; Statista.

The **GDP growth** decreased or was even negative in the BRICS over the past few years, except for China. Moreover, the figure shows dips in the years 2009 and 2012 as a consequence of recent crises. However, except for Russia, these global crises did not cause lasting damage to the economies. In contrast to the German economy which expanded by 74% between 1999 and 2014, South Africa and Brazil achieved growth rates of 149% and 282%, respectively, Russia even 950%. Therefore, the figure explains vividly why these economies are referred to as *emerging* or *rising powers.*[220]

---

[216] Cf. *Schmalz/Ebenau* (2014), p. 44-45.
[217] Cf. *Bieling* (2014), p. 381.
[218] Cf. *Weinlich/Fues* (2014), p. 299.
[219] Cf. *Claar* (2014), p. 197.
[220] For these terms, cf. *Nölke et al.* (2014), p. 9; *Stephen* (2013), p. 3.

Regardless of the recent decrease in growth and unaffected of current transformations, the economic potential of particularly the BRICS economies remains immense, as Table 2-3 shows. The forecasts of the economic development are based on GDP figures in constant 2014 $ billion to ensure purchasing power parity (PPP). Although projection models include numerous assumptions and, thus, are subject to uncertainties, all BRICS countries are expected to have a higher GDP than Germany in 2050, except for the smallest of the five economies: South Africa. However, the South African economy is expected to expand by 343% until 2050, whereas the outlook anticipates not more than 75% growth for Germany in the same period.

	Brazil	Russia	India	China	South Africa	Germany
GDP 2014 [$ billion, PPP]	3,072.61	3,558.64	7,277.28	17,632.01	683.15	3,621.36
GDP 2020 [$ billion, PPP] (growth 2014-2020)	3,590.35 (+17%)	3,920.56 (+10%)	10,535.98 (+45%)	25,449.18 (+44%)	807.56 (+18%)	3,972.51 (+10%)
GDP 2050 [$ billion, PPP] (growth 2014-2050)	9,164.31 (+198%)	7,574.65 (+113%)	42,205.37 (+480%)	61,079.12 (+246%)	3,026.38 (+343%)	6,338.00 (+75%)

Table 2-3: GDP forecast for BRICS countries vs. Germany
Sources: *IMF* (2014); *PwC* (2015b).

One of the aspects to be considered in GDP estimates is the countries' **human resources**. Table 2-4 describes the demographic structure and prospective development for the BRICS and Germany. While the population is assumed to decrease in Germany and Russia until 2050, strong growth could boost the economies in Brazil, India and South Africa. In addition, these countries may benefit from a considerable increase in working population, as the share of people aged under 15 was between 24% and 31% in 2014.

	Brazil	Russia	India	China	South Africa	Germany
Population 2014 [million]	202.77	143.70	1,259.70	1,367.52	54.00	82.57
GDP per capita 2014 [$, PPP]	15,153.18	24,764.37	5,776.99	12,893.42	12,650.93	43,858.06
Population 2050 [million] (growth 2014-2050)	231.12 (+10%)	120.90 (-16%)	1,620.05 (+29%)	1,384.98 (+1%)	63.41 (+17%)	72.57 (-12%)
GDP per capita 2050 [$, PPP]	39,651.74	62,652.19	26,051.89	44,101.08	47,727.17	87,336.36
Population below age of 15 in 2014	24%	16%	31%	16%	29%	13%

Table 2-4: Demographic development in BRICS countries vs. Germany
Sources: Datastream; Statista; Population Reference Bureau; *United Nations* (2013b); *IMF* (2014); *PwC* (2015b).

Hence, the demographic figures help to explain the particular GDP potentials in Brazil, India and South Africa.

This section has outlined the (prospective) role of emerging economies (on the basis of the BRICS countries) in the current and future global economy. The following section 2.2.3 presents accounting-related characteristics of emerging economies.

2.2.3 Accounting characteristics

2.2.3.1 Introduction

As illustrated in the previous sections, the large number of countries which could be labeled as *emerging economies* are no homogenous group, but rather each country has its **individual characteristics**, such as geographical area, historical, socio-economic, cultural and political features.[221] Consequently, generalizations for some or all emerging economies seem difficult. Nevertheless, this section discusses influencing factors which typically shape accounting characteristics in emerging economies and, thus, also determine financial reporting practices in these countries.

Ahmed/Nicholls (1994) argue that annual report information provided by companies from less developed countries suffer from several factors of these countries' **accounting environments**. The following statement summarizes major characteristics which might lead to non-compliance with existing financial reporting regulation and, therefore, affect financial reporting practices in emerging economies:

> "*In developing countries, while there are considerable incentives for voluntary disclosures in corporate annual reports, there are also reasons for not complying with mandatory disclosure regulations, including inadequate regulatory framework and enforcement mechanisms, and a lack of both an effective capital market and an accounting profession. Therefore, the assumption that all companies will disclose all mandatory information may not be true in these countries.*"[222]

The following presentation of major emblematic accounting characteristics in emerging economies focuses on economic policies (section 2.2.3.2), culture (section 2.2.3.3), historical development and accounting origins (section 2.2.3.4), accounting regulation and enforcement (section 2.2.3.5), accounting education (section 2.2.3.6) as well as financing system and capital markets (section 2.2.3.7). These sections include the presentation of both accounting systems and practices in emerging economies. The accounting practice is the actual application of the implemented accounting systems.[223] In line with the previous section, the analysis of the accounting characteristics also uses the example of the BRICS countries.

---

221 Cf. *Ezzamel/Xiao* (2011), p. 327.

222 *Ahmed/Nicholls* (1994), p. 62.

223 Cf. *Reisloh* (2011), p. 6.

2.2.3.2 Economic policies

In general, every company accounts for its business transactions what makes accounting necessary in the first place. How these business transactions are coordinated and resources are allocated within an economy depends, inter alia, on the **type of the economy** and the **policies** which the responsible governments pursue. Although large emerging economies, such as Brazil, India or China, are deemed to have implemented market economies, where resources are allocated efficiently through market mechanisms, a closer look reveals that this view is not that clear.[224] *May* (2014) argues that the strong influence of **reciprocity**[225] interferes with market principles in large emerging economies and, thus, not solely markets coordinate these economies, but also negotiations and agreements, which lead to interdependencies between parties.[226] Hence, emerging economies have developed specific forms of market economies. For example, according to *Schneider* (2009) *hierarchical market economies* are common in Latin America, where hierarchies determine business transactions, rather than market mechanisms or legal rules. Moreover, *Nölke/Vliegenthart* (2009) refer to transformational countries in Central and Eastern Europe as *dependent market economies*, as corporate relationships are controlled by foreign multinationals. Moreover, reciprocity-based collectives (e.g., family businesses) regulate the economies of countries such as Brazil, India and China, where less formal (e.g., governmental) institutions have been established due to the strength of such informal organizations.[227] As a consequence, an increased level of **ownership concentration** is deemed to be a typical characteristic of numerous emerging economies.[228] In particular, *Schiehll et al.* (2013) argue: "*Most listed companies in emerging markets have a concentrated ownership structure [...]*"[229]. Taking the above arguments into account, a crucial prerequisite ensuring that markets, including price mechanisms, are functioning efficiently is **transparency**.[230] As one of its main objectives, this study aims at investigating, as to what extent companies in emerging economies contribute to market transparency by reporting high-quality information.

In contrast to reciprocity-dominated economies, also the strong **influence of the state** and government can deter the establishment of a functional market economy. In Russia, for example, the government supported the creation of large state-owned companies in the strategic oil and gas industry.[231] Also the Chinese economy has a high percentage of state-owned corporations and in India the state reserves the right to control industries regarded as relevant for the country's national security.[232] These characteristics come along with tremendous risks and challenges for investors.

---

[224] Cf. *May* (2014), p. 85.

[225] Reciprocity generally describes symmetric exchange relationships, in which a party who receives something from another party is required to return something of equivalent value, as the typical example of present and counter-present illustrates, cf. *Weiner* (1980), p. 73.

[226] Cf. here and in the following *May* (2014), p. 88.

[227] Cf. *May* (2014), p. 97.

[228] Cf. amongst others *Haniffa/Cooke* (2002), p. 320; *Schiehll et al.* (2013), p. 339.

[229] Cf. *Schiehll et al.* (2013), p. 355.

[230] Cf. *May* (2014), p. 89.

[231] Cf. *Rosefielde* (2007), p. 185.

[232] Cf. *Tomlinson* (2013), p. 223-225; *Estrin/Prevezer* (2011), p. 47-49.

2.2.3.3 Culture

A country's **national culture** influences its accounting and financial reporting systems in different ways.[233] On the one hand, culture affects the creation, development and implementation of political and legal systems of a country which again determine the framework and regulation of financial reporting.[234] On the other hand, the national culture - including national values and attitudes - affects how the preparer of a financial report interprets and, thus, applies financial reporting rules.[235]

To operationalize the abstract term *culture*, researchers frequently refer to the cultural dimensions by *Hofstede*: power distance, individualism vs. collectivism, masculinity vs. femininity, uncertainty avoidance, long-term vs. short-term orientation and indulgence vs. restraint.[236] In a subsequent step, *Gray* (1988) links these cultural dimensions to accounting systems and, thereby, derives a country's cultural impact on its financial reporting practices.[237] *Gray* identifies four **accounting values**. First, there are differences across countries, whether accountants rely on their own professional judgment or rather strictly stick to a given set of rules (**professionalism vs. statutory control**). Second, accounting systems either require companies to prepare uniform and consistent accounts or rather grant entities a certain degree of flexibility to adjust accounts to the company's specific environment (**uniformity vs. flexibility**). Third, the attitude towards the fact that the future is uncertain differs considerably across cultures resulting in an either cautious or rather optimistic assessment (**conservatism vs. optimism**). The fourth accounting value is of particular interest to this study, since it is directly related to financial reporting. *Gray* distinguishes between those cultures which are willing to disclose information openly to the public and those which treat corporate information more confidentially and prefer to provide information only to closely related interest groups (**secrecy vs. transparency**). Referring to *Hofstede's* cultural dimensions, secrecy is particularly associated with high levels of uncertainty avoidance, power distance and collectivism. Besides secrecy, also the value of conservatism generally "*[...] impl[ies] a cautious approach to corporate financial reporting [...]*"[238], although secrecy affects a company's actual reporting practice and conservatism rather than its measurement approach.

Although a general evaluation of all emerging economies is obviously not possible, as each country has its individual culture, *Borker* (2013) identifies at least groups of emerging economies which share similar cultural characteristics.[239] Only a few of them, however, are characterized by a **favorable reporting profile**, which would require a focus on professionalism, optimism, flexibility and, in particular, transparency, as it is the case for the U.S., for example.[240] A considerable number of emerging countries (e.g., Brazil, Russia,

---

[233] Cf. *Nobes* (1998), p. 175; *Borker* (2012), p. 313-322.

[234] Cf. *Ding et al.* (2005), p. 334; *Borker* (2013), p. 674.

[235] Cf. *Borker* (2013), p. 674; *Gray* (1988), p. 8.

[236] Cf. *Hofstede* (1980b), p. 43; *Hofstede* (2001), p. 351; *Hofstede et al.* (2010), p. 280. The cultural dimension are used, among others, by *Nobes* (1998); *Hope* (2003); *Borker* (2012); *Borker* (2013).

[237] Cf. here and in this paragraph *Gray* (1988), p. 8-11.

[238] *Gray* (1988), p. 11.

[239] Cf. *Borker* (2013), 680.

[240] Cf. *Borker* (2013), 679-680.

China, Egypt, Philippines) tend to have high scores in *Hofstede's* dimensions collectivism, power distance and uncertainty avoidance.[241] This can be interpreted (in accordance with *Gray's* accounting values) as these countries prefer uniform accounting systems without discretion to report individually on separate business transactions.[242] Furthermore, the strongly pronounced collectivism, power distance and uncertainty avoidance decrease the level of accounting professionalism.[243] As a consequence of low accounting professionalism, accounting practices are questionable and the power of authorities (e.g., to define accounting regulation) is strengthened. The observation that numerous emerging economies seek to keep corporate information secret might particularly influence financial reporting activities so that companies provide solely few information.[244] In addition, *Doupnik* (2008) argues that strong uncertainty avoidance and collectivism are associated with earnings management, particularly earnings smoothing.[245]

Table 2-5 shows that the BRICS countries' characteristics barely match with the favorable reporting profile.

	Favorable reporting profile	Brazil	Russia	India	China	South Africa
Professionalism vs. statutory control	Professionalism	Statutory control	Statutory control	Professionalism	Professionalism/Statutory control	Professionalism/Statutory control
Uniformity vs. flexibility	Flexibility	Uniformity	Uniformity	Flexibility/ Uniformity	Uniformity	Flexibility/ Uniformity
Conservatism vs. optimism	Optimism	Conservatism	Conservatism	Optimism/ Conservatism	Optimism/ Conservatism	Optimism/ Conservatism
Secrecy vs. transparency	Transparency	Secrecy	Secrecy	Transparency/Secrecy	Secrecy	Transparency/Secrecy

Table 2-5: BRICS countries' cultural accounting values according to *Gray* (1988)
Based on *Hofstede* (1980b), p. 51-54; *Borker* (2012), p. 321; *Borker* (2013), p. 679.

Particularly the accounting profiles of Russia and Brazil might deter transparent and comprehensive reporting in those countries, while India seems to have a more reporting-friendly cultural environment.[246] In line with the favorable reporting profile, the South African accounting values show, at least to some extent, pronounced optimism and transparency.

---

[241] Cf. *Perera* (1989), p. 53-54; *Borker* (2012), p. 316; *Borker* (2013), p. 677-678.
[242] Cf. *Borker* (2013), p. 678.
[243] Cf. here and in the following *Perera* (1989), p. 52-54.
[244] Cf. *Hope* (2003), p. 221; *Doupnik/Salter* (1995), p. 392.
[245] Cf. *Doupnik* (2008), p. 338.
[246] Cf. *Borker* (2012), p. 321.

2.2.3.4 Historical development and accounting origins

The accounting systems of many emerging economies have been shaped by the accounting systems of countries which used to be related to the emerging economy.[247] This relationship can derive from different foundations, such as colonial history, trading partners, or role-model for an accounting system in a market-based economy. Until the middle of the 20th century a number of today's emerging economies were dominated by **colonial powers** so that the accounting system of the colonial state was frequently close to that of the colonial master or even a full copy, as the example of the British colonial empire and its former colonial states Hong Kong, Malaysia, Singapore as well as India illustrates.[248] However, not only colonial relations also **trading partners** influenced accounting systems of emerging countries. In the case of Brazil, for example, the USA were the country's most important trading partner in the 1950s when American automobile companies started to produce cars in Brazil.[249] The effect was that the U.S. accounting model influenced the Brazilian one and also Brazilian accounting education was adjusted to the American approach.

In the so-called **transformational countries** (e.g., the former Soviet states and China) accounting was supposed to primarily support the economic policy as well as to ensure that the state controls all production factors.[250] Strict regulations did not leave any room for discretion and the actual economic substance of transactions was of minor interest, as entities prepared reports for administration offices instead of various market participants.[251] After the collapse of the centrally-planned economic system the transformation towards market economies raised the need of a revised accounting system.[252] As there were already established and generally accepted accounting systems in other countries, transitional economies had the possibility to use other economies as a role-model and adopt their existing accounting systems and rules.[253] Particularly, the well-established International Accounting Standards (IAS) and the succeeding IFRS, respectively, were adopted by multiple countries or at least influenced the development of an own set of rules.[254] China, for instance, issued four sets of accounting standards since 1992 with continuously increasing consistency with IAS/IFRS.[255]

The literature particularly distinguishes Continental European and Anglo-Saxon (also British-American) accounting influences. According to the two regimes' traditionally dominant accounting characteristics, **Anglo-Saxon** regimes provide financial reporting regulations which tend to require more disclosures and less prudence for recognition than **Continental European** regimes.[256] Regarding the impact of the accounting system type

247 Cf. here and in the following *Radebaugh et al.* (2006), p. 72; *Nobes* (1998), p. 170.
248 Cf. *Ball et al.* (2003), p. 238-240.
249 Cf. here and in the following *Rodrigues et al.* (2012), p. 18.
250 Cf. *Adhikari/Wang* (1995), p. 27.
251 Cf. *Nobes* (2012), p. 283; *Sun* (2013), p. 36-37; *Peng/van der Laan Smith* (2010), p. 17-18.
252 Cf. *McGee/Preobragenskaya* (2005), p. 3.
253 Cf. *Ball et al.* (2003), p. 238-240.
254 Cf. *Steinbach/Tang* (2014), p. 32-33.
255 Cf. *Liu et al.* (2011), p. 663.
256 Cf. *Nobes* (1998), p. 168; *Nobes/Parker* (2012), p. 43.

on the financial reporting quality, *Lopes* (2011) argues that the value relevance of financial reporting would be lower in countries with the Continental European model.[257]

A country's historical development also determines its **legal system**. The literature discusses controversially, as to what extent legal systems are associated with the quality of financial reporting.[258] Legal systems and, thus, particularly investor protection in emerging economies are frequently characterized as *weak*.[259] However, this generalization appears problematic, since legal families and traditions differ across emerging economies. *La Porta et al.* (1998) finds the strongest legal protection of investors for common law countries (English legal tradition) and the weakest one for French-civil-law countries, whereas the investor protection in German- and Scandinavian-civil-law countries is in between.[260] Moreover, accounting research frequently deals with the assumption "*[...] that common law countries produce higher quality financial reports than civil law countries.*"[261]

2.2.3.5 Accounting regulation and enforcement

A common set of financial reporting regulation can be regarded as the basis for reliable comparisons of financial reporting practices among countries. Over the past few years, the **IFRS** have been established as generally-accepted reporting regulation in an increasing number of countries all over the world.[262] Table 2-6 presents the IFRS adoption in each of the BRICS countries for listed companies. The overview shows that the financial reporting regulation in all five countries is based on the IFRS to varying degrees. Except for China and India, the IFRS are already required for the financial statements (FS) of listed companies. While there are ongoing efforts to (further) implement IFRS in Russia and India, the IFRS are already fully adopted in Brazil and South Africa for a considerable period of time. However, the IFRS implementation is subject to an endorsement process to be transferred into national law in numerous countries.[263] The endorsement process can modify the IFRS, e.g. reduce accounting choices allowed by IFRS or add disclosure requirements. In addition to IFRS, companies may have to comply with other accounting regulation including specific reporting requirements (e.g., by national laws or stock exchanges).[264]

---

[257] Cf. *Lopes* (2011), p. 341.

[258] Cf. *Bushman/Smith* (2003), p. 75; *Lindahl/Schadewitz* (2013), p. 242.

[259] Cf. *Bushman/Smith* (2001), p. 298; *Füss* (2004), p. 66-67; *Krishnamurti et al.* (2005), p. 435; *Doidge et al.* (2007), p. 34; *Chen et al.* (2011), p. 1259.

[260] Cf. *La Porta et al.* (1998), p. 1113; *Krishnamurti et al.* (2005), p. 442.

[261] Cf. *Lindahl/Schadewitz* (2013), p. 243.

[262] For an overview of global IFRS adoption, cf. *PwC* (2014). For detailed insights on the adoption of IFRS and IFRS for SMEs by private firms in 110 countries, cf. *Saucke* (2015).

[263] Cf. here and in the following *Steinbach/Tang* (2014), p. 34.

[264] Cf. e.g. *PwC* (2014), p. 44; paragraph 3.4 of the *JSE* Listings Requirements.

	Brazil	Russia	India	China	South Africa
IFRS for listed companies	Required for consolidated FS in addition to Brazilian GAAP	Required for consolidated and individual FS	Dominant Indian GAAP; IFRS option for some companies is rarely used	No, but Chinese GAAP has largely converged with IFRS	Required for consolidated and individual FS
IFRS version	IFRS as published by the IASB, but some options not allowed	IFRS as published by the IASB	IFRS as published by the IASB	-	IFRS as published by the IASB
Year of transition	2010	2011	2 phases: 2016-2017 (planned)	-	2005
Prospective IFRS implementation	Already adopted	Further convergence with IFRS also for local accounting standards	Expected convergence to IFRS with some exemptions and changes in the near future	Local GAAP is continuously amended to be in line with IFRS principles, but no adoption plans	Already adopted

Table 2-6: IFRS adoption in BRICS countries
Sources: *Grant Thornton* (2010), p. 14; *PwC* (2014); *PwC* (2015a).

Furthermore, the impact of a country's **tax system** on financial reporting practices depends on the relation between tax accounts and financial accounts. In general, tax accounts can be fully independent, fully dependent or partially dependent from financial accounts.[265] The closer the relationship between accounting and tax system, the higher the influence of the tax system on accounting and, thus, on the information provided in financial statements. According to *Ali/Hwang* (2000), the lower the dependency between tax and financial accounts, the higher the quality of information in financial reports.[266]

	Brazil	Russia	India	China	South Africa
Relation between tax accounts and financial accounts	Dependent: From 2015 IFRS as basis for tax calculation[267]	Independent: Specific tax rules	Quasi-dependent: Statutory filings (Indian GAAP) with tax law adjustments as basis for tax calculation	Quasi-dependent: Statutory filings (Chinese GAAP) with tax law adjustments as basis for tax calculation	Quasi-dependent: Statutory filings (IFRS allowed) with tax law adjustments as basis for tax calculation

Table 2-7: Tax regimes in BRICS countries
Source: *PwC* (2014).

Among the BRICS countries, this relation differs considerably, as Table 2-7 shows. While, for example, companies in Russia prepare their tax accounts according to specific

265 Cf. here and in the following *Nobes* (2014), p. 25.

266 Cf. *Ali/Hwang* (2000), p. 2.

267 Before 2015, the introduction of IFRS in Brazil had led to a segregation of financial and tax accounting, as tax regulation was independent from the IFRS (cf. *Lopes* (2011), p. 343) so that the former tax-oriented accounting culture had been losing its strength, cf. *Carvalho/Salotti* (2013), p. 237-238.

tax rules, Brazilian entities calculate their taxable profits on the basis of their IFRS results from calendar year 2015 on.[268]

Uncertainty, as to what extent a company indeed complies with accounting regulation, poses a severe risk to users of financial reports. **Auditors** are able to contribute to enhanced levels of compliance. However, *Brown et al.* (2014) find that the quality of the auditors' working environment (e.g., education and licensing requirements) tends to be lower in emerging economies than in developed countries.[269] According to empirical research, big audit firms may affect disclosure compliance positively.[270]

Furthermore, the existence of **enforcement** mechanisms ensures that companies comply with the existing accounting regulation. However, empirical investigations suggest a relatively poor compliance of companies in less developed countries.[271] For entities from Bangladesh, for instance, *Ahmed/Nicholls* (1994) find that

> "*[...] none of the sampled companies complied with the existing financial regulations.*"[272]

Similarly, *Santos et al.* (2014) provide evidence for a low level of compliance with mandatory IFRS by Brazilian companies in their first year of IFRS adoption.[273] Table 2-8 reveals that there are **enforcement institutions** in all of the BRICS countries including regulators, stock exchanges and auditing oversight bodies. The institutions are mostly a part of public enforcement (e.g., state-funded security market regulators) rather than private enforcement (private litigation).[274] Private self-regulatory bodies could enhance the degree of accounting professionalism concerning both development and enforcement of accounting regulation.[275] However, *Brown et al.* (2014) provide empirical evidence that the enforcement environment tends to be weaker in emerging economies than in developed countries.[276] Their evaluation of the enforcement activity by independent bodies considers, inter alia, whether the enforcement body provides reports about its review of financial statements and whether enforcement actions are taken.[277] The results suggest relatively low enforcement scores for the BRICS countries (ranging from 6 to 16 points), whereas the highest score is reached by the U.S. (24 points).[278] A reason for a lower enforcement quality could be that regulators are less active and, thus, struggle to "[...] *promote the quality of financial reporting information by encouraging and assisting firms to provide the required information, identifying cases where suitable information has not been provided and taking action to ensure defective reporting is corrected.*"[279] Overall, the enforcement envi-

[268] Cf. *PwC* (2014), p. 45 and 132-133.
[269] Cf. *Brown et al.* (2014), p. 19-20.
[270] Cf. *Ahmed/Nicholls* (1994), p. 62; *Iatridis* (2012), p. 109-111.
[271] Cf. amongst others *Ahmed/Nicholls* (1994), p. 62; *Ali et al.* (2004), p. 183.
[272] *Ahmed/Nicholls* (1994), p. 62.
[273] Cf. *Santos et al.* (2014), p. 174.
[274] Cf. *Brown et al.* (2014), p. 2.
[275] Cf. *Saudagaran/Diga* (1998), p. 58.
[276] Cf. *Brown et al.* (2014), p. 19-20.
[277] Cf. *Brown et al.* (2014), p. 10.
[278] Cf. *Brown et al.* (2014), p. 19-20.
[279] *Brown et al.* (2014), p. 8.

ronment may be weaker in emerging economies than in developed countries due to a lack of professional attitude towards financial reporting and relatively poor mechanisms to enforce accounting rules.[280]

	Brazil	Russia	India	China	South Africa
Regulator	Securities and Exchange Commission (CVM) (for public entities); professional accountancy organization CFC (for non-public entities)	Federal Commission on the Securities Market (FCSM); Federal Service for Financial Markets of the Russian Federation	Securities and Exchange Board of India (SEBI)	Ministry of Finance; China Securities Regulatory Commission	Financial Services Board (FSB); Company and Intellectual Property Commission (CIPC)
Stock exchange	BM&FBOVESPA	Moscow Exchange	National Stock Exchange of India Ltd; Bombay Stock Exchange	Shanghai Stock Exchange	Johannesburg Stock Exchange
Auditing oversight body	Securities and Exchange Commission (CVM)	The Ministry of Finance of Russian Federation	The Institute of Chartered Accountants of India	Ministry of Finance; China Securities Regulatory Commission	Independent Regulatory Board for Auditors (IRBA)

Table 2-8: Enforcement bodies in BRICS countries
Sources: *IFRS Foundation* (2013a); *Brown et al.* (2014), p. 32-38; *IMF* (2015b), p. 8.

Furthermore, (international) investors may face the problem that companies in emerging economies report information in the local language, e.g. ad-hoc messages are sometimes initially published in the local language and translated into English only after a certain period of time. As a consequence, investors might have less protection against the managers' self-interests than in developed countries.[281] Hence, investment appears more risky so that investors either abandon investments in emerging economies or demand an adequate risk premium.

2.2.3.6 Accounting education

A prerequisite for high-quality accounting information are well-educated accounting professionals involved in the preparation of this information. The analysis of the **accounting education** may be particularly interesting for the analysis of accounting practices in less developed countries.[282] *Nobes* (2014) argues that their accounting education is related to factors, such as a country's colonial history and level of economic development in these countries. *Parry/Groves* (1990) provide evidence for a lower level of education practices and professional expertise in less developed countries.[283] In line with this observation, there are several reasons for a lower accounting education in emerging economies than in developed countries.

---

280 Cf. *de Lima et al.* (2010), p. 257; *Iatridis* (2012), p. 103; *Nobes* (2014), p. 24-30.
281 Cf. *Bushman/Smith* (2001), p. 295.
282 Cf. here and in the following *Nobes* (2014), p. 27.
283 Cf. *Parry/Groves* (1990), p. 134; *Nobes* (1998), p. 182.

Education in emerging economies is challenging due to the rapidly developing economic environment, the discrepancy between recent trends and old traditions regarding education and the lack of resources.[284] With respect to the BRICS, particularly the changes in the countries' accounting systems (e.g., the shift towards IFRS) are coming along with tremendous changes in their education systems. For example, adjusting the education of auditors to IFRS poses a major challenge,[285] as there is a shortage of qualified teachers and even the availability of teaching materials in the local language may cause difficulty.[286] Moreover, the national contexts and the perception of accounting in a society determine how international accounting standards are taught and, thus, affect the eventual application of these standards.[287] Nonetheless, the emerging economies have made considerable efforts to improve and internationalize their education system and the status quo can only be evaluated individually for each country.[288]

2.2.3.7 Financing systems and capital markets

Also dominant **financing systems** influence accounting and financial reporting practices in emerging economies. The two most pronounced financing system types are banking-oriented systems with bank loans as key financing instrument and capital market-oriented models, where equity is the entities' main funding source.[289] According to the literature, creditors have direct access to corporate information in banking-oriented systems, whereas shareholders in capital-market systems rather have to rely on company publications as source of information.[290] In line with this view, *Nobes* (2014) classifies providers of resources as *insiders* or *outsiders* depending on their relationship to the company:

> "*For example, insurance companies and unit trusts normally have widely diversified portfolios, so that any particular holding does not constitute a large proportion of a company's capital. Therefore, such institutions should perhaps be counted as outsiders. By contrast, 'insiders' such as governments, banks, families and other companies are all likely to have close, long-term relationships with their investees. This will involve the private provision of timely and frequent accounting information.*"[291]

According to *Nobes* (2014), the existence of dominant outsiders in combination with a strong equity focus (capital market-oriented) leads to a situation in which financial reporting becomes particularly important.[292] However, this inference holds only true in culturally self-sufficient countries, whereas in culturally dominated countries (e.g., emerging

---

[284] Cf. *Albu et al.* (2012), p. 52.
[285] Cf. *McGee/Preobragenskaya* (2005), p. 109.
[286] Cf. *Carvalho/Salotti* (2013), p. 240-241.
[287] Cf. *Albu et al.* (2012), p. 51.
[288] Cf. *Carvalho/Salotti* (2013), p. 213; *Steinbach/Tang* (2014), p. 38.
[289] Cf. *Wöhe/Döring* (2013), p. 541-547.
[290] Cf. among others *Ball et al.* (2000), p. 3; *Nobes* (2012), 34-35; *Ali/Hwang* (2000), p. 3-4.
[291] *Nobes* (2014), p. 21.
[292] Cf. *Nobes* (2014), p. 21.

economies which are culturally dominated by former colonial masters[293]), reporting practices are rather determined by the dominant cultural influence.[294]

Mulyaningsih (2014) finds differences between banking systems in developed and less developed countries.[295] Only developed countries have mature markets, where the penetration of banks is deeper than in developing countries. Furthermore, financial institutions in developed countries have more diverse businesses resulting in lower competitive pressure, but also increased risks of non-interest activities.

Choi/Meek (2011) state that the **capital markets** in emerging economies are generally not on the same level as developed capital markets.[296] However, *Füss* (2004) finds in a discriminant analysis that some emerging economies' capital markets (particularly stock markets in, amongst others, Chile, Mexico and Malaysia) show very similar characteristics to those of developed countries.[297] Capital markets gained in importance among companies in emerging economies as a crucial financing instrument in times of rapid growth.[298] Particularly in Brazil, India and China the number of companies listed on equity markets rose enormously over the past decades.[299] Traditionally, investor protection is more pronounced in common law countries (e.g., USA, UK) leading to a stronger capital market orientation, while in civil law countries (e.g., France, Germany) banking oriented financing is wide-spread.[300] Consequently, also the capital market systems of emerging economies might be influenced by their legal system and the legal system of influencing countries, respectively, such as former colonial masters.

On the whole, *Choi/Meek* (2011) posit that the capital market orientation in most emerging economies is lower than in major developed capital markets.[301] The observation that overall investor protection in most emerging economies is weaker than in developed economies has complicated the development of capital markets.[302] One reason for weaker investor protection is considerable cost to ensure a high-quality institutional infrastructure.[303] Moreover, missing or relatively weak governance systems and legal uncertainties are hindering the creation of effective and reliable legal systems.[304]

---

[293] Cf. section 2.2.3.4.
[294] Cf. *Nobes* (1998), p. 183-184.
[295] Cf. here and in the following *Mulyaningsih* (2014), p. 22-23.
[296] Cf. *Choi/Meek* (2011), p. 158.
[297] Cf. *Füss* (2004), p. 68 and p. 123.
[298] Cf. *Radebaugh et al.* (2006), p. 19.
[299] Cf. *Pilz* (2008), p. 91; *Liu et al.* (2011), p. 662.
[300] Cf. *La Porta et al.* (1997), p. 1131-1132 and 1138.
[301] Cf. *Choi/Meek* (2011), p. 158.
[302] Cf. *Chen et al.* (2011), p. 1259; *Füss* (2004), p. 66-67; *Bushman/Smith* (2001), p. 298.
[303] Cf. *Doidge et al.* (2007), p. 34.
[304] Cf. *Young et al.* (2008), p. 198.

2.3 Financial reporting environment in Brazil, South Africa and Germany

2.3.1 Overview

While section 2.2.3 has revealed which accounting characteristics determine the reporting environment of emerging economies in general, section 2.3 focuses on the financial reporting environment of this study's **sample countries Brazil**, **South Africa** and **Germany**. There are several reasons for the selection of the three countries.

In line with the focus of this study, the empirical investigation analyzes financial reporting practices in **emerging economies** (Brazil and South Africa) on the one hand and a **developed country** (Germany), on the other. The emerging economies Brazil and South Africa are selected, since they are on a similar economic level. In line with the description of the BRICS countries in section 2.2.2, *Iatridis* (2012) underpins: "*South Africa and Brazil exhibit a comparable GDP at purchasing power parity per capita.*"[305] As part of the BRICS countries, Brazil and South Africa have gained particular investor attention over the past few years. Although the economic importance of all three sample countries is supported by the performance of the countries' major stock market indices over the last years, the indices in Brazil (Ibovespa) and South Africa (FTSE/JSE All Share) show the typical rapid economic growth of emerging economies outperforming the German index (DAX30). Figure 2-7 illustrates the development of these indices between 1996 and 2014. After the Brazilian index advanced even about 2.5 times faster than the South African counterpart between 1996 and 2009, it has experienced some setbacks over the past few years so that the FTSE/JSE All Share outperformed Ibovespa in 2014 (compared to 1996 as base year).

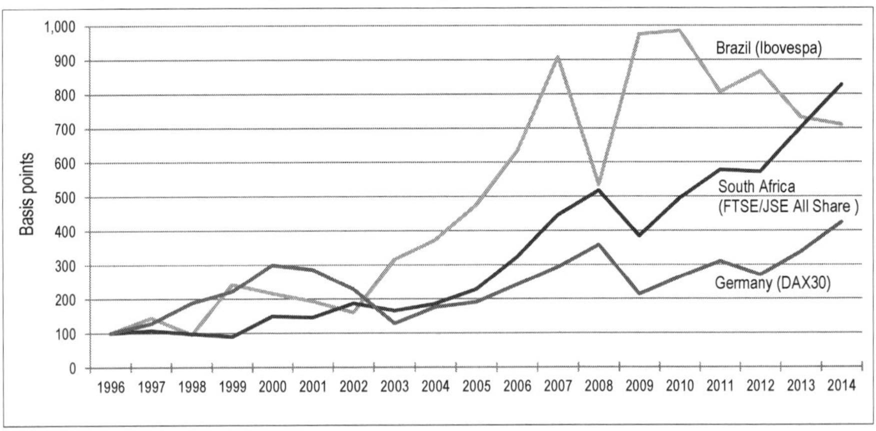

Figure 2-7: Performance development of stock market indices with base year 1996 (=100 basis points) Data source: Thomson Reuters Datastream.

[305] *Iatridis* (2012), p. 103.

Moreover, the fact that all sample companies from the three selected countries have to comply with the IFRS enhances the comparability of the empirical results. In line with the Brazilian and South African **IFRS adoption** in 2010 and 2005,[306] the IFRS are required in Germany for consolidated financial statements of companies with securities traded in a regulated market in Europe since 1 January 2005.[307] However, the countries' financial reporting regulations are not limited to the IFRS, but comprise additional reporting requirements. In particular, Germany is chosen as an adequate **developed country** benchmark, as there are well-established mandatory and voluntary financial reporting activities by companies and the country has an own far-reaching financial reporting history. For example, the German Accounting Standards (GAS) require companies to provide certain information in their management reports. Moreover, this study's selected companies publish annual reports in English in the three countries so that international investors can use and compare the annual reports as a basis for their decisions.

Further, this study's capital market analysis requires companies whose shares are traded actively at stock exchanges. The **capital markets** in the three sample countries show considerable trading activity. In particular, trading at the major stock exchanges in Brazil and South Africa has gained momentum over the past years. The annual trading value of company shares on the Brazilian *BM&FBOVESPA* and the *Johannesburg Stock Exchange (JSE)* increased by about 700% and 350% between 2000 and 2012.[308] During the same period, the *Deutsche Börse* in Germany lost about half of its equity trading value, which still exceeds the trading values of the *BM&FBOVESPA* and the JSE substantially. In line with *Nobes* (2014), the disclosure of corporate information is particularly important in case of strong equity markets.[309]

Important financial reporting characteristics of the sample countries are presented in the following country profiles of Brazil (section 2.3.2), South Africa (section 2.3.3) and Germany (section 2.3.4). The country profiles describe the sample countries' economic policies, historical development, national culture, accounting education, financing systems, financial reporting regulation and enforcement. Section 2.3.5 provides an integrated conclusion of the three countries' financial reporting environments and identifies major differences.

2.3.2 Brazil

The Brazilian economy is a typical example for reciprocity-dominated emerging economies, in which not only liberal market mechanisms determine market coordination, but also personal relationships between economic and state players. In particular, strong state-economic collectives, so-called *clans*, which are characterized by shared values, loyalty and personal trust, take over the market coordination, whereas in traditional liberal market

[306] Cf. section 2.2.3.5.

[307] Cf. Regulation (EC) No 1606/2002 of the European Parliament and of the Council of 19 July 2002 on the application of international accounting standards.

[308] Cf. here and in the following *World Federation of Exchanges* (2015). Currencies translated according to year-end exchange rates from Thomson Reuters Datastream.

[309] Cf. *Nobes* (2014), p. 21.

economies this function is ensured by the enforcement of legal claims.[310] Similarly, among Brazilian companies so-called *grupos economicos* coordinate the inter-company relations. However, there is a considerable amount of family-owned and family-run companies in Brazil, which are barely interested in intensive coordination with other entities.[311] The family businesses frequently have long traditions and make decisions rather internally and independently. However, unlike family-dominated economies in the 19th century, strong Brazilian families represent organizational units, which impede market mechanisms.[312] Consequently, the **ownership concentration** of companies is traditionally high in Brazil.[313] The personality- and charisma-oriented leadership models also shape Brazilian **policies**, which are closely-linked to the economic areas, as mentioned before.[314] Moreover, massive bureaucracy is costly and inefficient with more than 260.000 employees only in state-level administration; however, it keeps the state-supported economic system going, as a collapse could turn the current system into a hardly functioning system.[315] On the whole, the dominance of reciprocity and the high ownership concentration in Brazil impair market efficiency. The country's legal regime is regarded as poor.[316]

With respect to Brazil's **historical development**, the Portuguese colonization from the early 16th until the late 19th century has not only affected the country's language, but also other areas including the accounting system.[317] The Portuguese colonizers and other **Continental Europeans** brought a Continental accounting structure to Brazil.[318] Regarding the impact of the accounting system type on financial reporting quality, *Lopes* (2011) argues that the value relevance of financial reporting would be lower in countries with the Continental European model than in Anglo-Saxon countries.[319] In particular, Brazilian companies are said to traditionally rather comply with the regulation of their Continental European system than indeed provide decision useful information.[320]

Section 2.2.3.3 has revealed that the Brazilian national **culture** not contributes to a transparent financial reporting environment. According to *Hofstede's* cultural dimensions, the Brazilian culture is characterized by pronounced collectivism, power distance and uncertainty avoidance, whereas neither masculinity nor femininity is particularly dominant.[321] The country's dominant cultural accounting values (according to *Gray* (1988)) are statutory control, uniformity, conservatism and secrecy, which are entirely contrary to a favor-

310 Cf. *Lopes et al.* (2007), p. 2; *de Lima et al.* (2010), p. 257; *May* (2014), p. 91-92.
311 Cf. here and in the following *Schiehll et al.* (2013), p. 339; *May* (2014), p. 91-92.
312 Cf. *May* (2014), p. 96.
313 Cf. *Lopes/de Alencar* (2010), p. 459; *Schiehll et al.* (2013), p. 339.
314 Cf. *May* (2014), p. 91-92.
315 Cf. *May* (2014), p. 92.
316 Cf. *Lopes et al.* (2007), p. 2.
317 Cf. *Lockhart* (1983), p. 184 and 419.
318 Cf. *Rodrigues et al.* (2011), p.113; *Lopes* (2011), p. 341. For a detailed description of Brazilian accounting in the context of political, economic and social transformations between 1860 and 1964, see *Rodrigues et al.* (2011).
319 Cf. *Lopes* (2011), p. 341.
320 Cf. *da Costa* (1993), p.13.
321 Cf. *Hofstede* (1980b), p. 51-54.

able accounting value profile.[322] Thus, the national culture could be a reason for relatively low financial reporting quality when comparing to countries with a more reporting-friendly cultural profile.

The **accounting education** in Brazil has changed considerably after the implementation of IFRS.[323] Brazil adopted IFRS not only for consolidated but also for individual financial statements influencing, inter alia, tax payments and dividends.[324] Hence, "*[...] a true revolution in Brazil's approach to accounting education [...]*"[325] was necessary, as the demand for well-educated accounting professionals increased.[326] The result was a higher number of accounting students,[327] a more active professional accounting community, more accounting seminars and the publication of accounting journals. Before IFRS adoption, Brazilian universities frequently taught accounting "*[...] as a tool to calculate taxes and not as an instrument to reduce information asymmetry between investors and firms.*"[328] Specific areas, such as fair values, had not even been part of the curriculum, although they are required by law.[329] The role and function of the accountants, called *contador* in Brazil, and their profession have become more comprehensive after 2008. Accountants became responsible e.g. for valuations and measurements including, for example, depreciation rates or historical costs which had been regulated in the tax rules before. Moreover, for the first time accounting students learned to consider the underlying economic processes behind transactions, instead of solely referring to contractual arrangements. Thus, accountants and accounting students initially questioned IFRS skeptically, as IFRS appeared to be subjective and prone to manipulation. As classes had been rather technical before focusing on record-keeping and double-entry procedures, new classes, including discussions of the accounting issues and the underlying philosophy, as well as teaching materials were required. On the whole, the IFRS introduction is a severe challenge for accounting education in Brazil.

Brazil's **economic development** has affected the companies' financing system and, consequently, also financial reporting in the country. After the *lost decade* of the 1980's, which was dominated by severe macroeconomic problems (e.g., double-digit inflation rates and a lack of private funding),[330] the situation improved with the start of the so-called *Real plan* in the mid-1990's, when inflation was reduced and the capital market activity gained momentum. At the beginning of the 21st century companies were able to fund their activities through both local debt as well as local equity capital leading to a considerable increase in IPOs. Moreover, rating agencies raised their assessment of Brazil to investment

[322] A financial reporting favorable accounting value profile would include the characteristics professionalism, flexibility, optimism and particularly transparency.

[323] Cf. *Carvalho/Salotti* (2013), p. 237-238.

[324] Cf. *Carvalho/Salotti* (2013), p. 235.

[325] *Carvalho/Salotti* (2013), p. 239.

[326] Cf. here and in the following *Lopes* (2011), p. 342.

[327] In particular, the University of São Paulo focuses on accounting academia with a considerable number of programmes and publications, cf. *Lopes* (2011), p. 342.

[328] *Lopes* (2011), p. 344.

[329] Cf. here and in this paragraph *Lopes* (2011), p. 344-346.

[330] Cf. here and in the following *Rodrigues et al.* (2012), p. 21; *Lopes* (2011), p. 342-343.

grade and ownership concentration decreased. Hence, corporate reports gained in importance during this time.

Overall, however, the country's financing system is classified as **bank-oriented** in line with the French civil law tradition of Brazil.[331] Thus, private banks are predominantly used for funding rather than capital markets.[332] Particularly prior to the IFRS implementation in 2010, a relatively small number of banks had been responsible for the capital supply of Brazilian companies.[333] *Ali/Hwang* (2000) find a lower level for financial reports in countries with bank-oriented systems.[334] In particular for Brazil, *Lopes et al.* (2007) argue that "*[...] Brazilian firms rely on private deals to obtain funding which clearly reduces the informativeness of accounting reports*"[335]

In Brazil, the *National Congress* transfers regulatory power to the *National Monetary Council*,[336] which supervises *the Securities and Exchange Commission (CVM)* and the Brazilian *Central Bank*.[337] The *CVM* is concerned with the **financial reporting regulation** and enforcement for stock exchange listed companies (registered with the *CVM*).[338] The *CVM* enforces the accounting standards, interpretations and guidance issued by the *Brazilian Accounting Pronouncements Committee (CPC)*.[339] Being a government agency, the *CVM* further has the legal power to complement the financial reporting regulation for listed companies by additional *CVM* instructions.[340]

The *CVM's* **enforcement** process includes the review of financial statements for compliance on the basis of a sample as well as in case of triggering events.[341] The *CVM* can impose sanctions, such as restatements and fines for violations of the law or *CVM* instructions. However, the enforcement of accounting standards is regarded as weak in Brazil. One reason is the fact that not only the *CVM* is responsible for enforcement, but the enforcement of accounting standards is scattered across different institutions resulting in inefficiencies. For example, Brazil's professional accountancy organization *CFC* is concerned with the enforcement for non-public entities. In their international study, also *Brown et al.* (2014) find a relatively weak enforcement regime in Brazil.[342]

In the following, the fundamental IFRS adoption is outlined and additional *CVM* reporting requirements for Brazilian listed companies are presented. Other financial reporting

331 Cf. *Krishnamurti et al.* (2005), p. 442.

332 Cf. *de Lima et al.* (2010), p. 257.

333 Cf. *Lopes* (2011), p. 340.

334 Cf. *Ali/Hwang* (2000), p. 20.

335 *Lopes et al.* (2007), p. 2.

336 Law 4595/64.

337 *IFRS Foundation* (2013a), p. 1. The Brazilian *Central Bank* is concerned with the regulation of financial institutions including the issuance of specific accounting standards for companies from the financial industry, cf. *Lopes* (2011), p. 341.

338 Cf. *United Nations* (2007), p. 20; *IFRS Foundation* (2013a), p. 1.

339 Cf. *IASB* (2010) and *IFRS Foundation* (2013a), p. 1. The *CPC* was established in 2005 as the first individual accounting standard-setting body, cf. *IASB* (2010).

340 Cf. *United Nations* (2007), p. 20; *Deloitte* (2012), p. 19.

341 Cf. here and in the following *The World Bank* (2005), p. 20.

342 Cf. *Brown et al.* (2014), p. 19.

requirements in Brazil (e.g., listing requirements by the *BM&FBOVESPA*) are of minor importance for this study. In December 2007 the Brazilian National Congress amended the Brazilian Corporate Law, which establishes accounting principles and standards in Brazil,[343] to converge Brazilian accounting standards with **IFRS** (Law 11.638/07). After several steps of IFRS adoption between 2006 and 2010,[344] IFRS application finally became, inter alia, mandatory for the consolidated financial statements of all companies regulated by the *CVM* beginning with financial years ending 31 December 2010 and virtually replaced the former Brazilian GAAP.[345]

The introduction of IFRS came along with tremendous changes for accounting regulation and, therefore, for various groups concerned with the preparation or use of corporate reporting.[346] Major changes were the measurement on the basis of market values and the introduction of the impairment test for certain assets. Although the IFRS have been widely adopted as issued by the IASB, there are some **adjustments**.[347] For example, the revaluation options for property, plant and equipment under IAS 16 as well as for intangible assets under IAS 38 have not been endorsed. Further modifications are the obligatory use of the equity method to account for investments in subsidiaries, associates and joint ventures in the companies' individual financial statements, the prohibition of early adoption as well as some alterations to IFRIC guidance.

In addition to the IFRS, Brazilian listed companies have to comply with the regulation of the *CVM*.[348] Public corporations are required to publish important financial information on a quarterly basis.[349] Moreover, they have to disclose material information, which may influence the decisions of investors, immediately via so-called *Relevant Facts*.[350] Regarding annual financial information, all companies controlled by the *CVM* are required to publish their audited annual financial statements (including two year comparative figures) in both the official Gazette as well as an additional newspaper.[351]

In particular, *CVM* Instruction No. 480 requires public corporations to publish online *CVM's* **Reference Form**, which has to be updated once a year entirely and in case of considerable changes within seven days.[352] As general principles, companies shall provide information, which "*[...] is true, complete, and consistent [...] [and does] not mislead the investor.*"[353] Moreover, the disclosed information has to "*[...] be written in a simple, clear,*

---

343 Cf. *Deloitte* (2012), p. 19.

344 Cf. here and in the following *Lopes* (2011), p. 343-344.

345 Cf. *CVM* Instruction No. 457; *Lopes* (2011), p. 343. Individual financial statements have to be prepared according to Brazilian GAAP, which, however, has been fully converged with IFRS since 2010, *IFRS Foundation* (2013a), p. 2.

346 Cf. here and in the following *Deutsch-Brasilianische Industrie- und Handelskammer* (2012), p. 28.

347 Cf. here and in the following *IFRS Foundation* (2013a), p. 4.

348 For an overview of country-specific regulations in Brazil including laws, *CVM* instructions, resolutions and legal opinions, cf. *CVM* (2015).

349 Cf. article 14 of the *CVM* Instruction No. 296.

350 Cf. article 3 of the *CVM* Instruction No. 358.

351 Cf. *EY* (2011), p. 9.

352 Cf. article 24 of the *CVM* Instruction No. 480.

353 Article 14 of the *CVM* Instruction No. 480.

objective, concise language."[354] The issuer of the Reference Form further has to indicate, whether a piece of information is a factual information, interpretation, opinion, projection or estimate.[355] Since companies have to provide information about numerous sensitive issues in their Reference Forms, the document is of particular importance to the entities' stakeholders and *CVM* Instruction No. 480 emphasizes that the Reference Form's disclosures particularly help investors to evaluate company securities.[356] Hence, the Reference Form is commonly referred to as *CVM annual report*.[357] The catalogue of disclosure requirements includes, inter alia, the following reporting categories:

- a description of a company's risk factors (no. 4.1);
- the competition conditions in each operating market (no. 7.3(a)(ii));
- general guidelines for the potential disclosure of projections (no. 11);
- remuneration policy (no. 13.1); and
- breakdown of human resources (no. 14.1(a)).[358]

In more detail, the *CVM* requires, inter alia, the disclosure of the following **specific information in the Reference Form**. Companies are required to disclose the aggregated remuneration of the supervisory board, statutory board and audit committee.[359] As part of information on human resources, the Reference Form has to include the number of employees per position and geographic region, number of outsourced employees as well as the prevailing turnover rate.[360] The Reference Form shall also shed light on the operating activities of a company. For instance, entities must describe, separately for each operational segment, characteristics of the production process, revenues, profit or loss, any potential seasonality as well as main input factors and raw materials.[361] These examples show that the Reference Form does not only address typical information needs of investors and financial analysts regarding financial information, but also includes sensitive non-financial information.

Furthermore, a central element in Brazilian financial reporting for companies regulated by the *CVM* is the **statement of added value (DVA)** as part of the annual financial statements.[362] Ever since Law 11638 changed the so-called *Corporate Law* 6404/1976 fundamentally in 2007, listed companies are required to prepare statements of added value. Similar to the sustainability performance indicator *Economic Value Generated and Distributed*, used by the *Global Reporting Initiative (GRI)*, the DVA shall analyze the distribution of a company's value among those stakeholders, who generated the value, such as employees (e.g., salaries), government (e.g., taxes), shareholders (e.g., dividends).

[354] Article 15 of the *CVM* Instruction No. 480.
[355] Cf. article 19 of the *CVM* Instruction No. 480.
[356] Cf. article 17 of the *CVM* Instruction No. 480.
[357] Cf. e.g. *Vale* (2015).
[358] Cf. annex 24 of the *CVM* Instruction No. 480.
[359] Cf. annex 24, no. 13.2 of the *CVM* Instruction No. 480.
[360] Cf. annex 24, no. 14.1 of the *CVM* Instruction No. 480.
[361] Cf. annex 24, no. 7.3 of the *CVM* Instruction No. 480.
[362] Cf. here and in this paragraph *Machado et al.* (2015), p. 58.

2.3.3 South Africa

During the apartheid era, South African **economic policy** was variable, as politicians alternated their policies between trade liberalization, on the one hand, and protectionism, on the other.[363] In the 1970s and 1980s companies could particularly take advantage of low labor costs due to the system of racial segregation, which might be one reason for today's strength of trade unions in South Africa. After the end of the apartheid regime in 1994, South Africa has undertaken several steps to overcome its **social and economic problems**. Amongst other actions, politicians pursued a liberalization strategy and a more export-friendly trade policy.[364] However, the political change outpaced the economic development resulting in poverty and unemployment.[365] The country's economic growth could not compete with that of countries, such as Brazil and China, and the economy fell short of the government's growth target of five percent over the past few years.[366] South Africa faced challenges such as massive trade union protests, the shrinking of the traditional mining industry, the fact that growth is limited to technological and knowledge-based sectors (which hardly boost exports) as well as a difficult relation between state and corporations.[367] These political and **historical developments** need to be considered when analyzing and interpreting the country's corporate financial reporting activities. As a consequence of the experiences during the apartheid era, various social issues play an important role in financial reporting by South African companies.[368] For example, South African companies publish integrated reports including sustainability information, as the descriptions below specify.

According to *Hofstede's* model, South Africa's **culture** is characterized by relatively strong individualism, masculinity, power distance and lower uncertainty avoidance.[369] In line with the classification of the BRICS countries' national cultures in section 2.2.3.3, the cultural accounting values according to *Gray* (1988) are, to some extent, consistent with the favorable reporting profile. In particular, the characteristics *optimism* and *transparency* may form the cultural basis for high-quality financial reporting.

The framework for higher **accounting education** in South Africa is delegated to professional accounting bodies.[370] In line with professional demands, the curriculum focuses on practice, technical complexity, contextualization and professional skills. As a consequence, however, students hardly learn conceptual and critical thinking as well as scholastic skills. Although graduates can be immediately productive in the economy, critics argue that the teacher-centered pedagogy might not be appropriate for long-term career success.[371] In particular, the introduction of the more principles-based IFRS requires a more conceptual

[363] Cf. here and in the following *Claar* (2014), p. 196.
[364] Cf. *Nel* (2001), p. 1009; *Claar* (2014), p. 196.
[365] Cf. *Hammond et al.* (2012), p. 347.
[366] Cf. *Nel* (2001), p. 1009; *Claar* (2014), p. 197 and 205.
[367] Cf. *Nel* (2001), p. 1003; *Claar* (2014), p. 197 and 203-205.
[368] Cf. e.g. *van Schalkwyk* (2013), p. 19; *Be One South Africa* (2015).
[369] Cf. *Hofstede* (1980b), p. 51-54.
[370] Cf. here and in the following *van der Merwe et al.* (2014), p. 279 and 285.
[371] Cf. *Coetzee/Schmulian* (2012), p. 83.

framework-based than a rules-based teaching approach.[372] Due to the earlier adoption of IFRS in South Africa than in Brazil, the country's accounting education has had more time "*[...] to incorporate the development and assessment of accounting students' broader professional skills, competencies, and thought processes.*"[373]

Being a former British colony, South Africa has an Anglo-Saxon tradition and belongs to the legal category of common-law countries.[374] The **financing systems** of common-law countries are generally characterized as capital market-oriented with active stock markets, numerous investors, shareholder orientation and strong investor protection resulting in an increased level of FRQ.[375] In line with this common-law tradition, capital market funding is also dominant in South Africa.[376] Therefore, the country's financial reporting practices could be expected to be more transparent and FRQ to be higher than in civil law countries.[377]

With respect to accounting regulation, the **financial reporting requirements** of listed companies in South Africa derive from several sources, which are presented in the following. South Africa supports the development of **IAS/IFRS** since 1976.[378] The *South African Accounting Practices Board (APB)* decided to harmonize local South African (SA) GAAP with IFRS in 1995.[379] Hence, South Africa has been a so-called *early adopter* of IFRS and also one of the first emerging economies adopting the international standards. The *APB* issued IFRS as SA GAAP in 2003 without amendment which was used by listed, unlisted and private companies. The *JSE* even required companies to use the actual IFRS instead of the harmonized SA GAAP from 1 January 2005 on. For financial years starting on or after 1 December 2012 companies have to use either IFRS or IFRS for SMEs (if an entity falls within its scope) in accordance with new Companies Act Regulations (under the **Companies Act 2008**), which were adopted by the government in 2011. Thus, the Companies Act (issued by the South African Department of Trade and Industry) sets a general legal IFRS framework for all entities regardless of type or size.[380] However, the Companies Act includes further reporting requirements. It stipulates, for instance, that a social and ethics committee has to monitor a company's activities regarding the ten United Nations Global Compact Principles and report on these matters at the company's annual meeting.[381] Further, *regulated companies*[382] have to publish a list of shareholders holding at least a 5% stake in the company according to section 56(7) of the Companies Act 2008. Be-

---

[372] Cf. *Coetzee/Schmulian* (2013), p. 249.

[373] *Coetzee/Schmulian* (2013), p. 248.

[374] Cf. *Ball et al.* (2000), p. 13 and 20; *Iatridis* (2012), p. 101. However, some researchers do not classify South Africa as common law country, cf. e.g. *Bhattacharya et al.* (2003), p. 655.

[375] Cf. *Ball et al.* (2000), p. 46-49; *Iatridis* (2012), p. 103.

[376] Cf. *Iatridis* (2012), p. 115.

[377] Cf. *Ball et al.* (2000), p. 47; *Krishnamurti et al.* (2005), p. 442; *Iatridis* (2012), p. 103.

[378] Cf. *Coetzee/Schmulian* (2013), p. 243.

[379] Cf. here and in the following *IFRS Foundation* (2013b), p. 2; Regulation 27(4) to the Companies Act 2008.

[380] Cf. Regulation 27(4) to the Companies Act 2008.

[381] Cf. Regulation 43(5) to the Companies Act 2008.

[382] Regulated companies are all public companies as well as certain state-owned and private companies, cf. section 117(1)(i) in conjunction with 118(1) of the Companies Act 2008.

sides these statutory regulations, South African companies face additional financial reporting regulation, as presented in Table 2-9.

	Companies Act 71 of 2008	International Integrated Reporting Framework by the IIRC	King Report 2009 (King III)	JSE Listing Requirements (LR)
Focus	Stipulation of general legal framework (particularly, IFRS focus)	Framework for reports based on integrated thinking (different factors of value creation)	Corporate impact on communities; sustainability and risk-related issues	Prescription of minimum disclosure standards for listed companies
Effective date of current version	1 May 2011	December 2013	1 March 2010	30 September 2014
Binding character	Binding by law	Not legally binding; guidance for integrated report preparation	Not legally binding; comply or explain approach, if JSE-listed	Mandatory, if listed on the JSE

Table 2-9: Financial reporting regulation in South Africa

South Africa has not only been one of the first IFRS-adopting countries, but also one of the first which anticipated an increasing importance of **integrated reporting** as a response to the growing number and volume of both statutory as well as voluntary reports by companies (e.g., corporate governance reports, remuneration reports, sustainability reports).[383] Integrated reports, therefore, shall concisely explain the interdependencies of the issues included in the different reports.[384] The integrated report is further supposed to consider both financial as well as non-financial information. The **Integrated Reporting (<IR>) Framework**, issued by the *International Integrated Reporting Council (IIRC)*, provides *"[...] guidance on how to prepare an integrated report."*[385] It is the long term vision of the *IIRC* to establish <IR> as the primary norm for corporate reporting based on integrated thinking.[386] Taking into consideration various factors which contribute to a company's value creation, the <IR> distinguishes six categories of capital (financial, manufactured, intellectual, human, social and relationship as well as natural capital).[387] Eventually, the result of the integrated reporting process shall be a

> *"[...] holistic and integrated representation of the company's performance in terms of both its finance and its sustainability [...]"*[388].

The principles-based <IR> Framework requires the description of a company's business model by explaining how the firm converts its key inputs into outputs through its business activities, and how this leads to outcomes in terms of a change in the different capitals.[389] The fact that the company shall also provide corresponding objectives, risks and

---

[383] Cf. *Kajüter et al.* (2013), p. 199.

[384] Cf. here and in the following The International <IR> Framework, p. 2.

[385] *Integrated Reporting Committee of South Africa* (2014), p. 1.

[386] Cf. The International <IR> Framework, p. 2. For an overview of *IIRC's The International <IR> Framework*, cf. *Kajüter* (2014a).

[387] Cf. paragraph 2.15 of The International <IR> Framework.

[388] Cf. King Code of Governance for South Africa 2009, p. 54.

[389] Cf. paragraph. 2.23 of The International <IR> Framework.

opportunities reveals the idea of integrated thinking.[390] However, the stipulation of principles gives the preparer of an integrated report considerable room for discretion.[391] Since 2010, listed South African companies prepare their annual reports as integrated reports.[392] As trailblazer of the integrated reporting development, South African companies, listed on the *Johannesburg Stock Exchange (JSE)* have to prepare integrated reports or explain why they deviate from this requirement.[393] This approach is referred to as *comply or explain.*[394]

The King Report on Governance for South Africa and the King Report and Code of Governance Principles 2009, known as **"King III"**, is the third code of corporate governance principles and practices and the result of a process which started with the formation of the King Committee on Corporate Governance in 1992.[395] The King Committee for King III consisted of practitioners, researchers and experts in the fields of different sub committees (e.g., accounting and auditing; risk management; compliance and stakeholder relationships).[396] After King I and King II already addressed sustainability topics,[397] King III particularly emphasizes "*leadership, sustainability, and corporate citizenship*"[398]. Unlike the developer of statutory corporate governance regulations, such as the Sarbanes-Oxley Act in the U.S., the developers of the King Report opted for a voluntary basis, since a mandatory "*one size fits all*" approach could not be adequate for the variety of companies.[399] The *JSE* requires listed companies to address all 75 principles of the King III code and explain those principles which are not applied.[400] This *comply or explain* rule allows managers to decide that the (full) compliance with a particular requirement is not in the best interests of their company "*[...] and still achieve the objective of the overarching corporate governance principles of fairness, accountability, responsibility and transparency.*"[401]

Besides the integrated reporting perspective and the King III declaration, the **JSE Listing Requirements** oblige companies to provide a minimum level of company disclosures. Inter alia, annual financial statements have to "*[...] fairly present the financial position, changes in equity, results of operations and cash flows of the group.*"[402] Moreover, the catalogue contains a comprehensive list of requirements public companies have to fulfill to be listed on the *JSE*. The *JSE* Listing Requirements do not only refer to annual reports, but

---

390 Cf. *Integrated Reporting Committee of South Africa* (2014), p. 28.

391 Cf. *Kajüter* (2014a), p. 225.

392 For an overview of the integrated reporting development in South Africa, cf. *Hoffman* (2012).

393 Cf. *JSE* Listing Requirements, p. 425, in conjunction with chapter 9 of the King Code of Governance for South Africa 2009 (p. 48-49); *EY* (2014), p. 5.

394 Cf. King Code of Governance for South Africa 2009, p. 4. In spite of the *comply or explain* approach, the literature frequently labels integrated reporting in South Africa as *mandatory*, cf. e.g. *Güleş* (2014), p. 26; *Hoffman* (2012), p. 2.

395 Cf. King Code of Governance for South Africa 2009.

396 Cf. King Code of Governance for South Africa 2009, p. 4.

397 Cf. *Ioannou/Serafeim* (2014), p. 7.

398 Cf. King Code of Governance for South Africa 2009, p. 9.

399 Cf. King Code of Governance for South Africa 2009, p. 5-7.

400 Cf. Paragraph 8.63(a) of the *JSE* Listing Requirements.

401 King Code of Governance for South Africa 2009, p. 6.

402 Paragraph 8.62(e) of the *JSE* Listing Requirements.

also other reporting instruments, such as cautionary announcements, trading updates and interim reports.[403]

The practical application of the above described sources of regulations is illustrated by the following example which is taken from the integrated report 2014 of the company *Aveng*. The company's integrated report captures separate reports (annual financial statements, sustainability overview, corporate governance report and remuneration report). Table 2-10 describes the contents, relationship to other reports, regulation and extent of assurance for each report.

	Integrated report	Annual financial statements	Sustainability overview	Corporate governance	Remuneration
Contents	Material issues, performance and outlook	Audit committee, directors' and auditors' reports; consolidated FS	Safety; health and wellness; environment; HR; social investment	Corporate governance report; King III compliance register	Remuneration policy (for shareholders' approval); remuneration report
Relationship between sub reports	Cross-references across the suite of reports	Summarized set of FS is included in integrated report	Key elements are incorporated into integrated report	Version of corporate governance report included in integrated report	Contained within integrated report
Regulation	King III, <IR> Framework	IFRS; Companies Act; JSE Listing Requirements	B-BBEE Codes of Good Practice; Mining Charter; Construction Sector Charter; Carbon Disclosure Project	King III; Companies Act; JSE Listing Requirements	Remuneration policy; King III; Companies Act
Assurance	By the Board, audit committee, sub-committees	External audit; internal audit and controls; management and governance oversight	Independent assurance report on selected sustainability information; limited assurance on selected metrics	Internal audit; annual board assessments	Internal controls; management and governance oversight

Table 2-10: Example of the suite of reports in South African integrated reports
Following *Aveng's* Annual Integrated Report 2014, p. 2 (abridged).

The example of *Aveng's* integrated report shows that, in addition to the described regulations, South African companies apply **other sources of regulation**, for instance, industry-specific reporting requirements. Various safety, health and environment and human resource policies and frameworks call for further reporting activities by the companies. Although they provide this additional information mostly on a voluntary basis, the entities may face considerable pressure to comply with the requirements. According to *Marius Ungerer*, for example, compliance with the principles of the Broad-Based Black Empowerment Act 2003 (B-BBEE) "*[...] is essential for doing work with the government and big business.*"[404] The B-BBEE was launched by the South African government in 2003 to enhance the economic opportunities of people disadvantaged during the apartheid era.[405] Its

403 Cf. *JSE* Listing Requirements.
404 Quoted from *Van Schalkwyk* (2013), p. 19.
405 Cf. here and in the following *Be One South Africa* (2015).

Codes of Good Practice, revised in 2013, emphasize the elements of ownership, management control, skills development, enterprise and supplier development as well as socio-economic development. An example for a sector-specific set of rules is the Broad-Based Socio-Economic Empowerment Charter for the South African Mining Industry, which proposes responsible behavior among mining companies. However, this set of rules can be regarded as mandatory, as it is released by the *South African Department of Mineral Resources* and non-compliance may result, inter alia, in the suspension or cancellation of granted mining permits.[406]

The two main **enforcement institutions** in South Africa are the *Company and Intellectual Property Commission* (CIPC) and the *JSE*.[407] The CIPC is responsible for the companies' compliance with the disclosure requirements of the Companies Act. In addition, the *JSE* enforces the disclosures according to its particular Listing Requirements for listed companies. According to the *JSE* Listing Requirements, non-compliance may lead to sanctions, such as fines or suspension of listing.[408] In line with other emerging economies, however, the enforcement is found to be relatively weak in South Africa.[409]

2.3.4 Germany

After World War II, liberal reforms of the **economic policy** in West Germany paved the way for the so-called *social market economy*.[410] The social market economy aims at combining a competitive market economy with social progress.[411] The approach is regarded as basis for economic growth and a high level of employment in Germany.[412] Moreover, Germany's economic policy is concerned with the strong export orientation[413] of the economy as well as with the development of the labor market, which has been reformed intensively over the past decades.[414] Concerning the impact of the latest global financial crisis on Germany, the *OECD* concludes: "*In the face of the global financial crisis, the German economy has proved remarkably resilient, outperforming other large, high-income European economies.*"[415]

Along with the growth of the industrialized German economy, Germany has a long-standing accounting and financial reporting **history** which dates back to the 14th century, when already economic transactions were recorded in account books.[416] As the formation of a united state of Germany called for a unitary commercial law, the *General German*

---

406 Cf. section 3 of the Broad-Based Socio-Economic Empowerment Charter for the South African Mining Industry in conjunction with section 47 of the Mineral and Petroleum Resources Development Act.

407 Cf. here and in the following *IMF* (2015b), p. 8.

408 Cf. Paragraph 1.20 to 1.22 of the *JSE* Listing Requirements.

409 Cf. *Brown et al.* (2014), p. 19.

410 Cf. *Giersch et al.* (1994), p. 58.

411 Cf. *Müller-Armack* (1976), p. 245.

412 Cf. *Giersch et al.* (1994), p. 2-7; *Muresan* (2014), p. 99.

413 Cf. *Muresan* (2014), p. 326.

414 Cf. *Muresan* (2014), p. 329.

415 *OECD* (2014), p. 2.

416 Cf. here and in the following *Fülbier/Klein* (2013), p. 3-4.

Commercial Code (ADHGB)[417] was issued in 1861, which was the predecessor of today's *Commercial Code* (HGB), the German legislature's codification of financial reporting regulation.[418] A particular characteristic of the HGB was the formulation of leading accounting principles called *generally accepted principles on proper bookkeeping* (GoB).[419]

Based on *Hofstede's* cultural dimensions, Germany's national **culture** is characterized by relatively small power distance, but relatively strong individualism and uncertainty avoidance as well as pronounced masculinity.[420] The German accounting values according to *Gray* (1988) are not clear regarding any of the four key dimensions (professionalism/statutory control, flexibility/uniformity, conservatism/optimism and transparency/secrecy).[421] Consequently, however, the German accounting culture is, to some extent, characterized by all of the optimal accounting values. Thus, the German cultural environment could enhance the quality of German financial reports. In spite of the tendency towards an individualist German society, the German business culture is also affected by collectivism, particularly with respect to employees.[422] The strong position of employees (e.g., participation in supervisory bodies, pronounced employment protection) as well as other contract partners of companies contribute to Germany's **stakeholder-orientated** accounting approach. Financial reporting in Germany, therefore, may not solely focus on the information needs of equity investors, but also consider those of other stakeholders.

The **accounting education** in Germany is traditionally dominated by a technical as well as legal view.[423] Thus, legal compliance is generally an important issue. Moreover, the education in accountancy has been generally regarded as leading in comparison to other countries.[424] In particular, the requirements to become a German statutory auditor are regarded as high.[425] Due to the strong position of the traditional German Commercial Code, the accounting education emphasizes both international and national accounting standards.[426]

In line with the **financing system** of other civil law countries, German companies predominantly obtain financial resources through bank-financing, rather than dominant equity capital-markets. Although Germany used to have developed capital markets at the beginning of the 20th century, these had difficulty to regain their dominant role after World War II and even today stock market capitalization of listed companies is still relatively low in comparison to other developed countries (e.g., UK and U.S.).[427] Following

[417] Allgemeines Deutsches Handelsgesetzbuch.
[418] Cf. *Ernstberger/Vogler* (2008), p. 345.
[419] Cf. *Fülbier/Klein* (2013), p. 4.
[420] Cf. *Hofstede* (1980b), p. 51-54.
[421] Cf. *Borker* (2012), p. 321.
[422] Cf. here and in the following *Fülbier/Klein* (2013), p. 8 and 12.
[423] Cf. here and in the following *Becker/Messner* (2005), p. 419.
[424] Cf. *Coenenberg et al.* (1999), p. 386.
[425] Cf. *Coenenberg et al.* (1999), p. 371.
[426] Cf. *Becker/Messner* (2005), p. 419.
[427] Cf. *Fülbier/Klein* (2013), p. 8-9.

the literature, the fact that Germany is a civil-law country with dominant bank-financing could lower FRQ.[428]

As mentioned before, the legal basis of financial reporting regulation in Germany is the Commercial Code (**HGB**). Thus, the HGB also regulates the application of **IFRS**. The adoption of IFRS in Germany was part of a harmonization process of financial reporting in the European Union (EU). The EU paved the way for the adoption of IFRS as a common European financial reporting standard in 2002 through its Regulation No. 1606/2002.[429] The regulation led to an amendment of the HGB, so that section 315a I and II HGB require the application of IFRS, as endorsed by the EU, for consolidated financial statements of publicly traded companies since 1 January 2005.[430]

In addition to IFRS, the HGB regulates the disclosure of additional information. The HGB requires medium-sized and large corporations to prepare a separate **management report** in addition to their financial statements since 1985;[431] however, the attention of the management report as important reporting instrument increased notably over the past few years amongst publicly-traded companies.[432] Besides the financial statements, the management report is regarded as *the second pillar of accounting* and is provided as part of the companies' annual reports. The management report complements the financial statements by providing e.g. qualitative and forward-looking disclosures. In general, the consolidated management report is supposed to describe and analyze the course of business and economic position of the corporate group including, inter alia, important financial and non-financial performance indicators and explain essential risks and opportunities.[433]

As the HGB contains only rudimentary requirements of the management report, the **German Accounting Standards (GAS)** concretize its requirements. In particular, **GAS 20**, labeled *group management report*, captures various areas of sensitive company information (e.g., risk information), which are derived from the information needs of legitimate interest groups, such as shareholders, creditors, financial analysts, employees, customers as well as the general public.[434] Moreover, listed entities shall elaborate, as to what extent they comply with the **German Corporate Governance Code** (DCGK), which provides a set of "*[...] recommendations and suggestions, internationally and nationally acknowledged standards for good and responsible corporate governance.*"[435] For example, the DCGK requires the disclosure of each management board member's remuneration.[436]

---

[428] Cf. *Ball et al.* (2000), p. 47; *Krishnamurti et al.* (2005), p. 442; *Iatridis* (2012), p. 103.

[429] Cf. *Haller* (2002), p. 154-155.

[430] Non-publicly traded companies can choose to prepare their consolidated financial statements either under IFRS or German Commercial Code, cf. section 315a(3) HGB. For individual financial statements, the German Commercial Code remains mandatory and additional individual IFRS financial statements are solely allowed for disclosure, cf. section 325(2a) HGB.

[431] Cf. section 264(1) HGB. The different size categories are codified in section 267 HGB.

[432] Cf. here and in the following *Fink et al.* (2013), p. 3.

[433] Cf. section 315(1) no. 1 HGB.

[434] Cf. *Fink et al.* (2013), p. 11.

[435] *Regierungskommission Deutscher Corporate Governance Kodex* (2015). The DCGK was developed by the *DCGK Commission*, a self-regulating and independent body of the economy. After completion of the final code, the *Commission* handed the code over to the German government in 2002, however, still re-

Unlike the HGB, the German Accounting Standards are not a law. However, GAS-conform reporting is assumed to comply with the *generally accepted principles on proper bookkeeping* (GoB) for group accounting,[437] which again are required by the HGB.[438] Auditors are supposed to report non-compliance with the GAS in their audit reports.[439] Moreover, the **enforcement** authority *Financial Reporting Enforcement Panel (FREP)* is not only concerned with IFRS and HGB-conform reporting, but also with the compliance of the GAS.[440] In case of non-compliance, the governmental *German Financial Supervisory Authority (BaFin)* may take further legal actions. *Brown et al.* (2014) provide evidence of a relatively high quality of enforcement in Germany.[441]

Companies listed in the so-called *Prime Standard* on the Frankfurt Stock Exchange have to comply with additional **listing requirements**. These listing requirements include, inter alia, specific disclosure obligations. For example, annual financial statements have to be prepared in both German and English.[442] Moreover, the stock exchange replaced mandatory quertly reporting by the requirement to publish interim management statements for the first and third quarter for Prime Standard companies in Novemner 2015.[443] These interim management statements have to "*[...] outline the crucial events and transactions of the issuer's company within the period covered by the statement and their effects on the issuer's financial situation as well as describe the issuer's financial situation and operating results within the period covered by the statement.*"[444]

2.3.5 Conclusion

The country profiles have revealed both similarities and differences among the financial reporting characteristics in Brazil, South Africa and Germany. In all three countries, the **historical development** has shaped the financial reporting environment. As a result of their colonial past, Brazil and South Africa are classified as civil law and common law country, respectively. Germany belongs to the group of Continental European civil law countries. Bank-oriented **financing systems** are traditionally found in civil law countries.[445] Such systems are characterized by the fact that "*[...] banks have direct access to company information, reducing the demand for published information [...]*"[446] and, thus, FRQ might be lower in Brazil and Germany than in South Africa. Moreover, the traditionally high **ownership concentration** of Brazilian companies (e.g., in family businesses)

views it regularly. Cf. in this footnote *Regierungskommission Deutscher Corporate Governance Kodex* (2015).

436 Cf. no. 4.2.4 of the DCGK.

437 Cf. GAS 20, p. 4; section 342(2) HGB; *Küting/Weber* (2012), p. 8.

438 Cf. section 297(2) sentence 1 HGB.

439 Cf. *KPMG* (2013), p. 6.

440 Cf. here and in the following *Meyer* (2010), p. 153-158.

441 Cf. *Brown et al.* (2014), p. 19.

442 Cf. Exchange Rules for the Frankfurter Wertpapierbörse (FWB), article 50(1).

443 Cf. Exchange Rules for the FWB, article 51a(1). In addition, the publication of half-yearly financial reports is required by law according to section 37w of the German Securities Trading Act.

444 Exchange Rules for the FWB, article 51a(2).

445 Cf. *La Porta et al.* (1997), p. 1131 and 1137.

446 *Ali/Hwang* (2000), p. 4.

is assumed to influence the entities' financial reporting practices. *Lopes/de Alencar* (2010) argue that the high ownership concentration lowers the need for corporate disclosures, as the dominant block holders obtain insider information.[447]

Although all of the sample countries have adopted IFRS, the countries' additional **financial reporting regulations** differ. The *CVM* requires Brazilian listed companies to disclose additional information and particularly to report on sensitive issues in their Reference Forms. South Africa pursues an integrated reporting approach and listed companies face several regulatory sources with a focus on sustainability and corporate governance issues. The importance of these aspects can be explained by the political developments and social problems in the history of South Africa. The German Commercial Code particularly requires medium-sized and large companies to prepare management reports. This comprehensive financial reporting instrument captures the information needs of numerous user groups, which is in line with the stakeholder-oriented corporate governance model in Germany.

The analysis of the countries' **national cultures** has shown that the Brazilian cultural accounting values (according to *Gray* (1988)) are contrary to a favorable accounting value profile,[448] whereas the South Africa and German accounting values meet the optimal portfolio criteria at least to some extent including the important characteristics *optimism* and *transparency*. Thus, a higher FRQ may be expected in Germany and South Africa than in Brazil on the basis of the countries' cultural characteristics.

The analysis shows differences between the financial reporting environments of the emerging economies (Brazil and South Africa) and the developed country (Germany). In contrast to Germany, Brazil and South Africa are affected by their colonial history and have a less established national financial reporting regulation. Moreover, the quality of enforcement and auditors is assumed to be lower in the two emerging economies than in Germany. *Brown et al.* (2014) find considerably stronger **enforcement mechanisms** in Germany (score of 21 points for year 2008) than in Brazil (8 points) and South Africa (10 points).[449] Their study further suggests a higher quality of the **auditors' working environment** in Germany (score of 23 points for year 2008) than in Brazil (15 points) and South Africa (19 points). The review of the **accounting education** in the three countries further suggests a lower level of education in the two emerging economies than in Germany.

In spite of the fact that Brazil and South Africa are both emerging economies, there are also considerable differences between their financial reporting environments. In particular, the Brazilian characteristics show typical features of emerging economies,[450] which are presumably associated with a poor institutional environment and poor transparency in Brazil.[451] These characteristics are consistent with the observation by *Anderson* (1999) that

---

447 Cf. *Lopes/de Alencar* (2010), p. 459.

448 A favorable accounting value profile includes the characteristics professionalism, flexibility, optimism and transparency.

449 Cf. here and in the following *Brown et al.* (2014), p. 19.

450 Cf. section 2.2.3.

451 Cf. *Lopes et al.* (2007), p. 2; *de Lima et al.* (2010), p. 257.

"*[...] the quality of disclosure by Brazilian firms is perceived to be low.*"[452] This study investigates the actual financial reporting practices in the three countries and discusses how the country-specific characteristics are related to the observed FRQ.

[452] *Anderson* (1999), p. 54.

3 Review of prior research

3.1 Overview of research approaches

Besides within-country analyses in Brazil, South Africa and Germany, this study compares accounting practices across the three economies and, therefore, is part of **international comparative research.**[453] To conduct studies in this field, researchers "*[...] compare specific issues or phenomena in two or more countries, societies or cultures [...]*"[454]. The following sections provide an overview of the prior literature relevant to this study's research objectives. Analyzing the state of the research area is crucial to identify research gaps and, therefore, the necessity for further research. Moreover, it allows the classification of this study within the scope of existing research.

As illustrated in Figure 3-1, **empirical accounting research** distinguishes between descriptive (also: descriptive/comparative) and effect-oriented studies.[455] The three research objectives of this study can be assigned to these two categories. The first objective is to describe financial reporting practice by measuring FRQ[456] using both indirect as well as direct measurement techniques. This is part of descriptive research. In contrast, the identification of determinants of FRQ as well as the observation of capital market consequences belong to the category of effect-oriented studies.

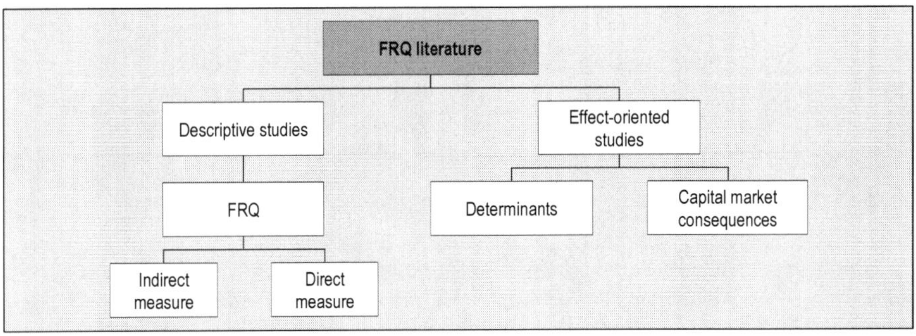

Figure 3-1: Systematization of the FRQ literature

[453] Although the literature sometimes distinguishes between *international comparative research* and *cross-national research*, this study uses the prefixes *inter* and *cross* interchangeably as synonyms referring to studies crossing national boundaries, cf. *Hantrais* (2009), p. 3. *Grootings* (1986) regards *cross-national research* as deductive and descriptive, whereas *international comparative research* would be more analytical with a focus on the relationship between macro- and micro-levels of societal phenomena, cf. *Grootings* (1986), p. 285-286; *Hantrais* (1999), p. 97.

[454] *Hantrais* (2009), p. 2.

[455] For the comparison of descriptive and effect-oriented research, cf. *Oberdörster* (2009), p. 28.

[456] The literature review uses the term *financial reporting quality (FRQ)* to refer to different financial reporting proxies throughout the literature, which might not measure FRQ in the sense of this study, but, for instance, rather capture the scope or quantity of disclosure. Similarly, *Leuz/Verrecchia* (2000) do not distinguish between quantity and quality of disclosure, cf. *Leuz/Verrecchia* (2000), p. 92.

However, some studies may belong to more than one category. For example, empirical studies could describe FRQ by indirect and/or direct measurement techniques and, in addition, investigate determinants and/or capital market consequences.

In general, **descriptive research** characterizes and compares accounting practices.[457] With regard to FRQ, descriptive studies describe financial reporting practices in detail on the basis of selected FRQ measures. Following *van Beest et al.* (2009), the study distinguishes between indirect and direct measures of FRQ.[458] As explained in section 2.1.3, common indirect measures typically use accounting models based on financial data to determine FRQ (e.g., accruals models), but also other (e.g., readability) attributes are applied as indirect FRQ proxies. Direct measures, in contrast, assess FRQ through a more comprehensive analysis of the information provided by companies. Direct measure studies frequently use content analyses (e.g., of annual report elements) to operationalize FRQ, but also surveys and expert interviews are potential measurement methods.[459] In a second step, descriptive studies may compare observed phenomena, for instance, across companies, research periods and/or reporting environments.

Unlike descriptive research, **effect-oriented studies** not only describe accounting practices, but they analyze economic consequences.[460] *Coenenberg/Haller* (1993) distinguish three types of effect-oriented studies. First, **determinants** of accounting practices are analyzed to investigate how providers of accounting information anticipate economic consequences in their financial reporting choices (ex post consequences). This approach to explain accounting observations is based on the positive accounting theory according to *Watts/Zimmerman* (1978).[461] This study follows the described research type by analyzing determinants which affect managers' reporting decisions and, thus, determine the FRQ of their companies. The second type of effect-oriented studies examines, as to what extent particularly **accounting regulations** influence certain accounting decisions by companies (e.g., investment and financing decisions). The third type encompasses studies which investigate the **benefit of accounting information** to its users. Accounting information is considered useful, if it changes or confirms the users' expectations on future economic consequences (a priori consequences). Following this approach, this study analyzes the decisions of capital market participants as reactions on the FRQ provided by companies.

The following literature review is structured according to Figure 3-1 and, therefore, presents studies measuring FRQ (section 3.2), both indirectly and directly, studies investigating determinants of FRQ (section 3.3) as well as studies examining capital market consequences of FRQ (section 3.4). Each of these sections sheds light on the reviewed studies' research sample, research period, methodology and main results. In line with the focus of this study, this literature review presents research on **emerging economies**. In addition, these studies are compared to existing research on **developed countries**. Finally, the literature's implications for this study are described (section 3.5).

---

[457] Cf. *Gassen* (2007), p. 358-359.

[458] Cf. *van Beest et al.* (2009), p. 27.

[459] Cf. *van Beest et al.* (2009), p. 27.

[460] Cf. here and in this paragraph *Coenenberg/Haller* (1993), p. 561-562; *Oberdörster* (2009), p. 28-29.

[461] For an overview of the positive accounting theory, cf. section 4.1.5.3.

3.2 Financial reporting practice

3.2.1 Indirect measure studies

A multitude of prior studies use indirect proxies to measure FRQ. However, only few studies apply indirect measures solely to describe financial reporting practice, but researchers mostly use them as a data base for additional effect-oriented studies (e.g., the impact of IFRS adoption on FRQ). Hence, this overview also includes studies, where the description of observed FRQ of entities is not the only and possibly not the primary objective. In the following, first research involving emerging economies is presented. Second, major developed country studies are described briefly. Moreover, the section distinguishes studies investigating a single country from those examining multiple countries.

Emerging economy studies:

According to *Lopes et al.* (2007) the **emerging economy** of Brazil provides a **single-country setting** which is characterized by enormous incentives for managers to manipulate earnings (inter alia, due to poor investor protection). They apply five proxies from the prior literature to compare the earnings management of Brazilian companies with and without U.S. cross listing for the sample period 1995-2003.[462] Based on the descriptive results of the earnings management proxies, the FRQ between the companies with and without U.S. cross-listing does not differ considerably. The study calculates the earnings management proxies for the entire sample period, but does not analyze the FRQ development over the years. Thus, the effects of specific years are not considered so that comparisons of the calculated proxies might be difficult. Moreover, there is considerable variation in the number of company-year observations hampering comparability. Hence, the interpretation of the results as well as the comparison between cross-listed and non-cross-listed companies appears difficult.

In their **cross-country study**, *Chen et al.* (2011) measure FRQ of private companies from 21 emerging economies. For the sample period 2002-2005, they apply three frequently used FRQ proxies: a version of the discretionary accruals proxy by *Jones* (1991) (*Kothari et al.* (2005)), accruals quality (*Dechow/Dichev* (2002)) and revenue-based FRQ proxy (*McNichols/Stubben* (2008) and *Stubben* (2010)).[463] The results for the discretionary accruals are described in more detail, as they can be compared to other existing studies as well as to the empirical results of this study. *Chen et al.* (2011) provide a discretionary accruals mean (median) value of 0.100 (0.056).[464] However, the study only presents the proxies' descriptive statistics for the entire sample, but neither compares FRQ across the sample countries nor over time. In addition, the interpretation of the results is difficult, as the number of sample companies per country differs considerably ranging from 24 (Eritrea) to 1,307 (Thailand). Furthermore, the findings for private companies are not inevi-

---

[462] Cf. here and in the following *Lopes et al.* (2007), p. 1 and 15. As the study investigates a period before mandatory IFRS introduction in 2010 (cf. *PwC* (2014)), the analyzed Brazilian companies apply Brazilian GAAP.

[463] Cf. *Chen et al.* (2011), p. 1264-1265. For an overview of FRQ measures, cf. section 2.1.3.

[464] Cf. *Chen et al.* (2011), p. 1266.

tably transferable to publicly traded companies, as the motives for earnings management, for instance, may be different.

The studies by *Bhattacharya et al.* (2003) and *Leuz et al.* (2003) investigate the quality of earnings in both emerging economies and developed countries. While *Bhattacharya et al.* (2003) analyze 34 countries during the period from 1986 to 1998, *Leuz et al.* (2003) use a sample of 31 countries (1990-1999). Both studies aggregate the results of different indirect FRQ proxies to calculate an overall opacity and earnings management proxy, respectively. Moreover, both studies rank all of the 34 and 31 sample countries according to the calculated earnings proxies.

However, the country rankings according to the measures applied by *Leuz et al.* (2003) present heterogeneous results. While, for instance, the results of the two earnings smoothing proxies imply similar earnings management levels for South African and German companies, the two earnings discretion proxies indicate that German companies engage considerably more in earnings management than entities from South Africa.[465] Considering these heterogeneous results of the individual earnings management proxies, the interpretation of the aggregated earnings management score seems difficult. Moreover, the number of company-year observations per country differs considerably ranging from 429 (Philippines) to 16,475 (Japan) hampering comparability.

Also the country ranking based on the earnings opacity proxies used by *Bhattacharya et al.* (2003) provides mixed results. For example, Brazil is one of the countries with the least loss avoidance and earnings smoothing activities, yet, has one of the highest ranks regarding earnings aggressiveness.[466] Furthermore, the rankings for Germany vary considerably across the results of the three FRQ proxies of the study, whereas the results for South Africa are relatively homogeneous. The aggregated earnings opacity ranking suggests that Brazilian companies (rank 4 out of 34) provide a higher FRQ than German (rank 15 out of 34) and South African (rank 25 out of 34) companies.

Although both studies operationalize the quality of earnings, the findings are not consistent. While *Leuz et al.* (2003), for example, find Portugal to be among the countries with the lowest FRQ (pronounced earnings management), *Bhattacharya et al.* (2003) classify the country as high FRQ according to their overall earnings opacity score. The results suggest that each indirect proxy captures different aspects of FRQ. Thus, the aggregation of multiple proxies into an overall earnings quality score seems difficult to interpret.

Overall, the existing studies provide mixed results regarding indirect measures of FRQ in emerging economies, particularly earnings management proxies. In particular, it is still unclear whether FRQ in emerging economies is systematically lower than in developed countries. Moreover, most studies have been conducted a considerable time ago and their results might be obsolete. Thus, additional research measuring FRQ indirectly in emerging economies can contribute to the literature.

Table 3-1 summarizes major studies which analyze FRQ in emerging economies on a descriptive level through the use of indirect measurement techniques.

---

465 Cf. *Leuz et al.* (2003), p. 514-515. Brazil is not included in the study.

466 Cf. here and in the following *Bhattacharya et al.* (2003), p. 660.

Study	Sample and period	Methodology	Selected results
***Bhattacharya et al.* (2003)**	Industrial companies from 34 developed countries and emerging economies (58,653 company years) (1986-1998)	FRQ is measured by 3 dimensions of earnings opacity: (1) accruals-based earnings aggressiveness; (2) loss avoidance proxy; (3) earnings smoothing proxy.	The results rank the countries of the study according to their measured earnings opacity. The findings for each country differ considerably across the used proxies. Overall, FRQ tends to be lower in emerging economies than in developed countries.
***Leuz et al.* (2003)**	8,616 non-financial companies from 31 developed countries and emerging economies (70,955 company years) (1990-1999)	FRQ is measured by five earnings management proxies: (1) Accrual component (Dechow et al. (1995)); (2) Smoothing and the correlation between changes in accounting accruals and operating cash flows; (3) Earnings discretion according to magnitude of accruals; (4) ratio of small profits to small losses (Burgstahler/Dichev (1997)); (5) aggregated earnings management score.	The different earnings management measures show a heterogeneous distribution of the country scores. The mixed results reveal no systematic differences in earnings management between emerging and developed economies. According to the descriptive cluster analysis companies in countries with developed equity markets, dispersed ownership structures, strong investor rights, and strong legal enforcement engage in less earnings management.
***Lopes et al.* (2007)**	Listed Brazilian companies with and without U.S. cross-listing (1995-2003)	FRQ is measured by 5 earnings management proxies based on the literature: (1) relation between operating income and cash flow; (2) correlation between changes in accruals and operating cash flows; (3) magnitude of accruals; (4) ratio of small profits to small losses; (5) ratio of non-discretionary earnings to net earnings.	The study provides descriptive results of the calculated earnings management metrics, which are compared between companies with and without U.S. cross-listing. However, the descriptive results suggest no considerable FRQ differences between companies with and without U.S. cross-listing.
***Chen et al.* (2011)**	6,727 private companies from 21 emerging economies (2002-2005)	FRQ is measured by 3 proxies: (1) discretionary accruals (Kothari et al. (2005)); (2) revenue-based measure (McNichols/Stubben (2008) and Stubben (2010)); (3) measure by Dechow/Dichev (2002).	The study shows descriptive statistics for the FRQ proxies in use. The discretionary accruals mean (median) value is 0.100 (0.056). The results remain robust when using signed FRQ measures instead of the absolute values of the residuals.

Table 3-1: Indirect measure studies of emerging economies

Developed country studies:

Regarding **developed countries**, there are a large number of **single-country studies**. However, U.S. based accounting research traditionally has a dominant position. Representing U.S. studies on FRQ, *Francis et al.* (2008), *Biddle et al.* (2009) as well as *Hribar et al.* (2014) measure FRQ through the use of well-established proxies. The descriptive results present the distributions of the different indirect FRQ proxies. For example, *Hribar et al.* (2014) compare their new unexplained audit fees proxy to the other earnings quality proxies. *Francis et al.* (2008) calculate a discretionary accruals mean (median) value of 0.0465 (0.0397) suggesting considerably less earnings management and, therefore, a higher FRQ than for the emerging economies in the study by *Chen et al.* (2011).[467] Another single-country investigation is conducted by *Ball/Shivakumar* (2005) who use a large UK sample of public and private companies.

Salewski et al. (2014) use a German sample to describe the earnings management of German GAAP and IFRS adopting companies (proxied by the discretionary accruals measure

[467] Cf. *Francis et al.* (2008), p. 71.

as defined by *Kothari et al.* (2005)) during the period between 1995 and 2012.[468] The total values of the IFRS companies' discretionary accruals indicate a higher FRQ than for the emerging economy sample by *Chen et al.* (2011), however, a lower FRQ than for the U.S. sample by *Francis et al.* (2008).[469]

In their **cross-country study**, *Ball et al.* (2000) calculate FRQ metrics measuring the timeliness and conservatism of income for companies from seven civil law and common law countries between 1985 and 1995. Their finding that the FRQ of common law countries tends to be higher than in civil law countries is in line with the descriptive results by *Leuz et al.* (2003) including both developed and emerging economies.[470] Moreover, a number of studies compare the FRQ in terms of earnings management of companies before and after IAS/IFRS adoption. Using multi-country samples, *Barth et al.* (2008) and *Chen et al.* (2010) find that companies tend to engage less in earnings management in the post-adoption period.[471]

Apart from financial metrics as indirect FRQ proxies, the literature uses **readability measures** to assess (a particular aspect of) FRQ.[472] *Biddle et al.* (2009) and *Li* (2008) use the so-called *Fog index* to measure the readability of U.S. annual reports. They provide evidence that the readability of the reports is generally very low,[473] which is consistent with *Courtis* (1995) arguing that readability research has

> "*[...] consistently revealed annual report prose passages to be at a reading ease level of difficult to very difficult, and beyond the fluent comprehension skills of about 90 per cent of the adult population and about 40 per cent of the investor population.*"[474]

A summary of the studies applying indirect measures of FRQ in a developed country setting is presented in Table 3-2.

Study	Sample and period	Methodology	Selected results
***Ball et al.* (2000)**	Companies from 7 civil and common law countries (40,359 company years) (1985-1995)	The study analyzes differences in timeliness and conservatism of income. It measures the flow of market valued economic income into book-valued accounting income using the change in market value of equity as a proxy for economic income.	Common-law countries' accounting incomes are less *smoothed* and more timely than code law countries' incomes due to greater income conservatism. Conservatism is found to differ across countries according to institutional arrangements.
***Ball/Shivakumar* (2005)**	Large sample of UK private and public companies (1990-2000)	FRQ proxies: (1) a time-series measure of timely loss recognition (Basu (1997)); (2) relation between accruals and cash flow from operations.	According to both proxies the quality of private-company earnings is lower than of public companies, although earnings are prepared under the same regulation.
		-Table is continued on the next page-	

468 Cf. *Salewski et al.* (2014), p. 1.
469 Cf. *Salewski et al.* (2014), p. 33.
470 Cf. *Ball et al.* (2000), p. 2 and 16.
471 Cf. *Barth et al.* (2008), p. 496-497; *Chen et al.* (2010), p. 221.
472 Cf. section 2.1.3.
473 Cf. *Li* (2008), p. 228; *Biddle et al.* (2009), p. 119.
474 *Courtis* (1995), p. 5.

Barth et al. (2008)	IAS- and non-IAS-adopting companies from 21 countries (1994-2003)	FRQ is measured by (1) 4 earnings management proxies; (2) coefficient on large negative income as proxy for timely loss recognition; (3) 3 value relevance metrics.	Companies adopting IAS engage less in earnings smoothing and management than non-IAS-adopting companies, recognize losses in a more timely manner and show accounting amounts of increased value relevance.
Francis et al. (2008)	677 U.S. companies (2001)	The study measures FRQ in terms of earnings quality proxied by four measures (accruals quality; earnings variability; absolute abnormal earnings; combined measure).	The descriptive results present and compare the distributions of the different indirect FRQ proxies. The total value of the companies' average (median) abnormal accruals is 0.0465 (0.0397).
Li (2008)	Large sample of U.S. companies (1993-2003)	The study measures the readability of 10-K annual reports using the Fog readability proxy.	The results indicate that the readability of the analyzed annual reports is generally very low. The MD&A and the Notes are considerably easier to read as the entire annual report.
Biddle et al. (2009)	Large sample of U.S. non-financial companies (1993-2005)	FRQ is measured by: (1) accruals quality (Dechow/Dichev (2002)); (2) accruals quality (Wysocki (2008)); (3) Fog readability index (Li (2008)); (4) summary FRQ index.	The descriptive statistics present the results of the four FRQ measures. The distribution of the Fog index ranges from 16.16 to 25.65 with a mean (median) of 19.31 (19.15). The distributions of the accruals quality proxies differ considerably.
Chen et al. (2010)	Publicly listed companies in 15 EU member states (2000-2007)	FRQ is measured by: (1) earnings management proxies (earnings smoothing; managing earnings towards targets; magnitude of discretionary accruals; accruals quality); (2) timely loss recognition.	The absolute value of the discretionary accruals decreases in the IAS /IFRS adoption period indicating less earnings management in line with expectations.
Salewski et al. (2014)	Listed German companies (3,095 company years) (1995-2012)	The study analyzes the FRQ of both German GAAP and IFRS applying companies in terms of earnings management proxied by discretionary accruals (Kothari et al. (2005)).	The mean and median discretionary accruals of German GAAP companies are lower than of IFRS companies. The total value of the IFRS companies' average (median) discretionary accruals is 0.087 (0.048).
Hribar et al. (2014)	Large sample of U.S. companies (2000-2010)	A new unexplained audit fees proxy is tested against two existing measures: (1) accrual quality (Dechow/Dichev (2002)); (2) earnings smoothness (Francis et al. (2004)).	The descriptive results present distributions of the different indirect FRQ proxies and compare the unexplained audit fees proxy to the other earnings quality proxies. The distributions of the accrual quality and earnings smoothness proxies are similar.

Table 3-2: Indirect measure studies of developed countries

As the above overview indicates, there are only relatively few studies measuring FRQ indirectly in emerging economies, whereas there is plenty of research on developed countries. Moreover, the analysis of the studies' descriptive results has shown that the different FRQ proxies in use, particularly earnings management proxies, provide heterogeneous results. Therefore, it is questionable whether these proxies measure FRQ consistently. Consequently, also the aggregation of individual FRQ proxies seems problematic so that each proxy should be interpreted individually.

The reviewed indirect measure studies focus on different aspects of FRQ. Thus, comparisons between emerging and developed economies are difficult. Although some discretionary accruals studies suggest an increased FRQ in developed countries, others indicate no systematic difference between the FRQ in emerging and developed economies. Additional comparative research could contribute to the literature through the indirect measurement of FRQ in both emerging and developed economies on a consistent basis. Moreover, the readability of corporate reports is widely unexplored in emerging economies.

3.2.2 Direct measure studies

In line with this study's classification into indirect and direct FRQ measures, particularly content analyses of corporate reports are regarded as direct measuring technique.[475] These content analyses are frequently based on a **disclosure index** which provides rules to categorize the analyzed contents.[476] Also analyst evaluations are commonly used to measure FRQ directly.

Emerging economy studies:

Overall, **single-country research** which focuses on one **emerging economy** applying direct measures of FRQ is scarce. In Brazil, *de Lima et al.* (2010) assess FRQ on the basis of an *International Accounting Standards Convergence Index*. Although most of the 37 disclosure index items represent mandatory disclosure requirements (for all companies with shares listed on the São Paulo Stock Exchange), the sample companies' average compliance with the disclosure index items is heterogeneous.[477] While, for example, solely 6.8% of the companies comply with the item *disclosure of the criteria followed to determine the economic depreciation rates*, 100% publish the required cash flow statement. However, the study focuses on IAS/IFRS-related disclosure requirements and does not consider additional reporting activities. Moreover, the disclosure index comprises only relatively few disclosure items.

Since 2012, *EY* initiates an annual **integrated report** competition which aims at benchmarking the FRQ of companies listed on the *JSE* in South Africa. The survey-based research considers the following evaluation criteria: seven guiding principles and eight content elements derived from the <IR> Framework issued by the *IIRC* as well as the extent to which the <IR> concepts are incorporated.[478] Overall, *EY* (2015) finds companies to make increasingly use of cross-referencing and include less repetitions of information in their integrated reports in line with the integrated reporting approach.[479] However, the study criticizes a lack of substance in some reports, such as a lack of meaningful KPIs and too much emphasis on the companies' past performance. Furthermore, the *Chartered Secretaries Southern Africa* (2015) conducts *Integrated Reporting Awards*, where judges evaluate reports, which have been entered voluntarily by companies from South Africa and other African countries.[480] However, the results suffer from a self-selection bias, because companies choose whether to participate in the competition or not. Moreover, both integrated reporting contests are subject to enormous subjectivity, as FRQ is based on the opinion of experts.

---

475 Cf. section 2.1.3.

476 Cf. *Krippendorff* (2013), p. 157. For a detailed description of disclosure index measures, cf. section 5.2.2.

477 Cf. here and in the following *de Lima et al.* (2010), p. 276.

478 Cf. *EY* (2015), p. 28.

479 Cf. here and in the folowing *EY* (2015), p. 15.

480 Cf. here and in the following *Chartered Secretaries Southern Africa* (2015).

The so-called *World Survey* is a **cross-country study** by *Tonkin* (1989), who compares the annual report quality of 200 large companies from 28 countries. The study's weighted coding scheme is based on the sub-categories (1) disclosure in financial statements (*accounting*), (2) disclosure in non-financial statements and (3) timeliness of the release of annual accounts.[481] The aggregated results present the highest average FRQ for UK companies.[482] South Africa is the highest-ranked emerging economy with an aggregated score of 48.5% which exceeds Germany's score of 37.5%. In particular, South African entities have a better average timeliness of the annual report release, whereas German companies provide a higher quality of non-financial disclosures (25.7%) than South African companies (24.7%).

Cahan et al. (2005) use the disclosure index by *Botosan* (1997) in a cross-country study, to examine the FRQ of the sample companies' annual reports (financial year 1998/1999). Their sample consists of 216 companies from 17 countries, which are part of the *Fortune* magazine's Global 500 largest companies in 1998.[483] However, only few sample companies are from emerging economies. The disclosure score range (from 21 to 85) indicates substantial variation in the FRQ of the sample companies, although the sample comprises only large companies.[484] Relatively poor FRQ is found for the categories non-financials and prospective information, whereas the average score for background information is relatively high. Regarding this study's sample countries Brazil and Germany, *Cahan et al.* (2005) find that the average FRQ is higher in Brazil (average score of 50) than in Germany (average score of 42).[485] However, the finding might not be representative, as the sample includes solely one Brazilian entity.

To analyze the annual reports of companies from 34 countries, *Francis et al.* (2005b) use a voluntary version of the disclosure rating by the Center of International Financial Analysis and Research (CIFAR) for the financial year 1991 or 1993.[486] Unlike other disclosure indices, the CIFAR model does not include the categories non-financial, risk and forward-looking information. The results show the highest FRQ for Sweden with an average score of 83.65.[487] In line with the results by *Tonkin* (1989), the FRQ of UK companies is on a similar level (83.49). Concerning this study's sample countries, the South African mean score (76.00) exceeds the German one (66.42). With a mean score of 55.33 the Brazilian companies' FRQ is one of the lowest in the sample.

Overall, yet, none of the above studies analyze general FRQ differences between emerging and developed economies. Furthermore, they investigate the companies' disclosures on the basis of differing criteria for FRQ and mostly before the adoption of IAS/IFRS in numerous countries. Thus, this study contributes to the literature by using a comprehensive disclosure index to measure FRQ and investigating recent annual reports.

---

481 Cf. *Tonkin* (1989), p. 28.

482 Cf. here and in the following *Tonkin* (1989), p. 48.

483 Cf. *Cahan et al.* (2005), p. 76.

484 Cf. here and in the following *Cahan et al.* (2005), p. 80.

485 Cf. here and in the following *Cahan et al.* (2005), p. 82.

486 Cf. here and in the following *Francis et al.* (2005b), p. 1130. The CIFAR index considers 90 mandatory as well as voluntary disclosure items in seven categories.

487 Cf. here and in the following *Francis et al.* (2005b), p. 1133.

In contrast to the analysis of the reporting contents, there are annual report competitions focusing on different aspects. For instance, the *Vision Awards* by the *League of American Communications Professionals* emphasize the **design**, quality of texts and message of annual reports.[488] Moreover, the international *Annual Report Competition (ARC) Awards* is conducted by judges who evaluate the reports regarding, inter alia, cover design, clarity of written text and the quality of communicating the company's spirit.[489]

The literature review reveals that direct FRQ measure studies vary considerably concerning measurement method, sample and research focus. Thus, the results of prior research are hardly comparable. In particular, existing studies provide mixed results regarding differences between the FRQ in emerging and developed economies.

Table 3-3 summarizes the direct measure studies conducted in emerging economies.

Study	Sample and period	Methodology	Selected results
Tonkin (1989)	200 large companies from 28 developed countries and emerging economies (1986/1987)	This World Survey evaluates the entities' annual reports on the basis of a weighted scoring scheme. It distinguishes the sub-categories (1) disclosure in financial statements; (2) disclosure in non-financial statements; and (3) timeliness of the release of annual accounts.	UK companies are found to provide the highest aggregated disclosure quality. South Africa is the emerging economy with the highest aggregated score of 48.5% exceeding Germany's score of 37.5%. However, German companies provide a higher quality of non-financial disclosures (25.7%) than South African companies (24.7%).
Cahan et al. (2005)	216 large companies from the U.S. and 16 other developed countries and emerging economies (1999)	Using the voluntary disclosure index by Botosan (1997), the study evaluates the annual report FRQ of 216 out of the Fortune magazine's Global 500 largest companies. In particular, it examines, whether FRQ is associated with the global diversification of operations and financing.	The results suggest a higher average FRQ than found by Botosan (1997). With a disclosure score range from 21 to 85 there is a substantial variation in FRQ across the sample companies. The highest score per country is found for Sweden.
Francis et al. (2005b)	484 companies from 34 developed countries and emerging economies outside the U.S. (1991/1993)	To determine the FRQ of the companies' annual reports, the study uses voluntary disclosure metrics based on the CIFAR disclosure rating.	The results show the highest average FRQ for Sweden (83.65). Moreover, the mean score is higher in South Africa (76.00) than in Germany (66.42) and Brazil (55.33).
de Lima et al. (2010)	54 Brazilian companies listed on the São Paulo Stock Exchange (2009)	The study measures FRQ by an IAS/IFRS convergence index.	The descriptive results show considerable heterogeneity regarding the compliance with different disclosure index related to mandatory IAS/IFRS requirements.
University of Cape Town/EY (2015)	100 South African companies listed on the JSE (with highest market capitalization) (financial year 2014)	The FRQ of the integrated annual reports is analyzed by a survey on the basis of a mark plan, which includes 7 guiding principles, 8 content elements derived from the <IR> Framework as well as the extent to which the <IR> concepts are incorporated.	Besides a ranking of the integrated reports (best report by *Liberty Holdings Ltd*), benchmarking identifies positive trends (e.g., increased use of cross-referencing and less repetition of information) as well as negative trends (e.g., lack of substance in some reports and too much emphasis on past performance).

Table 3-3: Direct measure studies of emerging economies

488 Cf. *Gazdar* (2014), p. 129.
489 Cf. *MerComm* (2015).

Developed country studies:

In the **developed country** literature, *Cerf* (1961) is regarded as the first researcher who uses a disclosure index to examine, which annual report disclosures meet investors' information needs in a U.S. setting.[490] This weighted disclosure index with 31 disclosure items (based on a self-conducted analysis of the information needs of financial decision makers) was the basis for FRQ measures in later studies, e.g. by *Singhvi/Desai* (1971) as well as *Botosan* (1997).[491] While numerous studies use the readily available FAF/AIMR[492] disclosure ranking based on financial analyst evaluations (e.g., *Lang/Lundholm* (1993) and *Healy et al.* (1999)), *Botosan* (1997) constructs an own voluntary disclosure index based on prior disclosure research.[493] She finds a considerable range of the companies' disclosure scores arguing that high-quality reports include both qualitative and quantitative information on the company's products and markets, multiple non-financial statistics as well as forecasts regarding profit, revenue and future trends.[494]

Using a disclosure index which builds on the index by Botosan (1997), *Francis et al.* (2008) find a moderate total voluntary FRQ of U.S. companies (average score of 46.95%) and a considerably lower FRQ for the category *projected information* (33.51%).[495] In line with this result, also *Beretta/Bozzolan* (2004) find poor forward-looking disclosures on the expected impact of identified risks on the company's future performance.[496]

Furthermore, disclosure indices serve also as a basis for annual report *beauty contests* hosted by business journals in different countries.[497] One of the most comprehensive content analyses of annual reports is the competition **"Best Annual Report"** (BAR) conducted annually by the *Research Team Baetge* of the *University of Münster*. In 2015, they evaluated the 2014 annual reports of 100 companies listed in major German stock exchange indices on the basis of a disclosure index with more than 300 criteria.[498] The fact that the scores range from 27.91% to 74.81% suggests, at most, a moderate overall FRQ.[499] Also *Oberdörster* (2009) uses the BAR scores as FRQ measures in her investigation of German companies during the same sample period from 1997 until 2005. The results show that the scores of the average total FRQ (increases from 43.47% in 1997 to 56.46% in 2005) considerably exceed those of the categories risk (ranging from 17.67% to 30.60%) and forward-looking disclosures (ranging from 14.82% to 41.53%).[500] In line with *Beretta/Bozzolan* (2004) and *Francis et al.* (2008), therefore, companies seem not willing to reveal high-quality prospective information. Another annual report contest is based on the **Value Reporting** disclosure index by the University of Zurich (VRZ) which is used

[490] Cf. e.g. *Fremgen* (1963), p. 465.
[491] Cf. *Cerf* (1961), p. 29.
[492] Financial Analyst Federation of the Association for Investment Management and Research.
[493] Cf. *Botosan* (1997), p. 331.
[494] Cf. *Botosan* (1997), p. 334-335.
[495] Cf. *Francis et al.* (2008), p. 71-72 and 81.
[496] Cf. *Beretta/Bozzolan* (2004), p. 277-278.
[497] Cf. *Daske/Gebhardt* (2006), p. 462.
[498] Cf. *University of Münster (Research Team Baetge)* (2015); *BILANZ* (2015).
[499] Cf. here and in the following *BILANZ* (2015).
[500] Cf. here and in the following *Oberdörster* (2009), p. 113-115.

by *Eugster* (2014) to measure the quality of voluntary information in annual reports in nine categories.[501] The trend analysis shows an increase in median FRQ from 38% in 1999 to 53% in 2008.[502]

The above direct measure studies in developed countries are summarized in Table 3-4.

Study	Sample and period	Methodology	Selected results
Cerf **(1961)**	527 U.S. companies (1956/1957)	Cerf (1961) uses a weighted index with 31 disclosure items to evaluate annual reports. The item selection is based on a self-conducted investigation of the information needs of financial decision makers.	The calculated scores for each company range from 5.88 to 83.05. Larger companies (according to both asset size and number of shareholders) as well as companies traded on the NYSE provide increased average scores.
Botosan **(1997)**	122 U.S. companies (1990)	The study investigates the quality of voluntary disclosures in the 1990 annual reports published by 122 U.S. companies with high and low analyst following. FRQ is measured by a self-constructed disclosure index.	The results suggest considerable heterogeneity in voluntary FRQ. The findings reveal that companies with high analyst following provide information of higher average FRQ than companies with low analyst following.
Beretta/Bozzolan **(2004)**	85 Italian listed non-financial companies (2001)	To measure the quality of risk disclosures in annual reports' MD&A sections, the study develops disclosure indices for each of the following categories: (1) disclosure quantity; (2) content type (risk factor); (3) expected impacts of considered factors; (4) type of measures; and (5) approach to disclose identified risks.	The average number of reported risk factors is 75, of which 35.9% concern the companies' strategies. Solely 15.5% of risk disclosures provide details on the expected impact of the identified risks on the company's future performance. 16.2% of risk disclosures deal with risk-management programs to deal with risks, whereas 49.5% are concerned with actions or decisions already taken.
Francis et al. **(2008)**	677 U.S. companies (2001)	For its content analysis of annual reports and 10-K filings, the study uses a self-constructed disclosure index which includes the categories (1) summary of historical results; (2) other financial measures; (3) non-financial measures; (4) projected information.	The results indicate substantial variation in the sample companies' voluntary FRQ. The average relative score (scaled by maximum score) is 46.95%. The mean relative scores for the categories non-financial measures and projected information are 45.49% and 33.51%.
Oberdörster **(2009)**	656 German companies (1997-2005)	The investigation analyses the FRQ of different parts of the annual report distinguishing German GAAP and international GAAP reports. The study uses the results of *Baetge's* BAR contest as FRQ proxy.	The results suggest that FRQ of multiple reporting categories is insufficient, particularly for risk and forward looking disclosures. The development of the annual reports' overall FRQ shows an increase from a score of 43.47% in 1997 to 56.46% in 2005.
Eugster **(2014)**	Swiss companies (1,039 company years) (1999-2008)	To measure voluntary FRQ of Swiss companies' annual reports, the study uses the VAR index by the University of Zurich, which consists of 9 indices.	The reached scores, which range from 5% to 88%, and the total standard deviation of 14% suggest massive variation of voluntary FRQ. The results show an increase in median FRQ from 38% in 1999 to 53% in 2008.
Baetge's "Best Annual Report" 2015/BILANZ **(2015)**	100 companies listed in major German stock exchange indices (financial year 2014)	The evaluation of the companies' annual reports is based on a content analysis using a disclosure index with more than 300 criteria. A company's FRQ is measured by its total score of the disclosure index.	The results present a ranking of the companies according to their total FRQ (reached scores). The company with the highest FRQ is *Deutsche Telekom AG* (74.81%). The disclosure index scores range from 27.91% to 74.81% suggesting a moderate FRQ.

Table 3-4: Direct measure studies of developed countries

501 Cf. *Eugster* (2014), p. 8.

502 Cf. *Eugster* (2014), p. 39.

The literature review reveals several shortcomings of prior research as well as research gaps. In line with the review of indirect measure studies, there are only a few recent direct measure studies investigating emerging economies. The fact that some countries in cross-country studies are represented by solely very few companies affects the studies' results negatively. Moreover, prior research does not find a consensus whether FRQ differs between emerging economies and developed countries. These mixed results may have several reasons, such as different sample periods and operationalizations of FRQ. In particular, studies focus on different aspects of financial reporting (e.g., risk disclosures). Moreover, some disclosure indices capture only very few criteria of FRQ, for example, as only a few disclosure items are included. Hence, a comprehensive study could analyze FRQ in more detail and, thereby, shed light on the role of FRQ in emerging economies in contrast to developed countries. Furthermore, most studies do not interpret the disclosure index (sub) scores thoroughly, but rather seem to seek an easy way to generate a FRQ score as basis for additional analyses.

In addition to the above studies, there is a considerable amount of literature concerned with specific areas of financial reporting which shall not be included in this literature review, such as forward-looking disclosures (e.g., *Barth* (2009)), management commentary (e.g., *Kajüter* (2013)) or sustainability reporting in BRIC countries (e.g., *Alon et al.* (2010)). The reviewed studies present descriptions of the quality of corporate reporting and provide insights into financial reporting practices in national and international settings, however, not potential effects. Thus, the following sections give an overview of studies investigating which determinants influence FRQ and present studies exploring capital market effects of FRQ.

3.3 Determinants of financial reporting quality

Research on the determinants of FRQ has been conducted in numerous single country as well as cross-country settings. However, only few studies focus on emerging economies. The following literature review includes studies with different measures of FRQ in line with this study's multidimensional understanding of FRQ.

Emerging economy studies:

Using a **single-country** and **emerging economy setting**, *Haniffa/Cooke* (2002) investigate the effect of corporate governance, the cultural background of decision makers as well as other company characteristics on voluntary disclosures in annual reports of Malaysian listed companies. The study measures FRQ by a disclosure index based on prior research.[503] Besides FRQ as dependent variable, the multivariate regression model includes a selection of explanatory variables.[504] The results show a lower FRQ, the more members of a dominant shareholding family are on the company's board and the more concentrated the shareholder structure is.[505] The findings are reasonable, since such family members and large block holders might have access to internal information and, thus, are less de-

[503] Cf. *Haniffa/Cooke* (2002), p. 330.

[504] Cf. *Haniffa/Cooke* (2002), p. 331-333.

[505] Cf. here and in the following *Haniffa/Cooke* (2002), p. 339.

pendent on information published in annual reports. Following the same argumentation, the significant positive association between the concentration of large institutional shareholders and FRQ seems counterintuitive. The identified positive relationship between fraction of foreign investors and FRQ in the emerging economy of Malaysia "*[...] supports the argument that obtaining foreign funds means a greater need for disclosure to monitor actions by management.*"[506] In line with prior studies' results, FRQ is positively related to profitability and FRQ differs according to industry.[507] However, the results do not show any cultural effects on FRQ.

For a Chinese sample of 110 listed companies, *Wang et al.* (2008) analyze the relation between the FRQ of the companies' 2005 annual reports (measured by a self-constructed and literature based disclosure index with 79 items) and potential influencing factors of FRQ. The OLS regression model finds significant relations between overall FRQ and the following determinants: company size, state ownership, profitability and auditor (Big-4/non-Big-4).[508] Consistent with the results by *Haniffa/Cooke* (2002), foreign ownership is positively related to FRQ. *Wang et al.* (2008) find no association between leverage and FRQ on a statistically significant level.

Also *Bokpin* (2013) uses an emerging economy setting to provide further evidence on the determinants of corporate disclosure. The study's sample encompasses 27 companies listed on the Ghana Stock Exchange.[509] In a low disclosure environment, FRQ is measured by the total score of a disclosure index which comprises the categories financial disclosure, governance and voluntary information.[510] The results of the computed regression model show positive relations between FRQ and company size as well as company age on a highly significant level.[511] Consistent with prior research, profitability as well as engagement of Big-4 auditor are positively associated with FRQ. A marginally significant negative relationship is found for leverage.

Schiehll et al. (2013) explore the determinants of voluntary executive stock option disclosure for a sample of 68 Brazilian listed companies. The study uses six highly correlated disclosure indices to operationalize voluntary executive stock option disclosure.[512] The results show that board size, the presence of a compensation committee and Big-4 auditing firm are positively and significantly related to the level of disclosure, whereas leverage and profitability are no significant determinants.[513] Moreover, the results are mixed for ownership concentration as a determinant in Brazil, as only some of the regression models as well as robustness tests support that a higher ownership concentration is associated with a lower disclosure level for companies.[514]

---

506 *Haniffa/Cooke* (2002), p. 339.
507 Cf. here and in the following *Haniffa/Cooke* (2002), p. 340.
508 Cf. here and in the following *Wang et al.* (2008), p. 23.
509 Cf. *Bokpin* (2013), p. 127.
510 Cf. *Bokpin* (2013), p. 136.
511 Cf. here and in the following *Bokpin* (2013), p. 138.
512 Cf. *Schiehll et al.* (2013), p. 342.
513 Cf. *Schiehll et al.* (2013), p. 350.
514 Cf. *Schiehll et al.* (2013), p. 352.

In a **cross-country setting** with companies from 42 developed and emerging economies, *Hope* (2003) investigates the influence of legal origin, culture and company-specific determinants on the FRQ of annual reports. He uses CIFAR disclosure scores (for financial years 1991 and 1993) as proxy for FRQ and cultural values by *Hofstede* as measures for national culture, although the cultural values had been determined about 15 years prior to the disclosure scores.[515] The regression results provide evidence that culture is one important explanatory variable of FRQ amongst others.[516] Overall FRQ tends to be higher in common law countries.[517] Regarding company-specific determinants, the results show that larger and cross-listed companies provide significantly higher FRQ.

Iatridis (2012) investigates this study's sample countries Brazil and South Africa from an auditing perspective. He measures the FRQ (in terms of earnings management and conservatism) of 270 companies from South Africa and 228 companies from Brazil.[518] The results show that companies being audited by big auditors reveal lower discretionary accruals and higher conservatism.[519] In addition, larger companies are found to engage less in earnings management than smaller ones.

On the whole, prior research on the determinants of FRQ in emerging economies is scarce, widely obsolete, uses different research approaches and provides inconsistent results. In line with the discussion of descriptive FRQ research before, also the determinant studies use different indirect and direct methods to measure FRQ, which focus on particular aspects of FRQ and vary regarding complexity and comprehensibility. Also the studies' selection of potential determinants varies considerably depending on the research focus. Thus, the research results are difficult to compare and interpretations have to take the study's individual setting into account. Nonetheless, the literature review has identified some determinants, which seem to particularly affect FRQ in emerging economies. Several studies suggest that company size, profitability, ownership concentration, cross-listing and audit firm are deemed to be pronounced determinants in emerging economies. However, the findings are not consistent among the reviewed studies so that additional research can contribute to the identification of determinants in emerging economies by using a setting of both emerging and developed economies. Although various studies suggest an important role of a company's ownership structure in emerging economies, the findings concerning the relation between ownership concentration and FRQ are mixed.[520] The literature review further suggests that leverage is no significant determinant of FRQ in emerging economies.

Table 3-5 summarizes the determinant studies involving emerging economies, which have been under review.

---

515 Cf. *Hope* (2003), p. 219 and 239.

516 Cf. *Hope* (2003), p. 241-242.

517 Cf. here and in the following *Hope* (2003), p. 234-236.

518 Cf. *Iatridis* (2012), p. 101 and 108.

519 Cf. here and in the following *Iatridis* (2012), p. 109-111.

520 For ownership concentration in emerging economies, cf. section 2.2.3.2.

Study	Sample	Methodology	Selected results
Haniffa/Cooke (2002)	167 listed companies from Malaysia (1995)	The regression model includes voluntary FRQ (measured by a disclosure index based on prior research) as dependent variable and a selection of explanatory variables from the categories corporate governance, culture and other company characteristics.	FRQ is negatively associated with family members on the board and ownership concentration, whereas the regression results do not support any assumed cultural effects. FRQ further increases with higher profitability and foreign investors. Moreover, FRQ differs according to industry.
Hope (2003)	Companies from 42 developed countries and emerging economies, 1,992 company years (1991; 1993)	The study calculates different regression models to investigate the relation between FRQ (proxied by CIFAR disclosure scores) as dependent variable and legal origin, culture (proxied by the cultural values by *Hofstede*) and company-specific factors as independent variables.	The results indicate that both legal origin as well as culture are important explanatory variables of FRQ. FRQ is found to be higher in common law countries. Moreover, the results show that larger, cross-listed and low leverage companies provide significantly higher FRQ.
Wang et al. (2008)	110 Chinese listed companies (2005)	The study measures FRQ with a self-constructed 79 items disclosure index (based on prior literature) and regresses FRQ on potential determinants (OLS regression).	Significant positive relations are found between overall FRQ and the following determinants: company size, state ownership, foreign ownership, profitability and auditor, however, not for leverage.
Iatridis (2012)	270 South African and 228 Brazilian listed companies (2005-2010)	FRQ in terms of earnings management and conservatism is measured by: (1) discretionary accruals based on Jones (1991); (2) operating income; (3) change in operating income.	Companies being audited by big auditors show lower discretionary accruals and higher conservatism. Larger companies engage less in earnings management than smaller ones.
Bokpin (2013)	27 companies listed on the Ghana Stock Exchange (2003-2008)	The study computes a regression model to investigate disclosure determinants. As dependent variable the model uses the total score of the applied disclosure index.	The positive relations between FRQ and company size as well as company age are highly significant. Significant relations are also found for the determinants profitability (positive sign), audit type (positive sign) and leverage (negative sign).
Schiehll et al. (2013)	68 Brazilian listed companies (2007)	The study regresses six direct measures of voluntary executive stock option disclosure (based on six disclosure indices) on selected governance-related determinants.	The results show a lower disclosure level for companies with a higher ownership concentration. Moreover, board size, presence of a compensation committee and Big-4 auditing firm are positively and significantly related to the level of disclosure. Leverage and profitability are no significant determinants.

Table 3-5: Determinants studies of emerging economies

Developed country studies:

Numerous studies investigate the determinants of FRQ in several **developed countries**. However, a comparison of their results is difficult, as the studies vary regarding sample period and size, selection of variables as well as FRQ measurement technique. While, amongst others, *Firth* (1979), *Cooke* (1991), *Wallace et al.* (1994), *Hossain et al.* (1995), *Al-Najjar/Abed* (2014), *Dainelli et al.* (2013) analyze the determinants of annual report disclosures, *Cohen* (2008) examines the influence of 12 potential determinants on four indirect proxies of FRQ (cash flow and accruals-based). Moreover, the type and number of analyzed determinants differ considerably. For example, *Cooke* (1991) focuses on a company's size, stock market listing and industry category,[521] whereas *Al-Najjar/Abed*

[521] Cf. *Cooke* (1991), p. 174.

(2014) include the variables company size, leverage, performance, operating cash flow to lagged total assets, cross-listing, competition rate, block holder ownership and other corporate governance variables.[522]

Based on significance tests and OLS regression models, the studies provide mixed results. In particular, the determinants company size and industry category are found to be associated with FRQ.[523] Some of the studies further provide evidence that a company's FRQ is related to its profitability, ownership concentration, auditing firm, listing status and leverage.[524] The meta-analysis by *Ahmed/Courtis* (1999) integrate 29 annual report disclosure studies and support positive relations between FRQ and size, listing status and leverage.[525] However, profitability and auditor size are not found to be associated with FRQ.[526]

The reviewed research is summarized in Table 3-6.

Study	Sample	Methodology	Selected results
***Firth* (1979)**	UK companies (80 companies for listing analysis and 100 companies for size and auditor analysis) (1976)	The study uses significance tests to investigate the relation between a company's size, listing and auditor on its 1976 annual report disclosures (measured by content analysis using a 48-items disclosure index).	The results present statistically significant positive relations between FRQ and both company size as well as share listing, whereas a company's auditor type is not found to be significantly associated with its FRQ.
***Cooke* (1991)**	48 Japanese companies (1988)	The study's linear regression model uses voluntary FRQ in annual reports (disclosure index proxy) as dependent and selected influencing factors as independent variables.	The most pronounced relation is found between FRQ and company size. The results also show industry effects on FRQ. Further, a company's listing status is a significant explanatory variable.
***Wallace et al.* (1994)**	50 Spanish companies (1991)	The study uses an OLS regression model to investigate the relation between FRQ and company characteristics following prior research. The study applies a mandatory disclosure index to measure the FRQ of annual reports.	The results show that Spanish companies, which are larger and stock exchange listed, provide significantly higher disclosure levels. Moreover, liquidity is negatively associated with FRQ.
***Hossain et al.* (1995)**	55 companies listed on the New Zealand Stock Exchange (of which 15 are simultaneously listed overseas) (1991)	The regression model investigates the influence of selected determinants on the FRQ of the sample companies' 1991 annual reports (measured by a 95 items disclosure index).	FRQ is related to company size, leverage and foreign listing suggesting that companies additionally listed overseas have a higher FRQ than those only listed on the domestic stock exchange.
***Ahmed/Courtis* (1999)**	Meta-analysis of 29 annual report disclosure studies (1968-1997)	The meta study assimilates the analyzed studies capturing 2,473 annual reports. On this basis, the study reinvestigates the association between FRQ as dependent variable and company characteristics identified by prior research as independent variables.	The results confirm positive relations between FRQ and the determinants size, listing status and leverage. However, profitability and auditor size are not found to be significantly associated with FRQ.

-Table is continued on the next page-

[522] *Al-Najjar/Abed* (2014), p. 586.
[523] Cf. *Cooke* (1991), p. 184-186; *Wallace et al.* (1994), p. 51; *Hossain et al.* (1995), p. 80; *Cohen* (2008), p. 81-82; *Al-Najjar/Abed* (2014), p. 589; *Dainelli et al.* (2013), p. 274-275.
[524] Cf. *Hossain et al.* (1995), p. 80; *Cohen* (2008), p. 81-82; *Al-Najjar/Abed* (2014), p. 589; *Dainelli et al.* (2013), p. 274-275.
[525] Cf. *Ahmed/Courtis* (1999), p. 53-54.
[526] Cf. *Ahmed/Courtis* (1999), p. 55.

***Cohen* (2008)**	2,857 U.S. companies (1987-2003)	The study regresses four indirect FRQ proxies (cash flow- and accruals-based) on 12 potential determinants of FRQ.	Higher FRQ with increasing size, ownership dispersion, capital intensity, leverage and decreasing sales margin. Also industry competition is significantly related to FRQ. Age (time since listing) is not significantly associated with FRQ.
***Al-Najjar/Abed* (2014)**	238 UK listed companies (2006)	*Al-Najjar/Abed* (2014) use computerized content analysis to measure the FRQ of voluntary information in annual reports. The regression model examines the relation between FRQ and corporate governance indicators and other determinants.	There is a significant negative association between FRQ and block holder ownership. The results also show that disclosure is significantly and positively related to company size, cross-listing status, operating cash flow and negatively to performance.
***Dainelli et al.* (2013)**	120 listed Italian companies (2010)	A regression model is calculated to investigate the relation between voluntary FRQ (measured by number of performance indicators disclosed in 2010 annual report) and profitability as well as other control variables.	The results show that more profitable, larger (proxied by market capitalization) and riskier companies have an increased disclosure level. Also industry effects are found.

Table 3-6: Determinants studies of developed countries

On the whole, relatively few studies investigate determinants of FRQ in emerging economies compared to the large number of studies in developed countries. Similar to the financial reporting practice studies, most determinants studies have been conducted a considerable time ago. As the national and international reporting environments have developed continuously over the past years, additional up-to-date research can provide useful insights. Overall, the literature investigates a number of different determinants. However, some studies only consider few potential determinants in their models, which may lead to omitted variables. Although there are specific determinants found to be significant in both emerging and developed economies, some determinants seem to be more pronounced in either emerging or developed economies countries. While in developed countries particularly the effects of company size and industry on FRQ are suggested to be strong, emerging economy studies emphasize the importance of ownership concentration, cross-listings, profitability and auditor type for the companies' FRQ. The literature review further suggests that the effect of company age may be more pronounced in emerging economies. Hence, an emerging economy environment may create different motives for companies to provide a high FRQ. As a consequence, country effects in emerging economies can be expected due to a different institutional and cultural environment than in developed countries.

After reviewing the literature on the description of observed FRQ and on the identification of associated determinants, the following section presents prior research on the economic consequences of FRQ in both emerging economies and developed countries.

3.4 Capital market consequences of financial reporting quality

In the accounting literature, there is a large number of studies concerned with potential capital market consequences of FRQ. These studies can be either **analytical** or **empirical** in nature.[527] The advantages and disadvantages of both research methods are summarized in the following statement by *Beyer et al.* (2010), who identify a considerable clash between analytical and empirical studies:

> "*The analytical models examined are often very focused and detailed, more so than could reasonably be tested using empirical methods. In contrast, the empirical studies are often very broad (relative to analytical models), but lack the necessary in-depth analysis.*"[528]

In line with this study's research approach, the literature review presents only empirical studies in the following. Empirical accounting research analyzes different capital market effects of FRQ. Inter alia, studies investigate the effect of financial reporting on the implied cost of equity capital[529] and information asymmetries. In particular, information asymmetries are commonly regarded as a component of the cost of equity capital and lower information asymmetries reduce the cost of equity capital according to economic theory.[530] While this literature review provides an overview of studies measuring various capital market effects, this study's empirical investigation analyzes the relation between FRQ and information asymmetries.

Emerging economy studies:

In an **emerging economy** setting (**single-country**), *Lopes/de Alencar* (2010) examine the relation between voluntary FRQ and the cost of equity of Brazilian companies. Based on a disclosure index (analyzing published information from annual reports, websites, São Paulo Stock Exchange filings and CVM files), the study uses panel data for the 50 most liquid shares listed on the *BM&FBOVESPA* for the years 1998, 2000, 2002, 2004 and 2005.[531] The regression model (based on Botosan (1997)) provides evidence that there is a significant negative association between disclosures and cost of equity.[532] The effect is stronger for companies with low analyst following and a dispersed ownership structure implying that particularly these companies might reduce their costs of capital by providing an increased level of disclosures.

---

[527] For a comprehensive review of both analytical as well as empirical research on economic consequences of disclosure, cf. also *Healy/Palepu* (2001), *Botosan* (2006) and *Beyer et al.* (2010).

[528] *Beyer et al.* (2010), p. 335.

[529] There are also studies exploring the relation between FRQ and cost of debt. For example, Sengupta (1998) finds that companies with high FRQ have lower cost of debt. cf. *Sengupta* (1998), p. 472-473.

[530] Cf. *Verrecchia* (2001), p. 164. However, there is analytical research suggesting that information asymmetries do not generally reduce the cost of capital. *Lambert et al.* (2012) provide the theoretical evidence that information asymmetries do not affect cost of capital in a market of perfect competition; however, if markets are not perfectly competitive, information asymmetries are found to influence cost of capital, cf. *Lambert et al.* (2012), p. 21. Further, *Hughes et al.* (2007) use an analytical model to show that information asymmetries only affect the marketwide risk premium and have no cross-sectional effect on a company's cost of capital, cf. *Hughes et al.* (2007), p. 723.

[531] Cf. *Lopes/de Alencar* (2010), p. 444-446.

[532] Cf. here and in the following *Lopes/de Alencar* (2010), p. 462-463.

The study by *de Lima et al.* (2010) examines whether changes in FRQ due to the shift from local GAAP to IFRS influences the cost of equity of Brazilian listed companies. The study operationalizes FRQ by several measures of accounting convergence, inter alia, a compliance index and the increase in annual report disclosures.[533] However, the study provides no evidence that the companies' costs of capital are related to any of the convergence measures.[534] The results do not suggest that higher FRQ results in a reduction in the costs of capital. Also *Bhattacharyya et al.* (2005) use the shift to a new financial reporting regulation to study the influence of the corporate governance disclosures of listed Indian companies on their beta value (as cost of capital proxy). They use an event study design including a control group of companies, which are not required to apply the new corporate governance rules.[535] The study finds that the beta values of the experimental group companies are significantly lower after the introduction of the regulation.

Francis et al. (2005b) use a **cross-country** sample to investigate the relationship between FRQ (based on CIFAR annual report disclosure scores) and the cost of equity capital. The findings suggest that companies with higher FRQ enjoy lower cost of equity.[536] Similarly, *Daske et al.* (2008) choose an international sample with companies from 26 countries to explore the economic consequences (in terms of market liquidity, cost of capital and Tobin's q) of mandatory IFRS adoption (which is assumed to increase FRQ). On the basis of a difference-in-difference design, the study compares more than 3,100 companies required to adopt IFRS (treatment sample) with about 17,000 non-IFRS companies (benchmark sample).[537] The results show a statistically significant increase in market liquidity and decrease in the costs of capital of the treatment companies after IFRS adoption.[538]

Investigating South African and Brazilian listed companies, *Iatridis* (2012) provides evidence that more earnings management (lower FRQ) by the Brazilian companies is significantly associated with higher costs of equity. In contrast, the relation is not significant for the South African entities.[539] However, *Iatridis* (2012) investigates capital market effects from an auditor's perspective and does not focus on the relation between indirect measures of FRQ and costs of equity. The regression model might not be adequate to isolate the influence of FRQ on the cost of equity. Thus, additional research, which is specifically concerned with the companies' FRQ in Brazil and South Africa can contribute to the literature by reexamining the results by *Iatridis* (2012).

On the whole, the literature provides some empirical evidence of capital market effects of FRQ in emerging economies. Although mostly a negative effect of FRQ on the costs of equity is suggested, this finding is not supported by all studies, which leaves room for ad-

533 Cf. *de Lima et al.* (2010), p. 267.

534 Cf. *de Lima et al.* (2010), p. 252.

535 Cf. here and in the following *Bhattacharyya et al.* (2005), p. 7 and 15-16.

536 Cf. *Francis et al.* (2005b). Already *Francis et al.* (2004) have investigated the relation between cost of equity capital and seven corporate attributes including accrual quality measured by the *Dechow/Dichev* (2002) model. They find that particularly accrual quality is of relevance for a company's cost of capital, as entities with lower accrual quality bear larger costs of equity, cf. *Francis et al.* (2004), p. 967.

537 Cf. *Daske et al.* (2008), p. 1086-1087 and 1103.

538 Cf. *Daske et al.* (2008), p. 1131.

539 Cf. *Iatridis* (2012), p. 114.

ditional research. Moreover, comparative research focusing on multiple emerging economies is very scarce and only a few studies have been conducted over the past few years. Cross-country research mostly does not distinguish between emerging and developed economies. Furthermore, not only the studies' approaches to measure FRQ, but also the operationalizations of capital market consequences differ considerably.

Table 3-7 summarizes the capital market studies involving emerging economies.

Study	Sample	Methodology	Selected results
***Bhattacharyya et al.* (2005)**	134 Indian listed companies (1998-2002)	Using an event study design and conducting significance tests, the investigation explores the influence of the introduction of mandatory corporate governance reporting regulation on the beta values of the companies (as proxy for cost of capital).	The results show a reduction in beta values in the post-regulation period suggesting that companies indeed provide a higher FRQ.
***Francis et al.* (2005b)**	484 companies from 34 developed countries and emerging economies outside the U.S. (1991/1993)	Francis et al. (2005b) use a multiple country sample to explore the relationship between FRQ (based on CIFAR annual report disclosure scores) and the cost of equity capital (approach by Easton (2004)).	The regression results provide evidence that higher FRQ is associated with lower costs of debt and equity.
***Daske et al.* (2008)**	3,100 companies from 26 developed countries and emerging economies (2001-2005)	The study examines the economic consequences (in terms of market liquidity, cost of capital and Tobin's q) of IFRS adoption. Using a difference-in-difference design the study compares the FRQ of IFRS adopters (treatment sample) and non-IFRS adopters (benchmark sample).	The study finds a statistically significant increase in market liquidity and decrease in the costs of capital of the treatment companies after IFRS adoption.
***de Lima et al.* (2010)**	54 Brazilian companies listed on the São Paulo Stock Exchange (2009)	The study examines the association between changes in FRQ due to IAS/IFRS adoption and capital market effects (cost of capital and market liquidity). FRQ is measured by: (1) convergence index (IAS/IFRS compliance); (2) increase in disclosure; (3) increase in earnings quality.	While none of the FRQ measures is significantly related to cost of capital, there is a statistically significant association between FRQ and market liquidity. The result suggests that the greater a company's compliance, the lower its trading costs and greater its liquidity.
***Lopes/de Alencar* (2010)**	50 Brazilian listed companies (1998, 2000, 2002, 2004 and 2005)	The study investigates the relation between voluntary FRQ (disclosure index measure) and the cost of equity capital of the companies on the basis of the regression model by Botosan (1997).	The regression results show a significant negative association between disclosure and cost of equity capital. The effect is stronger for companies with a low analyst following and a dispersed ownership structure.
***Iatridis* (2012)**	270 South African and 228 Brazilian listed companies (2005-2010)	The study investigates the relation between FRQ (in terms of earnings management and conservatism) and cost of equity (proxied by constant growth model) on the basis of OLS regressions.	For Brazil, earnings management is significantly associated with higher cost of equity. However, the relation is not significant for South Africa.

Table 3-7: Capital market studies of emerging economies

Developed country studies:

In contrast to the small number of emerging economy studies, plenty of research has been conducted in **developed countries**. As one of the first investigations, *Botosan* (1997) finds a negative and highly significant relation between disclosure index-based FRQ and the cost of equity for U.S. companies with low analyst following.[540] This finding indicates that companies in a low information environment can lower their cost of capital through increased disclosure levels. A negative association between cost of equity and FRQ is also found by *Botosan/Plumlee* (2002) using a U.S. sample as well as by *Hail* (2002) for a sample of Swiss companies. Contrary to the main findings of numerous earlier studies, *Eugster* (2014) does not confirm that higher voluntary disclosure quality leads to a lower cost of equity using a sample of 173 Swiss companies. After controlling for dynamic endogeneity, simultaneity and unobserved heterogeneity, no significant negative relation between voluntary disclosure quality and cost of equity could be found.[541]

Moreover, a number of studies use indirect measures of FRQ (particularly earnings management proxies) to examine the relation between FRQ and cost of capital. While *Bhattacharya et al.* (2012) provide evidence for a relation between FRQ and cost of capital (mediated by information asymmetry),[542] *Core et al.* (2008) do not find evidence that FRQ is related to cost of capital.[543] Moreover, prior research examines the relation between the switch to increased accounting standards (higher FRQ) and economic consequences. *Leuz/Verrecchia* (2000) find that companies following an international reporting strategy have significantly lower bid-ask spreads and higher median trading volume suggesting lower information asymmetries, while there is no significant difference in share price volatility.[544] *Baetge et al.* (2010) analyze the relation between FRQ and both the precision and variation of the analysts' EPS forecasts when German listed companies switch from local GAAP to international GAAP. The FRQ of the companies' notes is positively associated with the precision of the analysts' EPS forecasts (particularly for companies applying German GAAP).[545] However, the overall FRQ is found to have only a weak influence on the variance of EPS forecasts.[546]

A summary of the capital market studies conducted in developed countries is presented in Table 3-8.

Study	Sample	Methodology	Selected results
Botosan (1997)	122 U.S. companies (1990)	The study regresses cost of equity capital (proxied by earnings/book-value approach) on FRQ (disclosure index analysis of annual reports), market beta and market value. The regression model distinguishes between companies with low and high analyst following.	The results show a negative and highly significant relation between FRQ and cost of capital for companies with low analyst following. However, such a significant association is neither found for the overall sample nor for companies with high analyst following.
		-Table is continued on the next page-	

[540] Cf. *Botosan* (1997), p. 345
[541] Cf. *Eugster* (2014), p. 1.
[542] Cf. *Bhattacharya et al.* (2012), p. 459-460 and 476.
[543] Cf. *Core et al.* (2008), p. 20-21.
[544] Cf. *Leuz/Verrecchia* (2000), p. 121.
[545] Cf. *Baetge et al.* (2010), p. 98.
[546] Cf. *Baetge et al.* (2010), p. 99.

***Leuz/Verrecchia* (2000)**	102 German listed companies (1997/1998)	The study investigates the effect of an increased level of disclosure (proxied by commitment to international accounting standards) on the information asymmetry component of the cost of capital. Information asymmetries are measured by: (1) bid-ask-spreads; (2) trading volume; and (3) volatility.	Companies which follow an international reporting strategy have significantly lower bid-ask spreads and higher median trading volume. However, there is no significant effect on share price volatility.
***Botosan/Plumlee* (2002)**	668 U.S. companies (1985-1996)	Botosan/Plumlee (2002) use a sample of 668 U.S. companies from 43 different industries to compute an OLS regression model including cost of equity capital (estimated by a dividend discount model) as dependent and FRQ (measured through AIMR annual report rankings) as independent variable as well as control variables.	As expected, the regression results confirm a negative association between FRQ and cost of equity capital. Contradictory to expectations, more timely disclosures are found to be positively associated with the cost of equity capital. Moreover, the study provides no evidence that the level of investor relations activities affects costs of capital.
***Hail* (2002)**	73 Swiss listed companies (1997/1998)	The study regresses the companies' implied cost of capital (proxied by ex-ante residual income model) on the companies' voluntary FRQ (measured by VRZ rating).	According to the regression results, FRQ is negatively and highly significantly related to cost of equity capital suggesting that companies with increased disclosure levels enjoy lower costs of capital.
***Core et al.* (2008)**	U.S. companies, 93,093 company years (1970-2001)	The study reinvestigates the influence of accruals quality (indirect FRQ measure) on implied cost of capital, as found by Francis et al. (2005a). Cost of capital effects are computed based on both time-series as well as cross-sectional regression models.	The results refute that accruals quality is a priced risk in the returns expected by investors. Thus, a company's accruals quality (FRQ) is not found to be related to its implied cost of capital.
***Baetge et al.* (2010)**	German companies, 1,889 and 1,652 company years, respectively (1997-2005)	The investigation examines the relation between FRQ (measured by BAR results) of German companies' consolidated management reports and notes, on the one hand, and the precision as well as variance of analysts' EPS forecasts, on the other, before and after the companies' switch from German GAAP to IFRS or U.S. GAAP.	The FRQ of the companies' notes is positively associated with the precision of analysts' EPS forecasts (particularly for German GAAP entities). The effect of the notes' disclosure quality on the EPS forecasts is suggested to be stronger than the effect of management report disclosure quality. Overall FRQ has solely a weak effect on the variance of EPS- forecasts.
***Bhattacharya et al.* (2012)**	U.S. companies, 12,648 company years (1993-2005)	The study investigates a direct and indirect relation between three indirect FRQ proxies and cost of capital. FRQ is measured by (1) accruals quality; (2) absolute abnormal accruals; and (3) composite measure. Information asymmetries are assumed to mediate the FRQ- costs of capital relation.	The results provide evidence for both direct as well as indirect relations between FRQ and cost of capital. However, the direct association is economically more pronounced.
***Eugster* (2014)**	173 Swiss companies (1999-2008)	In line with Hail (2002), the study uses a Swiss sample and measures FRQ through the VRZ rating. Cost of equity capital is estimated by the use of implied cost of capital models.	After controlling for dynamic endogeneity, simultaneity and unobserved heterogeneity, no significant negative relation between voluntary disclosure quality and cost of equity capital is found.

Table 3-8: Capital market studies of developed countries

Although capital market effects are deemed to be easier to detect in emerging economy environments, the vast majority of research has been conducted in developed countries. It is questionable whether the results of the developed country studies are transferable to emerging economies due to their specific characteristics. In particular, numerous studies investigate the relation between FRQ and cost of equity. However, neither for developed nor for emerging economy settings a consensus has been found regarding this relationship. Moreover, only a few studies investigate economic consequences in terms of information asymmetries in an emerging economy setting. As the operationalizations of FRQ differ considerably across the existing literature, the results are difficult to compare. Furthermore, there is a lack of up-to-date research, as financial reporting practices as well as capital market behavior may change over time.

3.5 Implications for this study

On the basis of the prior literature including its deficiencies and limitations, this section identifies the existing research gaps, which are addressed in this study. Therefore, the literature review determines the focus of this thesis and, thus, affects not only the theory-based development of research hypotheses in the following chapter four, but also the study's methodological approaches which are presented in chapter five.

The literature review has shown that only a few studies compare the results of **indirect FRQ measures** across different countries on a descriptive level. In particular, there is hardly any empirical evidence on FRQ in terms of earnings management and readability of financial reports in a comparative setting including emerging economies. Moreover, existing descriptive studies provide heterogeneous results for different indirect FRQ proxies, as the country rankings by *Bhattacharya et al.* (2003) reveal. Most studies using indirect FRQ proxies investigate the effects of FRQ and do not provide descriptive results. Hence, this study contributes to the existing literature in light of the lack of descriptive research. Also the studies applying **direct FRQ measures** show heterogeneous cross-country results regarding the observed FRQ. While, for instance, *Cahan et al.* (2005) find a higher FRQ in Brazil than in Germany, *Francis et al.* (2005b) provide evidence of the opposite. As all of the reviewed studies claim to measure FRQ despite different measures (e.g., indirect accruals-based proxies or direct disclosure index measures), the calculation of correlations between the results of different measures can provide evidence, as to what extent the different measurement techniques provide consistent evaluations of FRQ.[547]

The reasons for inconsistent results of prior FRQ research can be manifold, including, inter alia, different **sample periods**. In particular, there are only a few recent studies. For example, the cross-country investigations by *Leuz et al.* (2003), *Cahan et al.* (2005) and *Francis et al.* (2005b) examine pre-IFRS research periods. FRQ developments since IFRS introduction are widely unexplored across multiple countries. As financial reporting practices may change over time, particularly in rapidly developing emerging economies, an up-to-date empirical investigation is able to provide new insights.

Moreover, the **sample sizes** differ enormously across prior studies. If cross-country studies capture emerging economies at all, they frequently include solely a few companies from these economies in their samples. For instance, the Brazilian and South African results in *Francis et al.* (2005b) are based on 10 and 22 companies, respectively. *Cahan et al.* (2005)

547 Prior research provides mixed results regarding the correlation between indirect and direct measures of FRQ, cf. e.g. *Bhattacharya et al.* (2003), p. 659; *Salewski et al.* (2014), p. 31.

provides results for Brazil based on one single entity only. Thus, cross-country studies capturing a large number of countries are frequently prone to selection bias, as only a few companies from one country or cross-listed companies are selected.[548] In addition, small country samples mitigate comparability, reliability and statistical significance of empirical results. Thus, a study's sample size could allow reliable statistical analyses on both within-country as well as cross-country level. **Within-country studies** provide empirical insights for a particular country and are able to complement cross-country research, as they are able to control for differences in financial reporting incentives (e.g., institutional structures),[549] "*[...] that are difficult to adequately control in cross-country work.*"[550]

The research results are further determined by the applied FRQ **measurement method**. These measures of FRQ vary considerably across studies. In particular, the use of **disclosure indices** is not consistent in the literature, as some disclosure indices are more comprehensive than others. While the disclosure index by *Francis et al.* (2008), for instance, comprises 25 disclosure index items, the results of *Baetge's* BAR competition are based on more than 300 disclosure index items, which allows the detailed examination of multiple facets of the reported information. However, most prior studies do not present such an analysis of the quality of several financial reporting areas (e.g., forward-looking reporting) or focus on specific reporting issues and, therefore, disregard other areas of reporting. The use of a self-constructed disclosure index offers advantages over direct FRQ measures based on **analyst ratings** (e.g., *FAF/AIMR* ranking), which might be biased through the subjective evaluation of analysts.[551] *Lang/Lundholm* (1993) express limitations of their findings due to the fact that "*[...] the data are based on analysts' ratings rather than the disclosures themselves.*"[552] On the whole, the reviewed studies use a large number of different FRQ measures indicating that measuring FRQ is difficult and that various operationalizations of FRQ appear feasible.[553] Therefore, the application of multiple FRQ measurement techniques allows capturing different dimensions of the abstract notion of FRQ.

Comparisons between the disclosure levels identified in different studies are also difficult, since some investigations focus on **voluntary** disclosures (e.g., *Eugster* (2014)), whereas other studies consider (additionally) **mandatory** disclosures (e.g., *Wallace et al.* (1994); *Hope* (2003)). Overall, there is no recent study which provides a comprehensive comparison of directly-measured FRQ in both emerging economies and developed countries. Moreover, *Beyer et al.* (2010) point out that "*[...] to date, little is known about the relations between firms' voluntary disclosure policies, mandatory disclosure requirements, and the information produced by security analysts.*"[554] Hence, a study could shed light on voluntary and mandatory disclosures by measuring the quality of both companies' overall and voluntary disclosures separately.

548 Cf. *Lopes/de Alencar* (2010), p. 444.
549 Cf. *de Lima et al.* (2010), p. 254.
550 *Holthausen* (2003), p. 282.
551 Cf. *Lang/Lundholm* (1993), p. 269.
552 *Lang/Lundholm* (1993), p. 269.
553 Cf. section 2.1.3.
554 *Beyer et al.* (2010), p. 335.

In addition to the description of financial reporting practices, empirical research investigates the **determinants of FRQ**. While *Chen et al.* (2014) identify the need for determinant studies even in developed countries, there are barely any recent studies on the determinants of FRQ in emerging economies.[555] However, a determinant study in emerging economies is of particular interest, since the particular environment in emerging economies (cf. section 2.2.3) could affect the role of the determinants. The literature review has identified some determinants being more pronounced in emerging economies than in developed countries, yet, comparisons of different studies are difficult and empirical evidence is weak. On the whole, it remains unclear, as to what extent determinants of FRQ differ between emerging economies and developed countries.

Additional research is further required, as the literature review shows **heterogeneous results** for multiple determinants of FRQ. For example, prior research does not find a consensus on the influence of a company's ownership structure, profitability and industry on its FRQ. The findings by *Haniffa/Cooke* (2002) and *Wang et al.* (2008) suggest that **ownership structure** affects disclosure practices in emerging economies significantly. The description of the emerging economies' accounting environments in sections 2.2.3 has shown that the effect of ownership structure on FRQ may be stronger in emerging economies than in developed countries due to cultural and historical developments. Examples are family-owned businesses in Brazil, aftereffects of colonial times or state interventions (e.g., state-owned companies). However, there is no consensus among existing studies that ownership concentration is in fact a significant determinant of FRQ. Hence, additional research can shed light on this discussion.

In line with the results by *Bokpin* (2013), the influence of **company age** as determinant of FRQ might be easier to detect in a setting with both emerging economies and developed countries. In particular, the share of younger companies is higher in emerging economies than in developed countries with a large number of well-established entities.[556] Hence, the role of company age can be investigated adequately. Furthermore, prior research finds **cross-listing** and **audit firm** to be significant determinants of FRQ in emerging economies. Thus, future research has to consider the influence of these factors (e.g., by excluding cross-listed companies or controlling for these determinants).

A general problem of prior determinant studies is that the selection of analyzed determinants varies considerably. Some studies focus on only few determinants which may be of interest to the study's particular research focus, yet, omit other **potential determinants**. Hence, studies are supposed to capture all major determinants influencing FRQ to provide evidence of factors influencing FRQ.

In line with the determinants studies, also **capital market effects of FRQ** have been mostly investigated in developed countries. In particular, numerous studies investigate economic consequences in terms of cost of capital, whereas fewer investigations focus on information asymmetries. However, neither for developed countries nor for emerging economies empirical research finds a general consensus on the relation between FRQ and

[555] Cf. *Chen et al.* (2014), p. 18.
[556] Cf. *Bokpin* (2013), p. 136.

these economic consequences. On the one hand, since studies have provided empirical evidence of a negative relationship between FRQ and cost of capital *Botosan* (1997). On the other hand, a considerable amount of research has not found that increased FRQ is associated with lower cost of capital. With respect to Brazil, for example, *Lopes/de Alencar* (2010) indicate a negative relation between FRQ and cost of capital, whereas *de Lima et al.* (2010) do not provide evidence for this relation.

The observation that the negative effect of FRQ on cost of capital is more pronounced among companies with low analyst following and a dispersed ownership is in line with expectations.[557] As described in section 2.1.1, companies bear the costs of financial reporting, as long as these costs do not exceed the resulting benefits. Thus, companies with a relatively large number of investors and low analyst following are assumed to provide increased FRQ to inform their investors and, thereby, lower the company's costs of capital. Thus a favorable setting to examine capital market consequences may include **emerging economies**, as analyst following tends to be lower than in developed countries. Moreover, economic consequences are supposed to be easier to identify in emerging economies due to a lower FRQ there[558]:

> "*[...] the economic consequences of an increased reporting strategy should be easier to detect when the disclosure environment is low.*"[559]

Following this argumentation, *Lopes/de Alencar* (2010), for example, choose the emerging economy of Brazil as an adequate research environment to detect capital market effects, since disclosure level is low and variation in disclosures is high.[560]

On the whole, the literature review has shown that research on the FRQ in emerging economies is very scarce compared to the larger number of studies in developed countries (particularly U.S. studies). Single emerging economies are only examined sporadically and even the prominent BRICS countries are largely uninvestigated. Cross-country studies focusing on FRQ in multiple emerging economies (e.g., *Chen et al.* (2011), *Iatridis* (2012)) are rare cases. The analysis of financial reporting practices in emerging economies is rather included in cross-country studies involving both developed and emerging economies (e.g., *Bhattacharya et al.* (2003), *Leuz et al.* (2003)). Although there are numerous reasons that financial reporting practice in emerging economies differs from financial reporting practice in developed countries,[561] there is poor empirical evidence of actual differences and associated effects. Therefore, a comparative up-to-date study in an emerging economy/developed economy setting can fill existing research gaps regarding descriptive observations, determinants and capital market consequences of FRQ.

---

557 Cf. *Botosan* (1997), p. 345.

558 Cf. e.g. *Bhattacharya et al.* (2003), p. 660.

559 *Hail* (2002), p. 766.

560 Cf. *Lopes/de Alencar* (2010), p. 444.

561 Cf. section 2.2.3.

4 Theory and hypotheses development

4.1 Conceptual framework and theoretical foundation

4.1.1 Introduction

Although chapter three has shown that a multitude of studies investigate financial reporting quality, most studies lack a sound theoretical foundation. An explanation may be that

"*[...] there is no comprehensive, or unifying, theory of disclosure [...]*"[562].

In particular, prior studies about determinants of FRQ frequently do not explain their selection of analyzed influencing factors on the basis of an underlying theoretical model.[563] Therefore, this chapter describes the theoretical foundation of the study and develops a conceptual framework to derive the research hypotheses, which are tested in the empirical investigation. The study's research objective is based on the **positive accounting theory** that aims at explaining and predicting actual accounting practices (in contrast to normative research).[564] In particular, the empirical investigation discovers the financial reporting activities of Brazilian, South African and German companies.

As a theoretical starting point, the **general systems theory** posits that companies (also organizations) are social systems, which are surrounded by a wider environment.[565] Systems, regardless if mechanical, biological or social, exist of at least two interrelated elements. However, the system shall not be evaluated as the sum of its separate elements, but rather as a totality. A social system interacts with its environment in a way that it receives input from the environment, uses this input according to individual objectives and, eventually, provides outputs to the environment. Researchers apply this system approach to businesses to explain the increasing complexity of organizations.[566] In particular, systems theory can also be applied to a company's reporting system or its responsible accounting employees. The system of the company interacts with the environment to keep the company, as a social system, running.[567] However, systems theory is not directly applicable to this study as a theoretical foundation, since it does not support the existence of universal relations (e.g., between country characteristics and FRQ). The theory rather focuses on so-called *single cases* considering solely one organization and one situation (single case approach).[568] However, both contingency theory as well as the societal effects approach are built on the notions of system theory and are introduced in the following.[569]

Using the construct of **contingency theory** (section 4.1.2) as an overall conceptual frame, different theoretical approaches influence financial reporting practice and quality, respec-

[562] *Verrecchia* (2001), p. 98.
[563] Cf. *Nobes* (1998), p. 162.
[564] Cf. *Watts/Zimmerman* (1986), p. 2. As part of this study's theoretical foundation, positive accounting theory and political costs are discussed in section 4.1.5.3.
[565] Cf. here and in the following *Kast/Rosenzweig* (1972), p. 450.
[566] Cf. *Carlisle* (1973), p. 48-49.
[567] Cf. *Reisloh* (2011), p. 93.
[568] Cf. *Brose* (1984), p. 231; *Reisloh* (2011), p. 93.
[569] Cf. *Kast/Rosenzweig* (1972), p. 459.

tively. The **culture approach** captures the relation between national culture and accounting (section 4.1.3). In addition, the **societal effects approach** considers the association between institutional context factors (e.g., financing system or legal system) and corporate reporting practices (4.1.4). Moreover, particularly **institutionalism** (section 4.1.5) serves as a theoretical foundation for the development of this study's research hypotheses (section 4.2). Thus, the culture and societal effects approaches are presented relatively briefly. In particular, the empirical investigation does not distinguish between multiple cultural and societal factors, but rather aggregates these factors into a country effect for each sample country (Brazil, South Africa and Germany).

4.1.2 Contingency theory as conceptual basis

Derived from systems theory, contingency theory regards organizations as **open systems**, whose outcome always depends on various factors, such as the influence of environmental aspects on the organization's activities and success.[570] Thus, a company's success always depends on particular factors:

> "*Contingency theorists believe that the best way is always specific to the nature of a task and the task environment.*"[571]

The (management) accounting literature picked up contingency theory in the 1970s, although it had been developed earlier.[572] The contingency approach gives up the formerly predominant idea that there is *a best way* to organize all companies (universalistic approach) and rather considers all relevant **situational factors**, before deciding for an organizational structure or a management course.[573] For instance, the stability of the environment may impact a company's organizational structure:

> "*Firms facing a stable, certain environment may find bureaucratic organization structure adequate for achievement of proper integration and differentiation, while a more uncertain environment would preclude effective use of the same form.*"[574]

With respect to this study, a company's most favorable accounting practice is dependent - contingent - upon **internal and external circumstances**.[575] As illustrated in Figure 4-1, contingency theory is a compromise in between the *universalistic approach* and systems theory's *single case approach*. While the single case approach denies the transfer of a company's management course to another one, the universalistic approach proposes universal solutions disregarding a company's particular influencing variables.[576]

In line with this study's research questions, contingency theory assumes that the behavior of organizations is associated with the particular circumstances and configuration of these

[570] Cf. *Jenner* (2001), p. 79-80.
[571] *Sorge* (1991), p. 161.
[572] Cf. *Otley* (1980), p. 413. Initial publications on contingency theory were, inter alia, *Woodward* (1958); *Udy Jr* (1959); *Stinchcombe* (1959).
[573] Cf. *Thompson* (1967), p. 27-28; *Tosi et al.* (1973), p. 27.
[574] *Tosi et al.* (1973), p. 27.
[575] Cf. *Otley* (1980), p. 413-416.
[576] Cf. *Brose* (1984), p. 231; *Jenner* (2001), p. 79.

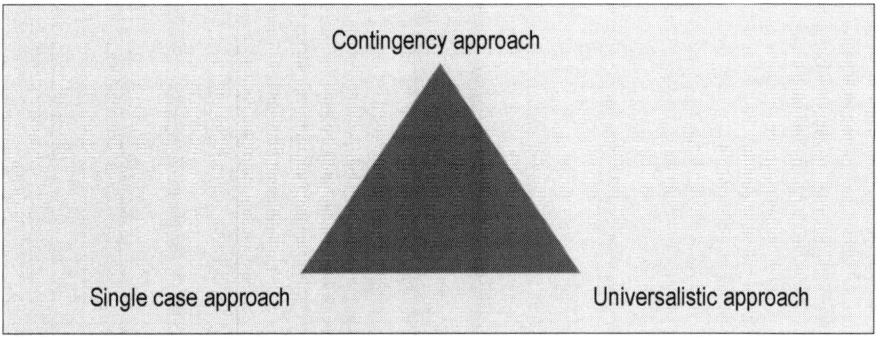

Figure 4-1: Single case, universalistic and contingency approach
Adopted from *Hellriegel/Slocum* (1976), p. 6.

organizations. The contingency approach allows to identify influencing factors, measure an organization's configuration and, unlike the single case approach, to transfer results to other organizations with corresponding configurations.[577] Moreover, researchers are able to formulate and test contingency hypotheses.[578]

The literature uses the contingency approach frequently due to its intuitive and wide-ranging applicability to a considerable number of settings.[579] In spite of its popularity, **critics** reverse these advantages arguing that contingency theory would be too loose to be regarded as a *real* theory, which provides an exact concept and theoretical implications.[580] Moreover, the contingency approach neither concretizes how to model a certain relationship nor how to determine relevant influencing variables. From a methodological perspective, the contingency approach runs the risk that assumed relationships are not modelled appropriately and results could be distorted; for instance, if context variables are interdependent, causal relations between variables remain unclear or environmental influencing factors are regarded as deterministic.[581] Therefore, this investigation uses the contingency approach rather as a meta-theory to conceptualize different phenomena in a conceptual framework than as actual theoretical basis.[582]

Applying general contingency theory to this study, internal and external factors influence the entity's financial reporting practices. In contrast to external factors, internal factors are regarded as company-specific characteristics (e.g., company size). With their model, *Doupnik/Salter* (1995) explain the impact of the external environment on the accounting practices of a company. Figure 4-2 illustrates that they emphasize **culture** (represented by four independent variables derived from *Hofstede* (1980a)) and **institutional structures** (operationalized by six independent institutional variables, e.g. legal system) as relevant

577 Cf. *Otley* (1980), p. 422; *Jenner* (2001), p. 80-82.
578 Cf. *Otley* (1980), p. 414.
579 Cf. *Schmidt* (1997), p. 758; *Donaldson* (1999), p. 51-52. *Jenner* (2001), p. 79.
580 Cf. here and in the following *Ulrich* (1993), p. 123; *Schmidt* (1997), p. 45; *Wolf* (2013), p. 219.
581 Cf. *Jenner* (2001), p. 81-82.
582 Cf. *Raffée* (1993), p. 37-40; *Reisloh* (2011), p. 99.

external factors influencing accounting practices.[583] However, the cultural variables do not only impact accounting practices directly, but also have an indirect effect via the institutional factors.

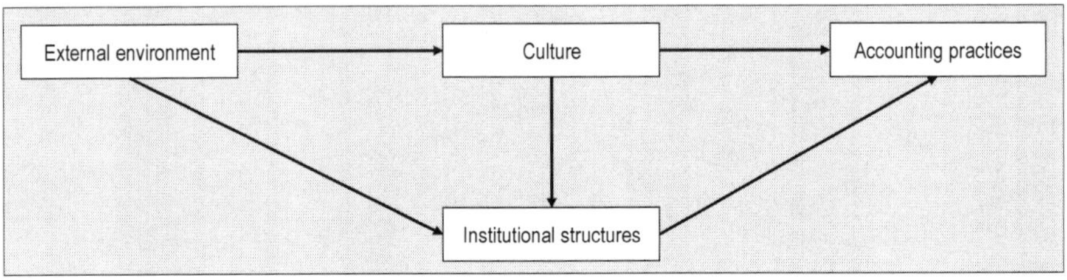

Figure 4-2: Impacts on accounting practices
Adapted from *Nobes* (1998), p. 163, following *Doupnik/Salter* (1995), p. 192.

Following *Doupnik/Salter* (1995), Figure 4-3 includes the culture approach and the societal effects approach (institutional factors) in this study's conceptual framework to explain the external influencing factors of financial reporting practice. In addition the framework includes a number of internal (company-specific) context factors, which are explained on the theoretical basis of **institutionalism**.

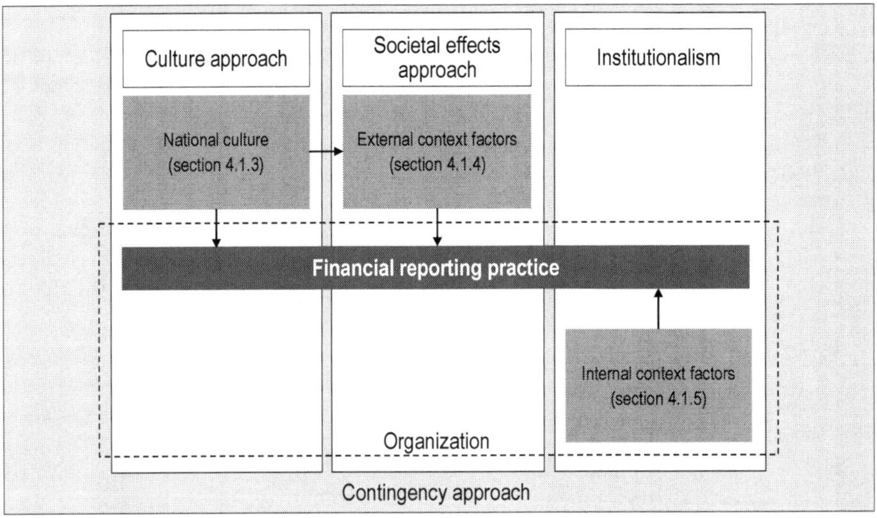

Figure 4-3: Basic conceptual framework
Following *Morgan* (2006), p. 42-49; *Reisloh* (2011), p. 144.

[583] Cf. *Doupnik/Salter* (1995), p. 192; *Nobes* (1998), p. 163-164.

4.1.3 Culture approach

To explain international differences in financial reporting practice, the accounting literature identifies a country's culture as an important factor.[584] However, no universally accepted definition of *culture* has been found and this abstract term is used in different contexts of human interaction.[585] While corporate culture, for instance, encompasses a set of common norms and attitudes determining the employees' behavior in an organization,[586] **national culture** captures the values, attitudes, behavioral patterns or concepts which are shared by the people of a sovereign nation.[587] In fact, groups of human beings do not only share the same culture, but also set their culture themselves.[588] In line with these definitions, the study focuses on national culture (referred to as *culture* in the following).

Although culture is difficult to operationalize, researchers have developed cultural models to measure national culture. On a conceptual basis, *Kluckhohn/Strodtbeck* (1961) propose that every human society finds its individual answers to a certain number of universal problems based on the people's stable values.[589] As such values differ across societies, researchers are able to detect cultural differences:

> "*[...] there is a systematic variation in the realm of cultural phenomena which is both as definite and as essential as the demonstrated systematic variation in physical and biological phenomena.*"[590]

In general, all possible solutions to a certain problem are inherent in every society. However, each society deals with universal problems in a different way.[591] According to *Kluckhohn/Strodtbeck* (1961) researchers shall scrutinize the following five basic problems to determine the **society's individual cultural values**. (1) First, the time orientation of human beings differs with regard to their focus either on the past, present or future. (2) Further, human beings decide about their relation to their natural environment, which can be characterized by mastery, submission or harmony. (3) The relationship between individuals might differ as well. They either interact as equals, the relation is dominated by a strong hierarchy, or the individual merit determines how human beings interact. (4) Moreover, human beings behave differently according to their individual motivation. This motivation can be either internal so that individuals value their own activities, or external suggesting that also others approve individual achievements, or in between these extremes. (5) Finally, the human nature is considered to be good, bad (also *evil*), or a mixture of both.

---

584 Cf. among others *Doupnik/Salter* (1995); *Nobes* (1998); *Ding et al.* (2005), p. 327; *Doupnik* (2008), p. 318; *Nobes* (2012), p. 25; *Borker* (2012), p. 313.

585 Cf. *Child* (1981), p. 304-306.

586 Cf. *Wien/Franzke* (2014), p. 11-13.

587 Cf. *Choi/Meek* (2011), p. 34; *Dahl* (2004), p. 1-2.

588 Cf. *Dahl* (2004), p. 1.

589 Cf. *Hills* (2002), p. 2. Similar value-based culture approaches are developed, amongst others, by *Rokeach* (1979); *Schwartz* (1992). For an overview of theoretical studies on value orientation, cf. *Torres* (1999), p. 41.

590 *Kluckhohn/Strodtbeck* (1961), p. 3.

591 Cf. here and in the following *Kluckhohn/Strodtbeck* (1961); *Hills* (2002), p. 4-5.

Hence, the *preferred solutions* to the aforementioned problems reflect the cultural values of a society. These cultural values have also implications for this study, since they can affect a company's financial reporting practices. For instance, a future-oriented entity might report more prospective information than entities with a focus on the past. Furthermore, externally motivated preparers of corporate reports might provide a higher level of information to get approval by the company's stakeholders, whereas internally motivated decision makers might disclose less information.

In addition to the mere theoretical thoughts by *Kluckhohn/Strodtbeck* (1961), other researchers provide empirical evidence on cultural differences. One of the most comprehensive cultural studies was conducted by *Hofstede* (1980a) on the basis of questionnaires, answered by the employees of a multinational corporation in 40 countries.[592] He defines culture, as

> "*[...] the collective programming of the mind which distinguishes the member of one group or category of people from another.*"[593]

Hofstede substantiates this concept of collective programming by positioning culture between the non-programmable human nature, on the one side, and the personality of individuals, on the other.[594] Hence, this study investigates, as to what extent the different *programming of the minds* of the *groups* of Brazilian, South African and German people leads to differences in financial reporting practices.

Hofstede identifies a total of six **cultural dimensions** to describe national culture:[595]

(1) individualism versus collectivism, the relationship between the individual and the group;

(2) power distance, social inequality including relationships with authority;

(3) masculinity versus femininity, social implications of being born male or female;

(4) uncertainty avoidance, the ability to deal with uncertainty, the control of aggression and the expression of emotion;

(5) long-term orientation versus short-term orientation; and

(6) indulgence versus restraint.

Although these cultural dimensions generally refer to societies as a whole, *Hofstede* (1984) himself detects that culture particularly affects general management and planning aspects. He finds, for example, a country's attitude towards masculinity versus femininity determines which jobs men tend to take in this country and which are commonly taken by

592 Cf. *Hofstede* (1980a); *Hofstede* (1980b), p. 44.

593 *Hofstede* (1980a), p. 25.

594 Cf. *Hofstede et al.* (2010), p. 6; *Dahl* (2004), p. 3.

595 Initially, *Hofstede* identified four cultural dimensions in his study, cf. *Hofstede* (1980b), p. 43. He added the dimensions *long-term vs. short-term orientation* and *indulgence vs. restraint* later, cf. *Hofstede* (2001), p. 351; *Hofstede et al.* (2010), p. 280. The following overview is adapted from *Borker* (2012), p. 315.

women.[596] In a next step, *Gray* (1988) links *Hofstede*'s cultural dimensions to accounting attitude.[597] In particular, he derives four accounting values:[598]

(1) professionalism versus statutory control;

(2) uniformity versus flexibility;

(3) conservatism versus optimism; and

(4) secrecy versus transparency.

The four **accounting values** have already been discussed with respect to the BRICS countries' characteristics in section 2.2.3.3. From a more theoretical perspective, Table 4-1 describes the relation between the cultural dimensions by *Hofstede* and the accounting values according to *Gray*. (1) A tendency to *professional* judgments by individuals and self-regulating systems (e.g., by private bodies) are assumed in a culture of individualism and indulgency, which supports individual decisions.[599] (2) *Uniformity* is negatively influenced by individualism and indulgence so that highly individualistic and indulgent societies have rather *flexible* accounting practices. Uniform accounting practices are common in cultures with a preference for high power distance among social relationships, uncertainty avoidance and long-term orientation. (3) Whether accountants measure corporate assets *conservatively* or *optimistically* depends, inter alia, on their attitude towards long-term thinking and uncertainty avoidance. Traditionally companies from Continental European countries, dominated by long-term orientation and high concern of uncertainty, report cautiously calculated profits.[600] Thus, these companies tend to hold hidden reserves.[601]

	Professionalism	Uniformity	Conservatism	Secrecy
Individualism	+	-	-	-
Uncertainty avoidance	-	+	+	+
Power distance	-	+	+	+
Masculinity	0	0	-	-
Long-term orientation	-	+	+	+
Indulgence vs. restraint	+	-	-	-
Positive relationships are shown by (+), inverse relationships by (-) and indeterminate relationships by (0)				

Table 4-1: Relations between *Hofstede*'s cultural dimensions and *Gray*'s accounting values Following *Borker* (2013), p. 676.

(4) The fourth accounting variable *secrecy versus transparency* is of particular interest to this study's empirical investigation of corporate disclosures, since reporting practices largely depend on the willingness to provide information. Secrecy-oriented companies put emphasis on the confidentiality of information and rather constrain their disclosures, whereas

596 Cf. *Hofstede* (1984), p. 98.
597 Cf. *Gray* (1988), p. 1.
598 Cf. *Gray* (1988), p. 8.
599 Cf. *Gray* (1988), p. 8.
600 Cf. *Gray* (1988), p. 10.
601 Cf. *Nobes* (2012), p. 38-41.

transparent entities follow a publicly accountable approach.[602] Secrecy is associated with a high degree of uncertainty avoidance, power distance and long-term orientation. Hence, only the accounting values (3) *conservatism versus optimism* and (4) *secrecy versus transparency* impact the companies' measurements and disclosures and, thus, accounting practice, as illustrated in Figure 4-4. The accounting values *professionalism versus statutory control* and *uniformity versus flexibility* rather affect the accounting system.

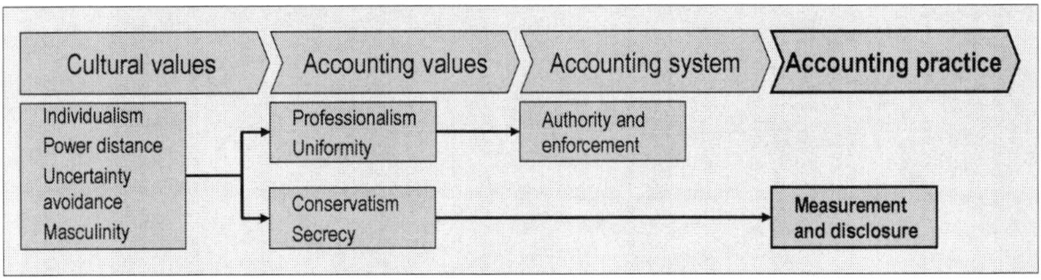

Figure 4-4: Impact of cultural and accounting values on accounting practice
Following *Deegan/Unerman* (2011), p. 139.

In addition to the direct influence of accounting values, *Gray* (1988) argues that societal values influence institutional characteristics and, therefore, also impact accounting practices indirectly.[603] The following section discusses the societal effects approach in more detail.

4.1.4 Societal effects approach

Besides the culture approach, the societal effects approach is the second pillar of this study's contingency theory-based conceptual framework.[604] According to the societal effects approach not only national culture shapes organizational processes. National societal effects including both human and institutional factors, which again may be affected by the national culture, influence organizational processes as well.[605] Differences in organizations across countries also result from the particular environment of a society in which organizations emerge and operate.[606] According to *Sorge* (1991):

> "*Societal differences in organizing and generating human resources, and the pursuit of different business strategies, are reciprocally related. An economy and society becomes populated by specific institutionalized organizational and human resource forms and practices, because economic niches and business strategies are different, and vice versa.*"[607]

Maurice et al. (1980) examine human organization and interactions in similar factories located in France, West Germany and Great Britain by focusing on processes, such as ed-

[602] Cf. *Borker* (2013), p. 678.
[603] Cf. *Gray* (1988), p. 7.
[604] Cf. section 4.1.2.
[605] Cf. *Sorge* (1991), p. 163; *Sorge* (1996), p. 83-84.
[606] Cf. *Maurice et al.* (1980), p. 59.
[607] *Sorge* (1991), p. 163.

ucating, training and recruiting. Criticizing the contingency approach, they "*[...] do not want to add additional, vaguely specified cultural variables as a residual to contingency explanations.*"[608] Instead, the investigation sheds light on differences concerning societal processes performed by different employee groups, e.g. how the bundling of work tasks affects the competences and qualifications of employees in the three countries.[609]

The societal effects approach suggests that there are **stable characteristics in a society**, which influence a company's organization and activities so that it is feasible to observe cross-national institutional differences.[610] *Lane* (1989) argues that although companies pursue the same organizational objectives, the attempts how to achieve these objectives differ depending on the societal institutions in each country.[611] With regard to financial reporting, the preparer of a financial report decides from a personal individual perspective what to report. However, the decision is affected by the entity's institutional environment, including e.g. accounting standards or the legal system. However, the relationship between the reporting entity and its institutional environment is interdependent, because the entity itself might influence relevant accounting standards, too, through lobbying activities or by establishing accounting best practices.[612]

In this study, cross-country differences in financial reporting practices due to societal effects are primarily considered in terms of **institutional characteristics**. Although the empirical investigation aggregates the country influence in solely one country variable, the institutional factors economic policies, accounting regulation and enforcement, accounting education, tax and legal system, financial system as well as capital markets are regarded as influencing factors, which are described for emerging economies throughout section 2.2.3. The institutional environments of the sample countries Brazil, South Africa and Germany are further outlined in the country profiles in section 2.3.

4.1.5 Institutionalism

4.1.5.1 Introduction

The third pillar of the study's conceptual framework is labeled as **institutionalism.**[613] Although it is only one part of the conceptual framework, which affects financial reporting practices, institutional theories are the main theoretical foundation for the subsequent hypotheses development. On the one hand, these theories allow general hypotheses regarding a company's financial reporting practices that are based on economic theory. On the other hand, institutionalism serves as a theoretical basis to explain the influence of company-specific context factors on corporate financial reporting.

---

608 *Maurice et al.* (1980), p. 61.
609 Cf. *Maurice et al.* (1980), p. 80-83.
610 Cf. *Lane* (1989), p. 31; *Bhimani* (2005), p. 254.
611 Cf. *Lane* (1989), p. 37-38; *Reisloh* (2011), p. 103.
612 Cf. *Reisloh* (2011), p. 102.
613 Cf. section 4.1.2.

Institutionalism is concerned with the role of institutions and explains, why and how institutions matter in numerous areas, such as economic as well as social life.[614] First institutional thoughts reach back to Aristotle and his analysis of different regime types (politeia). In the 19th century institutional economists responded to the universal claims of the classical economists that it is essential to consider the historical, social and institutional context to explain economic as well as social behavior. Further, empirical investigations, rather than mere philosophical ideas, would contribute to understanding.

The modern form of **new institutionalism** developed in the 1980s is used across a number of scientific disciplines. Institutions are assumed to play an important role to explain human interactions and are regarded as

> *"[...] shared rules and typifications that identify categories of social actors and their appropriate activities or relationships."*[615]

In line with this definition, researchers emphasize that such institutional rules are not only durable, as they are passed largely unmodified from one generation to another, but also binding, as individuals obey these social rules.[616] *W. Richard Scott* generally uses the term *institution* to capture all kinds of rules-based and relatively durable actions so that, for instance, society, state, laws, values, organizations and roles could be subordinated to institutions.[617]

In line with this study's research objectives, one reason for the emergence of new institutionalism was the upcoming interest to compare institutions across countries. Depending on the discipline, different forms of institutional theories have been developed. This study picks up theoretical approaches from both economics as well as sociology. While **new institutional economics** is derived from economics and, thus, takes the economic perspective, **new institutional sociology** presents the sociological counterpart. Figure 4-5 gives an overview of the institutionalism-based theoretical foundation derived from both institutional economics and institutional sociology.

---

[614] Cf. here and in the following *Encyclopædia Britannica Online* (2015).

[615] *Barley/Tolbert* (1997), p. 96.

[616] Cf. *Zucker* (1977), p. 741-742; *Senge* (2006), p. 35.

[617] *Scott* (2014) distinguishes institutions according to their function and argues that institutions' mechanisms of action can be of regulative, normative and cultural-cognitive nature. Similar to the rules in team sports, the *regulative* element in institutions refers to the establishment of rules, the monitoring of conformal behavior and sanctions in terms of rewards or punishments, cf. here and in the following *Scott* (2014), p. 60-70; *Senge* (2006), p. 39. *Normative* institutions manage to make societal players act in a certain way due to norms and values. The *cultural-cognitive* dimension refers to the social reality detecting institutions, such as belief systems, meaning systems, cultural frames and common scripts. Just as the term *scripts* suggests, societal actors' behaviors based on cognitive institutions are routine and programmed actions. Being taken for granted, these actions would never be questioned and are an integral part of a society's self-conception.

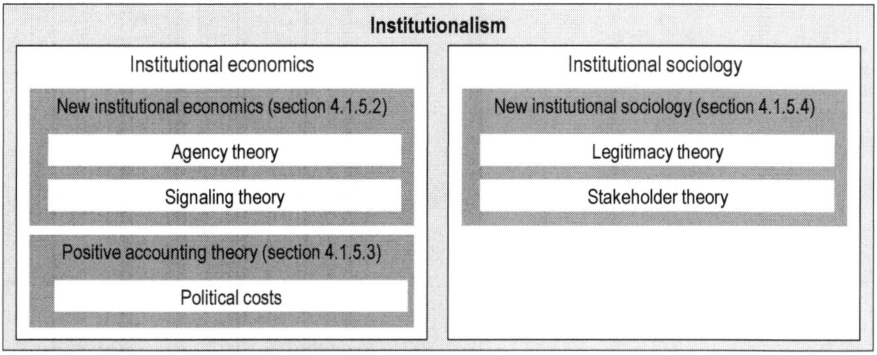

Figure 4-5: Institutionalism as theoretical foundation

New institutional economic thoughts are particularly reflected in the so-called **agency theory**, which is based on the relationship between a better informed party (the agent) and a less informed party (the principal). In the same setting as agency theory, **signaling theory** hypothesizes whether the better informed party conveys information to the other party (section 4.1.5.2.2). Based on the considerations of positive accounting theory, **political costs** arise when politics strongly interfere with organizations (section 4.1.5.3). Due to limitations of institutional economics, the additional sociological approaches deal with societal and ethical aspects. **Legitimacy theory** focuses on the societal acceptance of a company (section 4.1.5.4.2), whereas **stakeholder theory** is concerned with the interests of an entity's stakeholders (section 4.1.5.4.3). The following sections deal with the different approaches in more detail.

4.1.5.2 New institutional economics

4.1.5.2.1 Basic assumptions of new institutional economics

The emergence of new institutional economics[618] benefited from the incapability of the neoclassical theory to explain the development of complex institutions, e.g. concerning companies.[619] In particular, some **neoclassical assumptions** lost acceptance among researchers, foremost the idea that individuals with unlimited information act rationally in a perfect market at all times.[620] As a modification of neoclassical economic theory, new institutional economics is a family of theories including different streams,[621] all of which are based on the four basic assumptions of the neoclassical theory as well as additional new

---

618 The term *new institutional economics* goes back to *Williamson*, cf. *Williamson* (1975), p. 1.

619 Cf. *Wolf* (2013), p. 334-335.

620 *Erlei et al.* (2007), p. 46-47.

621 Major theoretical streams of new institutional economics are property-right theory, transaction costs theory and agency theory (cf. section 4.1.5.2.2), cf. *Picot* (1991), p. 153; *Erlei et al.* (2007), p. 69, 103 and 223; *Wolf* (2013), p. 338-371. For a comparative analysis of all three theories by the case of oil field unitization, cf. *Kim/Mahoney* (2005).

assumptions.[622] In line with the model of a *homo oeconomicus* who acts rational at all times,[623] the approach rests on the following four neoclassical assumptions:[624]

(1) scarcity of resources;

(2) methodological individualism;

(3) individual utility maximization; and

(4) stability of utility functions.

In a setting of scarce resources, each homo oeconomicus makes individual decisions aiming at the maximization of its individual utility, which is represented by stable utility functions. In addition to this neoclassical foundation, the **new assumptions** of new institutional economics are:[625]

(5) unequal distribution of information, knowledge, and capabilities;

(6) prevalent information structure;

(7) friction losses in economic processes;

(8) numerous interdependencies;

(9) rules regulating the possession and exchange of goods; and

(10) prevalence of institutions.

The fact that the information and expertise of each individual differs leads to an economy based on labor division. All actors intend to specialize and exchange goods on the basis of reliable rules, whereby interdependencies arise. In line with the design of this study, researchers shall further consider the specific prevailing information context, as **information asymmetries** impede the efficient coordination of resources. Moreover, new institutional economics incorporates the existence of institutions when explaining economic activities.

On the basis of these assumptions, new institutional economic theory pursues the objective to explain both the emergence and the characteristics of **institutions** and, in particular, organizations.[626] Furthermore, this theory investigates the economic results of institutional arrangements. The approach regards institutions as surrogates for markets which are, unlike neoclassical theory suggests, not perfect. Advocates of new institutional economics analyze the economic efficiency of institutions on the basis of the aforementioned economic considerations as well as cost-benefit-calculations.

The following section presents the basics of agency and signaling theory, which are built on the described assumptions of new institutional economics.

---

[622] Cf. *Wolf* (2013), p. 333-338.

[623] Cf. *Göbel* (2002), p. 49. For a detailed description of the homo oeconomicus model, cf. *Erlei et al.* (2007), p. 2-6.

[624] Cf. *Wolf* (2013), p. 337.

[625] Cf. *Wolf* (2013), p. 337-338.

[626] Cf. here and in the following *Wolf* (2013), p. 335-336.

4.1.5.2.2 Agency and signaling theory

Being part of new institutional economics, agency theory is concerned with relationships between distinctive situations and systems.[627] In the broadest sense, agency relationships always occur when one individual, referred to as **principal**, is dependent on the behavior of another individual, called **agent.**[628] In particular, agency theory puts emphasis on contractual relations, e.g. between an entity's managers, on the one hand, and its investors, on the other.[629] In this setting, a manager represents an agent, whose duties are determined by the owner of the entity (the principal). Another typical principal-agent relationship exists between a buyer and a seller, since the buyer depends on the seller to give him an appropriate consideration for the purchase price.[630] *Jensen/Meckling* define a principal-agent relationship as

> "*[...] a contract under which one or more persons (the principal(s)) engage another person (the agent) to perform some service on their behalf which involves delegating some decision making authority to the agent.*"[631]

Figure 4-6 illustrates that **information** is distributed **asymmetrically** among the two parties, because the agent has an information advantage over the principal. Based on the assumptions of new institutional economics,[632] principal and agent are both acting as a *homo oeconomicus* and pursue individual self interests.[633] With regard to actual businesses, it depends on the behavior of the manager, as to what extent the investor's business objectives are achieved.

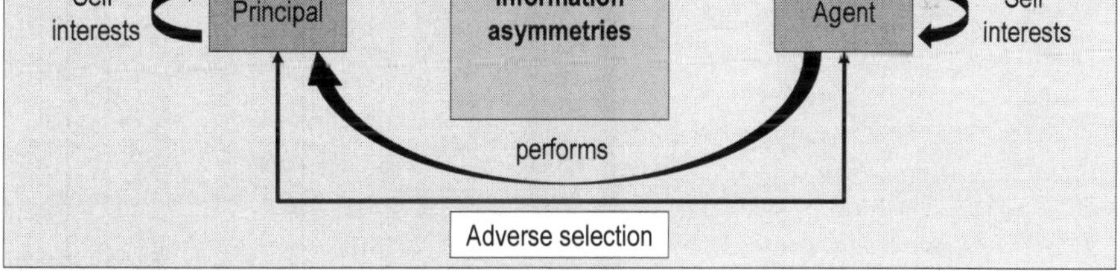

Figure 4-6: Basic principal-agent relationship
Own illustration based on *Nurmi* (2006), p. 93-94.

[627] Cf. *Williamson* (2000), p. 595.
[628] Cf. *Pratt/Zeckhauser* (1985), p. 2.
[629] Cf. here and in the following *Ewert/Wagenhofer* (2014), p. 357-359.
[630] Cf. *Göbel* (2002), p. 99.
[631] *Jensen/Meckling* (1976), p. 308.
[632] Cf. section 4.1.5.2.1.
[633] Cf. *Göbel* (2002), p. 100.

As long as both contractual partners pursue the same individual objectives, the agent's behavior is in line with the principal's interests.[634] Otherwise, the agent has incentives to act opportunistically. If there was a state of perfect information, however, opportunistic behavior by the agents would not be expected, since the principal would notice unfavorable actions by the agent immediately and respond accordingly.

Moreover, agency theory characterizes the principal-agent relationship as follows:[635] The agent is able to affect both the principal's and the agent's achievements. The principal tries to evaluate the outcome of the agent's behavior, yet, is not able to determine whether the agent's efforts or exogenous factors are responsible for that very outcome. The interests of the two parties differ, as managers, for instance, might aim at building a personal *empire*, whereas investors pursue the increase of the company value.

The assumed information asymmetries between principal and agent leads to multiple **information problems**, which are summarized in Table 4-2. Before the parties sign the contract, the principal is neither able to assess the agent's characteristics nor to evaluate the quality of the services offered by the agent (hidden characteristics).[636] In accordance with *Akerlof* (1970), this information problem may trigger the collapse of entire markets, e.g. the market for contracts between managers and investors, as principals refrain from entering into uncertain contracts or are solely willing to pay the lowest prices.[637] This phenomenon is called **adverse selection**. After the conclusion of the contract, the principal has difficulty in observing the agent's behavior (hidden action) or can hardly evaluate the observed actions (hidden information).[638] Thus, the agent has incentives not to act in line with the principal's interests resulting in **moral hazard**. For instance, moral hazard occurs when managers shirk their responsibilities, knowing that their actual actions are hidden. Benefiting from hidden information, managers could further make self-serving decisions, e.g. to gain fringe benefits, which the principal does not know of. The adverse selection and moral hazard problems are also displayed in above Figure 4-6.

Time of origin	Type of problem	Problem	Potential solutions	
			Principal	Agent
Before contract conclusion	Hidden characteristics	Adverse selection	Screening	Signaling
After contract conclusion	Hidden action	Moral hazard (e.g., shirking)	Monitoring	Reporting
	Hidden information	Moral hazard (e.g., self-serving decisions)		

Table 4-2: Problems and potential solutions in principal-agent relationships
Following *Göbel* (2002), p. 100 and 110; *Barth* (2009), p. 92.

[634] Cf. here and in the following *Meinhövel* (2005), p. 67-68.
[635] Cf. here and in the following *Subramaniam* (2006), p. 59; *Meinhövel* (2005), p. 68.
[636] Cf. *Göbel* (2002), p. 101.
[637] Cf. *Akerlof* (1970), p. 488-500.
[638] Cf. here and in the following *Göbel* (2002), p. 101-103.

To overcome the described agency problems, the literature comes up with several **potential solutions**, such as the harmonization of the parties' interests or the mitigation of the self-interested behavior of the homo oeconomicus through trust-building.[639] In addition, Table 4-2 provides approaches to reduce information asymmetries between principal and agent, which are of particular relevance to this study. Before entering into a contract, on the one hand, the principal may put efforts into **screening** activities to find and hire the *best* agent. Potential agents, on the other hand, have the opportunity to provide information about themselves through **signaling** and, thus, lower information asymmetries before contract conclusion. This approach to lower information asymmetry through signaling information to others is also referred to as signaling theory.[640] However, also after both parties have entered into a contract, there are measures to reduce information asymmetries. While the principal may **monitor** the agent's actions, the agent might lower the principal's concerns through **reporting** those activities which the agent has conducted. The fact that Table 4-2 explicitly names reporting as potential solution for moral hazard problems indicates the importance of agency theory for this study's research focus. The following section discusses, how and as to what extent financial reporting is able to mitigate problems in principal-agent relationships.

4.1.5.2.3 Financial reporting as solution for agency problems

The previous section suggested four potential solutions for agency problems: (1) screening and (2) monitoring by the principal, as well as (3) signaling and (4) reporting by the agent. All of these actions are approaches to overcome the agency problems by the reduction of information asymmetries. However, taking these actions is associated with additional costs. These **agency costs** generally occur whenever one individual delegates decision-making authorities to another individual.[641] Figure 4-7 shows the main model of the agency cost theory[642] including the exemplary relation between a manager as agent and shareholder as principal. The illustration suggests that not only the principal's activities to control the agent cause costs, but also the agent bears costs to guarantee the principal to act in the principal's interest. Hence, agency costs comprise screening costs to thoroughly select an agent before the contract conclusion, monitoring costs arising from the principal's effort to monitor the agent's actions as well as bonding costs as the agent has to give an account for the performed actions.[643] In spite of all security mechanisms, however, the principal cannot expect the agent to act in exactly the principal's interest at all times. The difference between the optimal performance for the principal and the actual performance is called *residual loss*.

---

639 Cf. *Göbel* (2002), p. 110.

640 Cf. *Morris* (1987), p. 48.

641 Cf. *Wolf* (2013), p. 364.

642 The basic constellation of the agency cost theory is similar to that of transaction cost theory, although the type of interaction differs. While the latter analyzes the horizontal relation between two trading partners, agency cost theory posits a vertical relationship between principal and agent, cf. *Wolf* (2013), p. 368.

643 Cf. here and in the following *Wolf* (2013), p. 370.

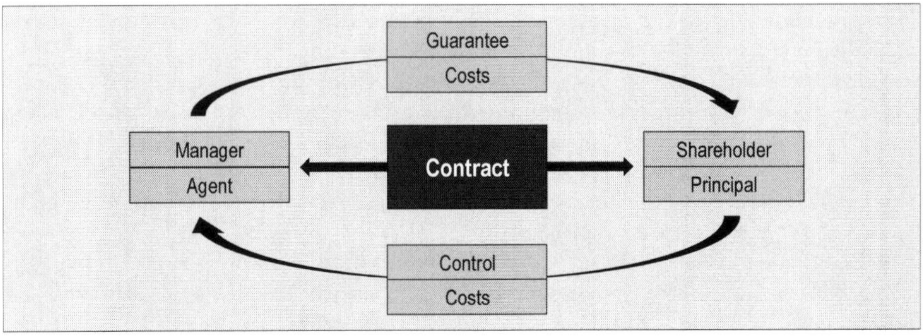

Figure 4-7: Main model of agency cost theory
Following *Wolf* (2013), p. 365.

This study investigates the role of (high-quality) financial reporting regarding the relation between company managers who prepare corporate reports as agents (also referred to as *companies* or *entities*), on the one hand, and existing or potential owners of the company (also referred to as *investors* or *shareholders*) as well as other stakeholders representing the principals, on the other hand. The investment into the company, i.e. the purchase of company shares, is regarded as contract conclusion. Hence, the suggested solutions to overcome, or at least mitigate, agency problems before contract conclusion refer to potential investors, while solutions after contract conclusion focus on existing investors. Hence, the first potential solution incorporates all **screening** efforts by potential investors to collect information about the target company.[644] Existing shareholders could aim at **monitoring** their agents' activities.[645] This may, for example, include the implementation of internal control or reporting systems. Moreover, the company owners are able to engage internal auditors or the supervisory board to control their agents.

Financial reporting represents a measure which the company (the agent) can conduct to reduce information asymmetries. The company has an interest to persuade potential investors to invest into the company by providing corporate reports which credibly signal the quality of the investors' potential investment (**signaling**). The higher the quality of the reports, the more convincing is the signal. In accordance with *Akerlof* (1970), for example, investors may be willing to pay a higher purchase price on the basis of high-quality information provided through financial reporting than without this information. However, such signals are only credible, if it is too costly for the agent to send out false signals. For example, if the agent reports a company value which is higher than the actual company value, the agent's consequences (e.g., the termination of the responsible manager's contract) have to cause higher costs for the agent than ensuring a credible report.[646]

However, the company has not only an incentive to attract potential investors, but also to satisfy the information needs of existing shareholders through **reporting**. After contract conclusion, the agent provides transparent corporate reports to inform the existing inves-

[644] Cf. *Göbel* (2002), p. 110.
[645] Cf. here and in the following *Göbel* (2002), p. 112.
[646] Cf. *Göbel* (2002), p. 111.

tors of a company and, thus, lower information asymmetries between principals and agents. The agents might be intrinsically motivated to demonstrate that, for instance, pleasing results have not been the result of exogenous effects, but of the agent's own work.[647]

A similar, however, more focused theory based on agency thought is the so-called **capital need theory**. It emphasizes the objective of entities to attract providers of capital.[648] Hence, companies publish information voluntarily to lower the premium on capital costs, which capital providers demand for uncertainty. The capital needs theory suggests that companies which aim at raising additional capital (e.g., strongly growing corporations) have an above-average level of disclosures.[649] Nonetheless, the main idea of this approach is also covered by signaling theory which argues that companies engage in reporting activities to reduce information asymmetries between the company and its investors and, thus, reduce their costs of capital.

4.1.5.3 Positive accounting theory and political costs

In accounting research, a crucial distinction can be made between normative and positive research. While normative research describes how the world should ideally be, positive accounting research with its positive accounting theory aims at both explaining and predicting accounting phenomena.[650] In the 1970s, U.S. accounting researchers came up with positive accounting theory,[651] which was particularly developed and promoted by *Watts/Zimmerman*.[652] Although **normative accounting research** pursues important objectives, e.g. to suggest improved accounting standards to regulatory bodies or standard setters, it has experienced a considerable decline in the literature during the past decades. One of the reasons for this development is that the methodology of normative studies does not fully capture what actually determines current accounting practices.[653] Thus, it is easier for **positive accounting research** to derive recommendations of practical relevance than for normative accounting research. Advocates of positive accounting research criticize that normative studies do not verify whether predicted phenomena can actually be observed in accounting practice and, therefore, abandon an important source of knowledge.[654] Positive accounting theory, in contrast, helps to better understand observable behavior and enables decision makers to both predict and explain the consequences of their decisions. This study examines, inter alia, what affects managers' decisions, for instance, to disclose certain information. As the study analyzes actual financial reporting practices by the sample companies, it is classified into the category of positive accounting research.

647 Cf. *Göbel* (2002), p. 113.
648 Cf. here and in the following *Abd-Elsalam/Weetman* (2003), p. 66.
649 Cf. *AbuGhazaleh et al.* (2012), p. 213.
650 Cf. *Watts* (1995), p. 297.
651 Cf. *Haller* (1988), p. 398.
652 Cf. among others *Watts/Zimmerman* (1986); *Watts/Zimmerman* (1990).
653 Cf. here and in the following *Watts* (1995), p. 301.
654 Cf. *Ball/Brown* (1968), p. 159.

Beyond the empirical focus on accounting reality, positive accounting theory provides a conceptual and microeconomic theoretical basis for empirical investigations.[655] For this purpose, positive accounting theory relies on **cost-benefit analyses** comparing the benefit of reported financial information to the corresponding costs.[656] Hence, an accounting practice is solely regarded as favorable, if its benefits exceed its direct and indirect costs.[657] The corresponding benefits of accounting information are more complex to measure, as different user groups interpret a certain piece of reported information differently and, thus, every user group attaches more or less value to it than another user group.[658] An approach to quantify the benefits of reporting is to compute the decrease in a firm's cost of capital resulting from reduced information asymmetries due to disclosure.[659]

The above paragraph reveals that positive accounting theory generally picks up the idea of existing information asymmetries and takes particularly cost-benefit considerations into account. In more detail, the positive accounting theory distinguishes between contract-oriented and process-oriented approaches. The **contract-oriented approach**, on the one hand, aims at investigating what influences the accounting and financial reporting decisions of managers.[660] It is based on both the idea that a company consists of a conglomerate of contracts (contracting theory) and on agency theoretical thought. One of the main hypotheses argues that the managers' earnings management depends on both their remuneration arrangements (bonus plan hypothesis) and the company's debt-to-equity ratio (debt/equity hypothesis). Empirical research confirms that managers report higher company earnings, the higher the earnings-based bonus and company's leverage.[661]

The **process-oriented approach**, on the other hand, analyzes the political processes behind the development of (accounting) regulation (political process approach).[662] In particular, researchers investigate which forces and drivers influence the setting of new (financial reporting) standards. They assume that managers engage in lobbying to reach more favorable rules for their company. In that way, they try to avoid **political costs** arising from, e.g. taxation, environmental constraints or the denial of grants. Hence, political costs generally occur when regulating and (governmental) supervisory bodies influence the companies' activities.[663] *Watts/Zimmerman* (1990) argue that particularly large companies fight political costs:

> "*The political cost hypothesis predicts that large firms rather than small firms are more likely to use accounting choices that reduce reported profits. Size is a proxy variable for political attention. Underlying this hypothesis is the assumption that it is costly for individuals to become informed about whether accounting profits really*

655 Cf. *Haller* (1994), p. 598.
656 Cf. *Verrecchia* (1983), p. 181 and *Leftwich et al.* (1981), p. 51.
657 Cf. *Haller* (1994), p. 598.
658 Cf. *Baetge et al.* (2014), p. 130.
659 Cf. *Leuz/Verrecchia* (2000), p. 92.
660 Cf. here and in the following *Haller* (1994), p. 599-600.
661 Cf. *Haller* (1988), p. 399.
662 Cf. here and in the following *Haller* (1994), p. 600-601.
663 Cf. *Han/Wang* (1998), p. 104.

represent monopoly profits and to 'contract' with others in the political process to enact laws and regulations that enhance their welfare."[664]

This *size hypothesis* is based on the assumption that political costs increase with company size, as, for example, larger companies have to pay higher taxes, are exposed to higher demands by trade unions and are of particular public interest.[665] Besides size, particularly a company's industry is assumed to influence its political costs.[666] This suggests that larger corporations and "*politically sensitive companies*"[667] (e.g., regulation requires the chemical industry to meet certain environmental requirements) provide an increased level of disclosures to avoid political costs.

Although the positive accounting theory is of fundamental interest to this study, it is not without controversy. **Critics** argue that theory shall not only describe the current state (e.g., of reporting practice), but also suggest solutions for existing problems. The latter, yet, would not be achieved by the positive accounting theory.[668] Moreover, *Watts/Zimmermann* posit that the theory would be free of value judgment, as it solely describes and explains accounting activities.[669] However, all generated hypotheses are based on the unverifiable assumption that individuals act according to cost-benefit considerations.[670] A main point of criticism is also the fact that the theory solely examines the contractual relationship between managers and capital providers to investigate factors influencing accounting policy, whereas it disregards other contractual relationships between the entity and, for example, its suppliers or customers.[671] To analyze such influencing factors, the positive accounting theory defines proxy variables such as the existence of a bonus plan (bonus plan hypothesis) or the debt-to-equity ratio (debt/equity hypothesis). Critics question, whether these proxies are indeed appropriate and whether additional differentiations, (e.g., between different types of bonus plans) might be necessary. Overall, however, the positive accounting theory contributes to the theoretical foundation of accounting research, as it is a new and vigorous attempt to capture as well as explain financial reporting practices.[672]

---

664 *Watts/Zimmerman* (1990), p. 139.
665 Cf. *Haller* (1994), p. 601.
666 Cf. *Watts/Zimmerman* (1990), p. 140.
667 *Deegan/Unerman* (2011), p. 300. The literature frequently mentions oil corporations as example for sensitive companies, cf. *Watts/Zimmerman* (1978), p. 115-116; *Verrecchia* (1983), p. 182; *Milne* (2002), p. 374.
668 Cf. *Sterling* (1990), p. 129; *Chambers* (1993), p. 24.
669 Cf. *Watts/Zimmerman* (1990), p. 146.
670 Cf. *Chambers* (1993), p. 9-11.
671 Cf. here and in the following *Haller* (1994), p. 605.
672 Cf. *Demski* (1988), p. 628.

4.1.5.4 New institutional sociology

4.1.5.4.1 Basic assumptions of new institutional sociology

The theory of new institutional economics aims at explaining the allocation of resources on the basis of traditional economics' assumptions, however, lacks to consider societal and ethical behavior based on moral concepts.[673] Due to these restrictions of economic theories, this study uses also sociological approaches as theoretical basis. Following a long tradition of institutions in sociological theory to explain human behavior, U.S.-American organizational researchers refined societal institutionalism over the past few decades.[674] They ignore traditional institutional ideas of individuals embedded in habits and culture as well as classical bureaucratic organizations, as proposed by *Max Weber*, and rather stress the importance of **individual interests of humans** as drivers of social processes and, thus, reality. These recent approaches are used in different modern social sciences, such as political sciences and economics, and will be labelled as *new societal institutionalism* or *new institutional sociology* in the following.

Although new institutional economics and new institutional sociology share the same basis of institutionalism, the latter denies the premises of an individualism-oriented homo oeconomicus and emphasizes the relation between the described rationality-based behavior of individuals, on the one hand, and societal legitimacy, on the other.[675] In contrast, new institutional economics focuses on the relation between institutions and transaction costs.[676] Hence, the sociological counterparts to methodological individualism and homo oeconomicus in the new institutional economics are **methodological collectivism** and **homo sociologicus**.[677] However, sociologists question whether new institutional economics is indeed *institutionalist*, since a rationally-acting homo oeconomicus could not be influenced by social institutions.[678] From the sociological perspective, institutions are primarily regarded as given, exogenous beliefs in society, which companies may conform to.[679] How and why entities act according to these societal beliefs is the research objective of new institutional sociology. The theoretical construct according to which organizations in the same societal environment develop similar configurations is called **institutional isomorphism**.[680] *DiMaggio/Powell* (1983) define isomorphism as

> "*[...] a constraining process that forces one unit in a population to resemble other units that face the same set of environmental conditions. At the population level, such an approach suggests that organizational characteristics are modified in the direction of increasing comparability with environmental characteristics [...].*"[681]

---

673 Cf. *Schmid/Maurer* (2003), p. 18 and 22.
674 Cf. here and in the following *Hasse/Krücken* (2005), p. 5-7.
675 Cf. *Schmid/Maurer* (2003), p. 23; *Hasse/Krücken* (2005), p. 13.
676 Cf. *van der Steen* (2006), p. 7. For new institutional economics, cf. section 4.1.5.2.
677 Cf. *Meran* (1979), p. 35-46; *Dahrendorf* (2010), p. 19.
678 Cf. *Dugger* (1990), p. 424.
679 Cf. here and in the following *van der Steen* (2006), p. 7.
680 Cf. *DiMaggio/Powell* (1983), p. 147.
681 *DiMaggio/Powell* (1983), p. 149.

Entities from distinctive environments, therefore, tend to develop a particular optimum of organizational practices.[682] The early literature saw the environment as static and homogenous. However, this understanding changed over time, as organizations are in competition not only for resources, but also for institutional legitimacy in different demanding and changing environments. New institutional sociology primarily attempts to explain similarities among organizations rather than changes in organizations. *DiMaggio/Powell* (1983) identify three isomorphic change mechanisms, which lead to a growing assimilation of organizations: coercive, mimetic and normative isomorphism.[683] While coercive isomorphism occurs due to political impact and the objective to gain legitimacy, mimetic isomorphism is regarded as the organization's standard response to uncertainty; moreover, normative isomorphism results from the pressures of professionalization.

Hence, the main difference between new institutional economics and new institutional sociology is that the activities of organizations (e.g., companies) do not only depend on the rational behavior of individuals, but also on institutional and macro-structural influences, particularly the **norms and values of the society**.[684] On the basis of transaction cost economic thought, the new institutional economics focuses on the analysis of transaction costs which can be optimized through changes of an organization's governance structures.[685] The sociological approach, in contrast, emphasizes the external institutional pressure which drives individuals and organizations to increase their own legitimacy. Hence, it is able to explain the introduction of new practices in companies, such as the Balanced Scorecard or Activity Based Costing, as these are generally accepted and, thus, legitimate. However, the sociological approach is not able to shed light on how such new practices are implemented. Table 4-3 compares some of the key features of new institutional sociology with those of new institutional economics.

	New institutional economics	New institutional sociology
Unit of analysis	Transaction	Organization
Assumptions on individual	Bounded rational	Institutional determinism
Changes addressed	Governance structure	Institutionalized formal practices
Institutional focus	Efficiency	External legitimacy

Table 4-3: Comparison of new institutional economics and new institutional sociology
Following *van der Steen* (2006), p. 30.

For the investigation of corporate financial reporting quality, sociological thought is an important theoretical basis to explain particularly voluntary disclosure practices of companies due to societal norms and moral concepts. Thereby, companies manage to satisfy the information needs of stakeholder groups. For instance, the general public might demand information, as to what extent a chemical company complies with the societal expectations of environmental protection. These aspects are in the center of the **legitimacy**

[682] Cf. here and in the following *Hannan/Freeman* (1977), p. 930; *van der Steen* (2006), p. 15-17.
[683] For a detailed description of the three mechanisms, cf. *DiMaggio/Powell* (1983), p. 150-156.
[684] Cf. *Blaesing* (2013), p. 97.
[685] Cf. here and in the following *van der Steen* (2006), p. 30.

theory and **stakeholder theory**, which are presented in the following sections. Both theories belong to the so-called "*systems-oriented theories*"[686], as they assume that individuals act according to collective societal expectations and that companies, in particular, are influenced by their specific societal environment, but are also able to affect this environment.[687] Referring to institutional isomorphism, this study investigates, as to what extent companies from the same institutional environment show similar financial reporting practices, and qualities, respectively.

4.1.5.4.2 Legitimacy theory

According to the legitimacy theory a company has to ensure a certain level of legitimacy to guarantee its future existence, as the brief description by *O'Donovan* (2002) reveals:

> "*Legitimacy theory is based on the idea that in order to continue operating successfully, corporations must act within the bounds of what society identifies as socially acceptable behavior.*"[688]

Hence, companies always strive for societal legitimacy. In more detail, the abstract term *legitimacy* refers to the aggregated evaluation of past actions against shared and common values and, thus, does not depend on specific events.[689] Moreover, legitimacy is a social construction as perceived or assumed by society, which is created subjectively, however, can be possessed objectively:

> "***Legitimacy*** *is a generalized perception or assumption that the actions of an entity are desirable, proper, or appropriate within some socially constructed system of norms, values, beliefs, and definitions.*"[690]

Legitimacy theoretical thoughts are based on the existence of an uncodified **social contract**[691] requiring companies to act conform to laws, rights as well as **societal expectations**, which are either explicitly determined by laws or are implicit.[692] Regarding corporate reporting practices, societal expectations have changed considerably over the past decades.[693] It is not sufficient anymore to meet traditional expectations of only selected interest groups, such as investors (for example, by reporting the company's profit as "*all-inclusive criterion*"[694]), but also expectations of the society have to be addressed.[695] For instance, companies have incentives to comply with environmental and other sustainability

---

686 Cf. *Smith et al.* (2011), p. 430-431.

687 Cf. *Blaesing* (2013), p. 109-110.

688 *O'Donovan* (2002), p. 344.

689 Cf. here and in the following *Suchman* (1995), p. 574.

690 *Suchman* (1995), p. 574 (emphasis as in original).

691 Early ideas of a social contract go back to *Plato*'s *The Republic* explaining the nature of justice among the persons of a society, cf. *Weale* (2013), p. 3. The so-called *social contract theory*, however, was developed as part of modern moral and political theory, foremost by the later philosophers *Thomas Hobbes*, *John Locke* and *Jean-Jacques Rousseau*, cf. *Friend* (2015).

692 Cf. *Shocker/Sethi* (1973), p. 97; *Deegan et al.* (2000), p. 104-105; *O'Donovan* (2002), p. 344.

693 Cf. *Patten* (1992), p. 471; *Newson/Deegan* (2002), p. 184-194.

694 *Ramanathan* (1976), p. 516.

695 Cf. *Ramanathan* (1976), p. 516-517.

requirements, as society has effective sanctioning mechanisms (e.g., the boycott of products).[696] As a response to changes in societal expectations due to modifications of social values, managers may adjust their organizational structures to deal with the increased societal pressure for legitimation.[697]

Congruence between the activities of entities, on the one hand, and the expectations of society, on the other, leads to legitimacy among the society.[698] However, the more the company's actions and the society's expectations fall apart, the larger is the so-called **legitimacy gap**. To be regarded as legitimate, companies meet the society's expectations and, thus, reduce the legitimacy gap. In fact, for companies it is not crucial what actions they actually take, but rather what the society's perception of the entity's actions is.[699] Thus, companies can attempt to manage the perceptions of the society to manage their legitimacy.[700] As the society, however, has hardly any knowledge about the companies' actions, entities may engage in corporate reporting to inform society and demonstrate legitimate behavior.

According to *Dowling/Pfeffer* (1975) companies must put the **organizational focus** on the overlapping area of the three organizational dimensions (1) economic viability (earn at least cost of capital), (2) political-legal dimension (comply with laws) and (3) the socio-cultural expectations (act in line with social values) to obtain the "*license to operate*"[701], as shown in Figure 4-8.[702]

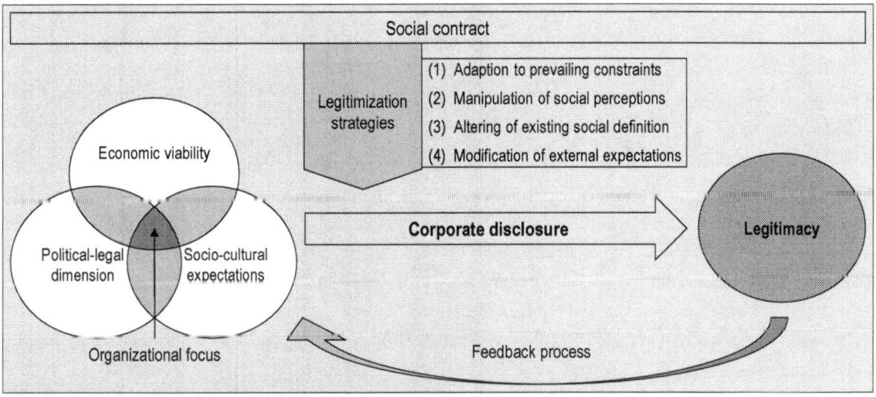

Figure 4-8: Relation between legitimacy theory and corporate disclosure
Following *Khor* (2003), p. 7-9, on the basis of *Dowling/Pfeffer* (1975); *Lindblom* (1994).

[696] Cf. *Newson/Deegan* (2002). For a detailed overview of sustainability reporting, cf. *Blaesing* (2013).
[697] Cf. *Dowling/Pfeffer* (1975), p. 124; *O'Donovan* (2002), p. 346.
[698] Cf. here and in the following *O'Donovan* (2002), p. 346-347.
[699] Cf. *Suchman* (1995), p. 574; *O'Donovan* (2002), p. 347.
[700] Cf. *Khor* (2003).
[701] *Deegan* (2000), p. 259.
[702] Cf. *Dowling/Pfeffer* (1975), p. 124; *Khor* (2003), p. 10.

This congruence area should be the focus of the company's reporting. Depending on its economic and social situation, the company tries to **extend**, **maintain** or **defend** legitimacy.[703] *Ashforth/Gibbs* (1990) argue that it is less problematic for an entity to maintain a certain degree of attained legitimacy than for entities entering a new field or are becoming established to extend legitimacy.[704] They further posit that also defending legitimacy comes along with severe problems when the attained legitimacy is threatened. *O'Donovan* (2002) breaks down these purposes to actions, which the company performs either **reactively**, particularly to repair its legitimacy during a crisis, or **proactively** to gain legitimacy ex ante.[705]

Based on the existence of a social contract, entities may pursue different **legitimization strategies** which are also shown in Figure 4-8. (1) First, companies have the opportunity to accept the societal definitions of legitimacy and, thus, change their own actions to conform to them (adaption to prevailing constraints).[706] (2) A different approach is to communicate in a way which suggests that the company identifies with legitimate values and institutions (manipulation of social perceptions). (3) A more difficult strategy is to actually change prevailing norms and values so that the entity's present practices are in line with the altered definition of social legitimacy. (4) The fourth legitimization strategy suggests entities to modify external expectations.[707]

Seeking legitimacy, companies are able to implement the described strategies separately, or in combination, through public **corporate disclosure** in different media (e.g., annual reports).[708] The feedback managers receive about their companies' legitimacy allows them to evaluate and possibly readjust their entities' organizational focus and reporting activities. On the whole, Figure 4-8 presents the link between legitimacy theory and corporate disclosure.

An **example** for a reactive attempt to repair legitimacy is the Australian mining and petroleum corporation *BHP*, which increased positive disclosures in the annual reports between 1983 and 1997 as a response to unfavorable events and societal perceptions. Also after the *Exxon Valdez* oil spill catastrophe in 1989 the company reacted with a higher level of environmental disclosures.[709] However, although this incident was limited to a single company, the environmental disclosures in the annual reports of North American oil companies increased significantly to legitimize the entities' businesses. This can be regarded as a proactive action by the oil companies, as they thereby seek to change the social contract before actually facing a particular threat.[710] Similarly, the U.S. tobacco industry faced pres-

---

[703] Cf. *Ashforth/Gibbs* (1990), p. 182.
[704] Cf. here and in the following *Ashforth/Gibbs* (1990), p. 182-184.
[705] Cf. *O'Donovan* (2002), p. 350.
[706] Cf. here and in the following *Dowling/Pfeffer* (1975), p, 127; *O'Donovan* (2002), p. 353-354; *Khor* (2003), p. 7.
[707] Cf. *Lindblom* (1994), p. 59.
[708] Cf. *Khor* (2003), p. 7.
[709] Cf. here and in the following *Patten* (1992), p. 474-475.
[710] Cf. *Khor* (2003), p. 11.

sure to provide comprehensive information proactively in times when a crisis seemed to be evolving.[711]

To implement a legitimization strategy through disclosure activities, entities particularly make use of **annual reports.**[712] In particular regarding environmental issues, managers consider annual reports a convenient medium to "*[...] respond to public pressure, especially in response to negative media reports [...]*"[713]. However, since stand-alone environmental reports and sustainability reports have emerged in the 1990s, some companies provide environmental information in these separate reports, rather than in the entities' annual reports.[714]

On the whole, the legitimacy theory has come up with similar implications as the political cost theory. While the political cost theory, however, is based on the assumptions of new institutional economics and assumes that managers maximize their individual utility, the legitimacy theory argues that managers' behavior is influenced by a social contract. The following section discusses the stakeholder theory as additional approach from the field of new institutional sociology.

4.1.5.4.3 Stakeholder theory

In the literature, the stakeholder theory is used as a theoretical basis for both **normative business ethics** research and **empirical management** investigations.[715] However, there is no consensus, whether stakeholder theory can be applied to these different disciplines separately, as this would mean a separation of the managers' ethics from their actions.[716] Although both perspectives assume differing interests of stakeholders, the ethical view evaluates the interests of all stakeholders as generally equally important to the company.[717] Consequently, it is the management's task to emphasize the ethical role of the company and treat all stakeholders equally, which may be to the detriment of economic objectives (e.g., profitability).[718] As such behavior is not consistent with actual management practices, the empirical management perspective is presented in the following as the relevant theoretical basis for this study.

Although both theories posit that entities have to fulfill **information needs**, legitimacy theory focuses on the disclosure of information to gain legitimacy among the general society, whereas the stakeholder theory distinguishes between different interest groups with specific information needs.[719] Hence, the stakeholder theory is not based on the existence

---

[711] Cf. *Pava/Krausz* (1997), p. 340; *O'Donovan* (2002), p. 350.

[712] For research on the relation between legitimacy theory and annual reporting pratices, cf. inter alia *Dowling/Pfeffer* (1975); *Lindblom* (1994); *Suchman* (1995); *Pava/Krausz* (1997); *Deegan et al.* (2000); *Deegan* (2002); *O'Donovan* (2002); *Unerman* (2000); *Deegan et al.* (2002); *Chu et al.* (2012); *Kent/Zunker* (2013); *Chan et al.* (2014).

[713] *O'Donovan* (2002), p. 351.

[714] Cf. *Unerman* (2000), p. 674; *Blaesing* (2013), p. 146-147.

[715] Cf. *Hasnas* (1998), p. 25.

[716] Cf. *Orij* (2010), p. 870.

[717] Cf. *Hasnas* (1998), p. 26.

[718] Cf. *Stoney/Winstanley* (2001), p. 608.

[719] Cf. *Donaldson/Preston* (1995), p. 67.

of one general social contract like legitimacy theory, but argues that there are different social contracts between the corporation and each stakeholder group.[720] Another major difference between legitimacy and stakeholder theory is the intrinsic motivation of a company. While legitimacy theory suggests that a company provides information solely due to moral requirements, stakeholder theory states that companies have an own interest to satisfy their stakeholders' information needs as prerequisite to run a successful business (e.g., the company depends on capital and labor resources to maximize the company value).[721]

According to *Freeman* (1984) a stakeholder of a company is

> "*[...] a person or group that can affect or is affected by the achievement of the organization's objectives.*"[722]

Besides obvious interest groups, such as stockholders and creditors, which are also mentioned by accounting standard setters,[723] also, among others, customers, suppliers, employees, communities and the general public belong to a company's stakeholders.[724] Every stakeholder group may be able to limit or reject the entity's access to resources, which are required by the company, such as capital or labor.[725] However, not all interest groups have the same "*stakeholder power*"[726]. Hence, corporations are particularly interested in cooperative relationships with stakeholders holding the most important resources which the corporation depends on.[727] *Clarkson* (1995) distinguishes between **primary** and **secondary stakeholders**. The continuing participation of primary stakeholders is vital for the company's long-term survival as a going concern.[728] These major stakeholders commonly include investors, employees, customers, suppliers as well as public stakeholders, such as the government or communities, which, for example, provide infrastructures and markets. Secondary stakeholders are not of existential relevance for the company, however, particularly the media and various special interest groups are, for instance, capable of damaging or enhancing the entity's image by influencing the public opinion.[729] Thus, also secondary stakeholders may be able to affect a company's achievements in line with the above definition by *Freeman* (1984).

To investigate the strategic management of stakeholders, *Ackermann/Eden* (2011) posit the need to prioritize between stakeholder groups on the basis of the two dimensions **power of stakeholders** and **interest of stakeholders**, as illustrated in Figure 4-9.

---

[720] Cf. *Deegan* (2002), p. 283; *Deegan/Unerman* (2011), p. 348.

[721] Cf. *Freeman et al.* (2010), p. 10-12.

[722] *Freeman* (1984), p. 46.

[723] According to the IFRS Conceptual Framework the primary interest groups of financial reporting are "*existing or potential investors, lenders and other creditors*", F.OB2.

[724] Cf. *van der Laan Smith et al.* (2005), p. 126-127.

[725] Cf. *Ullmann* (1985), p. 552.

[726] *Ullmann* (1985), p. 552.

[727] Cf. *van der Laan Smith et al.* (2005), p. 127.

[728] Cf. here and in the following *Clarkson* (1995), p. 106.

[729] Cf. *Clarkson* (1995), p. 107.

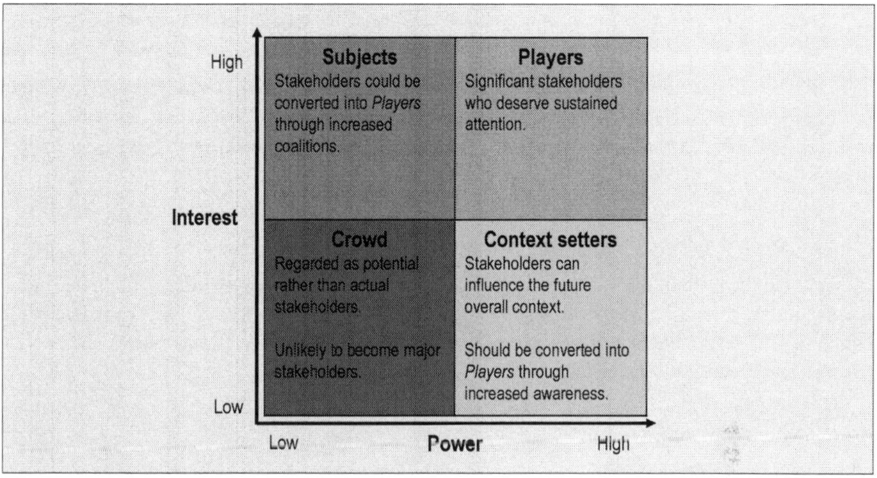

Figure 4-9: Importance of stakeholders
Following *Ackermann/Eden* (2011), p. 183.

They asked top management teams, which stakeholders are regarded as powerful to influence the entity's strategy and which stakeholders have a significant interest in the company.[730] The result was the positioning of different stakeholder stereotypes in a power-interest grid. *Players* and *Context setters* are the most relevant stakeholders for a company, since both groups have a high degree of power and, thus, are able either to support or to sabotage the company's business. Managers should try to raise the company's awareness among *Context setters*, since *Context setters* may largely determine the future setting of the entity's operating context. *Subjects* have a high interest in the company, but only low power (so far). However, the company can increase the power through coalitions to convert *Subjects* into *Players*. The *Crowd* category encompasses potential stakeholders, who neither show interest in the company nor have the power to influence it considerably.

The importance of stakeholder theory to this study is underpinned by *van der Laan Smith et al.* (2005), who find that stakeholder attributes are pronounced in **international contexts.**[731] Hence, it is reasonable to consider stakeholder attributes and particularities, which influence the decisions of managers, in this investigation.[732] The increasing importance of the stakeholder view leads to a reconsideration, though no objection, of the well-established shareholder value orientation, as the following statement by *Shaw* (2000) shows:

> *"A business will only be able to deliver sustained and sustainable shareholder value through continuous improvement and innovation by what is being increasingly referred to a 'stakeholder symbiosis'. Stakeholder symbiosis is the belief in the interde-*

[730] Cf. here and in the following *Ackermann/Eden* (2011), p. 182.
[731] Cf. *van der Laan Smith et al.* (2005), p. 147.
[732] Cf. *Orij* (2010), p. 871.

> *pendence of financial performance, customer loyalty, employee motivation and good corporate practice.*"[733]

The discussion on whether companies are supposed to put their shareholders or their stakeholders first to be successful is also picked up by *Akisik* (2011) who, however, examines the role of stakeholder theory in a particular **emerging economy setting** over the period from 1997 to 2006.[734] He assumes that

> "*[…] a good cooperation with stakeholders would have a positive impact on the creation of shareholder value in emerging market countries.*"[735]

In fact, he finds that stakeholder-related aspects (inter alia, stock market development, employment, managers' credibility, social responsibility and customer satisfaction), which frequently differ between emerging economies and developed countries, positively impact the shareholder value of entities.[736]

4.1.6 Summary

This section summarizes the above presented theoretical approaches, which present the basis for the subsequent development of hypotheses (section 4.2). In a second step, this theoretical foundation allows to refine this study's conceptual framework.

Institutionalism has been presented as the main theoretical foundation of this study. Institutions, which have a regulatory effect on human behavior, play a major role in both new institutional economics and new institutional sociology. However, there are considerable differences between these institutional streams of thought. **New institutional economics**, including the agency theory, picks up ideas of traditional economics and, therefore, emphasizes efficiency in organizational practices. Principals and agents act as rationalists pursuing their individual interests and, while doing so, have to consider the given environment. Considering the limitations of the new institutional economics, the **new institutional sociology** approach allows additional ethical and moral considerations, as it posits that organizations seek legitimacy "*as part of a larger social system*"[737]. Moreover, the approach assumes that people are satisfied and behave conform to what they regard as legitimate, which may also be derived from the environment as a source of practice.[738] While agency problems are concerned with difficulties in control mechanisms, the sociological view focuses on the regulating power of institutions determining, whether individuals (e.g., stakeholders of corporations) support the legitimacy of organizational practices. In addition, the **positive accounting theory** argues that entities attempt to avoid political costs which may arise when regulatory authorities interfere with a company's operations. How these institutionalism-based theoretical approaches might affect company-specific

---

[733] *Shaw* (2000), p. 37.
[734] Cf. *Akisik* (2011), p. 157.
[735] *Akisik* (2011), p. 158.
[736] Cf. *Akisik* (2011), p. 174-175.
[737] *Al Mamun et al.* (2013), p. 44.
[738] Cf. here and in the following *Al Mamun et al.* (2013), p. 44-45.

characteristics (which are selected as internal context factors) is explained separately for each characteristic in section 4.2.3.

Besides internal context factors, also factors outside of the company influence the financial reporting practice of a corporation. Of relevance for this cross-country investigation of financial reporting practices is **national culture** with its accounting-related operationalization by *Gray*'s accounting values. National culture affects both financial reporting practices directly and the design of a country's societal context factors. Referring to the **societal effects approach**, multiple external institutional context factors are assumed to influence financial reporting practice. Although a three-country study does not allow the separate analysis and evaluation of the countries' national culture and each institutional context factor, these external context factors may pose an important explanation for potential cross-country differences in the empirical results. All internal and external influencing factors cohere as essential parts of the contingency approach. Figure 4-10 present the refined conceptual framework of the study.

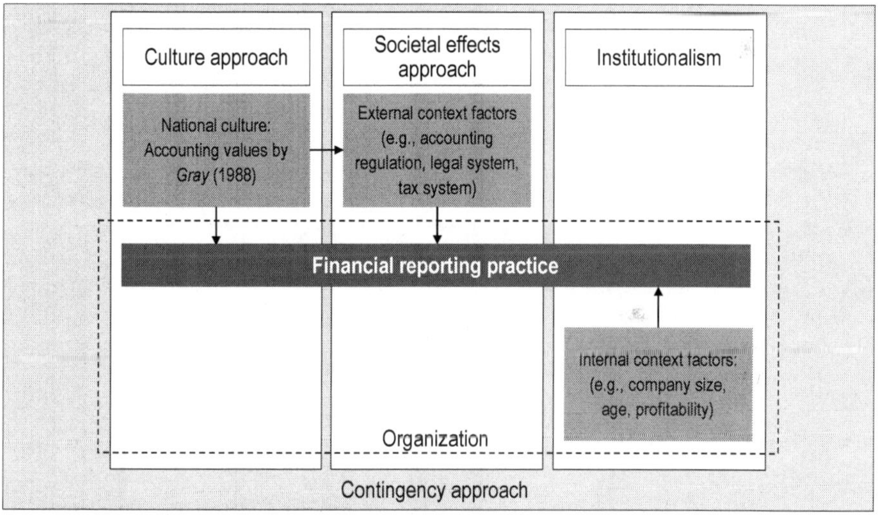

Figure 4-10: Refined conceptual framework
Following *Morgan* (2006), p. 42-49; *Reisloh* (2011), p. 166.

4.2 Hypotheses development

4.2.1 Introduction

The following sections derive the research hypotheses of the empirical investigation on the basis of both the described conceptual framework and the theoretical foundation. Hypotheses generally comprise a **null hypothesis** and an **alternative hypothesis** stating the exact opposite of the null hypothesis.[739] In line with this study's scientific approach of critical rationalism, the objective of statistical testing is to reject the null hypothesis and, thus, to keep the alternative hypothesis. Hence, the following sections solely display the alternative hypotheses, which are either **directed** or **undirected**. While directed hypotheses posit the direction of the relation between the analyzed variables (e.g., X and Y are positively associated), undirected hypotheses only state that those variables are associated, however, give no direction.[740]

The research hypotheses aim at explaining[741] the observed accounting practices and relationships. They are designed to shed light on the initially raised **research questions.**[742] Each **research hypothesis** can be assigned to at least one of the research questions. Thus, the development of the research hypotheses follows the three research fields of the study: (1) financial reporting practice, (2) determinants of financial reporting quality and (3) information asymmetries associated with financial reporting quality. The first group of hypotheses (section 4.2.2) is concerned with general expectations regarding financial reporting practices within and across the analyzed countries on the basis of the observed financial reporting quality. Hence, the hypotheses are directly linked to the research questions RQ1a and RQ1b. The second set of hypotheses (section 4.2.3) deals with the identification of determinants which influence financial reporting quality. These hypotheses shall provide answers to research question RQ2a and RQ2b. In addition, the third group of hypotheses (section 4.2.4) proposes potential capital market effects in terms of information asymmetries referring to research questions RQ3a and RQ3b.

4.2.2 Financial reporting practice

The research questions RQ1a and RQ1b are concerned with the financial reporting practices in Brazil, South Africa and Germany from a **within-country** as well as a cross-country perspective. On the basis of the contingency approach, several sources of influence on a company's financial reporting practice have been identified. While the national cultural and institutional environments affect the financial reporting activities of all companies within this environment, institutionalism explains the effect of company-specific context factors. These factors are unique to a company and, thus, determine differing incentives for entities and their managers to provide a certain level of disclosure. For example, a company's size might influence its individual financial reporting practices, as larger larger companies have higher agency costs than smaller companies according to agency

[739] Cf. *von Auer* (2013), p. 107-108.

[740] Cf. *Pospeschill* (2006), p. 171.

[741] Cf. *von Auer* (2013), p. 8.

[742] For the research questions, cf. section 1.1.

theory and, therefore, provide an increased financial reporting quality (FRQ).[743] Thus, differences in FRQ are assumed for each of the country samples Brazil, South Africa and Germany regardless of country characteristics (**hypothesis H1a**).

In addition to company-specific effects, the theoretical foundation also suggests **cross-country** effects on financial reporting practice. In particular, the culture and societal effects approaches state that external factors stemming from a country's national culture and institutional environment give rise to systematic differences in financial reporting practices across the three economies. Based on the description of the accounting environments in the three countries in chapter two, there are differences in national culture, based on differing accounting values according to *Gray* (1988), as well as institutional country specifications, such as national financial reporting regulation.[744] For example, prior research suggests that civil law countries are particularly stakeholder-oriented, as the relationships between the company and important stakeholders are closer than in common law countries, which rather focus on shareholder value.[745] In accordance with the stakeholder theory, thus, companies from civil law countries might particularly focus on stakeholders' information needs and, thus, provide different information than companies from common law countries. As this study investigates both civil law (Brazil and Germany) and common law countries (South Africa), differences in financial reporting practices across these countries are expected. Overall, therefore, it is hypothesized that financial reporting practices (based on FRQ) differ across the country samples (**hypothesis H1b**).

Based on the conceptual framework and the theoretical foundation the hypotheses H1a and H1b are as follows:

H1a	FRQ differs within each of the economies of Brazil, South Africa and Germany.
H1b	FRQ differs across the economies of Brazil, South Africa and Germany.

These general hypotheses concerning expected financial reporting practices may serve as a starting point for further, more detailed, analyses. In particular, not only differences in financial reporting practices in terms of total FRQ can be examined, but also differences regarding specific areas of financial reporting (e.g., important financial or non-financial information).[746] Moreover, this study analyzes in more detail, how financial reporting practices differ across Brazil, South Africa and Germany. For that purpose, the following section develops directed hypotheses concerning the FRQ in each country to capture country effects as one of the identified determinants.

[743] Cf. *Barth* (2009), p. 98-99. The theoretically derived effects of such company-specific determinants on FRQ are discussed in the following section 4.2.3.

[744] Cf. section 2.3.

[745] Cf. *Ball et al.* (2000), p. 2. For instance, the French company law particularly encourages the reconciliation of societal and stakeholder interests, cf. *Halpern* (2000), p. 5.

[746] For the results of this content-related analysis, cf. section 6.1.2.2.

4.2.3 Determinants of financial reporting quality

In line with the research questions RQ2a and RQ2b, the study investigates factors determining FRQ. Therefore, this section develops hypotheses concerning the relation between FRQ and important influencing factors which have been indicated by the conceptual framework. According to the culture and the societal effects approaches, a number of **country-specific factors** influence FRQ, such as cultural and institutional aspects. This study depicts the effects of these influencing factors in a country variable to determine the influence of each country. In particular, a country's cultural and institutional characteristics affect its level of stakeholder orientation, which is used to explain cross-country differences in this study.

The conceptual foundation of this thesis has shown that emerging economies in general and Brazil and South Africa in particular have grown rapidly over the past decades; however, their **stages of development** regarding economic strength as well as institutional environment are assumed to have not reached the level of developed countries, such as Germany.[747] Particularly, the German capital market activity and accounting environment (including, inter alia, accounting regulation, accounting education, enforcement) may have developed further than those in emerging economies. Thus, more developed countries are assumed to provide a higher FRQ. Although numerous researchers generally claim that FRQ is lower in emerging economies than in developed countries,[748] the literature review has revealed that empirical studies measuring FRQ indirectly as well as directly provide heterogeneous results.[749]

Regarding **cultural aspects**, the German and South African cultures are found to be more reporting-friendly than the Brazilian culture, as their cultural values according to *Gray* (1988) are, at least to some extent, in line with the optimal accounting values (including professionalism, flexibility, optimism and transparency).[750] In particular, the fact that both optimism and transparency are more pronounced in Germany and South Africa than in the rather conservative and secrecy-dominated culture in Brazil suggest differences in FRQ.

New institutional sociology perceives a company as an integral part of society, which attempts to legitimize its actions. In line with both legitimacy theory and stakeholder theory, a high level of **stakeholder orientation** of a society leads to increased pressure on the company to meet the stakeholders' expectations.[751] However, these expectations may differ between countries, as societal institutions (such as, norms and values) are specific to every society. *Ball et al.* (2000) argue that the level of stakeholder orientation in a society depends on its **corporate governance system**, which again is characterized by its **legal system**.[752] They posit that civil law countries have a *stakeholder governance model*, whereas

---

[747] For the financial reporting environment in Brazil, South Africa and Germany, cf. section 2.3.

[748] Cf. amongst others *Cooke/Wallace* (1990), p. 79; *Salter* (1998), p. 211; *Lopes et al.* (2007), p. 2; *Ball et al.* (2003), p. 235; *de Lima et al.* (2010), p. 257; *Iatridis* (2012), p. 103; *Nobes* (2014), p. 24-30.

[749] Cf. section 3.2

[750] *Borker* (2012)

[751] Cf. *Deegan* (2002), p. 295.

[752] Cf. *Ball et al.* (2000), p. 3; *Donaldson/Preston* (1995), p. 75.

common law countries pursue a *shareholder governance model.*[753] Hence, Brazilian and German entities (both civil law countries) might face greater pressure to meet the stakeholders' information needs than those from the common law country South Africa. Similarly, *van der Laan Smith et al.* (2005) distinguish two corporate governance structures: *contractarianism*, which regards a company as a combination of contracts, and *communitarianism*, seeing companies as social organizations.[754] According to the Anglo-American contractarianism approach an entity has to focus on its shareholders' interests (e.g., wealth maximization), the rather Continental European communitarian view emphasizes a company's social responsibilities towards multiple stakeholders. Consequently, these thoughts support a strong stakeholder orientation in Germany, which may lead to increased efforts to provide high FRQ to a company's stakeholders.

As additional corporate governance aspect, a country's dominant **board system** may also affect FRQ. The principal-agent theory suggests that in countries with mainly dualistic board systems (e.g., Germany) efforts to monitor the executives' activities are stronger, since the supervisory board is able to work more independently than in monistic systems (e.g., Brazil and South Africa), where board members rather perform a *self-supervision.*[755] If the monitoring results are reported by the company, a higher (corporate governance) FRQ could be assumed for countries with dualistic board systems.[756]

Based on the above discussion, it is hypothesized that country effects determine FRQ in Brazil, South Africa and Germany as follows:

H2a	FRQ is higher in Germany than in Brazil and South Africa.
H2b	FRQ is higher in South Africa than in Brazil.

Besides country effects, the study analyzes several **company-specific determinants**. The effect of these company-specific determinants on FRQ is explained on the basis of the theoretical foundation of institutionalism. As this theoretical foundation is the same in both emerging economies and developed countries the expected effects do not generally differ among the three sample countries. However, the above described distinctive characteristics of emerging economies give rise to differences in the manifestation of the determinants. Thus, the actual importance of certain company-specific determinants may be different in emerging economies due to their financial reporting environments. This study's hypotheses regarding company-specific determinants are derived in the following on the basis of the presented theories.

---

[753] Cf. section 4.1.5.4.3.

[754] Cf. here and in the following *van der Laan Smith et al.* (2005), p. 129-130.

[755] Cf. *Filiz* (2013), p. 153, 155 and 160; *Kostyuk* (2003), p. 104; *Lessambo* (2014), p. 131.

[756] However, research shows that supervisory board members might make operational decisions contradicting the objective of a separation of the management and supervisory powers, cf. *Kostyuk* (2003), p. 105. Moreover, supervisory board members might have a poor information basis due to the distance between operational and supervisory activities, cf. *Schewe* (2015), p. 93. These arguments mitigate the positive effect of dualistic board systems on FRQ.

Although numerous studies find strong positive associations between **company size** and the level of disclosure,[757] there is no universal explanation for these observations. Different aspects might play a decisive role. On the one hand, larger companies simply have more **resources** than smaller ones, which allow the establishment of comprehensive reporting systems. These systems include, inter alia, well-trained employees, developed internal control systems as well as large accounting departments with a modern technological infrastructure.[758] For smaller entities, similar reporting efforts would cause considerable additional costs, as data is not collected in a standardized manner.[759]

On the other hand, there are **theory-based explanations** for the relation between company size and financial reporting practices. The principal-agent theory argues that companies provide information to reduce existing information asymmetries between the entity's management and its stakeholders.[760] The larger and, thus, more complex a company, the larger are the information asymmetries and, consequently, the arising agency costs.[761] Hence, particularly larger corporations have an incentive to reduce existing information asymmetries through financial reporting. Furthermore, the positive accounting theory argues that larger companies are frequently facing an increased interest of the public as well as particular attention by authorities, which leads to the occurrence of political costs.[762] Thus, foremost larger companies attempt to avoid such political costs through adequate disclosures. In line with the above argumentation, therefore, it is hypothesized:

H3	FRQ is positively associated with company size.

In addition to size, also **company age** is assumed to affect FRQ.[763] The legitimacy theory argues that companies try to derive and secure their societal legitimacy. Although theory states that society may change its benevolence from time to time, society's expectations, as well as an entity's legitimacy might increase over time, as the company becomes gradually more integrated into society.[764] In addition, older companies have had more time to establish a reporting system including expertise, structures and processes to guarantee high quality information in their corporate reports than younger ones. Also *Owusu-Ansah* (1998) underpins that older companies are able to prepare reports more easily and further argues that older and, thus, well-established companies are less likely to suffer from competitive disadvantages when providing high-quality information than younger entities.[765]

[757] Cf. amongst others, *Firth* (1979); *Cooke* (1991); *Lang/Lundholm* (1993); *Wallace et al.* (1994); *Ahmed/Courtis* (1999); *Cahan et al.* (2005); *Cohen* (2008); *Iatridis* (2012); *Al-Najjar/Abed* (2014); *Bokpin* (2013); *Dainelli et al.* (2013).

[758] Cf. *Reisloh* (2011), p. 156.

[759] Cf. *Singhvi/Desai* (1971), p. 131.

[760] Cf. section 4.1.5.2.3.

[761] Cf. *Barth* (2009), p. 98-99.

[762] Cf. section 4.1.5.3.

[763] Cf. amongst others, *Cohen* (2008); *Bokpin* (2013).

[764] Cf. section 4.1.5.4.2.

[765] Cf. *Owusu-Ansah* (1998), p. 614.

Similarly, *Haniffa/Cooke* (2002) find the length of a company's listing as a determinant of voluntary disclosures.[766] Hence, the following hypothesis assumes:

H4 FRQ is positively associated with company age.

One of the most important criteria to evaluate the performance of managers is the company's **profitability**.[767] In accordance with signaling theory, executives provide increased disclosures to signal and explicate that the company managed by them is successful and, thereby, reduce agency costs.[768] Thus, financial reporting provides profitable companies the possibility to differentiate their entity from other (less profitable) companies. Moreover, stakeholder theory suggests that a company's success can only be ensured if it has access to its major stakeholders' resources.[769] Therefore, the entity has to meet the information needs of its stakeholders. This leads to the assumption that companies with a higher profitability have a higher level of FRQ (hypothesis H5).

Epstein/Palepu (1999) posit that "*[...] managers respond effectively to investors' information needs when the company is doing well [...]*". Also *Haniffa/Cooke* (2002) find a statistically significant positive relation between voluntary annual report information and profitability for a sample of listed companies from the emerging economy of Malaysia. However, besides a number of studies supporting H5, there are also prior determinants studies, which do not provide evidence of this relationship.[770] Insignificant results or even negative associations indicate that also other argumentations are feasible. On the one hand, profitable companies do not see any necessity to provide comprehensive information and, thereby, run the risk to reveal sensitive information to its competitors. On the other hand, companies with low profitability could attempt to justify their results by providing an increased level of disclosures. In line with the prevailing literature opinion, however, it is hypothesized that there is a positive relationship between FRQ and profitability:

H5 FRQ is positively associated with profitability.

Although numerous studies have investigated the relation between the stock market **valuation** of a company and its FRQ, the findings are mixed.[771] On the one hand, according to agency theory, particularly higher valued companies have an incentive to provide voluntary information to market participants to avoid price discounts, which may lead to a *market for lemons* as described by *Akerlof* (1970). However, a number of studies do not find such a positive relationship between company valuation and FRQ. Reasons might be that the additional disclosure costs (e.g., proprietary cost) outweigh the expected benefits.[772] On the other hand, signaling theory may suggest a different conclusion. Managers being convinced that a company is undervalued at the capital market might have an in-

[766] Cf. *Haniffa/Cooke* (2002), p. 332.
[767] Cf. *Cerf* (1961), p. 21.
[768] Cf. *Blaesing* (2013), p. 129.
[769] Cf. section 4.1.5.4.3.
[770] Cf. amongst others *Lang/Lundholm* (1993), p. 248.
[771] Cf. here and in the following *Chen et al.* (2014), p. 18.
[772] Cf. *Verrecchia* (1983), p. 192; *Healy/Palepu* (2001), p. 420.

centive to signal the actual value of the entity and reduce information asymmetries to increase its attractiveness for investors.[773] Following this argumentation hypothesis H6 expects a negative association between FRQ and company valuation. For a sample from the emerging economy of China, *Chen et al.* (2014) find a negative relation between company valuation and voluntary disclosures for entities which rely on the relationship-driven *guanxi* network.[774]

H6 FRQ is negatively associated with company valuation.

According to the capital asset pricing model (CAPM), equity investors expect a return on company stocks which consists of a risk-free rate of return plus a risk premium, which depends on the **systematic company risk.**[775] Unlike the unsystematic risk, capital market participants are not able to reduce the systematic risk through portfolio diversification.[776] The so-called beta value is a standardized measure of a stock's systematic risk, which is based on the correlation of the returns of a security and of the entire market. Beta values below one indicate securities with an inherent risk below the risk of the entire market, whereas securities above market risk have beta values higher than one. Following the principal agent theory, particularly companies with high beta factors attempt to reduce their risk premium by reducing information asymmetries between company and investors through increased FRQ.[777] For example, *Francis et al.* (2005a) find that accruals quality increases with higher beta values.[778] Hence the following relation is expected:

H7 FRQ is positively associated with systematic company risk.

Furthermore, the **ownership concentration** of a company is frequently subject to investigation throughout the financial reporting literature. Although prior research mostly agrees that the "*[...] ownership distribution has a significant influence on the quality of disclosure [...]*"[779], the literature discusses extensively, how ownership concentration affects disclosure practices.[780] **Dominant block holders** do not necessarily rely on corporate reports (e.g., annual reports) to reduce existing information asymmetries, but obtain information via other channels and frequently even before other stakeholders.[781] On the one hand, dominant block holders might use their power to prevent the publication of certain information for their own benefit (*opportunistic hypothesis*):[782] "*Instead of sharing information*

[773] Cf. *Dainelli et al.* (2013), p. 267.
[774] Cf. *Chen et al.* (2014), p. 18.
[775] Cf. *Deegan* (2000), p. 209.
[776] Cf. here and in the following *Wöhe/Döring* (2013), p. 636-637.
[777] Cf. section 4.1.5.2.3.
[778] Cf. *Francis et al.* (2005a), p. 297.
[779] *Singhvi/Desai* (1971), p. 132.
[780] Cf. *Jiang/Habib* (2009), p. 277. *Al-Najjar/Abed* (2014) give an overview of the mixed results on the relation between ownership concentration and FRQ in prior research, cf. *Al-Najjar/Abed* (2014), p. 580-582.
[781] Cf. *Al-Najjar/Abed* (2014), p. 583.
[782] Cf. *Jiang/Habib* (2009), p. 276.

with minority shareholder, large block holders may prefer less disclosure."[783] These arguments suggest that a high ownership concentration is negatively correlated with FRQ. On the other hand, strong block holders might be able to ensure high FRQ by monitoring the management (*efficient monitoring hypothesis*).[784] According to the latter argument, companies with large shareholder concentration would have an increased level of FRQ.

For companies with a **dispersed ownership structure**, financial reports may be an important medium to reach the large number of shareholders. A number of studies posit a lower likelihood of disclosures with increasing institutional ownership concentration and insider ownership.[785] For private companies, *Chen et al.* (2008) show that family-owned companies with a highly-concentrated ownership provide less voluntary information than non-family entities.[786] Similarly, *Cohen* (2008) find a negative correlation between ownership concentration and disclosure level.[787] *Jiang/Habib* (2009) provide further evidence of such an association for companies with dominant financial institutions as owners.[788] They emphasize that an emerging economy setting with pronounced ownership concentration contributes to the discussion on the effect of ownership concentration:

> "*Most studies regarding the relationship between ownership concentration and voluntary disclosure practices are conducted in Anglo-Saxon countries with relatively dispersed corporate ownership structure and transparent legal system.*"[789]

Investigating emerging economies with different legal origins, this study is able to shed additional light on the discussion. On the basis of the above arguments, the following relation is hypothesized:

H8	FRQ is negatively associated with ownership concentration.

Company characteristics, such as, inter alia, company size, company age, profitability, systematic risk, number of innovations or internationality can differ considerably according to the **industry**, in which an entity operates. While this study examines some of these attributes separately (as part of other hypotheses), the remaining industry effect is captured by the aggregated industry variable.[790] *Inchausti* (1997) argues that companies in the same industry publish similar information, as, on the basis of signaling theory, market participants could interpret it as a signal of *bad news*, if a company deviates from the industry's overall reporting strategy.[791]

Furthermore, **political costs** arise particularly in politically sensitive industries, which have negative repercussions for the society or the environment and, thus, are in the focus

[783] *Jiang/Habib* (2009), p. 277.
[784] *Shleifer/Vishny* (1986), p. 462; *Jiang/Habib* (2009), p. 276.
[785] Cf. amongst others *Ajinkya et al.* (2005), p. 343; *Karamanou/Vafeas* (2005), p. 465.
[786] Cf. *Chen et al.* (2008), p. 533.
[787] Cf. *Cohen* (2008), p. 81.
[788] Cf. *Jiang/Habib* (2009), p. 299.
[789] *Jiang/Habib* (2009), p. 276.
[790] Cf. *Blaesing* (2013), p. 134.
[791] Cf. *Inchausti* (1997), p. 56.

of supervisory authorities.[792] Typical examples are the automobile and mineral oil industries.[793] To avoid political costs, companies from such industries are expected to increasingly engage in financial reporting activities. Similarly, companies in these politically sensitive industries may also have to deal with considerable expectations by society, since their business activities tend to raise public concerns, e.g. concerning sustainability issues.[794] Legitimacy theory posits that entities have to gain society's legitimacy to ensure their access to resources.[795] Hence, a company's FRQ is expected to be affected by its industry category:

H9 FRQ differs across industries.

As stakeholder theory refers to companies' customers as primary stakeholders, companies might particularly address this stakeholder group in their corporate reports.[796] Consequently, the reporting activities of an entity would also be affected by its **customer basis**. Depending on whether a company sells its products and services primarily to business customers (B2B) or to end-consumers (B2C) companies may adjust their reporting practices resulting in differences in FRQ.[797] For example, end-consumers might have different information needs than B2B customers. In line with legitimacy theory, society might put less pressure on B2B entities, as their products do not affect end-consumers directly and sanctioning actions (e.g., boycott of products) are more difficult to seize. Customer orientation is included as an additional internal context factor. Prior empirical disclosure studies have not taken it into account or have not found significant disclosure differences in corporate reports of B2B and B2C companies, as the results by *Santema/van de Rijt* (2001) suggest.[798] This study investigates the following hypothesis:

H10 FRQ differs across customer bases.

Moreover, a company's **information environment** is assumed to affect its financial reporting activities and, thus, FRQ. The wider corporate information is spread, the more users are reached and, thus, managers' reporting efforts (e.g., to reduce information asymmetries) can be more effective.[799] Hence, this study investigates the association between a company's information environment and its FRQ. The hypotheses H11a and H11b are not directed, as effects in both directions are conceivable. On the one hand, signaling theory suggests a negative association, if entities with a low information environment seize the opportunity to inform investors via financial reports (e.g., annual reports), because hardly any other media are available. On the other hand, a high information level means that the company is in the spotlight of the wider society. According to

[792] Cf. *Blaesing* (2013), p. 134.
[793] Cf. *Verrecchia* (1983), p. 182; *Milne* (2002), p. 374.
[794] Cf. *Blaesing* (2013), p. 134.
[795] Cf. section 4.1.5.4.2.
[796] Cf. section 4.1.5.4.3.
[797] Cf. *Wanderley et al.* (2008), p. 376.
[798] Cf. *Santema/van de Rijt* (2001), p. 104.
[799] Cf. *Jeanjean/Stolowy* (2008), p. 482-484.

the legitimacy theory, the company would try to satisfy the arising expectations and, hence, provide high quality information. In the literature, for instance, *Botosan* (1997) explicitly distinguishes in her empirical disclosure study between entities with low and high analyst following and finds significant associations.[800] This study tests the following hypothesis:

H11	FRQ is associated with information environment.

4.2.4 Capital market consequences

In accordance with the research questions RQ3a and RQ3b, the capital market study analyzes the relationship between FRQ and information asymmetries. Principal-agent theory argues that agency costs occur when **information asymmetries** lead to adverse selection regarding, for instance, contracts between buyers and sellers of company stocks.[801] Capital market participants, such as investors and financial analysts, use information from corporate reports as a basis for their decisions. The efficient allocation of resources depends on the information provided by entities, which is in line with this study's empirical capital market investigation. However, companies would only provide information voluntarily, if benefits exceed the corresponding costs, as described in section 2.1.1. In the following, the role of financial reporting in a capital market environment is explained in more detail.

Commonly a large number of companies compete for the household savings in an economy to fund their businesses.[802] However, savers have difficulty in making investment decisions, i.e. "*[...] distinguishing good quality from bad [...]*"[803]. The first problem is that companies' information levels exceed the savers' information levels. *Akerlof* (1970) illustrates this **information problem** between a less informed party (e.g., saver) and a better informed party (e.g. management of a company) by the example of the used car market, where only the seller has the information, whether a car is a good car or a bad car, a so-called *lemon* (information asymmetry). He concludes that lemons drive the good cars out of the market, because potential buyers, who cannot identify non-lemons, are not willing to pay more for any car than the price of a lemon.[804] In analogy, investors might undervalue good potential investments.[805]

However, there are solutions to overcome such information asymmetries. First, companies may have incentives to provide all relevant information to investors voluntarily. Second, companies might also be required by regulation to disclose the information. Moreover, information intermediaries, such as financial analysts and rating agencies, are able to mitigate the information asymmetries by supplying investors with self-generated information. Figure 4-11 illustrates not only that information can flow directly (e.g., annual reports) and indirectly through information intermediaries from households to companies, but

800 Cf. *Botosan* (1997), p. 323.
801 Cf. section 4.1.5.2.2.
802 Cf. here and in the following *Healy/Palepu* (2001), p. 407.
803 *Akerlof* (1970), p. 500.
804 Cf. *Akerlof* (1970), p. 489.
805 Cf. here and in the following *Healy/Palepu* (2001), p. 408.

also capital can flow directly (e.g., private equity) and indirectly through financial intermediaries (e.g., banks) in reverse direction. Hence, this study's capital market investigation explores, how the disclosure of information by the reporting companies (flow of information) influence the capital market decisions (flow of capital).

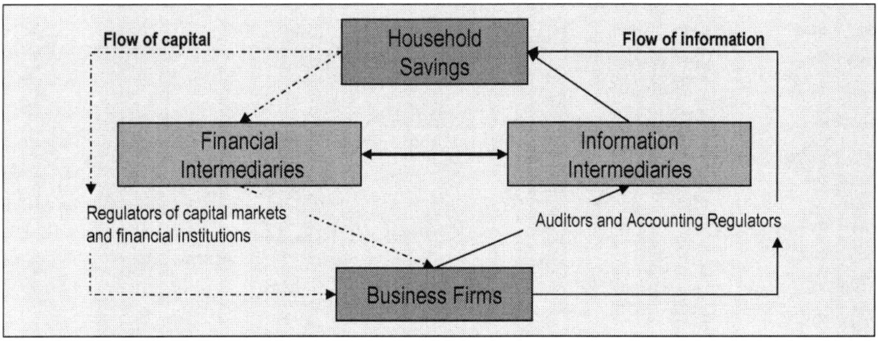

Figure 4-11: Financial and information flows in a capital market economy
Following *Healy/Palepu* (2001), p. 408.

On the whole, information asymmetries lead to adverse selection and cause agency costs according to theory.[806] This results in lower liquidity of the stocks so that companies have to issue share capital at discounted prices in order to attract or keep investors.[807] On the basis of signaling theory, *Leuz/Verrecchia* (2000) describe the relation between disclosure quality and the behavior of capital market participants, in particular equity capital investors, as follows:

> "*A commitment to increased levels of disclosure reduces the possibility of information asymmetries arising either between the firm and its shareholders or among potential buyers and sellers of firm shares. This, in turn, should reduce the discount at which firm shares are sold, and hence lower the costs of issuing capital.*"[808]

Consistent with this brief explanation, the reduction of information asymmetries lowers the uncertainty of investors, who, therefore, demand a lower risk premium for their investments so that also the company's costs of capital decrease.[809] Hence, this study investigates the relationship between the FRQ by a company's management (agent) and the corresponding information asymmetries for the investors (principals). In line with theory, hypothesis H12 assumes a **negative association** between FRQ and information asymmetries. However, no actual impact of FRQ on information asymmetries is claimed, as the causality between reporting and information asymmetries might be reversed.

The existence of incentives to provide information on the capital market is no recent phenomenon. Already in 1926, before extensive reporting requirements (particularly securi-

---

[806] Cf. section 4.1.5.2.2.
[807] Cf. *Leuz/Verrecchia* (2000), p. 92.
[808] *Leuz/Verrecchia* (2000), p. 92.
[809] Cf. *Hail* (2002), p. 743-745.

ties acts) became effective in the U.S. during the 1930s, 82% of the companies traded on the New York Stock Exchange voluntarily provided audited financial statements to satisfy the information needs of capital suppliers.[810] The fact that companies see the necessity of providing information to investors is also underpinned in mainstream media, such as *The New York Times* arguing that companies

> "*[...] realize that institutional investors prefer to put money into companies that provide lots of information and that good investor relations can help their stock price*"[811].

The literature review has shown that the accounting literature heavily investigates the question, as to whether and to what extent corporate reporting practices have an effect on capital market behavior.[812] However, neither in analytical nor in empirical research a consensus has been found, whether information asymmetries are in fact negatively associated with FRQ in line with theory. Nonetheless, based on agency theory, it is hypothesized as follows:

H12	FRQ is negatively associated with information asymmetries.

4.2.5 Summary

The last sections have developed hypotheses to be tested throughout the empirical investigation of this study. The theoretical foundation of these hypotheses is multifold. Figure 4-12 summarizes the formulated hypotheses according to the most relevant underlying theoretical basis. As illustrated in the conceptual framework, **institutionalism** serves as major theoretical foundation to develop hypotheses regarding the influence of company-specific context factors on financial reporting practice and, thus, quality (**determinant study**). According to institutionalism, the existence of institutions determines the behavior of individuals. While new institutional economics argues that individuals act rationally at all times on the basis of cost-benefit considerations, new institutional sociology limits the rational behavior as it assumes that individuals as well as organizations seek societal legitimacy and, therefore, considers also moral and ethical influences. In particular, agency theory, as part of new institutional economics, is not only an essential basis for the determinant study, but also provides the theoretical foundation for the assumed relation between FRQ and information asymmetries in hypothesis H12 (**capital market consequences**). One of the main objectives of this study is to identify differences in **financial reporting practice** between emerging economies and developed countries, in particular, between Brazil, South Africa and Germany. Based on institutionalism, hypothesis H1a expects FRQ differences within each country sample. To explain FRQ differences across the three countries (H1b), the study further applies the culture and societal effects approaches.

---

[810] Cf. *Elliott/Jacobson* (1995), p. 78-79.
[811] *Sweeney* (03.04.1994).
[812] Cf. section 3.4.

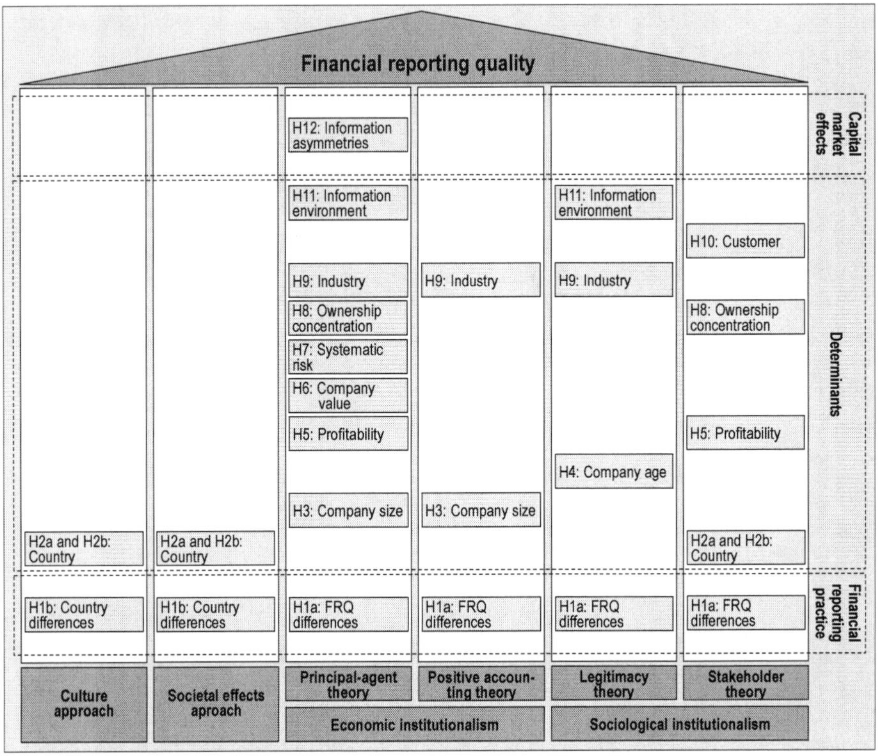

Figure 4-12: Overview of hypotheses and underlying theories
Following *Blaesing* (2013), p. 137.

5 Research design

Given the conceptual foundation of this study, the design of the empirical investigations in a cross-country setting is outlined throughout this chapter. After the description of the empirical field (section 5.1), section 5.2 describes the methodology of data collection for each of the three FRQ measures (accruals-based, disclosure index-based, readability measure). Section 5.3 presents the applied methods to analyze the collected data.

5.1 The empirical field

5.1.1 Sample selection

The study compares the FRQ in the two emerging economies Brazil and South Africa to the FRQ in Germany which is regarded as a developed country benchmark concerning comprehensive reporting activities.[813] The empirical investigation of FRQ requires a sample which is appropriate to describe financial reporting practices, to measure FRQ indirectly and directly, to determine influencing factors of FRQ as well as to analyze capital market consequences within and across the three economies. The selection of large companies is adequate, since these entities are meaningful for the economy and company data is largely available.

Therefore, the 50 largest companies in each of the countries (according to market capitalization on 31 December 2013) are selected so that the **total sample** comprises 150 companies.[814] The Brazilian sample companies are listed in the Bovespa IBrX 100 (Brazil 100 Index) on BM&FBOVESPA (Brazilian Securities, Commodities and Futures Exchange) in São Paulo. As shown in Table 5-1, the IBrX 100 comprises the 100 stocks most actively traded and best representative for the Brazilian equity market according to certain criteria.[815]

	Capital market (Stock exchange index)	Brazil (Bovespa IBrX)	South Africa (All-Share)	Germany (HDAX)
	Number of companies in indices	100	164	110
-	Thereof financial companies	- 16	- 36	- 9
-	Thereof cross-listed or head office in another country	- 32	- 17	- 8
-	Thereof English annual report not available	- 1		
=	Population	51	111	93
-	**Selection of sample companies**	**- 50**	**- 50**	**- 50**
=	Unconsidered companies in indices	1	61	43

Table 5-1: Sample selection summary

[813] For a detailed explanation of the selection of the sample countries, cf. section 2.3.1.

[814] Cf. indices and company data were retrieved from Thomson Reuters Datastream.

[815] Cf. *BM&FBOVESPA* (2014). For additional information on the Bovespa IBrX 100 index compilation, cf. *BM&FBOVESPA* (2015).

The South African stock index is the FTSE/JSE All Share of the Johannesburg Securities Exchange (JSE). It includes South African companies with the largest market capitalizations representing 99% of the entire capital market value.[816] On 31 December 2013, the index included 164 listed entities. The basis for the selection of the German companies is the HDAX index of the Deutsche Börse Group (Frankfurt Stock Exchange). It includes 110 listings which meet the required criteria regarding both order book turnover and free float market capitalization.[817]

The reasons for the preassigned **sample size** of 50 entities per country are multifold. First, the sample size shall allow statistical analyses and valid results for both the study's entire sample and within each country sample.[818] Second, the sample size shall guarantee that all sample companies are listed in the three selected indices. Third, a single researcher must be able to analyze the financial reporting practices of all sample companies, including the comprehensive disclosure index study, within a reasonable period of time.

As the study investigates financial reporting practices in Brazil, South Africa and Germany, a company's registered headquarter has to be in the sample country.[819] To further guarantee the same institutional environment for companies within one country and, thus, comparability of observed FRQ, all companies are excluded from the sample, which have to fulfill material additional disclosure requirements due to listings on other stock exchanges besides those in São Paulo, Johannesburg or Frankfurt.[820] In particular, companies listed on a stock market in the USA are excluded from the sample, as they are subject to additional corporate transparency requirements to improve investor protection.[821]

In line with the financial reporting literature, financial institutions are not considered in the sample, as their business models are distinctive and, thus, reporting requirements and contents diverge structurally from those of non-financial companies.[822] Hence, comparisons would hardly be feasible. However, real estate entities remain in the sample, if the companies' business activities are not dominated by typical activities of financial institu-

---

816 Cf. here and in the following *FTSE* (2015a); *FTSE* (2015b), p. 14. For additional information on FTSE/JSE Africa Index Series, cf. *Johannesburg Stock Exchange* (2004).

817 Cf. *Deutsche Börse AG* (2014), p. 25. The HDAX aggregates the selection indices DAX (30 entities), MDAX (50 entities) and TecDAX (30 entities). While the DAX consists of the 30 largest listed companies and the MDAX of the next 50 mid-cap companies, only stocks from the *technology* industry are included in the TecDAX.

818 For statistical significance and sample size, cf. section 5.3.3.2.

819 For this constraint, cf. *Oberdörster* (2009), p. 100.

820 For the potential impact of cross-listings, cf. *Hail/Leuz* (2009), p. 428; *Lindahl/Schadewitz* (2013), p. 262-263.

821 Cf. *Leuz/Oberholzer-Gee* (2006), p. 415. The study does not exclude entities trading American Depositary Receipts (ADRs) (U.S. dollar denominated certificates issued by a U.S. depository bank which evidence the ownership of shares of entities outside the United States, cf. *SEC* (2013)) of Level 1 on the OTC market in the U.S., as no major additional disclosures are required. However, companies listed on U.S. stock exchanges or issuing Level 2 ADRs which require to comply with comprehensive SEC regulation (e.g., SEC Form 20-F, cf. *SEC* (2013)) are excluded from the sample. For an overview of ADR programs in the U.S., cf. *Gande* (1997), p. 71.

822 Cf. amongst others *Botosan* (1997), p. 327; *Hail* (2002), p. 753; *Faulkender/Petersen* (2006), p. 51; *Oberdörster* (2009), p. 100-101; *Tang et al.* (2012), p. 12.

tions. In South Africa, for example, no real estate companies are selected, since their businesses are primarily concerned with financial investment management rather than the management of specific properties (e.g., shopping malls).

5.1.2 Sample description

5.1.2.1 Industry composition

The classification of the sample companies' industries is not only important to analyze empirical results across industries, but also to control for potential industry effects in the regression analyses and, thus, test the formulated hypotheses. However, the identification of homogeneous industry clusters for companies from three distinctive economies is not trivial. In light of the relatively small sample size, the number of industry categories shall ensure that every industry category is represented by several entities.

A detailed industry classification is provided by the four-digit numerical Standard Industrial Classification (SIC) codes of the U.S. government, which are assigned to each business entity on a systematic, uniform and comparable basis.[823] Following the SIC code industry aggregation as proposed by *French/Fama* (2010) (with minor adjustments), this study assigns the 150 sample companies to ten industry categories: (1) consumer non-durables and durables, (2) manufacturing, (3) energy and mining, (4) business equipment, (5) telecommunication, television and media, (6) wholesale and retail, (7) healthcare, (8) real estate, (9) transport and travel, and (10) construction.[824] Furthermore, the disregarded companies from the financial industry are excluded from the study on the basis of their SIC codes. Consequently, financial companies are not considered in the analyses.

Figure 5-1 shows that all industries are represented by at least 3% of the sample companies. Moreover, five categories similarly represent between 5% and 7% of the entities, whereas four categories subsume considerably larger percentages of companies.

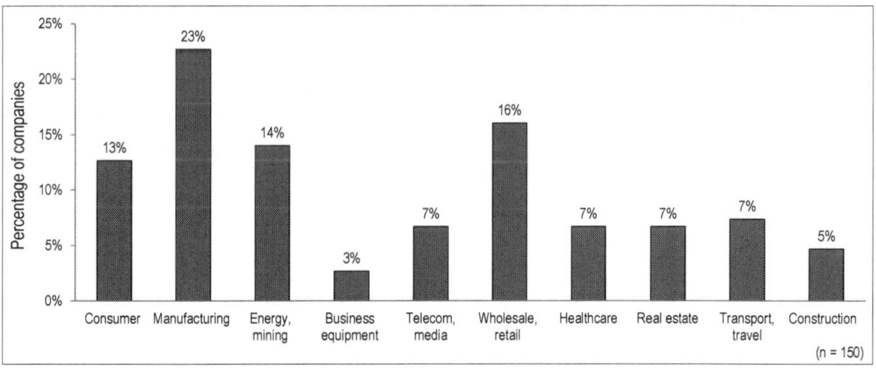

Figure 5-1: Industry composition of total sample

[823] Cf. *U.S. Small Business Administration* (2015).

[824] For this study's SIC code industry composition, cf. Appendix, Table A-2.

The largest category is manufacturing, which comprises 34 companies (23%). However, it is not surprising that the total sample's industry composition, as illustrated in Figure 5-1, does not match with the industry breakdown in each of the three countries. Figure 5-2 reveals that every economy is driven by different key industries. While the German economy is dominated by manufacturing businesses (particularly, from the automobile and chemical industry), a considerable number of Brazilian entities belong to the energy, wholesale and retail as well as real estate sectors. Besides wholesale and retail, manufacturing, consumer and mining are the key industries of the South African sample. The dominance of certain industries in the countries can also be explained by country characteristics. For instance, the wealth of natural resources allows extensive energy and mining activity in Brazil and South Africa.

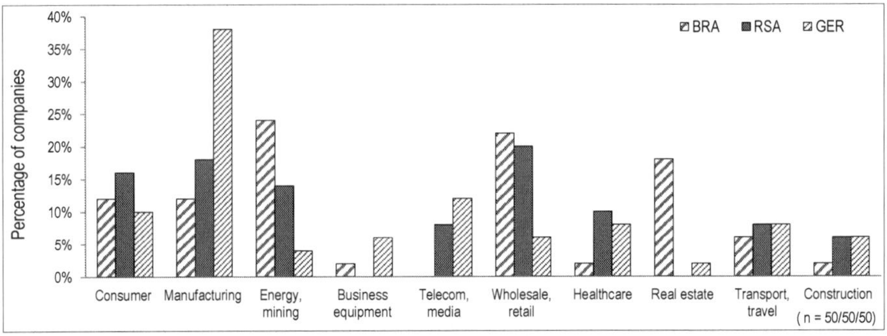

Figure 5-2: Industry composition of sample per country

With respect to this study's objective to compare emerging economies with developed countries, Figure 5-2 suggests characteristic industry compositions in the emerging economies Brazil and South Africa, on the one hand, and the industrialized Germany, on the other. It can be argued, for instance, that in highly developed countries, particularly specialized manufacturing and technology industries are capable of enhancing wealth, while the percentage of companies from such industries is lower in less developed economies. Instead, the share of companies from industries, such as wholesale and retail, consumer or mining is higher in the emerging economies of Brazil and South Africa than in Germany. Moreover, the rapid economic growth in emerging economies may directly boost both energy generation and the real estate business.

These trends are supported by the overall industry composition of listed non-financial companies in the three countries, as illustrated in Figure 5-3 which underpins that the selected samples are largely representative for the three countries' industry structures of listed companies. However, there are few deviations compared to the distribution of the sample industries. Although manufacturing with a share of about 25% is still the largest industry in Germany, the sample includes 38% manufacturing companies. Moreover, wholesale, retail and real estate are overrepresented in the Brazilian sample, while the business equipment sector is underrepresented in the samples of both South Africa and Germany. Apart from that, the relations are highly proportional to those in Figure 5-2.

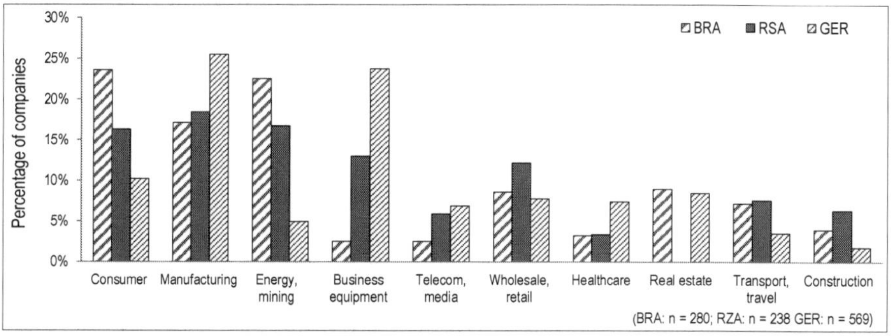

Figure 5-3: Overall industry composition of listed companies in Brazil, South Africa and Germany[825]

5.1.2.2 Company size

To further describe the companies included in the sample, the analysis of the entities' size is of particular interest. A company's size is not only associated with its importance to investors, the general society and other stakeholders, but researchers have also identified size as one of the key influencing factors for corporate financial reporting.[826] From a theoretical perspective, size correlates with complexity, which again causes agency costs according to the principal-agent theory.[827] Consequently, large companies could particularly strive to reduce complexity and agency costs through transparent corporate reporting. Moreover, as the size of an entity indicates its market power, the corresponding political and societal interest in the company can also give rise to political costs for the entity (positive accounting theory).[828] Thus, large companies could make increased efforts to provide information to these stakeholder groups and, thereby, lower political costs. Since there is no universal measure for company size, this section characterizes the sample by the four indicators market capitalization, total assets, total revenues and number of employees.[829]

The **market capitalization** of the sample companies, i.e. the value of the entities' shares, on 31 December 2013 reveals considerable heterogeneity between the companies from the emerging economies Brazil and South Africa, on the one hand, and from Germany, on the other. Figure 5-4 shows right-skewed distributions for the Brazilian and South African samples, where the majority of the companies have a market capitalization of less than

[825] Industry composition on 31 December 2013 retrieved from Thomson Reuters Datastream (excluding financial companies). In line with the South African sample selection, real estate companies from South Africa are excluded.

[826] For company size as a determinant of FRQ, cf. section 3.3.

[827] For the theoretical foundation of the principal-agent theory, cf. section 4.1.5.2.2.

[828] Cf. *Watts/Zimmerman* (1990), p. 139. For the theoretical foundation of the political cost theory, cf. section 4.1.5.3.

[829] Data for market capitalization, total assets, total revenues and number of employees on 31 December 2013 were primarily retrieved from Thomson Reuters Datastream and Compustat. Missing values were taken from the companies' annual reports. To guarantee comparability, all financial numbers are given in EUR. For currency translation, the following exchange rates on 31 December 2013 were used: BRL/EUR = 3.2510; ZAR/EUR = 14.4323 (Source: Thomson Reuters Datastream).

€ two billion. In contrast, all entities with a market capitalization of more than € 50 billion are in the German sample.

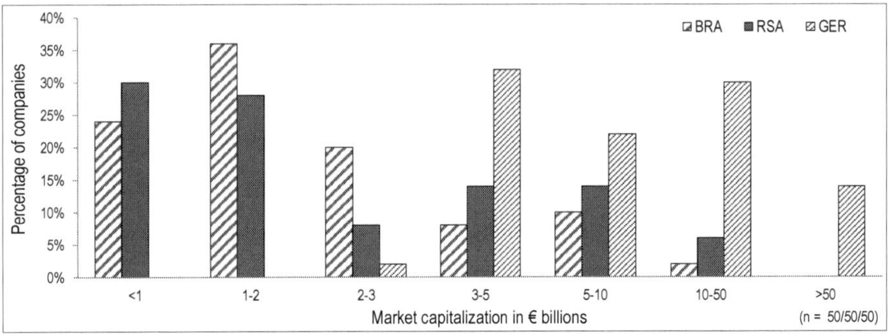

Figure 5-4: Distribution of sample companies' market capitalization per country

Furthermore, Table 5-2 provides additional insights into the sample's size characteristics in terms of market capitalization. The smallest company is *HRT Petroleo* (€ 83 million) from Brazil, whereas the largest one is the German automobile multinational *Volkswagen* (€ 92,904 million). While the medians of the Brazilian and South African samples are similar, the standard deviation of the South African sample (€ 5,976 million) is considerably higher than among the Brazilian entities (€ 2,332 million). This difference in variation between the two emerging economy samples is also illustrated by the fact that the South African 25% percentile and median are lower than the corresponding Brazilian numbers; however, South Africa has higher values regarding mean and 75% percentile. Thus, the South African sample includes a considerable number of both relatively small and large companies. Moreover, in all samples the mean value is above the median indicating that there are outliers with large market capitalizations. The market value dominance of the German sample is demonstrated by the fact that more than 75% of the Brazilian and South African entities have a lower market capitalization than the first quartile German company (25% percentile).

Sample	Min.	25% pctl.	Median	Mean	75% pctl.	Max.	Std. Dev.
Overall (n=150)	83	1,310	3,013	8,562	7,047	92,904	16,275
Brazil (n=50)	83	1,114	1,726	2,397	2,471	11,335	2,332
South Africa (n=50)	658	882	1,525	3,806	3,814	31,641	5,976
Germany (n=50)	2,949	4,260	7,587	19,483	27,231	92,904	23,950

Table 5-2: Description of sample companies' market capitalizations [in € millions]

In addition to market capitalization, Figure 5-5 shows the distribution of **total assets** on 31 December 2013 in the sample. The percentage of entities with total assets of less than € one billion is higher than the percentage of companies with market capitalization less than € one billion for the total sample. In more detail, there are more South African entities (42%), yet, less Brazilian companies (20%) compared to market capitalization.

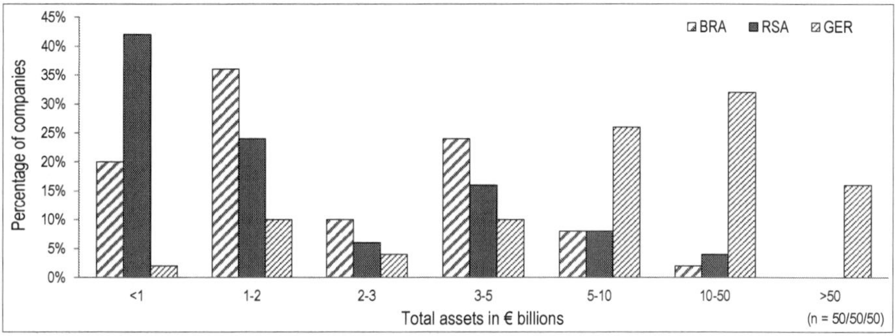

Figure 5-5: Distribution of sample companies' total assets per country

This indicates that South African companies with relatively low total assets tend to have higher market capitalizations than the corresponding Brazilian entities. Moreover, in terms of total assets, 16% of the German companies are classified into the three lower categories (less than € three billion), compared to 2% in terms of market capitalization. However, on the upper end of the distribution, there are even more German companies with total assets above € ten billion than in the market capitalization distribution.

In line with the above description, the statistics in Table 5-3 confirm that the standard deviation of total assets for the German sample is more than twice the standard deviation of market capitalization, while it is considerably lower for the South African companies. This suggests that there is no perfect correlation between the two size measures and, thus, a large amount of total assets is not generally necessary to reach a relatively high market value. Overall, also the total asset measure indicates that more than 75% of the Brazilian and South African sample companies are smaller than the German entities at the first quartile. While *Volkswagen* is also the largest company according to total assets, the entity with the smallest total assets is *Famous Brands*, a South African food service entity.

Sample	Min.	25% pctl.	Median	Mean	75% pctl.	Max.	Std. Dev.
Overall (n=150)	104	1,195	2,866	12,587	6,259	318,711	35,245
Brazil (n=50)	295	1,173	1,895	2,775	3,847	21,123	3,122
South Africa (n=50)	104	765	1,382	2,371	3,099	15,575	2,826
Germany (n=50)	791	4,656	9,686	32,614	32,349	318,711	55,742

Table 5-3: Description of sample companies' total assets [in € millions]

Furthermore, the companies' **total revenues** of the fiscal year characterize the size of the sample entities.[830] The distribution of revenues in the sample supports that there are massive size differences between the Brazilian and South African companies, on the one hand, and German ones, on the other (cf. Figure 5-6). However, the smaller half of the German sample is distributed similarly across all categories up to € ten billion, except for companies with less than € one billion (2%). Thus, these categories (between € 1 and € 10 billion) comprise numerous companies from both the emerging economies (Brazil and South Africa) and the developed Germany.

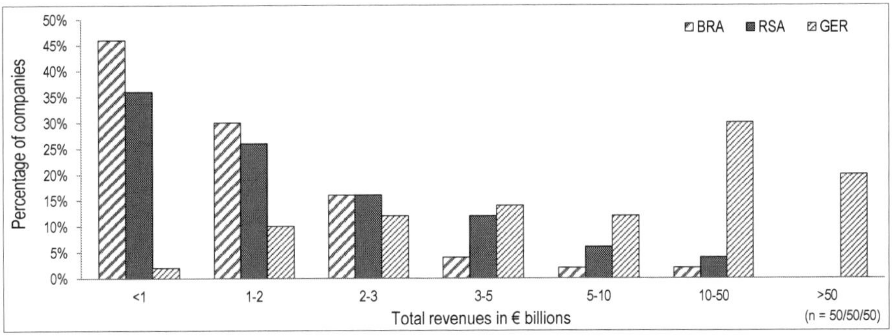

Figure 5-6: Distribution of sample companies' total revenues per country

Unlike suggested by the size measures market capitalization and total assets, most small companies with revenues of less than € one billion are from Brazil. Solely 8% of the Brazilian sample companies have revenues of more than € three billion, compared to 22% in the South African sample.

Table 5-4 indicates that *HRT Petroleo* is an extreme outlier in the sample with revenues of only € 1.48 million. Considering that the second largest company *EON* reports total revenues of € 122,450 million and only three entities reach a turnover of more than € 100,000 million, also *Volkswagen* is an outlier with revenues of € 197,007 million.

Sample	Min.	25% pctl.	Median	Mean	75% pctl.	Max.	Std. Dev.
Overall (n=150)	1	824	1,967	10,198	5,377	197,007	24,897
Brazil (n=50)	1	468	1,242	1,908	1,940	31,226	4,342
South Africa (n=50)	138	798	1,257	2,304	2,605	12,617	2,602
Germany (n=50)	603	2,961	10,432	26,384	34,638	197,007	37,960

Table 5-4: Description of sample companies' total revenues [in € millions]

830 In line with this study, revenues refer to fiscal years ended between 1 July 2013 and 30 June 2014. As revenue is a flow figure, currency translations are based on the average exchange rates: BRL/EUR = 2.9752; ZAR/EUR = 12.8091 (Source: Thomson Reuters Datastream).

Although the Brazilian companies are considerably smaller in the first quartile than the South African ones, the median and mean of both sub samples are relatively similar. The revenues of the median German company (€ 10,432 million) are more than 8 times higher than the median in the Brazilian and South African sub samples.

As non-financial indicator, total number of employees characterizes the sample from an additional perspective and, thus, relativizes conclusions from the proxies market capitalization, total assets and revenues.[831] For example, although the Brazilian company *BR Properties* has solely 77 employees, its total assets amount to € 4.8 billion (top 12% in the Brazilian sample). Hence, Figure 5-7 helps to comprehend a company's size and complexity. It further illustrates the range in employee numbers.

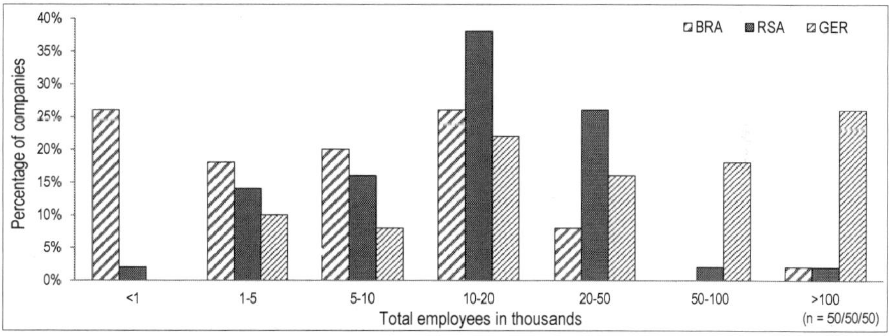

Figure 5-7: Distribution of sample companies' total employees per country

On the one hand, all sub samples include at least 10% of companies with less than 5,000 employees and, on the other hand, the largest entities employ more than 100,000 people in Brazil, South Africa and Germany.

Furthermore, Table 5-5 indicates that particularly the Brazilian sample includes small companies, as 25% of the companies have less than 925 employees. Compared to the other emerging economy, South Africa, the Brazilian entities are considerably smaller on average in spite of a higher maximum number by the largest entity.

Sample	Min.	25% pctl.	Median	Mean	75% pctl.	Max.	Std. Dev.
Overall (n=150)	22	5,919	12,607	38,001	28,765	563,000	78,540
Brazil (n=50)	22	925	6,252	11,825	12,355	185,000	26,383
South Africa (n=50)	183	7,617	12,558	18,154	23,906	106,371	18,565
Germany (n=50)	2,024	13,100	36,631	84,024	110,815	563,000	119,447

Table 5-5: Description of sample companies' total employees

831 Cf. *Blaesing* (2013), p. 143.

Table 5-5 further reveals that the variance in company size is even higher in Brazil than in South Africa, although the South African mean and median exceed the Brazilian numbers significantly. This underpins the large gap between small and large entities in Brazil. In terms of number of employees, the dominance of the German companies is still obvious, however, less pronounced. For instance, the German sample median is less than three times the South African median number and about six times the Brazilian median.

Being one of the most important determinants of FRQ according to prior literature, the analysis of the sample companies' sizes sheds light on an essential entity characteristic. It is obvious that the German sample includes considerably larger entities than the emerging economy samples. However, the distribution is not that clear between Brazil and South Africa. While South African entities are larger in terms of average market capitalization and number of employees, the Brazilian companies have higher values of total assets on average. The mean of revenues is similar for both sub samples. Overall, the size of the sample companies differs considerably both within each sub sample as well as across the three countries. Hence, statistical analyses have to control for company size.

The **correlation coefficients** of the four proxies for company size show medium and strong relations (cf. Table 5-6).[832] This suggests that all measures can be associated with company size. However, it might be worthwhile to use multiple proxies throughout the analyses and interpret these separately, as no correlation coefficients indicate perfect or very strong correlations of 0.8 or higher. The number of employees seems to be no adequate size proxy, as its correlations with the other measures are relatively low.

	Market capitalization	Total assets	Total revenues	Total employees
Market capitalization	1.000 -			
Total assets	0.675 *** (0.000)	1.000 -		
Total revenues	0.712 *** (0.000)	0.783 (0.000)	1.000 -	
Total employees	0.569 *** (0.000)	0.565 *** (0.000)	0.768 *** (0.000)	1.000 -

The table presents the Spearman correlation coefficients between the company size measures market capitalization, total assets, total revenues and total employees with p-values in parentheses for the total sample. *, ** and *** denote significance at the 10%, 5% and 1% level.

Table 5-6: Correlation analysis of different size measures for total sample

In addition to Table 5-6, the correlation coefficients for the country samples provide interesting insights. While the untabulated size proxy correlations for the German sub sample are relatively strong with significant values between 0.650 to 0.911 and the corresponding South African figures indicate significant medium relations on a stable level (between 0.409 and 0.662), the **size measures of the Brazilian sample** show interesting characteristics, as Table 5-7 reveals.

[832] For the interpretation of correlation coefficients, cf. section 5.3.3.2.

	Market capitalization	Total assets	Total revenues	Total employees
Market capitalization	1.000 -			
Total assets	0.206 (0.151)	1.000 -		
Total revenues	0.318 ** (0.024)	0.538 *** (0.000)	1.000 -	
Total employees	0.296 ** (0.037)	0.025 (0.862)	0.581 *** (0.000)	1.000 -

The table presents the Spearman correlation coefficients between the company size measures market capitalization, total assets, total revenues and total employees with p-values in parentheses for the Brazilian sample. *, ** and *** denote significance at the 10%, 5% and 1% level.

Table 5-7: Correlation analysis of different size measures for Brazilian sample

The correlations of the Brazilian size proxies differ fundamentally from those for South Africa and Germany. For instance, there is no significant association between a company's total assets and its market capitalization. Compared to the South African and German companies, Brazilian companies might be less dependent on assets to reach a high market capitalization. Only the medium relationships between total revenues and total assets (0.538) as well as between total revenues and total employees (0.581) are on a highly significant level ($p < 0.001$).

Based on the correlation analysis, total revenues appear to be the most appropriate size measure with pronounced correlations to the other size proxies and, therefore, are used in the empirical investigation. However, additional sensitivity analyses can apply the additional proxies to determine, whether the empirical results differ when using alternative size proxies (cf. sections 6.2.4). In particular, market capitalization is considered as alternative size proxy, as it is widely accepted as size measure in the literature.[833]

5.1.3 Research objects

After the selection and description of the 150 sample companies from Brazil, South Africa and Germany, this section determines the actual research objects in line with the study's research questions and developed hypotheses.

According to *Kromrey* (2009), research objects shall be (1) relevant for the study's purpose, (2) actually existing and (3) available.[834] As mentioned before, the study investigates the FRQ of sample companies on the basis of three FRQ measures. While the calculation of the accruals-based proxies uses **financials** retrieved from databases, both the disclosure index and the readability measure rely on the companies' **annual reports** for the financial year 2013 as research objects. While the disclosure index study analyzes the entire annual report, the readability measure particularly uses the **CEO/management's letter** to the

833 Cf. among others *Hail* (2002), p. 758; *Wang et al.* (2008), p. 21; *Loughran/McDonald* (2014), p. 1652.

834 Cf. *Kromrey* (2009), p. 317.

shareholders[835] in the annual reports as research object. Numerous prior studies provide evidence that these letters are important parts of the annual report, which are read thoroughly by investors and financial analysts and are able to influence their decisions.[836] The letters to the shareholders are not subject to regulation.[837] The management, therefore, "*[...] may use them strategically to manage the impressions shareholders have of the company.*"[838] Thus, managers are free to present voluntary information in coherent sentences using their characteristic language. Overall, a poor CEO/management's letter is assumed to "*[...] undermine the quality of financial reporting.*"[839] Hence, the textual sections of the CEO/management's letter to the shareholders allow cross-country comparisons and, therefore, are appropriate research objects to analyze FRQ in terms of readability.

Capital market participants as well as other (potential) interest groups of a company have several **sources of information**. To substantiate capital allocation decisions, investors and financial analysts, for instance, "*[...] might observe returns, study press releases, study the firm's principal industries, read the reports of other analysts, or chat with employees of the firm.*"[840] Within this *toolbox* of information instruments the **annual report** takes a special position, as the following statement by *Knutson* (1993) shows:

> "*At the top of every analyst's list (of financial reports used by analysts) is the annual report to shareholders. It is the major reporting document and every other financial report is in some respect subsidiary or supplementary to it.*"[841]

In line with the notion by *Knutson* (1993), a company's information in its annual report is found to be positively associated with disclosures by other reporting instruments.[842] Therefore, the investigation of the one reporting instrument *annual report* may serve as a measure of the overall disclosure level.[843] Also other researchers regard the annual report as "*the major medium*"[844] of corporate communication.[845] Particularly in emerging economies, where financial analysts may be less influential than in countries with more developed capital markets, annual reports may be the main source of information for investors.[846] Annual reports used to be regarded as a company's "*business card*"[847]. In fact, annual reports contain considerably more information than the mere contact details of a

---

835 If not available, the board's letter to the shareholders is used as research object.

836 Cf. emongst others *Bartlett/Chandler* (1997); *Baird/Zelin* (2000); *Hooghiemstra* (2010).

837 Cf. *Hooghiemstra* (2010), p. 275.

838 *Hooghiemstra* (2010), p. 275.

839 *Hooghiemstra* (2010), p. 277.

840 *Barry/Brown* (1985), p. 413.

841 *Knutson* (1993), p. 7.

842 Cf. *Lang/Lundholm* (1993), p. 258.

843 Cf. *Botosan* (1997), p. 329.

844 *Firth* (1979), p. 273.

845 Cf. amongst others *Firth* (1979), p. 273; *SRI International* (1987), p. 4-5; *Lang/Lundholm* (1993), p. 258; *Botosan* (1997), p. 331.

846 Cf. *Chen et al.* (2011), p. 1259.

847 *Baetge/Kirchhoff* (1997), p. 17.

company and can rather be seen as the description of an entity by its management including a multitude of detailed information.[848]

Although the structure of annual reports differs across countries and companies, some elements have been established as typical **components** of annual reports. In addition to financial statements and the CEO/management's letter, this study's analyzed annual reports include a management reporting section, which is used by the management to comment on the company's business activities. While there is a single annual report document for the South African and German sample companies, the annual report information of the Brazilian entities is provided in two documents. Thus, the research objects for the Brazilian sample consist of both the annual financial report and the *CVM* annual report (Reference Form).[849] The annual reports of the sample companies have been published in English and were available as PDF documents on the companies' websites.[850]

In light of the objective of the study, **annual reports** have several advantages over other research objects. First, all companies publish such reports annually on a **regular** basis, whereas irregular ad-hoc announcements of publicly traded companies, for instance, are less comparable between entities.[851] Second, companies use the annual report as a major reporting instrument and provide both mandatory and voluntary information on different reporting areas. While financial statements are prepared in accordance with **regulation**, management reporting leaves room for **voluntary** information.[852] Third, annual reports generally include both quantitative and qualitative information. **Quantitative** information (e.g., earnings per share) is particularly shown in the financial statements. Although there is only a fine line between quantitative and **qualitative** content, the latter is usually associated with verbal descriptions of, for example, corporate objectives or governance structures, but also verbal accounting explanations in the notes belong to the category of qualitative information. Finally, annual reports are not only concerned with the company's previous fiscal year, but also provide **forward-looking** information which is of particular interest to investors and other users. While the financial statements present information on the company's activities during the past financial year and may at most give indirect indications of the future development, the management report typically contains prospective information.[853]

5.1.4 Annual report characteristics

In line with the study's objective to provide an up-to-date description of financial reporting practice, the most recent available annual reports have been analyzed. Hence, the study investigates annual reports with **end of fiscal year** between 1 July 2013 and 30 June

848 Cf. *Baetge et al.* (2012), p. 59; *Pellens et al.* (2014), p. 949.

849 Cf. section 2.3.2.

850 Some entities also offer free print versions of their annual reports.

851 Cf. here and in the following *Pellens et al.* (2014), p. 949-950.

852 *Wagenhofer/Ewert* (2015) use the term *value reporting* or *business reporting* to refer to voluntary reporting in addition to the financial statements, which provides additional information for investors' company evaluations, cf. *Wagenhofer/Ewert* (2015), p. 13 and 356.

853 Cf. *Fink et al.* (2013), p. 3; *Freiberg* (2013), p. 59; *Pellens et al.* (2014), p. 950.

2014. As Figure 5-8 shows, the financial years of two thirds of the 150 companies end on 31 December 2013 including all Brazilian sample companies. 19 entities have fiscal years ending before this date and 31 choose a fiscal year end date in the first half of 2014, of which 16 South African companies have their balance sheet date on 30 June 2014.

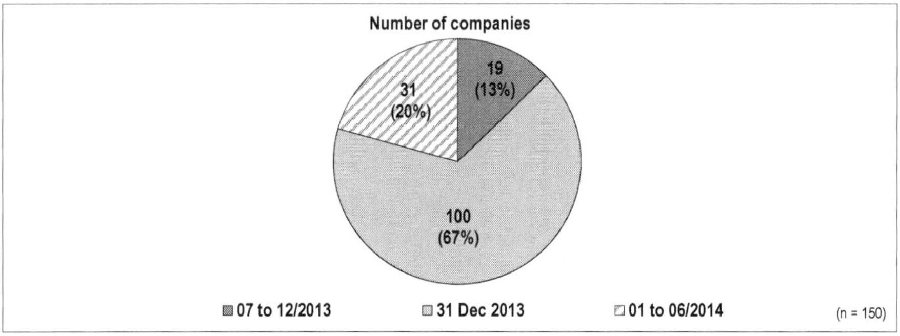

Figure 5-8: Fiscal year ends of sample companies

Regardless of a company's fiscal year end, agency theory suggests that users of annual reports attempt to obtain the information as soon as possible to use it as a basis for their decisions. Table 5-8 shows that the sample companies published their annual reports about 68 days on average after their balance sheet dates. Although eleven companies published their annual reports more than 100 days after their fiscal year ends, the standard deviation of 18.49 is relatively low. However, the Brazilian entities provide the report about 10 days earlier on average than those of the South African sample. German companies publish their annual reports on average about seven days earlier than the South African counterparts. As potential explanation, the integrated reporting design of the South African reports might be responsible for the extended period of report preparation, as integrated reports include information from various areas (e.g., sustainability) and the collection of this information may take additional time.

	Overall (n=137)	Brazil (n=37)[854]	South Africa (n=50)	Germany (n=50)
Days until publication	68.33	63.35	73.78	66.56

Table 5-8: Average number of days between end of financial year and publication of annual report

Almost all companies in the sample begin their annual reports with CEO/management's letters to the shareholders or statements and comments by the supervisory board. However, the overall structure of the annual reports differs across the countries. The **German annual reports** include, besides consolidated financial statements, group management reports which are required by HGB. Although there is no standardized structure, most

[854] The analysis refers to publication dates of the Brazilian annual financial reports. However, the date of publication was not available for 13 Brazilian companies.

reports label the sections of the management report according to the reporting topics required by HGB and GAS 20 (e.g., outlook, sustainability, risks and opportunities).[855]

The fact that the **South African** companies in the sample publish annual **integrated reports** also affects the structure of the reports. The majority of the South African sample follows the recommendations by the *IIRC* and the fourth generation of *GRI* Guidelines. Consequently, some of the recommended sections are found in most South African reports, such as *About this report, Scope of the report, Group profile* or an index showing where to find certain information in the report.

As mentioned above, the research object of the **Brazilian** sample consists of both the annual financial report and the CVM Reference Form. The **annual financial report** comprises, inter alia, the company's financial statements including the notes as well as a management report with qualitative and quantitative information on different issues in a non-standardized way. Further, the **Reference Form** has a standardized structure as required by the *CVM*.

5.2 Methodology of financial reporting quality measures

5.2.1 Accruals-based earnings management measure

5.2.1.1 Magnitude of accruals

As outlined in section 2.1.3, the accounting literature provides multiple indirect proxies to measure FRQ.[856] This study uses two accruals-based earnings management proxies: (1) the magnitude of accruals measure following *Leuz et al.* (2003) and (2) a modified version of the discretionary accruals model by *Jones* (1991) following *Kothari et al.* (2005). Researchers argue that earnings management reduces the decision usefulness of financial reporting information and, therefore, overall FRQ.[857] Both of this study's proxies are **discretionary accruals** models, which attempt "*[...] to investigate the manipulation of accruals to achieve earnings management goals [...].*"[858] Discretionary accruals arise when managers use the flexibility of financial reporting regulation to exert discretion and, thus, manage the company's earnings.[859] Hence, discretionary accruals models "*[...] focus on the opportunistic use of accruals to window-dress and mislead users of financial statements*"[860] *(opportunistic view).*[861]

The **magnitude of accruals proxy** (MACCR) measures the extent to which entities use discretion in their reported earnings.[862] *Leuz et al.* (2003) calculate this earnings discretion

[855] Cf. GAS 20.

[856] Cf. amongst others *Biddle et al.* (2009); *van Beest et al.* (2009); *Chen et al.* (2011); *Tang et al.* (2012); *Ma* (2012).

[857] Cf. *van Beest et al.* (2009), p. 6.

[858] *Dechow/Dichev* (2002), p. 36. For details on discretionary accruals, cf. section 2.1.3.

[859] Cf. *Dechow et al.* (2010), p. 358.

[860] *Dechow/Dichev* (2002), p. 36.

[861] For details on discretionary accruals, cf. section 2.1.3.

[862] Cf. here and in the following *Leuz et al.* (2003), p. 510.

measure as the ratio of the absolute value of accruals and the absolute value of the cash flow from operations (cf. equation (5.1)). Higher scores of the measure indicate more earnings management. Differences between companies (e.g., in company size or performance) are controlled for through scaling by the cash flow from operations.

$$(5.1)\quad MACCR_{i,t} = |TACCR_{i,t}|/|CFO_{i,t}|$$

where,

$TACCR_{i,t}$ = total accruals in year *t* for company *i*; and

$CFO_{i,t}$ = cash flow from operations in year *t* for company *i*.

Following *Hribar/Collins* (2002), this study computes total accruals directly from the statement of cash flows as earnings before extraordinary items and discontinued operations less cash flow from operations (cf. equation (5.2)).[863] *Hribar/Collins* (2002) show that this approach results in less noisy and less biased estimates than taking total accruals from the balance sheet (as proposed e.g. in the model by *Jones* (1991)). They argue that the balance sheet approach is based on the assumption that changes in the working capital accounts (balance sheet) are always linked to changes in the accrual component of revenues and expenses (income statement). This link, however, does not hold true when extraordinary events occur, such as reclassifications, acquisitions and divestures.

$$(5.2)\quad TACCR_i = EBXI_i - CFO_i$$

where,

$EBXI_i$ = earnings before extraordinary items and discontinued operations for company *i*; and

CFO_i = cash flow from operations for company *i*.

5.2.1.2 Modified-Jones model

The study's second accruals-based proxy is a modified version of the *Jones* (1991) model as defined by *Kothari et al.* (2005). The **original model** by *Jones* (1991) was the first approach to estimate discretionary accruals based on the notion that accruals are a linear function of revenue growth and property plant and equipment (PPE).[864] Revenue is an objective measure of the company's operations affecting accounts receivables, assets, payables and inventory (working capital accruals) and assumed to be relatively robust towards management manipulations.[865] In addition, PPE influences the part of total accruals, which is associated with nondiscretionary depreciation expense.[866] Thus, *Jones* (1991) uses

[863] Cf. here and in the following *Hribar/Collins* (2002), p. 106, 109 and 133.

[864] Cf. *Jones* (1991), p. 211; *Stubben* (2010), p. 698; *Kamarudin/Wan Ismail* (2014), p. 4-5.

[865] Cf. *Kamarudin/Wan Ismail* (2014), p. 4.

[866] Cf. *Kamarudin/Wan Ismail* (2014), p. 5.

changes in revenues and PPE to control for changes in nondiscretionary accruals, which are caused by changes in the entity's economic environment.[867] The regression residuals represent the discretionary accruals which cannot be explained by the variables of the economic environment. The *Jones* (1991) model has affected subsequent accrual models, as most of them are a variation of the model defined in equation (5.3).[868] All variables are scaled by total assets in t-1 to mitigate heteroskedasticity in residuals.[869]

$$(5.3) \quad TACCR_{i,t} = \alpha_0 + \alpha_1(\Delta REV_{i,t}) + \alpha_2(PPE_{i,t}) + \varepsilon_{i,t}$$

where,

$TACCR_{i,t}$ = total accruals in year *t* for company *i*;

$\Delta REV_{i,t}$ = revenues in year *t* less revenues in year *t-1* for company *i*;

$PPE_{i,t}$ = property, plant, and equipment in year *t* for company *i*; and

$\varepsilon_{i,t}$ = error term in year *t* for company *i*.

However, the described model has been subject to controversial discussion in the literature. In particular, *Dechow et al.* (1995) criticize the assumption that discretion is not exercised over revenues.[870] They argue that management is in fact able to exercise discretion to accrue revenues at the end of the fiscal year (no cash-in yet) and it would be disputable when revenues have to be recognized. This could result in an increase in both revenues and total accruals. To address this shortcoming, *Dechow et al.* (1995) modify the original *Jones* (1991) model as follows:

$$(5.4) \quad TACCR_{i,t} = \alpha_0 + \alpha_1(\Delta REV_{i,t} - \Delta REC_{i,t}) + \alpha_2(PPE_{i,t}) + \varepsilon_{i,t}$$

where,

$\Delta REC_{i,t}$ = net receivables in year *t* less net receivables in year *t-1* for company *i*; and

all other variables as defined above.[871]

The modified model by *Dechow et al.* (1995) subtracts change in accounts receivables from the change in revenues. Thus, the model is able to measure discretionary accruals adequately, even if companies manage earnings over revenues due to this modification. It is based on the assumption that earnings management is the reason for all changes in cred-

867 Cf. *Jones* (1991), p. 211.

868 *Jones* (1991) calculates total accruals as follows: *TACCR* = change in current assets - change in cash - change in current liabilities - depreciation and amortization expense.

869 Cf. *Kothari et al.* (2005), p. 173.

870 Cf. here and in the following *Dechow et al.* (1995), p. 199. Moreover, critics argue that the model by *Jones* (1991) suffers from errors in measurement and omitted variables leading to low statistical explanatory power, cf. *Christodoulou/Sarafidis* (2008), p. 2-5; *Dechow et al.* (2010), p. 358-359.

871 All variables are scaled by total assets in t-1.

it sales in the regarded period, as "*[...] it is easier to manage earnings by exercising discretion over the recognition of revenue on credit sales than it is to manage earnings by exercising discretion over the recognition of revenue on cash sales.*"[872]

The second accruals-based proxy of this study is the **modified-Jones model** as defined by *Kothari et al.* (2005) with an adjustment for the change in receivables as posited by *Dechow et al.* (1995). As illustrated in equation (5.5), *Kothari et al.* (2005) add a constant to the model by *Dechow et al.* (1995) to include an additional control for heteroskedasticity and to mitigate potential problems due to an omitted size variable.[873] Moreover, they argue "*[...] that discretionary accrual measures based on models without a constant term are less symmetric, making power of the test comparisons less clear-cut.*"[874]

$$(5.5) \quad TACCR_{i,t} = \alpha_0 + \alpha_1(1/TA_{i,t-1}) + \alpha_2(\Delta REV_{i,t} - \Delta REC_{i,t}) + \alpha_3(PPE_{i,t}) + \varepsilon_{i,t}$$

where,

$TACCR_{i,t}$ = total accruals for company *i* in year *t* (calculated as in equation (5.2));

$TA_{i,t-1}$ = total assets for company *i* in year *t-1*; and

all other variables as defined above.[875]

The discretionary accruals of each sample company for the financial year 2013 are the entities' residuals of the cross-sectional regressions per industry.[876] Moreover, the regression input variables are winsorized at the 1st and 99th percentiles to mitigate the influence of outliers.[877] Since the discretionary accruals are regression residuals, their average is zero by construction. Consistent with prior research, the calculation of the cross-sectional regressions per industry is based on a large sample to adequately capture industry effects. The study conducts the modified-Jones model using a universe comprising 949 listed companies from Brazil, South Africa and Germany, whose regression data are available on Thomson Reuters Datastream (including this study's 150 sample companies). The discretionary accruals are calculated for the entire sample to allow cross-country comparisons.

When interpreting the results of the accruals model, **unsigned** and **signed discretionary accruals** can be distinguished.[878] The latter show the direction of earnings management activities and, thus, indicate upward and downward earnings management (e.g., due to conservative accounting policy). Unsigned discretionary accruals equal the absolute value of the computed discretionary accruals. In line with the literature, this study views "*[...] upward and downward earnings management as equally problematic and, hence, rel[ies] on*

872 *Dechow et al.* (1995), p. 199.
873 Cf. *Kothari et al.* (2005), p. 173-174.
874 *Kothari et al.* (2005), p. 173.
875 All variables are scaled by total assets in t-1.
876 Cf. *Kothari et al.* (2005), p. 173. For the industry classification, cf. section 5.1.2.1.
877 Cf. *Stubben* (2010), p. 702.
878 Cf. here and in the following *Meyer* (2009), p. 35; *Epps/Guthrie* (2010), p. 69.

the absolute value of discretionary accruals."[879] Hence, the unsigned discretionary accruals are used as FRQ proxy. In line with *Kothari et al.* (2005), the calculated discretionary accruals are further multiplied by 100 for analysis.

5.2.2 Disclosure index measure

5.2.2.1 Basis of content analysis

Empirical investigations have a number of possibilities to obtain data on the research objects, such as, inter alia, surveys, data bases, experiments, interviews as well as content analyses.[880] In addition to the accruals-based proxy of FRQ, this study applies a self-constructed disclosure index and conducts a content analysis on the basis of this disclosure index to measure the quality of annual report information. This is considered a more direct approach of FRQ measurement than the accruals-based proxies.[881] In contrast to reactive research methods (e.g. surveys and interviews) which are frequently used in the literature to evaluate reporting quality, the content analysis belongs to the group of **non-reactive research techniques**, because the research subjects are unaware of being studied.[882] Hence, the results do not depend on the reactions and subjective evaluations of the survey participants and interviewees. Researchers prefer non-reactive methods over reactive ones, since no undue influence is able to distort the data during the collection process and the data sources are not able manipulate the data. Furthermore, content analysis is a fast-growing technique in quantitative research, as the use of computers have made content analyses *"quicker and easier"*[883]. Regarding this study, content analysis is further a convenient way to collect the data, as the annual reports are publicly available and can be examined at any time.

Although the literature provides plenty of definitions of content analysis, the following one, found by *Holsti* (1969), gets to the heart of this study:

> "*Content analysis is a phase of information-processing in which communication content is transformed, through objective and systematic application of categorization rules, into data that can be summarized and compared.*"[884]

Applying the definition to this study, the content analysis aims at processing the information provided in the corporate communication instrument *annual report*. As **categorization rules**, also referred to as "*system of categories*"[885], the investigation uses a comprehensive disclosure index which comprises the financial reporting aspects to be examined throughout the content analysis. A detailed set of consistent rules and procedures reduces the bias due to judgments by the researchers **(objectivity)**.[886] However, judgments can

---

[879] *Cahan* (2014), p. 121.
[880] Cf. *Krippendorff* (2013), p. 45.
[881] Cf. section 2.1.3.
[882] Cf. here and in the following *Krippendorff* (2013), p. 45-46.
[883] *Neuendorf* (2002), p. 1.
[884] Quoted from *Holsti* (1969), p. 3.
[885] *Krippendorff* (2013), p. 150.
[886] Cf. *Holsti* (1969), p. 3.

never be eliminated, as every content analysis requires researchers to decide whether a certain content has to be placed in category *A* or *B*. True objectivity can also not be achieved, because a *fact* is based on the socially agreed consensus by researchers.[887] In contrast to "*subjective analyst disclosure quality rankings*"[888] based on assessments by experts, *Beattie et al.* (2004) refer to disclosure index-based content analysis (as in this study) as a "*semi-objective approach*"[889]. Moreover, the a priori design of the disclosure index is in line with the requirement of objectivity. The researcher has to make all decisions (e.g., on coding rules) before the beginning of the actual data collection.[890] With respect to objectivity, it is further necessary to distinguish between **idiographic** and **nomothetic** research.[891] Nomothetic studies, such as this one, typically investigate multiple cases to identify generalizable and objective results. Idiographic approaches rather focus on a single phenomenon providing unique conclusions which are non-generalizable and subjective.

Furthermore, the content analysis of annual reports requires the **systematic** classification of information relevant to the research question on the basis of the disclosure index.[892] In line with the above definition, it is a primary objective of this investigation to **summarize** the main aspects of the examined annual reports. In accordance with the nomothetic approach, this allows the identification of generalizable conclusions through breaking down the large number of observations based on the disclosure index. In contrast, an idiographic research approach would rather focus "*[...] on a full and precise conclusion about a particular case [...].*"[893] Furthermore, the study's research questions put emphasis on **comparisons** within and across the selected country samples and, thus, the investigation aims at comparing the results of the content analysis. In line with *Berelson* (1971), who argues that by "*[...] definition content analysis calls for the quantification of content elements [...]*"[894], this study's content analysis transforms narrative text into a quantitative form to obtain a measure of FRQ, which can be statistically analyzed and compared.[895] Therefore, the disclosure index determines a coding scheme which assigns a certain amount of points to predefined disclosure contents.

In addition to the above definition, *Merten* (1995) does not solely regard content analysis as a research technique to obtain summarized data, but also posits the objective to, thereby, investigate the "*social reality*"[896]. Using the term *social*, he does not only refer to the

---

887 Cf. *Neuendorf* (2002), p. 11.

888 *Beattie et al.* (2004), p. 207.

889 *Beattie et al.* (2004), p. 208.

890 Cf. *Neuendorf* (2002), p. 11.

891 Cf. here and in the following *Neuendorf* (2002), p. 11.

892 *Krippendorff* (2013) subsumes the criteria objective and systematic under the requirements of replicability and validity, cf. *Krippendorff* (2013), p. 25. In this study, replicability is seen as a sub criterion of reliability. This study assesses the quality of the content analysis on the basis of both reliability and validity, cf. section 5.2.2.2.

893 *Neuendorf* (2002), p. 15.

894 *Berelson* (1971), p. 135. Although numerous researchers support this view (cf. e.g. *Kassarjian* (1977), p. 10; *Neuendorf* (2002), p. 10.), also qualitative content analysis techniques are described in the literature. For qualitative content analyses, cf. *Atteslander* (2010), p. 182.

895 Cf. *Milne/Adler* (1999), p. 237.

896 *Merten* (1995), p. 85.

social action of text preparation, which is always intended for particular recipients, but also to the fact that the text allows to draw inferences about the social context of the preparers of the text.[897] Figure 5-9 illustrates *Merten's* view that the underlying social reality can never be captured purely through content analysis, as surveys and observations transfer relevant aspects to the symbolic reality first (through writing). Since content analysis, in a next step, transforms the symbolic reality into data, it could be regarded as secondary research instrument.[898]

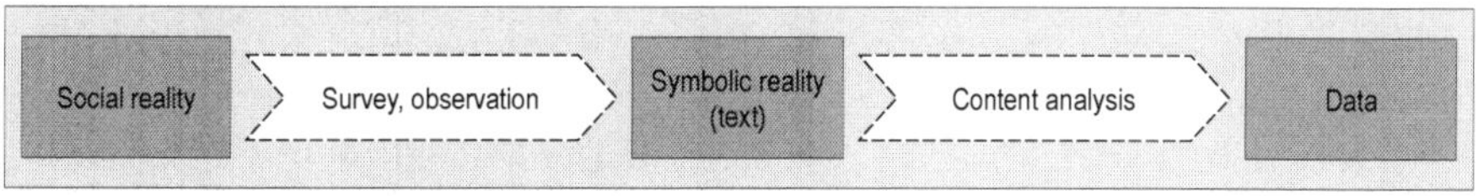

Figure 5-9: Levels of data collection
Following *Merten* (1995), p. 86.

Following *Merten's* understanding, *Atteslander* (2010) develops a social communication model and posits the explicit objective of content analyses to draw conclusions about both the origination and use of the analyzed text.[899] Also this study pursues this objective by conducting a content analysis on the basis of a disclosure index. The general steps of the content analysis are presented in the following.

The process of content analysis comprises up to nine different steps.[900] (1) Before the beginning of the actual analysis the researcher has to specify **theory** and **rationale** for the content analysis. With respect to this study, the content analysis is used to test hypotheses derived from the theoretical foundation and, thereby, elaborate on this study's research questions. (2) Second, variables used in the study are selected and defined (**conceptualizations**). This study's main variable is the construct of FRQ. (3) To **operationalize** the defined variables, proxies need to be selected, which shall match the conceptualizations. (4) The **coding scheme** differs depending on whether human or computer coding is applied. While both methods require a codebook including the explanation of all variable measures and transformation rules, a coding form is solely necessary for the human coding approach to write down observations. This study's coding scheme is based on the disclosure index' content categories which are presented in section 5.2.2.4. The disclosure index is complete, because all relevant text passages can be assigned to exactly one content category. This requires that the contents of (sub) categories do not overlap.[901] Information beyond the research questions have to be excluded from the disclosure index.[902] (5) The **sampling** process selects (e.g., randomly) a subset of units which shall be analyzed from the larger population.[903] This study's content analysis studies the annual reports of the

---

[897] Cf. here and in the following *Merten* (1995), p. 85-87.

[898] However, content analysis is commonly only referred to the process of directly analyzing a certain text and, thus, suggested to be a primary research instrument, cf. *Merten* (1995), p. 87.

[899] Cf. *Atteslander* (2010), p. 196.

[900] Cf. here and in this paragraph *Neuendorf* (2002), p. 50-51.

[901] Cf. *Kromrey* (2009), p. 314-315.

[902] Cf. *Rössler* (2010), p. 101; *Blaesing* (2013), p. 154.

[903] Cf. *Neuendorf* (2002), p. 83.

sample companies (selected in section 5.1.1). (6) During a **training and test** phase the researchers check, whether or not the coding can be done consistently and adjust the codebook or coding form if necessary. This is particularly important, if multiple researchers perform the (7) **coding**. This coding can be performed by either a computer-based approach or by human coding.[904] Computer-based approaches examine disclosures using machine learning algorithms.[905] Although computer-based approaches require less labor resources and can analyze a larger sample size than the human coding method,[906] this study uses the manual approach which has important advantages. Language can be complex and relevant information might be presented in multiple manners.[907] In addition, users of annual reports may encounter similar problems as the coder so that the approach is authentic. (8) If there is more than one coder, a **reliability figure** (e.g., relation between observed agreement and expected agreement[908]) can be calculated. (9) Finally, the possibilities to **report** the content analysis results depend, inter alia, on the used variables and feasible statistical methods (e.g., bivariate and/or multivariate techniques).

At the end of the content analysis process, the results are supposed to be both reliable as well as valid. The following section sheds light on these two central criteria of content analyses.

5.2.2.2 Reliability and validity of content analyses

To assess the quality of a research instrument both its reliability and its validity are important criteria. According to *Krippendorff* (2013):

> "*Content analysis is a research technique for making replicable and valid inferences from texts (or other meaningful matter) to the contexts of their use.*"[909]

He further specifies that a reliable research technique is supposed to provide replicable findings and, thus: "*Replicability is the most important form of reliability.*"[910] *Merten* (1995) subsumes **reliability** under *internal validity*, as it only refers to the quality of the measuring instrument, whereas *external validity* means that the analysis results correspond with social reality.[911] Concerning reliability, *Merten* distinguishes intersubjective reliability, temporal reliability and instrumental reliability.[912] According to the definition of **intersubjective reliability**, a research technique should still measure what it is supposed to

---

904 Cf. here and in the following *Milne/Adler* (1999), p. 243.

905 Cf. *Lerchenmüller* (2012), p. 20. For example, *Al-Najjar/Abed* (2014) evaluate the quality of voluntary forward-looking information in narrative sections of annual reports by automated keyword searches. For an overview of studies using computer-based methods, see *Lerchenmüller* (2012), p. 156-157.

906 Cf. *Beattie/Thomson* (2007), p. 140.

907 Cf. *Milne/Adler* (1999), p. 243; *Lerchenmüller* (2012), p. 16.

908 Cf. *Holsti* (1969), p. 140. For a detailed description of reliability figures, cf. amongst others *Holsti* (1969), p. 135-142; *Merten* (1995), p. 304-310.

909 *Krippendorff* (2013), p. 24.

910 *Krippendorff* (2013), p. 24.

911 Cf. here and in the following *Merten* (1995), p. 302-303.

912 Although largely following the argumentation of *Merten* (1995), *Krippendorff* (2013) uses the terms replicability, stability and accuracy instead of intersubjective reliability, temporal reliability and instrumental reliability, cf. *Krippendorff* (2013), p. 270-271.

measure, if it is conducted by different researchers (replicability). As the content analysis of this investigation is only coded by the author himself, the results are not biased by judgments of other coders. In contrast to intersubjective reliability, **temporal reliability** requires constant results, if the content analysis is repeated over time using the same research instrument (stability).[913] In particular, content analyses which code a large number of texts may be conducted over an extended period of time and, thus, run the risk that the results at the beginning differ from those at the end, e.g. due to fatigue or learning effects.[914] To guarantee stability of results in this study, the coding scheme has been tested using ten randomly selected annual reports from all sample companies so that the code book and coding form could be improved on the basis of this pretest. Additionally, the analyses of the first five annual reports of each country have been repeated at the end. Since the results of the re-collected data do not differ from those of the initial analysis, stability is assumed. **Instrumental reliability** describes a measuring technique's precision and effects of potential changes of the instrument (accuracy). *Krippendorff* (2013) refers to it as "*[...] the degree to which a process conforms to its specifications and yields what it is designed to yield.*"[915] To avoid inaccuracies during the coding process, this content analysis is based on an objective category system (disclosure index) and a code book including precise descriptions of each disclosure index item. Moreover, illustrative examples were determined for each item during the pretest.

In general, **validity** of a research instrument refers to the match between what the instrument shall measure (i.e., the social reality) and what it in fact measures.[916] While the above described reliability, as part of internal validity, focuses on the measuring process, external validity means that the entire results of the content analysis are valid. Therefore, reliability is a necessary, however, not sufficient condition for validity. However, it is not possible to verify validity, but only to falsify it through critical argumentation. If no objections to the validity of a research technique are raised, its validity can be assumed.[917] Consequently, external validity is also referred to as *generalizability*, as it is a prerequisite to extrapolate results to other settings or times.[918] Regarding this disclosure index study, valid results of the financial reporting measure are required to test the formulated hypotheses appropriately. To examine the external validity of the disclosure index measures, the results are compared to those of prior disclosure research, which investigate the same research subjects. The fact that other studies find similar disclosure quality levels for the sample companies (e.g., regarding the ranking of the companies within one country) indicates that the results of the content analysis are valid. Moreover, the consistency of the results across both disclosure index categories and across country samples suggests external validity.

913 Cf. *Merten* (1995), p. 303; *Neuendorf* (2002), p. 163.
914 Cf. *Blaesing* (2013), p. 163.
915 *Krippendorff* (2013), p. 271.
916 Cf. here and in the following *Merten* (1995), p. 310-311; *Krippendorff* (2013), p. 269.
917 Cf. *Zimmermann* (1972), p. 79.
918 Cf. *Neuendorf* (2002), p. 115.

5.2.2.3 Self-construction of disclosure index

As mentioned above, this study's content analysis uses a comprehensive disclosure index to analyze the contents of the sample companies' annual reports. According to *Hassan/Marston* (2010)

> "*[...] a disclosure index is a research instrument to measure the extent of information reported in a particular disclosure vehicle(s) by a particular entity(s) according to a list of selected items of information.*"[919]

Although the accounting literature uses such disclosure indices extensively, their construction differs greatly. In particular, variations occur regarding the degree of researcher involvement and the selected disclosure items included in the indices.[920] The **researcher involvement** depends on the extent to which the researcher selects and evaluates items.[921] No involvement means that indices from prior research or external organizations are used, whereas a fully involved researcher controls the entire construction process from the selection of disclosure items to scoring them.

This study uses a new **self-constructed disclosure index** to measure the FRQ of companies from Brazil, South Africa and Germany for several reasons. First, the results of adequate prior disclosure indices are not available for the selected sample companies in the investigated period or they focus on other research objects than the entire annual report (e.g., the chairman's statement, online publications, ad-hoc announcements or standalone sustainability reports).[922] Second, existing indices are affected by the **specific setting** which they are constructed for. For example, the disclosure indices *DSCORE* by *Botosan* (1997) or *Brazilian Disclosure Index* by *Lopes/de Alencar* (2010) cannot be applied in this study, since they are designed for particular research settings and are not sufficiently comprehensive for this study's research objective. Moreover, particularly older disclosure indices do not adequately capture recent financial reporting trends, such as sustainability disclosures or management commentary sections in annual reports.[923] Third, a self-constructed disclosure index allows capturing exactly those reporting (sub) categories and items which shall be analyzed within the chosen setting. This study's approach to construct a disclosure index has the advantage that the index does not solely rely on a single existing disclosure index, but takes into account the main aspects of multiple well-established disclosure measures. With respect to this study's cross-country setting, the self-construction assures that included disclosures are both relevant and (potentially) available in all three countries.[924]

The development of an own disclosure index comes along with a number of critical choices, such as: which items to select, computer-based or manual data analysis, weighted or

---

[919] *Hassan/Marston* (2010), p. 18.

[920] Cf. *Hassan/Marston* (2010), p. 19.

[921] Cf. here and in the following *Hassan/Marston* (2010), p. 19-21.

[922] Cf. e.g. *Beattie et al.* (2004), p. 209; *Marston/Polei* (2004), p. 308; *Hooghiemstra* (2010), p. 298; *Blaesing* (2013), p. 158.

[923] For the recent development and importance of sustainability reporting, cf. *Blaesing* (2013); *Kajüter* (2014b). For the management commentary discussion, cf. *Fink et al.* (2013); *Kajüter* (2013).

[924] Cf. *Marston/Shrives* (1991), p. 202.

unweighted, form of weighting.[925] These factors will determine the research design and, therefore, the results of the study. Although no existing disclosure index shall be applied directly in this study, prior disclosure indices serve as a **basis of the disclosure item selection**. This is similar to the approaches by *Firth* (1979) and *Hossain et al.* (1995), whose studies also rely on prior disclosure indices.[926] In particular, this study's disclosure index items are derived from the following research: BAR *by University of Münster (Research Team Baetge) (2015)*[927], VRZ by the *Department of Banking and Finance* (*University of Zurich*) (2014)[928], *Brazilian Disclosure Index* by *Lopes/de Alencar* (2010), annual report analysis framework by *Beattie et al.* (2004), *DISC* used by *Hail* (2002), scoring system by *Robb et al.* (2001), *DSCORE* used by *Botosan* (1997).

The quality of the annual report information largely depends on the information needs of the **legitimate user groups** of annual reports.[929] In line with this study's definition of FRQ, particularly investors and financial analysts as well as other legitimate stakeholders of the reporting entity are regarded as important users of annual reports. However, an evaluation of the quality of the disclosure index, based on the information needs of each interest group, does not seem practical.[930] In line with *Marston/Shrives* (1991), who argue that "*[...] information needs of different groups are likely to overlap [...]*"[931], this study applies a comprehensive disclosure index capturing the information needs of the legitimate user groups.[932] To ensure that the index captures annual report information consistent with these **information needs**, the following survey-based studies are considered: *Prigge* (2006), *Heumann* (2005), *Epstein/Palepu* (1999), *Chenhall/Juchau* (1977), *Buzby* (1974). Moreover, the *Jenkins Committee* (commissioned by the *American Institute of Certified Public Accountants (AICPA)*) published recommendations to improve business reporting.[933] These recommendations have attracted great attention in the accounting literature.[934] Hence, the disclosure index emphasizes disclosures the Jenkins Committee regards as essential, e.g. on forward-looking information.[935]

[925] Cf. *Lerchenmüller* (2012), p. 9.
[926] Cf. *Firth* (1979), p. 274.
[927] Cf. *University of Münster* (*Research Team Baetge)* (2015).
[928] Cf. *Department of Banking and Finance* (*University of Zurich*) (2014).
[929] Cf. section 2.1.2.
[930] Cf. *Blaesing* (2013), p. 156.
[931] Cf. *Marston/Shrives* (1991), p. 201.
[932] For example, the disclosure index content category *sustainability* addresses all stakeholders of a company despite differing information needs, cf. *Blaesing* (2013), p. 156. Furthermore, the disclosure index category *non-financials* explicitly concerns the stakeholder groups customers and suppliers, cf. Appendix, Table A-1.
[933] Cf. *AICPA* (1994).
[934] Cf. amongst others *Ferling* (1994); *Elliott/Jacobson* (1995), p. 77; *Jonas/Blanchet* (2000), p. 354-356; *Robb et al.* (2001), p. 72.
[935]Cf. *AICPA* (1994), p. 4.

5.2.2.4 Content categories

After describing the self-construction approach of this study's disclosure index, this section outlines the actual **contents** of the developed disclosure index. Obviously, the selection of the disclosure index items fundamentally determines the results of the content analysis:

> "*Since the categories contain the substance of the investigation, a content analysis can be no better than its system of categories.*"[936]

Therefore, the identification and choice of relevant items is one of the researcher's most important steps when creating an index. This can be particularly difficult, since there is no generally accepted theory or approach how to select items.[937] Nor does the literature agree upon an adequate number of items, as the number varies, for example, between 17 items in the disclosure index by *Barrett* (1976)[938] and more than 300 items comprised in the BAR index by *Baetge*[939]. Since this study aims for a detailed analysis of financial reporting practice in Brazil, South Africa and Germany, it applies a comprehensive disclosure index with a total of 285 items in seven reporting categories:[940]

(1) Background information;
(2) Important financials;
(3) Important non-financials;
(4) Sustainability information;
(5) Value based management;
(6) Forward-looking information; and
(7) Risks and opportunities.

The first category **background information** encompasses general information about a company (e.g., ownership structure) as well as insights into its business activities (e.g., products), its industry and operating markets, its macroeconomic environment as well as corporate governance characteristics.[941] The *background information* category further includes strategy-related information, such as an entity's strategic objectives, business model

---

[936] *Berelson* (1971), p. 147. For the importance of the disclosure items selection, cf. also *Marston/Shrives* (1991), p. 195.

[937] Cf. *Wallace et al.* (1994), p. 43.

[938] Cf. *Barrett* (1976), p. 25.

[939] Cf. *University of Münster* (*Research Team Baetge*) (2015).

[940] For the full disclosure index, cf. Appendix, Table A-1. The category selection is based on *Department of Banking and Finance* (*University of Zurich*) (2014), p. 2. Similar categories are found amongst others in *AICPA* (1994); *Botosan* (1997), p. 332; *University of Münster* (*Research Team Baetge*) (2015).

[941] Cf. e.g. *Heumann* (2005), p. 205-206; *Prigge* (2006), p. 93-105 and 121-126; *Lopes/de Alencar* (2010), p. 445; *Department of Banking and Finance* (*University of Zurich*) (2014), p. 5-6; *University of Münster* (*Research Team Baetge*) (2015), p. 2-3.

and core competencies.[942] In addition, the index captures the description of the entity's share price development.[943]

The category **important financials** covers figures which companies may typically provide in financial statements. To actually measure the quality of the provided information, the index explicitly distinguishes between qualitative description (e.g., of revenue development), quantitative description and explanation (e.g., give reasons for increase/decrease). Besides the analysis of the earnings situation (including revenues, order intake, profit, expenses as well as profit and loss indicators), also the vertical balance sheet structure (assets, liabilities and equity) is investigated.[944] Enabling users to identify the company's core earnings,[945] the index distinguishes, for instance, between operating and non-operating profits and requires a breakdown of profits according to business activities. Regarding an entity's financial position, the index covers, inter alia, disclosures on capital structure, financing activities and liquidity situation. Annual reports are further supposed to explain the impact of changes in the accounting regulation. Finally, the index investigates, as to what extent managers evaluate the economic position of their company.

In line with the recommendations by the *Jenkins Report*[946], the third category focuses on **important non-financials**. However, differentiation between financial and non-financial disclosures is not trivial in all cases. Non-financial business reporting does not imply that information can neither be denominated in monetary nor quantitative terms.[947] Revenue per employee, for instance, describes the relation of a financial (revenue) to a non-financial (number of employees) figure. Other ratios consist only of *non-financial* data, such as an oil company's ratio of dry holes to drilling attempts. In fact, *non-financials* can generally be found throughout the entire annual report of a company, e.g. in board letters, interviews as well as executive and management reports. Other typical non-financial measures include human resource assets, reject rate of goods produced, average hours of training, employee retention rate, employee and customer satisfaction.[948] *Fink et al.* (2013) argue that non-financial indicators are primarily qualitative figures, because their numeric measurability plays only a subordinate role.[949] Hence, the disclosure index includes - primarily qualitative - information on the human capital of an entity (e.g., employee satisfaction), its suppliers and customers (e.g., customer satisfaction), major corpo-

942 Cf. e.g. *Heumann* (2005), p. 203-205; *Prigge* (2006), p. 111-112; *Department of Banking and Finance* (*University of Zurich*) (2014), p. 5.

943 Cf. e.g. *Prigge* (2006), p. 126-127.

944 Cf. here and in the following *Prigge* (2006), p. 131-166; *Lopes/de Alencar* (2010), p. 446; *University of Münster* (*Research Team Baetge*) (2015), p. 4.

945 Cf. *AICPA* (1994), p. 61-62.

946 Cf. *AICPA* (1994), p. 4.

947 Cf. here and in the following *Elliott/Jacobson* (1995), p. 83.

948 Cf. also *Fink et al.* (2013), p. 147.

949 Cf. *Fink et al.* (2013), p. 146.

rate processes and brands.[950] Moreover, disclosures on research & development activities and on major investments are requested under *non-financials*.[951]

Following the structure of the VRZ index, the increasing importance of **sustainability information** is examined in an own category.[952] Through the disclosure of sustainability information, companies shed light on their practices in the three sustainability dimensions *economic*, *environmental* and *social* performance, which have been identified by the *Global Reporting Initiative (GRI)* as *triple bottom line*.[953] To fulfill the sustainability reporting categories of the disclosure index, annual reports have to provide information about all three triple bottom line areas on the basis of performance indicators included in *GRI's* most recent G4 Sustainability Reporting Guidelines.[954] Besides a qualitative description, the companies shall explain their sustainability activities thoroughly with the aid of quantitative figures. In addition, the disclosure index captures the management's comments on objectives, their achievement and actions regarding economic, environmental as well as social sustainability. However, the evaluation does not consider information which is already included in another disclosure index category. For instance, employee information, which is asked for under *non-financials*, is not captured by social sustainability information to avoid a double counting. Moreover, companies shall describe their overall sustainability strategy and explain how their triple bottom line categories interact, i.e. as to what degree their business activities cause interdependencies among the economic, environmental and social dimension. As part of general sustainability information, the entities are supposed to indicate, whether they make use of a sustainability framework for reporting purposes.[955] Finally, information on potential listings in sustainability indices may be interesting to stakeholders (particularly, capital market participants) and are considered in the sustainability category.

The category **value based management** primarily captures a company's management control as well as its remuneration practices.[956] It requires disclosures on value based management concepts (e.g., Economic Value Added (EVA)[957]) and corresponding key performance indicators used internally in management accounting. Concerning a company's compensation practice, the disclosure index investigates information about, inter alia, the underlying remuneration philosophy, compensation components as well as criteria for

---

950 Cf. here and in the following, *Heumann* (2005), p. 129-130 and 206-207; *Department of Banking and Finance* (*University of Zurich*) (2014), p. 7-8; *University of Münster* (*Research Team Baetge*) (2015), p. 5.

951 Cf. *Prigge* (2006), p. 113-121; *Department of Banking and Finance* (*University of Zurich*) (2014), p. 7-8; *University of Münster* (*Research Team Baetge*) (2015), p. 3.

952 Cf. *Department of Banking and Finance* (*University of Zurich*) (2014), p. 14. For the increasing importance of sustainability information, cf. *Blaesing* (2013).

953 Cf. *Global Reporting Initiative* (2013), p. 5.

954 For a description of the G4 performance indicators by the *GRI*, cf. *Global Reporting Initiative* (2013), p. 47-83; *Kajüter* (2014b).

955 Besides the most frequently applied Sustainability Reporting Guidelines by the *GRI*, also the Global Compact Principles by the *United Nations* (cf. *United Nations* (2015)) as well as the Sustainability Framework of the *World Bank*-related *International Finance Corporation (IFC)* (cf. *International Finance Corporation* (2015)) are examples for potential frameworks.

956 Cf. *Heumann* (2005), p. 139; *Department of Banking and Finance* (*University of Zurich*) (2014), p. 11.

957 For a detailed description of EVA, cf. *Kajüter* (2011), p. 461-463.

compensation. Moreover, it is analyzed whether the companies reveal the remuneration of each board member.

Numerous studies emphasize the importance of **forward-looking information** to stakeholders.[958] The disclosure index includes forecasts regarding revenues, earnings, earnings margins, value based indicators and dividends.[959] Moreover, the index analyzes important forecasts (e.g., on revenues) with respect ro regional or segmental differentiation, description of underlying assumptions and consideration of reference values. Furthermore, the *forward-looking information* category includes additional financial forecasts (e.g., for capital structure, liquidity and financing volume) as well as strategic and non-financial objectives (e.g., the company's future key markets and prospective investment volumes). Finally, the management's assessment of prospective economic trends is captured by the index.

The final content category covers **risk and opportunity** issues. Risks (opportunities) are regarded as potential future trends or events which might result in a deviation from forecasts or goals which is negative (positive) for the company.[960] The category includes, inter alia, a company's reporting on general risk management activities and strategies.[961] Besides an assessment of a company's overall risk situation, the disclosure index analyzes as to what extent the entities provide insights on material risks (e.g., industry risks). For each risk category, the index distinguishes qualitative and quantitative descriptions as well as the explanation of the risk's potential impact on the company. A special focus lies on financial risks which are analyzed in more detail. In addition, the entities' opportunity disclosures are investigated, yet, in less detail than their risk disclosures.

5.2.2.5 Mandatory vs. voluntary reporting

To determine cross-company differences, most disclosure index studies in developed countries investigate voluntary disclosures which imply larger variation than mandatory disclosures, because the companies do not have to comply with regulations.[962] In emerging economies, however, the regulatory environment might be low and existing rules may not be enforced strictly so that the investigation of mandatory disclosures appears worthwhile as well.[963] Unlike numerous prior investigations, this study manages to distinguish between **mandatory** and **voluntary disclosures**. According to *Marston/Shrives* (1991) the investigation of both types of information may be advisable, as

---

958 Cf. amongst others *AICPA* (1994), p. 4; *Botosan* (1997), p. 332; *Epstein/Palepu* (1999), p. 50; *Prigge* (2006), p. 201 and 240; *Barth* (2009).

959 Cf. here and in the following *Prigge* (2006), p. 191-210; *Lopes/de Alencar* (2010), p. 445; *Department of Banking and Finance* (*University of Zurich*) (2014), p. 13; *University of Münster* (*Research Team Baetge*) (2015), p. 7.

960 Cf. *Kajüter et al.* (2015), p. 515 on the basis of GAS 20.11.

961 Cf. here and in the following *Prigge* (2006), p. 170-190; *Department of Banking and Finance* (*University of Zurich*) (2014), p. 10; *University of Münster* (*Research Team Baetge*) (2015), p. 6.

962 Cf. *Lerchenmüller* (2012), p. 12.

963 Cf. *Ahmed/Nicholls* (1994), p. 62.

> "*[...] an index can include a mixture of items required by regulation and voluntary items if this suits the purpose of the research project.*"[964]

By doing so, this study is able to pursue two objectives. First, the disclosure index study captures major decision useful information, regardless whether mandatory or voluntary, to analyze the overall information provided by the companies (which is the basis for the users' decisions). Second, the study aims at investigating the efforts of an entity to provide high quality information in their annual reports in addition to mandatory disclosures. Thus, the investigation measures the **voluntary** disclosure level of the sample companies separately. However, it is not always trivial to distinguish mandatory from voluntary reporting.[965] For instance, some regulations require that certain information solely has to be disclosed, if it is material. However, there might be no clear threshold for materiality. Moreover, even if rules require disclosures on a certain topic (e.g., forward-looking information), the regulation might not concretize this requirement. Thus, prior studies have struggled to distinguish voluntary and mandatory information adequately (e.g., *Cooke/Wallace* (1989); *Inchausti* (1997)).

Although the vast majority of this study's disclosure index items belong to the group of voluntary information, single items are **explicitly required** to be reported in one or multiple sample countries, e.g. due to national laws. These items are labeled as *mandatory* and excluded from the voluntary disclosure index. If an item is labeled as *voluntary*, there is either no regulation concerning this issue or the disclosure index requires other or additional disclosures compared to those which are required by regulation.

Therefore, four disclosure indices are constructed in total. The first disclosure index captures relevant information provided in the annual reports including both mandatory and voluntary disclosures.[966] The other three indices capture solely voluntarily reported information. As voluntary disclosures differ among the three country samples, each country has an own **voluntary disclosure index**.

As described above, an item is solely classified as *mandatory*, if regulation explicitly requires its disclosure and non-compliance would probably entail significant legal consequences for the reporting entity. As all **sample companies** have to comply with **IFRS** (as adopted by their countries), e.g. the disclosure of a company's basic and diluted *earnings per share* according to IAS 33 is mandatory for all 150 sample companies, since their shares are traded on a public market (IAS 33.2). In addition to IFRS, the preparers of annual reports may have to consider country-specific disclosure requirements.

In **Brazil**, *CVM* Instruction No. 480 requires companies to report on several of the disclosure index topics. Only some of these rules, however, entirely meet a disclosure index item. For instance, the *CVM* explicitly requires to report a breakdown of debt according to maturity (less than 1 year, 3 years, 5 years),[967] which is also captured by quantitative

964 *Marston/Shrives* (1991), p. 195.
965 Cf. here and in the following *Lerchenmüller* (2012), p. 25-26.
966 Cf. section 5.2.2.5.
967 Cf. annex 24, no. 3.8 of the *CVM* Instruction No. 480.

disclosure index items.[968] Furthermore, *CVM* Instruction No. 480 stipulates that entities have to describe risk factors, e.g. risks related to the company's suppliers and clients.[969] The requirement of a "*description of risk factors related to the economy sectors in which the issuer operates*"[970] matches with a qualitative disclosure index item in the category *risks and opportunities*.[971]

In **South Africa**, for instance, *regulated companies* have to publish a list of those shareholders who hold at least a 5% stake in the company according to section 56(7) of the South African Companies Act. This disclosure requirement meets the disclosure index item *shareholder structure* in the category *background information*.[972] Although the South African sample companies prepare integrated reports, neither the requirements of the <IR> Framework nor the King III (comply-or-explain approach) are legally binding.[973] Thus, disclosure index items required by these regulations are not classified as mandatory. Overall, there are only relatively few differences between the South African voluntary and full disclosure indices.

With respect to **Germany**, the disclosure items required by the German Commercial Code (HGB) are mandatory. Moreover, this study classifies disclosure items as mandatory, which are explicitly required by the German Accounting Standards (GAS).[974] In particular, GAS 20 captures some specific disclosure items of the study. For example, GAS 20.70 requires entities to analyze revenues in detail (including a classification of revenues as well as the influence of product range and portfolio of services).[975] However, other requirements by the GAS leave considerable room for discretion so that no disclosure index item is fulfilled. For example, according to GAS 20.105-107, information on important non-financial KPIs shall be provided "*[...] to the extent that they are material for an understanding of the course of business and position [...]*"[976].

5.2.2.6 Weights

After the introduction of the disclosure index content categories and the differentiation between mandatory and voluntary disclosure items, this section deals with the weights assigned to these disclosure items. The literature discussion on the differentiation between **weighted** and **unweighted** disclosure indices is related to the dispute, whether disclosure indices measure disclosure quantity or quality.[977] Although *Botosan* (2004) argues that all disclosure index measures so far, "*[...] rest upon mere counts of disclosure items and the*

---

968 Cf. Appendix, Table A-1, items B.3.4.3 and B.3.4.4.

969 Cf. annex 24, no. 4 of the *CVM* Instruction No. 480.

970 Annex 24, no. 4.1 of the *CVM* Instruction No. 480.

971 Cf. Appendix, Table A-1, item G.6.3.

972 Cf. Appendix, Table A-1, item A.1.1.

973 Cf. section 2.3.3.

974 Cf. section 2.3.4.

975 This requirement meet disclosure index items B.1.1.1, B.1.1.2, and B.1.1.3, cf. Appendix, Table A-1.

976 GAS 20.105. In addition, GAS 20.106 determines that KPIs used for the internal management shall be disclosed and GAS 20.107 provides examples of non-financial KPIs.

977 Cf. among others *Marston/Shrives* (1991), p. 195; *Beattie et al.* (2004), p. 233; *Beretta/Bozzolan* (2004), p. 266; *Botosan* (2004), p. 290; *Lerchenmüller* (2012), p. 26.

maintained hypothesis that quantity and quality are positively related"[978], numerous studies attempt to measure disclosure quality through the use of weighted disclosure indices,[979] whereas "*[...] unweighted indices, by construction, can only measure the quantity of disclosure.*"[980] Already *Cerf* (1961) assigned weights to different items of information.[981] However, *Cooke/Wallace* (1989) point out that assigning weights to disclosure items can be misleading, because the importance of a disclosure item varies across entities, transactions, users, companies, industries, countries and times.[982]

This study's disclosure index includes explicit and implicit weights to not only measure the quantity of disclosures, but indeed the quality of financial reporting. Unlike indices which evaluate each disclosure item on a scale (e.g., the VRZ index uses grades ranging from 1 ("*no information*") to 6 ("*very good information*"))[983], this study basically uses a **binary coding scheme** to both reduce subjectivity and accelerate the coding process. Therefore, if the criteria of an item are met, generally one point is awarded; otherwise the item score is zero (1/0).[984] However, entities are expected to provide both qualitative and quantitative information about items (if both types of information are useful). The index weights qualitative and quantitative information explicitly with 0.5 points each:

	Criteria fulfilled	Criteria not fulfilled
Qualitative information about item	0.5	0
Quantitative information about item	0.5	0
Maximum score per item	$\sum = 1$	

Table 5-9: Scoring methodology of disclosure index items

In the reporting category *forward-looking information*, the disclosure index further weights the **precision of forecasts** (e.g., revenue forecasts) differently, "*[...] because precise information is more useful and may enhance management's reporting reputation and credibility.*"[985] For this purpose, three forecast precision categories are distinguished: (1) qualitative or comparative; (2) qualified-comparative[986]; and (3) point and interval forecasts.[987] Each of the three precision categories is regarded as one item and, thus, is rewarded one point, if

978 *Botosan* (2004), p. 290.

979 Cf. amongst others *Buzby* (1975), p. 21-23; *Coy et al.* (1993), p. 123-125; p. 205; *Botosan* (1997), p. 333-334; *Oberdörster* (2009), p. 88-100 (using the BAR index by *Baetge*). For an overview of studies using reporting quantity as a proxy for disclosure, see *Lerchenmüller* (2012), p. 154-155.

980 *Beretta/Bozzolan* (2008), p. 337.

981 Cf. *Cerf* (1961), p. 8-9.

982 Cf. *Cooke/Wallace* (1989), p. 51.

983 Cf. *Department of Banking and Finance* (*University of Zurich*) (2014).

984 Cf. *Barth* (2009), p. 125.

985 *Botosan* (1997), p. 334.

986 According to GAS 20.128 qualified-comparative forecasts shall illustrate both the direction and the intensity of the expected change in the projected key performance indicator (e.g., "*revenues will increase slightly*"). For qualified-comparative forecasts in detail, cf. also *Fink et al.* (2013), p. 169.

987 For the precision of forecasts, cf. *Barth* (2009), p. 19-23. A similar classification according to forecast precision is applied by the *BAR* index, cf. *Oberdörster* (2009), p. 95.

fulfilled, and zero otherwise (1/0). However, if a higher precision type is fulfilled, also the subordinate categories are rewarded with a point resulting in the following total scores:

Forecast precision	Total points awarded
No forecast	0
Qualitative description or comparative forecast	1
Qualified-comparative forecast	2
Point or interval forecast	3

Table 5-10: Scoring methodology for forecast precision

The selection of a certain number of items within one reporting sub category inevitably leads to **implicit weighting**, as "*[...] the unscaled aggregation of values is an implicit weighting scheme*"[988]. Taking into account that some reporting issues are considered more important from a stakeholder's perspective than others, important information (e.g., forecasts of future earnings[989]) is broken down into sub items which can be awarded additional points so that the fractions of the superordinate categories increase.[990] This approach leads to a disclosure index "*dominated by implicit weights*"[991] based on the thorough **selection of important disclosure items** which represent the users' actual information needs.

Table 5-11 shows how the total 285 items of the disclosure index are distributed among the seven reporting categories. As the maximum score of each item is one, the maximum total FRQ score amounts to 285. The implicit weights of the maximum score (in parentheses) indicate that most weight is put on *important financials* (27%), whereas the categories *value based management* and *sustainability information* have the lowest implicit weights (7%).

Financial reporting quality disclosure index	Number of items/Maximum score
1 Background information	33 (12%)
2 Important financials	77 (27%)
3 Important non-financials	44 (15%)
4 Sustainability information	20 (7%)
5 Value based management	21 (7%)
6 Forward-looking information	60 (21%)
7 Risks and opportunities	30 (11%)
Total FRQ	**285 (100%)**

Table 5-11: Disclosure index categories

988 *Salzman* (2003), p. 10-11.

989 *Prigge* (2006) finds that information on a company's prospective earnings is the most important category to capital market participants, cf. *Prigge* (2006), p. 201 and 240.

990 For a similar approach of breaking down disclosure elements into sub elements to differentiate the disclosure level of different annual reports in more detail, cf. *Buzby* (1974), p. 429-430.

991 Cf. *Elbannan/Elbannan* (2014), p. 64.

To demonstrate that the implicit weights are adequate to measure FRQ, they are compared to the weights of well-established disclosure indices in prior research. However, in the literature the reporting categories of disclosure indices and their corresponding weights vary considerably. While the VRZ index barely captures the retrospective development of important **financials** in its categories *trend analysis* (5%) and *management discussion and analysis of the financial statement (10%),* the BAR index 2015 shows a weight of 34% for the category "*report on economic position*", which predominantly includes disclosures on financials.

Moreover, the VRZ index attaches considerably less importance to **forward-looking** disclosures in its category *target figures and credibility* (10%) than the BAR index (32%). In between this range, this study's index weights *forward-looking* information with 21%. Also the weight for the category **risks and opportunities** with 11% is in between the values of VRZ (10%) and BAR (16%). *AICPA* (1994) emphasizes the importance of forward-looking information in corporate reports, as "*[...] users need a forward-looking perspective because their goal is to predict a company's financial future*"[992] which, inter alia, requires assessments of risks and opportunities.[993] The VRZ index' weights of the categories **non-financials** (20%) and **sustainability** (10%) exceed those of the BAR index, which captures these issues in other categories. This study's index includes these increasingly important categories explicitly with weights of 15% and 7%, respectively. Also **background information** (12%) and **value based management** (7%) are represented similarly as in other studies. Overall, the disclosure index weights are assumed to be in line with the information needs of major users, particularly, both investors and financial analysts.

With respect to the **voluntary disclosure indices** for each country, there are only minor differences between the weights per category of the voluntary indices and the full disclosure index. Table 5-12 presents the maximum scores (per reporting category) for the three voluntary country indices including the category weights (in parentheses). With a maximum score of 244 the German index shows the largest deviation (-14%) indicating more disclosure index items are required in Germany than in Brazil and South Africa.

Voluntary disclosure index	BRA	RSA	GER
1 Background information	29.0 (11%)	30.0 (12%)	28.0 (11%)
2 Important financials	63.5 (25%)	68.0 (25%)	60.0 (25%)
3 Important non-financials	39.5 (15%)	42.0 (16%)	40.0 (16%)
4 Sustainability information	20.0 (8%)	20.0 (7%)	20.0 (8%)
5 Value based management	17.0 (7%)	21.0 (8%)	13.0 (5%)
6 Forward-looking information	60.0 (23%)	60.0 (22%)	60.0 (25%)
7 Risks and opportunities	27.5 (11%)	28.0 (10%)	23.0 (9%)
Total FRQ	**256.5 (100%)**	**269.0 (100%)**	**244.0 (100%)**

Table 5-12: Maximum scores of voluntary disclosure indices per country

992 *AICPA* (1994), p. 19.
993 Cf. *AICPA* (1994), p. 19-20.

Moreover, the large number of disclosure items might reduce the importance of the weights, since "*[...] it has been found that the weighted and unweighted scores tend to give the same results where there are a large number of items.*"[994]

For each index, the total disclosure index score of FRQ is calculated as the ratio of total score awarded to the respective maximum score. This **relative measure** (in % of the maximum score) allows intuitive comparisons between, inter alia, entities, industries and countries. Further, the relative score of total FRQ can be analyzed in comparison to the relative scores of the seven reporting categories. Although it is generally assumed that all 285 disclosure items are relevant for the full disclosure index (*one size fits all approach*) to each of the large sample companies (rebuttable presumption),[995] entities shall not be penalized for not disclosing an item, which is obviously not relevant or applicable to its business activities.[996] Thus, if it is justified that a certain company disregards an item, the specific item is not considered in the disclosure index for this entity and the index is reduced by one item.

$$(5.6) \quad FRQ = \left(\textstyle\sum_{i=1}^{n} d_i\right) / M$$

where,

FRQ = disclosure index score of FRQ;

d_i = achieved score for disclosure item *i*;

n = number of disclosure items; and

M = maximum disclosure index score.

After the description of the disclosure index measure of FRQ, the following section presents the readability measure used as an additional measure of FRQ in this study.

5.2.3 Readability measure

Besides the accruals-based proxies and the disclosure index study, the third FRQ measure of this study is concerned with the readability of annual report narratives. In contrast to subjective analyst ratings, *Beattie et al.* (2004) classify both disclosure index studies and readability analyses as *semi-objective* methods to analyze narratives in annual reports (cf. Figure 5-10).

This study's readability analysis is twofold. First, it evaluates the overall readability of the reports on the basis of the *impression* criteria of the VRZ index. Second, the study applies two readability proxies which are commonly used throughout the disclosure literature: (1) *Fog* and (2) *Flesch Reading Ease* (FRE) indices.

994 *Beattie et al.* (2004), p. 210.

995 Cf. *Buzby* (1974), p. 429-430; *Blaesing* (2013), p. 161.

996 Cf. *Marston/Shrives* (1991), p. 204-205; *Abd-Elsalam/Weetman* (2003), p. 71.

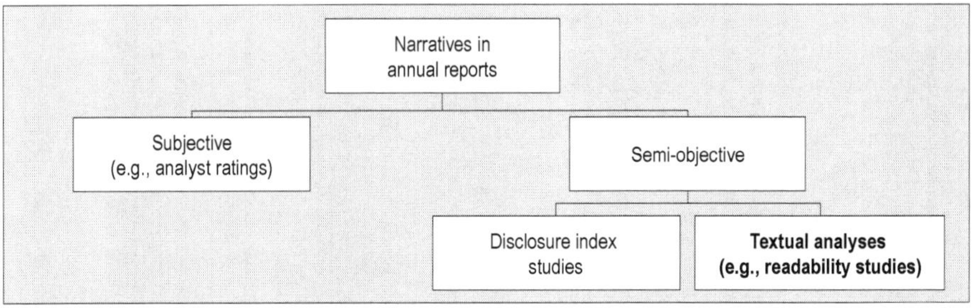

Figure 5-10: Analysis techniques of narratives in annual reports
Following *Beattie et al.* (2004), p. 209.

The first readability analysis is based on the VRZ index of the *Department of Banking and Finance* (*University of Zurich*) (2014). The readability of the entire annual report is evaluated on a **Likert scale**[997] ranging from 1 ("*very poor*") to 5 ("*very good*") with regard to the following aspects which are assessed separately:[998]

(1) clear-cut structure;

(2) understandable language and style of expression; and

(3) user-friendly use of figures and tables.

(1) The annual report's table of contents has to be clearly arranged to provide a clear-cut structure. Therefore, both the selection and the order of the sections are supposed to be comprehensible. Imprecise titles of sections impede the readability. Moreover, important information should be easy to find. Thus, it is analyzed whether or not the annual reports include sections concerned with the main content categories of the disclosure index. (2) The language is understandable, if it is precise and in fact *calls a spade a spade* (no boilerplates). A good readability is further assumed, if sentences are relatively short, provided information is immediately understandable and transitions between different sections are fluent. Furthermore, the explanation of technical terms improves the understandability of the language and, thus, the text's readability. (3) Preparers of annual reports should use meaningful figures and tables purposefully for an improved understanding of facts. Imprecise figures and tables may contradict this purpose. In particular, figures and tables should be self-explanatory and labelled adequately.

Besides this subjective assessment of the readability, the study applies two readability measures which belong to the aforementioned category of *semi-objective* analysis. Unlike the subjective evaluation on the basis of a Likert scale, these readability measures do not analyze the entire annual reports, but analyze the readability of the CEO/management's letter to the shareholders. As explained in section 5.1.3, this research object allows comparisons of the readability of textual elements across the sample countries.

[997] For details on Likert scale, cf. *Maurer/Pierce* (1998), p. 325.
[998] Cf. here and in the following *Department of Banking and Finance* (*University of Zurich*) (2014), p. 4.

In particular, the recent accounting literature increasingly applies the **Fog index** to measure financial disclosure readability.[999] Even the SEC in the U.S. contemplated the Fog proxy to detect poor readability of financial statements.[1000] The index determines a text's readability on the basis of two components: sentence length and word complexity.[1001] As presented in equation (5.7), the Fog index formula includes the sum of average word number per sentence and fraction of complex words multiplied by 0.4.[1002] A word is labeled as *complex*, if it has more than two syllables. However, *Loughran/McDonald* (2014) criticize that some "*[...] frequently used 'complex' words like company, operations, and management are not going to confuse consumers of SEC filings.*"[1003]

$$(5.7) \quad Fog\ index_i = (ASL_i + FCW_i) * 0.4$$

where,

ASL_i = average sentence length for company *i* (measured by average number of words per sentence); and

FCW_i = fraction of complex words (words with more than two syllables) for company *i*.

The Fog index scores are interpreted according to Table 5-13.[1004] Scores between 12 and 14 indicate ideal readability. While texts with scores between 8 and 10 are deemed to be *childish,* textual passages with a Fog index score of 18 or higher are regarded as *unreadable.*

Fog index score	8-10	10-12	12-14	14-18	≥18
Interpretation	Childish	Acceptable	Ideal	Difficult	Unreadable

Table 5-13: Interpretation of Fog index score
Based on *Li* (2008), p. 225.

As second well-accepted readability proxy, the study uses the **Flesch reading ease index** *(FRE).*[1005] Similar to the Fog index, the *FRE* index takes into account the sentence length and complexity of words. Besides the average sentence length (ASL_i), however, its formula includes the average number of syllables per word (cf. equation (5.8)).

$$(5.8) \quad Flesch\ Reading\ Ease_i = 206.835 - (1.015 * ASL_i) - (84.6 * ASW_i)$$

where,

ASW_i = average number of syllables per word

[999] Cf. amongst others *Li* (2008); *Loughran/McDonald* (2014); *Kumar* (2014); *Lundholm et al.* (2014); *Ertugrul et al.* (2015).
[1000] Cf. *Loughran/McDonald* (2014), p. 1644.
[1001] Cf. *Kumar* (2014), p. 4.
[1002] Cf. here and in the following *Ertugrul et al.* (2015), p. 8.
[1003] *Loughran/McDonald* (2014), p. 1645.
[1004] Cf. e.g. *Li* (2008), p. 225; *Ertugrul et al.* (2015), p. 8.
[1005] Cf. here and in the following *Flesch* (1948), p. 229; *Kumar* (2014), p. 4.

The FRE index assesses how easy it is to read a certain text passage.[1006] The formula in equation (5.8) has been developed for the English language and calculates a score ranging from 1 to 100. The reading ease increases with higher scores. A score of 64 is regarded as *plain English*. The following Table 5-14 provides an interpretation of FRE index scores.

Flesch reading ease score	0-30	30-50	50-60	60-70	70-80	80-90	90-100
Interpretation	Very difficult	Difficult	Fairly difficult	Standard	Fairly easy	Easy	Very easy

Table 5-14: Interpretation of Flesch reading ease score
Adopted from *Flesch* (1948), p. 230.

Despite a massive use of readability formulas in the literature, *Courtis* (1998) criticizes their simplicity.[1007] According to him, the indices are solely rough estimates of difficulty and capture only those aspects of a sentence, which are actually measurable in that way. Therefore, he criticizes that "*[…] other important matters such as syntax, style, format, graphic design, logic, conceptual density, human interest, organization and reinforcement are not considered.*"[1008]

5.3 Methods of analysis

5.3.1 Introduction

After presenting the methodology of the FRQ measures, the following description of the applied methods to analyze these FRQ measures follows the structure of the empirical study. After this general introduction into data analysis, the following section presents statistical techniques to analyze the collected data (FRQ measures) on a descriptive and univariate level (cf. section 5.3.2). The subsequent section is concerned with the methodology of the determinants study. It introduces the included variables and illustrates the applied statistical instruments, particularly both bivariate and multivariate analysis techniques (section 5.3.3). Furthermore, also the statistical foundation of the information asymmetry study, including the definition of the variables, is presented in a separate section (section 5.3.4).

Of particular importance is the **scale level** of the collected data, as it determines which statistical instruments of quantitative evaluation are applicable.[1009] *Cleff* (2015) distinguishes three main scale levels: (1) nominal, (2) ordinal, and (3) metric scale.[1010] The nominal scale simply assigns numbers to characteristics, however, does not rank the identified characteristics (e.g., "*1*" for male and "*2*" for female). In contrast, ordinally scaled data are categorized according to characteristics which allow a certain ranking (e.g., evaluation of a product offer on a scale from 1 "*very poor*" to 5 "*very good*"). While the distances

[1006] Cf. here and in the following *Kumar* (2014), p. 4.
[1007] Cf. here and in the following *Courtis* (1998), p. 460.
[1008] *Courtis* (1998), p. 460.
[1009] Cf. *Pospeschill* (2006), p. 22.
[1010] Cf. here and in the following *Cleff* (2015), p. 19-21.

between two consecutive ranks (e.g., between evaluation of "*4*" and "*5*") of ordinally scaled data cannot be interpreted, the metric scale allows such interpretations. For example a 30-year old person is not only older than a 29-year old person, but is exactly one year older (assuming identical birthdays).

The **scale level of disclosure index scores** is controversially discussed in the literature. To analyze the disclosure-based data on FRQ with the help of statistical methods, such as the interpretation of mean values and relationships between variables on the basis of parametric tests, the data must be scaled metrically.[1011] This implies for the results of disclosure indices that not only the rank of a score can be interpreted (e.g., the quality of report A is higher than of report B), but also the differences between the quality of reports (e.g., the quality of report A with a score of 200 points is twice as high as the quality of report B achieving 100 points). Despite critics who argue that disclosure indices measuring FRQ solely meet the criteria of ordinally scaled data,[1012] this study assumes the collected disclosure index data as metrically scaled in line with other research.[1013] In particular, the considerable number of observations and the comprehensiveness of the disclosure index, which allows a large number of potential "*rank levels*", fulfill criteria required as prerequisite for the application of metric analysis techniques.[1014] This view is further unproblematic, since studies show that parametric testing with ordinally scaled data provides reliable results, if the variables are normally distributed and fulfill the assumption of variance homogeneity (no heteroskedasticity).[1015] Moreover, this study mitigates concerns regarding the scale level of the data by conducting non-parametric significance tests, which do only require ordinally-scaled data.[1016] Finally, the study's descriptive statistics consider not only the mean, but also median values for interpretation.

Consistent with the literature, the results of the statistical tests include the p-value, which marks the test's **level of significance** (α) considering the following thresholds: α = 10% (*); α = 5% (**); α = 1% (***).[1017] The lower the significance level α, the lower the risk to dismiss the null hypothesis, although it is correct; however, the lower also the possibility to reject an incorrect null hypothesis.[1018] The study refers to test results on the 1% level as *highly significant*, whereas results on the 10% level are regarded as *marginally significant*.

5.3.2 Analysis of financial reporting practice by descriptive and univariate statistics

According to the research questions RQ1a and RQ1b, this study aims at a comprehensive analysis of prevailing financial reporting practices in Brazil, South Africa and Germany. For this purpose, the results of the data collection for the different FRQ measures (accru-

1011 Cf. *Pospeschill* (2006), p. 25.
1012 Cf. e.g. *Marston/Shrives* (1991), p. 199.
1013 Cf. *Francis et al.* (2008), p. 71; *de Lima et al.* (2010), p. 278; *Cleff* (2015), p. 21.
1014 Cf. *Opp/Schmidt* (1976), p. 35.
1015 Cf. *Gregoire/Driver* (1987), p. 159-165. For the relevance of normal distribution and heteroskedasticity, cf. section 5.3.3.2.
1016 Cf. *Firth* (1979), p. 277 279.
1017 Cf. *Pospeschill* (2006), p. 168.
1018 Cf. *von Auer* (2013), p. 123-127. For the development of null and alternative hypotheses, cf. 4.2.1.

als-based proxies, disclosure index measure and readability measure) are described on the basis of descriptive and univariate statistics.

Initially, **descriptive statistics** characterize the empirical observations on the basis of various location parameters, including minimum, maximum, mean, median, as well as quartiles for both absolute and relative distributions.[1019] In addition, the statistical variation of the distributions is described through standard variation. Numerous visualizations (e.g., bar charts and boxplot diagrams) complement the provided descriptive statistics for a better understanding.

Moreover, **univariate statistics** examine whether differences in the results of distinctive groups (particularly among the three country samples) are significant and, thus, allow a transfer of the results from the particular sample to the general population (inductive reasoning). In particular, this study applies the non-parametric Wilcoxon rank-sum test (also Mann-Whitney two-sample statistic or "U test") and Kruskal-Wallis test (also "H test") to examine, whether the distributions of sub samples differ significantly.[1020] While the Wilcoxon rank-sum test is only applicable to two samples, the Kruskal-Wallis test determines for C samples with n_i observations in the sample i, whether the samples belong to the same population. The significance tests contribute to find within- as well as cross-country differences in financial reporting practices and quality, which is one of this study's main objectives.[1021] As the Wilcoxon rank-sum and Kruskal-Wallis tests are both rank-based significance tests, they can be conducted using ordinally scaled data, which mitigates concerns regarding the scale level of the data in use.

5.3.3 Determinants analysis

5.3.3.1 Selection of variables

As the determinants study investigates which factors influence the quality of financial reporting, this study's FRQ measures are used as **dependent variables** in the determinants model. Besides the indirect accruals-based proxy and the Fog readability measure , particularly the full disclosure index score is included in the model. As additional sensitivity analysis, also the voluntary score is used as a measure for financial reporting quality.

The **independent variables** are the proxies for the determinants of FRQ which have been identified on the basis of prior literature and theoretical approaches in chapter four. Thus, the determinants study tests the hypotheses, developed in section 4.2.3, which suggest a directed or undirected relation between FRQ and each of the assumed determinants.

[1019] Cf. here and in the following *Cleff* (2015), p. 36-58. Descriptive statistics are also provided to describe variables included in the determinant study (cf. section 6.2) and information asymmetry study (section 6.3).

[1020] Cf. here and in the following, *Kruskal/Wallis* (1952), p. 584-608. For an overview of the Wilcoxon-Mann-Whitney, Kruskal-Wallis and other related tests, cf. *Kruskal/Wallis* (1952). For a general introduction to hypotheses testing, cf. *Auer/Rottmann* (2015), p. 353-408.

[1021] The significance tests are also used in the isolated determinants analysis, cf. section 6.2.2.

As explained in the hypotheses development section, the study captures differences in **country effects** between Brazil, South Africa and Germany by country variables. These country variables aggregate the influence of all country-specific factors which are not captured by other explanatory variables. The determinants regression model includes a country variable for Brazil and another one for South Africa which take the value of one if a company is from Brazil or South Africa, respectively, and 0 otherwise. As both variables are 0 for German entities, the results of the country variables have to be interpreted against the benchmark of the German setting. In line with the focus of the thesis, this allows comparisons between the two emerging economies and the developed Germany.

On the basis of the sample description in section 5.1.2.2, **company size** is operationalized by the amount of revenues during the financial year 2013. However, alternative size proxies, such as market capitalization and total assets are used in additional sensitivity analyses. Due to the considerable variance in the company size proxies across the sample companies and the fact that the values are not distributed equally, the determinants regression model uses the natural logarithms of the size measures. The data is received from Thomson Reuters Datastream.

Besides company size, **company age** is included in the model as additional determinant. It is computed as the number of years from the year of a company's foundation until the examined financial year 2013. Also earlier studies consider the influence of a company's age and, analogously, the number of years since a company's equity market listing.[1022] The year of foundation is taken from Thomson Reuters Datastream.[1023]

In line with prior empirical studies on disclosure quality, also the association between a company's financial reporting quality and its **profitability** is investigated.[1024] As profitability proxy the study uses return on equity (ROE) which is one of the most important performance indicators from the perspective of company owners. Following *Haniffa/Cooke* (2002) the ROE is computed as net income divided by the owners' total equity.[1025] ROE is calculated for the sample companies' financial year 2013 on the basis of data from Thomson Reuters Datastream. However, it should be considered that a company's ROE depends on its leverage when interpreting the results.[1026]

To determine, whether a company is over- or undervalued the literature provides several operationalizations of **company valuation**, such as Tobin's Q, price-earnings-ratio or

---

1022 Cf. *Barry/Brown* (1985), p. 412; *Haniffa/Cooke* (2002), p. 332.

1023 Missing values are replaced by company age calculations on the basis of information on the company websites.

1024 Cf. amongst others *Inchausti* (1997), p. 54; *Haniffa/Cooke* (2002), p. 332; *Dainelli et al.* (2013), p. 267.

1025 Cf. *Haniffa/Cooke* (2002), p. 332.

1026 Leverage is not included in the determinants study as additional independent variable for several reasons. First, the literature review has shown that leverage is of minor importance in emerging economies, cf. section 3.3. Second, leverage is an indicator for company risk which is already captured by the variable *systematic risk*. Third, prior research uses leverage as a proxy for stakeholder orientation, cf. *Bluesing* (2013), p. 201. However, stakeholder orientation is already operationalized by ownership concentration in this study.

price-book-ratio.[1027] In particular, the simple price-book value (relation of a company's current stock price to its book value per share), which considers both the assessment of future prospects and past costs, has proven useful in multiple studies.[1028] Therefore, this study uses the price-book-value at the end of the financial year 2013 as proxy for company valuation. The data is received from Thomson Reuters Datastream.

Furthermore, the determinants investigation tests the hypothesized relationship between an entity's financial reporting quality and its **systematic risk**. In line with prior research, the beta value of a company's stock measures its systematic risk in relation to the efficient market portfolio.[1029] It is defined as follows:[1030]

$$(5.9) \quad Beta = Cov(r_i;\ r_m)/Var(r_m)$$

where,

r_i = return on stock of company *i*; and

r_m = return of the market portfolio.

Data from Thomson Reuters Datastream allow the calculation of the average beta factor for the financial year 2013 on the basis of weekly beta values.

As discussed in the theoretical foundation, **ownership concentration** is assumed to have an influence on FRQ. With the so-called Herfindahl index[1031] the study uses a proxy for ownership concentration which is intuitive to interpret. The Herfindahl index adds up the squared fractions of each shareholder (cf. equation (5.10)).[1032] As the model weights larger shares more heavily due to squaring, a higher index stands for a higher level of concentration. The strongest concentration would be a Herfindahl index of 1, which means that a single shareholder holds all shares. Since the index weights the share of each company owner, the index is more meaningful than, for example, the mere number of investors whose shares exceed a certain threshold.[1033]

$$(5.10) \quad H = \sum_{i=1}^{N} a_i^2$$

where,

H = Herfindahl index as measure for ownership concentration;

[1027] Cf. *Capaul et al.* (1993), p.29; *Chen et al.* (2014), p. 22.

[1028] Cf. amongst others *Fama/French* (1992), p. 441; *Capaul et al.* (1993), p. 27.

[1029] Cf. *Francis et al.* (2005a), p. 297.

[1030] Cf. *Mankiw/Shapiro* (1984), p. 6.

[1031] For further characteristics of the Herfindahl index, cf. *Rhoades* (1993), p. 188.

[1032] Due to data availability, this study's Herfindahl index is based on the fractions of a company's five largest shareholders at the end of the financial year 2013. Data is taken from the companies' annual reports and websites as well as from Thomson Reuters Datastream.

[1033] In the literature ownership concentration is frequently determined through the identification of block holders with shares of more than e.g. 5% (cf. *Bertrand/Mullainathan* (2000), p. 44) or 25% (cf. *Elston/Goldberg* (2003), p. 1400).

a_i	= fraction of company shares of shareholder *i*; and
N	= total number of shareholders.

Furthermore, the study examines the relationship between the **customer basis** of a company and its FRQ. Following prior research it distinguishes between companies with mainly business-to-consumer (B2C) customers and those offering their products and services primarily to business-to-business (B2B) clients.[1034] The determinants regression model includes a dummy variable which takes the value of one for B2C companies and 0 for B2B entities.

Moreover, theory suggests that an entity's **information environment**, the extent of available information about the entity, affects its FRQ. The study uses two indicators for information level: **media coverage** and **analyst following**. While media coverage captures the extent of media attention which a company receives, analyst following represents the number of financial analysts evaluating the entity. To determine an entity's media coverage, the search engine *Google News* is searched for news on each sample company. The proxy is defined as the logarithmized number of *Google News* results. The second proxy, analyst following, is the number of I/B/E/S earnings per share (EPS) forecasts by analysts during the companies' financial year 2013.

Finally, the determinants model also analyzes industry-fixed effects. Following the SIC code industry categories by *French/Fama* (2010) as described in section 5.1.2.1,[1035] the determinants model includes a dummy variable for each of the 10 industry categories that is 1 if a company belongs to the industry and 0 otherwise. In the regression model, the industry *business equipment* is used as a benchmark category for the other industry results and, thus, is omitted from the regression results.

5.3.3.2 Bivariate correlation and multivariate analysis

The determinants study uses both bivariate correlations and multivariate regression techniques to analyze the relationship between FRQ and the determinants described in the previous section and, thereby, test the corresponding hypotheses H2 to H11.

The **bivariate correlation analysis** conducts an isolated analysis of the statistical relationship between each determinant variable and the corresponding FRQ measure through the computation of a correlation coefficient.[1036] This study uses *Spearman's* rank correlation coefficient *(Spearman's rho)*, which, in a first step, ranks all values of the variables X and Y, respectively, (assuming equal distances between the values of two consecutive ranks) and, second, calculates the correlation between X and Y.[1037] In contrast to correlations, such as *Pearson's* correlation, which measure the linear relationship between the values of two var-

[1034] Cf. *Santema/van de Rijt* (2001), p. 104. The classification is based on the customer group which is responsible for the majority of a company's revenues. The sample companies are categorized on the basis of the information provided in their annual reports.

[1035] For an overview of this study's industry categories, cf. Appendix, Table A-2.

[1036] Cf. *Auer/Rottmann* (2015), p. 92.

[1037] Cf. *Cleff* (2015), p. 102-104.

iables (X and Y), *Spearman's* correlation coefficient determines a monotonic relationship between two rank sequences (for X and Y).[1038] The advantage of *Spearman's* correlation over *Pearson's* correlation is that it requires only ordinally scaled variables,[1039] which lowers concerns regarding the metric scale of this study's data. Moreover, *Spearman's* correlation coefficient is robust to outliers.[1040] By construction, the value of *Spearman's* normalized correlation coefficient can range from -1 (perfect negative correlation) to +1 (perfect positive correlation).[1041] While there is no universal guideline regarding the interpretation of correlation coefficients between the two extremes -1 and +1, *Brosius* (2011) recommends the following guide values and interpretations:

Absolute value of the correlation coefficient	0	above 0 to 0.2	above 0.2 to 0.4	above 0.4 to 0.6	above 0.6 to 0.8	above 0.8 to below 1	1
Interpretation	No correlation	Very weak correlation	Weak correlation	Medium correlation	Strong correlation	Very strong correlation	Perfect correlation

Table 5-15: Interpretation of correlation coefficients
Following *Brosius* (2011), p. 523.

In addition to the correlation analysis, the **multivariate analysis** uses ordinary least squares (OLS) regressions to examine the relationships between FRQ (dependent or response variable) and the identified determinants (independent or explanatory variables).[1042] Equation (5.11) shows the full determinants model which regresses FRQ on the above described determinant proxies. The regression coefficients β_1 and β_2 describe the aggregated association of the Brazilian and South African financial reporting environment and FRQ in comparison to the German setting.

$$(5.11) \quad FRQ_i = \alpha + \beta_1 Country\_BRA_i + \beta_2 Country\_RSA_i + \beta_3 Company\ size_i + \beta_4 Company\ age_i + \beta_5 Profitability_i + \beta_6 Company\ valuation_i + \beta_7 Systematic\ risk_i + \beta_8 Ownership_i + \beta_9 Customer\ basis_i + \beta_{10} Media_i + \beta_{11} Analyst_i + \sum \beta_{12} Industry_i + \varepsilon_i$$

where,

FRQ_i = financial reporting quality measure for company *i*;

$Country\_BRA_i$ = dummy variable that is 1 for a Brazilian company *i* and 0 otherwise;

$Country\_RSA_i$ = dummy variable that is 1 for a South African company *i* and 0 otherwise;

$Company\ size_i$ = logarithmized revenues of company *i*;

$Company\ age_i$ = number of years since foundation of company *i*;

$Profitability_i$ = return on equity (ROE) of company *i*;

1038 Cf. *Pospeschill* (2006), p. 354-355.
1039 Cf. *Cleff* (2015), p. 102.
1040 Cf. *Auer/Rottmann* (2015), p. 104.
1041 Cf. here and in the following *Brosius* (2011), p. 523.
1042 Cf. *Cleff* (2015), p. 135.

$Company\ valuation_i$	= price-to-book-ratio of company *i's* stock;
$Systematic\ risk_i$	= beta value of company *i*;
$Ownership_i$	= Herfindahl concentration index for five largest company shares by owners of company *i*;
$Customer\ basis_i$	= dummy variable that is 1 if company *i* is B2C company and 0 if B2B company;
$Media_i$	= logarithmized number of online news concerning company *i*;
$Analyst_i$	= Number of EPS forecasts by analysts for company *i;*
$Industry_i$	= dummy variable that is 1 if company *i* belongs to the industry and 0 otherwise; and
ε_i	= error term for company *i*.

However, the application of the OLS regression model provides only valid results, if the following prerequisites are fulfilled. First, the regression residuals have to be identically distributed.[1043] Otherwise, the residuals would be dependent on the independent variables and the order of the observations (e.g., a systematic increase in residuals due to negligent data collection or when measuring later observations). This would indicate **heteroskedasticity**. However, the problem is mitigated through the estimation of *White*-corrected robust standard errors in the regression models.[1044]

Second, the residuals must be uncorrelated to avoid **autocorrelations**.[1045] However, autocorrelation is particularly a problem in time series analyses and, thus, less relevant for this study. Third, the regression model requires the explanatory variables to be independent from each other.[1046] Strong relationships between the explanatory variables cause **multicollinearity**, which biases the regression results. The example of two perfectly correlated explanatory variables shows that only one of them would be required, as the second variable does not add any explanatory value. This study's tests for multicollinearity are twofold: The correlation coefficients of the determinant variables are analyzed prior to the computation of the regression models and the variance inflation factor (VIF) is determined for every regression. A VIF above ten indicates the existence of multicollinearity.[1047] Almost all regression results throughout this thesis show VIF values below ten.

Fourth, the residuals of the regression model have to be normally distributed to allow valid significance tests.[1048] According to the central limit theorem, a minimum of 30 observations is sufficient to meet this criterion.[1049] As this study's regressions include at least 50

[1043] Cf. here and in the following *Backhaus et al.* (2016), p. 103.
[1044] Cf. *White* (1980), p. 817-838.
[1045] Cf. here and in the following *Backhaus et al.* (2016), p. 105.
[1046] Cf. here and in the following *Cleff* (2015), p. 160-162.
[1047] Cf. *Brosius* (2011), p. 583.
[1048] Cf. *Backhaus et al.* (2016), p. 110.
[1049] Cf. *Auer/Rottmann* (2015), p. 286 and 460.

observations, normal distribution is assumed. Furthermore, the F-statistic indicates in OLS regressions the overall significance of the regression model.[1050] Thus, a significant F-statistic suggests that the regression model is not only valid for the applied sample, but also for the underlying population.

5.3.4 Capital market analysis on the basis of information asymmetries

5.3.4.1 Conceptual considerations

As formulated in the research questions RQ3a and RQ3b, this study aims at providing evidence, whether information asymmetries on the capital market are associated with the level of FRQ. It is assumed that higher FRQ reduces a company's information asymmetry component of its **cost of equity**.[1051] The cost of equity can be calculated by discounting a company's expected future cash flows with the returns demanded by investors.[1052] This expected return consists of a risk-free interest rate and a company-specific risk premium which cannot be diversified. In efficient capital markets, hence, the release of useful information leads to a movement in share prices, as the investors revise their assumptions regarding future cash flows,[1053] and "*[...] unambiguously moves a firm's cost of capital closer to the risk-free rate.*"[1054]

To capture information asymmetries, the literature frequently focuses on the **liquidity of shares**,[1055] as lower liquidity levels are the result of costs caused by adverse selection in transactions between buyers and sellers of a company.[1056] Thus, companies facing illiquidity issue capital at a discount resulting in higher cost of capital. Companies have an incentive to reduce information asymmetries by providing high-quality information and, thereby, reduce the discount at which (illiquid) shares are traded leading to lower cost of equity.[1057] This study uses the relative bid-ask spreads, the fraction of zero return days and the illiquidity measure by *Amihud* (2002) as proxies for information asymmetries. To test the relationship between the companies' FRQ and information asymmetries, the regression model includes the information asymmetry measures as dependent variable.

Although some studies find that increased FRQ is able to reduce information asymmetries, there is no consensus in the literature on the **time window** when such effects occur.[1058] For instance, it could be assumed that capital market participants use information

---

[1050] Cf. here and in the following *Backhaus et al.* (2016), p. 86.

[1051] Cf. section 4.2.4.

[1052] Cf. here and in the following *Lambert et al.* (2007), p. 387.

[1053] Cf. *Deegan* (2000), p. 361.

[1054] *Lambert et al.* (2007), p. 387.

[1055] Cf. amongst others *Lesmond et al.* (1999), p. 1113; *Leuz/Verrecchia* (2000), p. 93; *Amihud* (2002), p. 31; *Goyenko et al.* (2009), p. 153; *Balakrishnan et al.* (2014), p. 2237. For an overview of liquidity measures, cf. *Balakrishnan et al.* (2014), p. 2271-2272.

[1056] Cf. here and in the following *Foucault et al.* (2013), p. 4-5, 120 and 379.

[1057] Cf. *Leuz/Verrecchia* (2000), p. 92.

[1058] For the use of different time lags when measuring capital market effects, cf. *Botosan* (1997), p. 341; *Stoll* (2000), p. 2484-2485; *Leuz/Verrecchia* (2000), p. 116; *Hail* (2002), p. 743; *Daske et al.* (2008), p. 1133; *Balakrishnan et al.* (2014), p. 2262.

immediately when published, after a certain period of time or over an extended period of time. Moreover, investors may already get access to annual report information before its official publication. To capture both long-term and short-term time lags of capital market reactions, the study measures information asymmetries during different time windows. While the main model focuses on a company's information asymmetries during its full financial year after the balance sheet date, the additional robustness tests also consider the capital market observations in each quarter of this financial year.

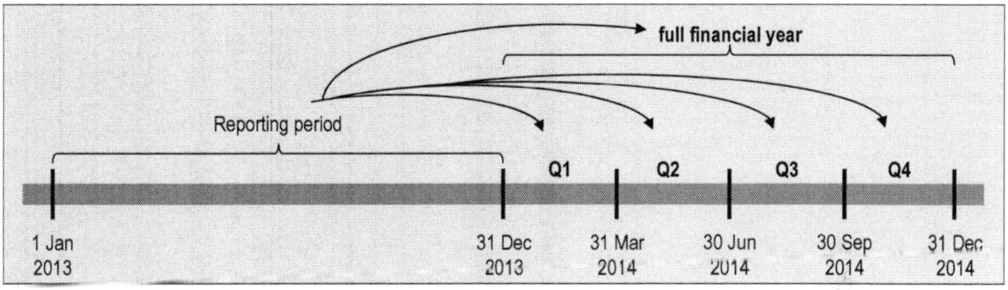

Figure 5-11: Analyzed time lags of capital market effects (fiscal year end on 31 December 2013)

For a company with 31 December as balance sheet date, Figure 5-11 illustrates that the study measures information asymmetries between 1 January and 31 December 2014 (full financial year), 1 January and 31 March 2014 (Q1), 1 April and 30 June 2014 (Q2), 1 July and 30 September 2014 (Q3) as well as 1 October and 31 December 2014 (Q4). For a company with balance sheet date 31 March 2014, the time windows are analogously postponed by a three months period.

5.3.4.2 Information asymmetries models and variables

The study calculates three separate proxies to measure information asymmetries: bid-ask spreads, zero return days and the illiquidity measure by *Amihud* (2002). In line with its extensive use in prior research, this study regards **bid-ask spreads (BAS)** as primary proxy for information asymmetries.[1059] *Bekaert et al.* (2007) argue that the BAS proxy is more precise than other liquidity proxies.[1060] In this study BAS are calculated as the mean relative spread between bid and ask prices of a company i over the period of expected capital market reactions (cf. equation (5.12)). *Lesmond* (2005) argues that the paucity of bid-ask spread data might require the use of other liquidity estimates in emerging markets.[1061] However, with respect to this study's sample, BAS are available from capital markets with relatively high trading volumes so that the BAS proxy can be applied.

[1059] Cf. amongst others *Healy et al.* (1999), p. 489; *Leuz/Verrecchia* (2000), p. 108; *Daske et al.* (2008), p. 1135.

[1060] Cf. *Bekaert et al.* (2007), p. 1785. An increased precision can particularly be assumed for intraday BAS. As intraday BAS are not available for this study, end-of-day BAS are used.

[1061] Cf. *Lesmond* (2005), p. 411.

$$BAS_i = (ask\ price_i - bid\ price_i)/((ask\ price_i + bid\ price_i)/2) \tag{5.12}$$

where,

BAS_i	= bid-ask spread for company *i*;
$ask\ price_i$	= closing ask price for company *i;* and
$bid\ price_i$	= closing bid price for company *i*.

In addition to BAS, the study uses the fraction of **zero-return days (zeros)** following *Lesmond et al.* (1999). Zeros is calculated as sum of zero-return days for a company during the selected period (e.g., full financial year 2014) divided by the number of total trading days for the company in that period (cf. equation (5.13)).[1062] Hence, the zeros measures for the sample companies are comparable, although the number of total trading days slightly differs between Brazil, South Africa and Germany. According to *Lesmond et al.* (1999), zero-return days occur when market participants decide not to trade because transaction costs exceed the value of new information which is not priced yet.[1063] Higher fractions of zero-return days indicate lower liquidity and, thus, higher information asymmetries. As the zero-return days computation requires solely a time series of daily returns, it can be applied in settings where data for other proxies are not available and, therefore, might be particularly useful for emerging market studies.[1064] Moreover, zeros is found to capture cross-country liquidity effects in emerging markets better than volume-based liquidity proxies.[1065]

$$Zeros_i = zero\text{-}return\ days_i\ /T_i \tag{5.13}$$

where,

$Zeros_i$	= fraction of zero-return days for company *i;*
$zero\text{-}return\ days_i$	= number of days with return = 0 in the regarded period for company *i*; and
T_i	= number of total trading days in the regarded period for company *i*.

The **Amihud (2002) illiquidity measure (AIM)** computes the ratio between the absolute value of the relative stock return and the value of the trading volume per day during a certain period of time, as illustrated in equation (5.14).[1066] It is multiplied by 1,000,000 for expositional purposes. The AIM shows the daily price response, if the trading value changes by 1,000 currency units, i.e. higher values suggest a stronger price reaction to the trades (in 1,000 currency units) and, thus, more illiquid shares. As days with low trading

[1062] Cf. *Goyenko et al.* (2009), p. 159.

[1063] Cf. *Lesmond et al.* (1999), p. 1115; *Daske et al.* (2008), p. 1133.

[1064] Cf. *Bekaert et al.* (2007), p. 1785.

[1065] Cf. *Lesmond* (2005), p. 411.

[1066] Cf. *Amihud* (2002), p. 32; *Balakrishnan et al.* (2014), p. 2271.

activity or no trading activity at all would incorrectly yield a price impact of zero, days with zero-returns are omitted from the calculation.[1067] The study uses the median of the calculated AIM proxy as basis for interpretation. In contrast to the bid-ask spreads measure, which is dependent on liquid capital markets to get reliable data (if the required microstructure data are available at all), the AIM proxy can also be used for less liquid markets without such data, particularly in emerging capital markets.[1068] *Goyenko et al.* (2009) find the AIM to be the best liquidity measure which considers the price impact of trades.[1069] *Lesmond* (2005) classifies the AIM proxy as one of the best to measure within-country liquidity in emerging markets.[1070]

$$(5.14)\quad AIM_i = |return_i| / (share\ price_i * trading\ volume_i) * 1{,}000{,}000$$

where,

AIM_i	= Amihud's illiquidity measure for company *i*;
$return_i$	= daily relative return for company *i*;
$share\ price_i$	= day-end share price for company *i;* and
$trading\ volume_i$	= number of traded company *i* shares.

To determine the relationship between information asymmetries and financial reporting quality, the **main regression model** uses the **BAS proxy** (as measure for information asymmetries), whereas the zeros proxy and AIM proxy, respectively, replace the BAS proxy in the additional robustness test regressions. Following the regression model by *Stoll* (2000), the main model regresses the logarithmized bid-ask spreads on the FRQ measure (e.g., total score of full disclosure index) and the control variables (cf. equation (5.15)). The selection of the independent control variables follows prior studies using this model (e.g., *Leuz/Verrecchia* (2000); *Stoll* (2000)) to allow consistent comparisons: company size, turnover volume, return volatility as well as mean share price. "*The rationale for these variables is based primarily on order processing and inventory considerations.*"[1071] In particular, an increase in company size and turnover volume suggests a higher probability of locating a counterparty and, thus, the risk of accepting inventory is reduced. The stock return volatility captures the risk of adverse changes in the price of stocks put into inventory. Stock price is also a risk proxy, as stocks with lower prices are assumed to be riskier. The reason for the use of logarithmized values is twofold. First, the variables are not distributed equally so that logarithms allow better comparisons of large and small values. Second, the approach eases the use of multiplicative linkages between variables.

Consistent with *Stoll* (2000), *company size* is operationalized in this capital market study by the companies' market capitalization at the beginning of the observation period. *Turn-*

[1067] Cf. *Daske et al.* (2008), p. 1133.
[1068] Cf. *Amihud* (2002), p. 32; *Balakrishnan et al.* (2014), p. 2271.
[1069] Cf. *Goyenko et al.* (2009), p. 169.
[1070] Cf. *Lesmond* (2005), p. 411.
[1071] *Stoll* (2000), p. 1480. Cf. also in the following, *Stoll* (2000), p. 1480.

over volume is measured as the daily trading volume divided by the company's market capitalization on that day. *Volatility* is computed as the standard deviation of stock returns and *share price* is the average share price. Since the thesis aims for a cross-country comparison, the regression includes country variables for both Brazil and South Africa, which allow a comparison against the regression results for Germany. To control for the influence of different industries, the model includes industry-fixed effects on the basis of ten industry groups following *French/Fama* (2010), as defined in section 5.1.2.1.[1072]

$$(5.15)\quad IA_i = \alpha + \beta_1 FRQ_i + \beta_2 \ln(Company\ size_i) + \beta_3 \ln(Turnover\ volume_i) + \beta_4 \ln(Volatility_i) + \beta_5 \ln(Share\ price_i) + \beta_6 Country\_BRA_i + \beta_7 Country\_RSA_i + \sum \beta_8 Industry_i + \varepsilon_i$$

where,

IA_i	= information asymmetry proxy for company *i*;
FRQ_i	= financial reporting quality measure for company *i*;
$Company\ size_i$	= market value of equity for company *i* at the beginning of the period;
$Turnover\ volume_i$	= mean value of daily trading volume for company *i* during the period;
$Volatility_i$	= standard deviation of daily returns for company *i* during the period;
$Share\ price_i$	= mean share price for company *i* during the period;
$Country\_BRA_i$	= dummy variable that is 1 for a Brazilian company *i* and 0 otherwise;
$Country\_RSA_i$	= dummy variable that is 1 for a South African company *i* and 0 otherwise;
$Industry_i$	= dummy variable that is 1 if company *i* belongs to the industry and 0 otherwise; and
ε_i	= error term for company *i*.

Although the regression model according to equation (5.15) considers country-fixed effects, it is not able to capture how an increase of FRQ in one of the three particular countries affects the relationship between FRQ and information asymmetries. To find such cross-country differences, the information asymmetry regression model has to include a term interacting FRQ with the country variables. Still using the results for the German companies as a benchmark, equation (5.16) defines the regression model including interaction terms for the Brazilian and South African sample companies.

[1072] For this study's industry classification, cf. Appendix, Table A-2.

$$(5.16)\quad IA_i = \alpha + \beta_1 FRQ_i + \beta_2 \ln(Company\ size_i) + \beta_3 \ln(Trading\ volume_i) + \beta_4 \ln(Volatility_i) + \beta_5 \ln(Share\ price_i) + \beta_6 Country\_BRA_i + \beta_7 Country\_RSA_i + \beta_8 FRQ_i * Country\_BRA_i + \beta_9 FRQ_i * Country\_RSA_i + \sum \beta_{10} Industry_i + \varepsilon_i$$

where,

$FRQ_i * Country\_BRA_i$= interaction term of FRQ_i and $Country\_BRA_i$ for company *i*;

$FRQ_i * Country\_RSA_i$= interaction term of FRQ_i and $Country\_RSA_i$ for company *i*; and

all other variables as defined above.

The validity of the regression results depends on the same prerequisites as those described in section 5.3.3.2 for the multivariate determinants analysis.

6 Empirical results

After the description of the empirical field including the sample selection as well as the presentation of the research methodology of the different studies in chapter five, this chapter presents the empirical results of the investigations. In particular, the research hypotheses, which have been developed in chapter four, are tested throughout this chapter. The structure of the empirical results follows this study's research objectives. First, section 6.1 describes financial reporting practices by presenting the descriptive results for each of the three measures of FRQ. Second, section 6.2 presents the results of the determinants study. Third, the results of the capital market study are presented in section 6.3. Finally, section 6.4 links and discusses the results of the three studies.

6.1 Financial reporting practice

After section 6.1.1 presents the results of the accruals-based proxies, section 6.1.2 shows the results of the annual report investigation including the analysis of the annual report size as well as the results of the content analysis on the basis of the disclosure index. Moreover, the findings of the readability analysis are presented in section 6.1.3. Section 6.1.4 compares the results of the three FRQ measures on the basis of correlation analyses and section 6.1.5 evaluates the analyzed financial reporting practice critically.

6.1.1 Accruals-based earnings management

6.1.1.1 Magnitude of accruals

In the following, the FRQ of the sample companies is analyzed on the basis of the accruals-based proxies introduced in section 5.2.1. While this section presents the results for the magnitude of accruals (MACCR) proxy, the following section shows the findings for the modified version of the discretionary accruals model by *Jones* (1991).

The results of the MACCR proxy (cf. Table 6-1) show that the MACCR medians of the South African (0.732) and German (0.809) companies are considerably higher than the corresponding value for the Brazilian sample (0.481). Although the MACCR proxy might also be affected by other factors than earnings management (e.g., an entity's business model and industry), the result suggests that South African and German companies tend to engage in more earnings management than their Brazilian counterparts. However, the fourth quartile of the Brazilian distribution includes outliers with particularly high MACCR values boosting the country's mean MACCR to 1.757, which is more than twice the other countries' mean values. This relatively high mean value is in line with the results by *Lopes et al.* (2007), who find an average MACCR for non-cross-listed Brazilian companies of 1.861.[1073]

[1073] Cf. *Lopes et al.* (2007), p. 12.

Magnitude of accruals (MACCR)							
Sample	Min.	25% pctl.	Median	Mean	75% pctl.	Max.	Std. Dev.
Total (n=150)	0.012	0.380	0.716	1.082	0.957	23.827	2.360
Brazil (n=50)	0.012	0.212	0.481	1.757	1.089	23.827	4.006
South Africa (n=50)	0.032	0.532	0.732	0.722	0.928	1.810	0.345
Germany (n=50)	0.107	0.598	0.809	0.767	0.973	1.597	0.280
Kruskal-Wallis test: p < 0.001							

Table 6-1: Earnings management (magnitude of accruals)

Although the German median and mean values exceed the South African ones, the descriptive statistics in Table 6-1 are relatively similar for both country samples. However, the standard variation is higher in South Africa (0.345) than in Germany (0.280), which could indicate more similar earnings management strategies in Germany. Consistent with this study's results, *Leuz et al.* (2003) find a similar median MACCR for Germany (0.848) and also their median value for South Africa (0.297) is below the German one.[1074] The larger difference between their South African and German medians may be explained by different samples and time periods as well as differing approaches to compute total accruals. The Kruskal-Wallis test ($p < 0.001$) shows that the sub samples differ significantly which is in line with hypothesis H1b expecting FRQ to differ across the three countries.

6.1.1.2 Modified-Jones model

The second accruals-based FRQ proxy of this study is the **modified-Jones model**, which determines discretionary accruals as residuals of cross-sectional industry regressions. Consistent with prior research, the modified-Jones model is conducted for a larger sample of 949 companies (universe sample) to consider industry effects in the regressions.[1075] The modified-*Jones* model characteristics and distribution of the discretionary accruals are consistent with prior research.[1076] In particular, the average explanatory power of the regressions (adj. R^2) indicates a good model quality considering its sample size when comparing to other studies.[1077] However, only the results for this study's **sample companies** are presented in the following.

1074 Cf. *Leuz et al.* (2003), p. 514-515. Note that *Leuz et al.* (2003) do not include companies from Brazil.

1075 Cf. section 5.2.1.2.

1076 Cf. *Kothari et al.* (2005), p. 176. For the universe sample statistics of the modified-Jones model regression estimates, cf. Appendix, Table A-6.

1077 *Dechow et al.* (2003), for example, find an adj. R^2 of 9.2% for their modified-*Jones* model, cf. *Dechow et al.* (2003), p. 360.

The analysis refers to the companies' unsigned discretionary accruals.[1078] Table 6-2 shows that German companies with a median of 2.3 seem to engage less in earnings management than Brazilian (2.8) and South African (3.8) sample entities. Thus, the results suggest that particularly South African companies tend to exercise discretion to manage earnings. However, the Brazilian entities show the largest mean value (5.2), which is consistent with their high maximum value. Moreover, the particularly high mean value for Brazil is in line with the results of the MACCR proxy.

Noticeably, the results provide evidence that the companies from the emerging economies Brazil and South Africa engage in more earnings management than those from Germany. This finding is in line with the assumption that a less developed accounting environment (e.g., weaker enforcement) in emerging economies allows more earnings management resulting in a lower FRQ. The observation that the mean discretionary accruals exceed the median values is consistent with the findings by *Salewski et al.* (2014) and *Chen et al.* (2011). Using a larger sample and another sample period, *Salewski et al.* (2014) show mean (median) discretionary accruals for German companies (IFRS adopters) of 8.7 (4.8).[1079] Also *Francis et al.* (2008) use a developed country setting investigating the earnings quality of 677 U.S. companies. Their results show mean and median discretionary accruals of 4.65 (3.97).[1080] For a sample of companies from emerging economies only, *Chen et al.* (2011) find mean (median) discretionary accruals of 10.0 (5.6).[1081] These high values for an emerging economy sample are in line with both expectations and this study's results.

Unsigned discretionary accruals							
Sample	**Min.**	**25% pctl.**	**Median**	**Mean**	**75% pctl.**	**Max.**	**Std. Dev.**
Total (n=150)	0.00	1.50	3.00	4.50	5.70	33.40	5.10
Brazil (n=50)	0.10	1.20	2.80	5.20	5.90	33.40	6.80
South Africa (n=50)	0.00	2.00	3.80	4.80	7.10	14.10	3.80
Germany (n=50)	0.00	1.10	2.30	3.70	4.40	19.40	4.20
Kruskal-Wallis test: p = 0.096							

Table 6-2: Earnings management (unsigned discretionary accruals)

[1078] For the results of the signed discretionary accruals, cf. Appendix, Table A-7. The results of the total sample indicate that there are more sample companies aiming at increasing earnings than attempting to decrease earnings. In particular, the distribution of the South African results suggests that companies use discretion particularly to reach higher earnings (optimistic policy) compared to the other samples. Moreover, cross-country differences can be assumed according to the Kruskal-Wallis test (p = 0.098).

[1079] Cf. *Salewski et al.* (2014), p. 33.

[1080] Cf. *Francis et al.* (2008), p. 72.

[1081] Cf. *Chen et al.* (2011), p. 1266.

Further, the Kruskal-Wallis test indicates that FRQ differs significantly across the three countries on the 10% level (p = 0.096) and, therefore, supports hypothesis H1b. However, this inference is only to some degree in line with the above results for the MACCR measure. The finding that South African entities show a higher discretionary accruals median than Brazilian entities is consistent with the results for the MACCR proxy. Unlike the MACCR findings, however, the unsigned discretionary accruals suggest that the median German company (2.3) uses even less discretion to manage earnings than the Brazilian median entity (2.8).

6.1.2 Annual reporting practice

This section presents the results of the annual report analysis. After section 6.1.2.1 describes the analyzed annual reports formally in terms of report size, section 6.1.2.2 provides the results of the content analysis on the basis of this study's self-constructed disclosure index.

6.1.2.1 Size of annual reports

Although the quality of annual report information can hardly be assessed by the number of the report's pages, this figure gives an indication for the report's disclosure quantity. Number of pages may represent, for instance, the size of the reporting entity, the complexity of its business model or the entity's effort to provide information to its addressees. Figure 6-1 illustrates the distribution of annual report pages in the three sample countries. It shows obvious gaps in report size from Brazilian reports[1082] with a median of 96 pages to South African reports (142 pages) and to German reports with a median of 223 pages per report. Moreover the report sizes are relatively similar within each country.

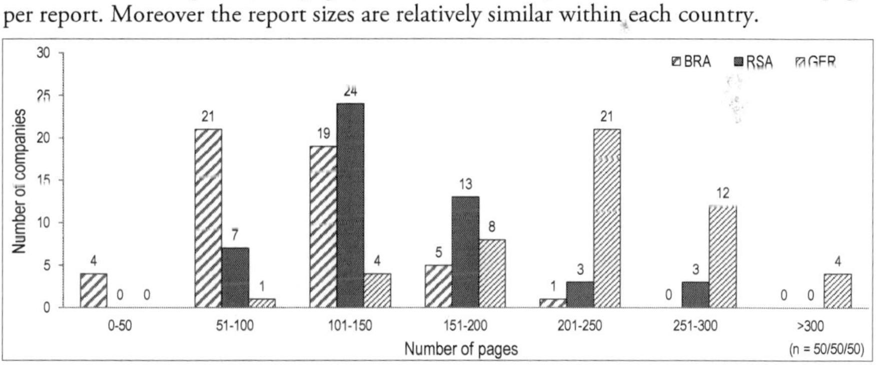

Figure 6-1: Number of pages in annual reports

While 40 Brazilian reports comprise between 51 and 150 pages, 37 South African reports range from 101 to 200 pages and 33 German companies report between 201 and 300 pages. This suggests that the annual report size is considerably higher for the developed

[1082] Excluding the Brazilian Reference Forms, as only relatively few pages of these standardized reports are relevant to this study.

Germany than in the emerging economies Brazil and South Africa. The differences in report size are consistent with the fact that also the companies are significantly larger in Germany.[1083]

In line with the additional descriptive statistics in Table 6-3, the smallest report is published by the Brazilian company *Lojas Americanas* (26 pages), whereas the German company *Siemens* prepares the largest report (371 pages).

Number of annual report pages							
Sample	**Min.**	**25% pctl.**	**Median**	**Mean**	**75% pctl.**	**Max.**	**Std. Dev.**
Total (n=150)	26.0	112.0	146.0	162.0	214.0	371.0	72.0
Brazil (n=50)	26.0	81.0	96.0	102.2	127.0	183.0	35.3
South Africa (n=50)	66.0	119.0	142.0	148.2	163.0	292.0	49.9
Germany (n=50)	88.0	200.0	223.0	229.2	272.0	371.0	63.0
Kruskal-Wallis test: p < 0.001							

Table 6-3: Distribution of number of annual report pages

The South African reports comprise significantly less pages than the German ones. This observation may not be intuitive, as the South African companies publish integrated reports which attempt to include a multitude of different areas of information.[1084] For instance, the integrated reports comprise the companies' sustainability reporting activities, whereas Brazilian and German companies may present this information in additional stand-alone sustainability reports. However, relatively small sizes of the South African reports are in line with the objective of integrated reporting to prepare concise reports focusing on essential issues.[1085]

Moreover, the Kruskal-Wallis test shows that the report sizes differ significantly ($p < 0.001$) across the three country samples. On average, the German reports are more than double the size of the Brazilian reports. In all three countries the median is lower than the mean of reported pages, which indicates that the distribution is right-skewed. This result suggests that there are considerable outliers at the upper page range in all three analyzed countries.

[1083] Cf. section 5.1.2.2.

[1084] Cf. section 2.3.3.

[1085] Cf. *Kajüter* (2014a), p. 75.

6.1.2.2 Content-related analysis of annual reports

6.1.2.2.1 Total financial reporting quality

After the analysis of the annual reports' size, the results of the content analysis on the basis of the disclosure index are presented in the following. While this section provides empirical evidence of the total FRQ provided in the annual reports, the following sections analyze the disclosure quality in the seven reporting categories in more detail. Moreover, the results are not only presented for the total sample, but also for each sub sample to analyze the financial reporting practices both within and across Brazil, South Africa and Germany.

The content analysis uses two types of disclosure indices. While the full disclosure index captures all disclosure items selected in accordance with the users' information needs, the voluntary disclosure index comprises only disclosure items which are reported voluntarily by the companies.[1086] The main results of the **full disclosure index** study are presented in Table 6-4. For the **total sample** the reached scores range from 13.0% to 68.4%. Thus, the score of the company with the best FRQ is more than five times higher than that of the company with the lowest FRQ. However, the maximum value of 68.4% suggests that even the best-performing entity has still considerable room to provide an annual report of even higher FRQ to its addressees. With a median score of 32.0% the median company in the sample does not meet sufficient disclosure items to reach one third of the maximum disclosure score. Overall, therefore, total FRQ can be characterized at most as moderate. The fact that the mean score (35.7%) exceeds the median score shows that the distribution is right-skewed including outliers with a relatively high total FRQ score.

Total FRQ (in % of maximum full disclosure index score)							
Sample	Min.	25% pctl.	Median	Mean	75% pctl.	Max.	Std. Dev.
Total (n=150)	13.0	26.8	32.0	35.7	44.4	68.4	12.8
Brazil (n=50)	13.0	20.0	25.6	25.5	31.1	39.8	6.8
South Africa (n=50)	19.3	27.9	31.4	32.0	35.6	45.8	6.3
Germany (n=50)	29.1	42.8	50.4	49.5	57.0	68.4	10.1
Kruskal-Wallis test: $p < 0.001$							

Table 6-4: Total FRQ (full disclosure study)

Furthermore, the main results of the full disclosure index study indicate a clear gap between the total FRQ of each **country sample**. The total FRQ in Brazil with a median score of 25.6% is lower than in South Africa with a median score of 31.4%. However, the total FRQ of both emerging companies is considerably lower than for the German sample, where the median company reaches a score of 50.4%. The corresponding average val-

[1086] Cf. section 5.2.2.5.

ues differ solely marginally from the median scores. The result of the Kruskal-Wallis test shows that the identified differences between the country's scores are statistically significant. These cross-country differences are further illustrated by Figure 6-2. The boxplot visualizes, inter alia, the range of the scores for each country as well as distances between the quartiles. In particular, it reveals that the score ranges of the second and third South African quartiles are lower than for Brazil and Germany, which indicates relatively homogenous disclosure qualities within the South African sample. In line with this observation, the South African distribution has the lowest standard deviation (6.3%) among all sub samples. Moreover, the illustration points out that in spite of the significant FRQ differences across the three countries not all Brazilian and South African companies provide a lower total FRQ than all German companies. In fact, numerous Brazilian and South African entities publish annual reports of higher total FRQ than German companies in the first (and partly second) quartiles.

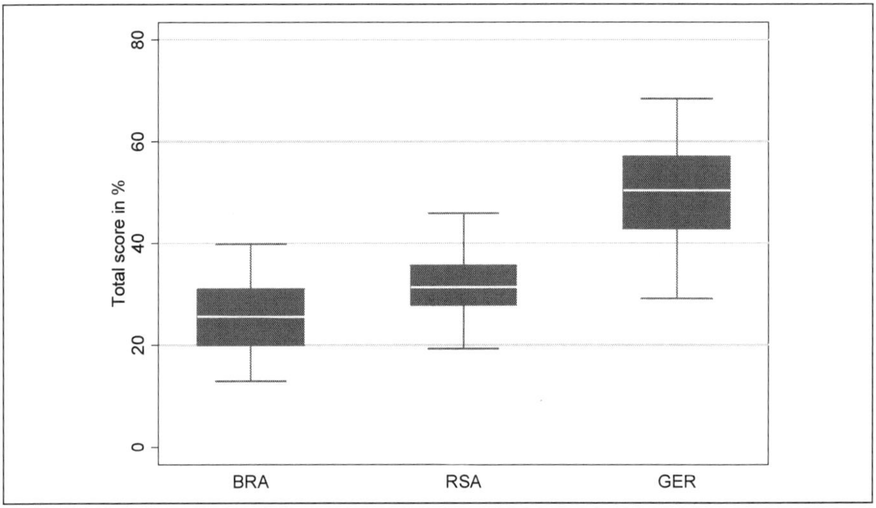

Figure 6-2: Total FRQ boxplot diagram (full disclosure study)

In addition to the results of the full disclosure index study, Table 6-5 presents the distribution of the **voluntary disclosure index** scores. As the voluntary disclosure indices do not include disclosure items which are required by regulation, the decrease in median and average scores in all (sub) samples is not surprising. Nonetheless, the general differences in FRQ across Brazil, South Africa and Germany remain unchanged. According to the Kruskal-Wallis test these differences are significant.

On the one hand, the gap between Brazilian and South African FRQ widens for the voluntary disclosures, since Brazilian companies face more mandatory disclosure index items (due to regulation in Brazil)[1087] than their South African counterparts. On the other hand,

[1087] For the financial reporting regulations in Brazil, South Africa and Germany, cf. section 2.3.

the FRQ gap between South Africa and Germany is reduced, as also German companies have to comply with more mandatory disclosure index items than South African companies. Since the results for the full and voluntary disclosure indices show solely minor differences and this study aims at providing insights into overall annual reporting practices, particularly the full disclosure index results are analyzed in the following.

Total FRQ (in % of maximum voluntary disclosure index score)							
Sample	Min.	25% pctl.	Median	Mean	75% pctl.	Max.	Std. Dev.
Total (n=150)	7.8	22.8	29.6	32.1	41.4	64.1	13.2
Brazil (n=50)	7.8	13.8	20.7	20.4	26.3	35.1	7.2
South Africa (n=50)	16.5	26.2	29.4	30.3	33.8	44.1	6.5
Germany (n=50)	26.4	38.9	45.4	45.7	54.3	64.1	10.1
Kruskal-Wallis test: $p < 0.001$							

Table 6-5: Total FRQ (voluntary disclosure study)

On the whole, there are substantial and significant variations in total FRQ across the three samples. In addition to the results for total FRQ, the following sections provide a more detailed analysis of the disclosure quality in each of the reporting categories: *background information*, *important financials*, *important non-financials*, *sustainability information*, *value based management*, *forward-looking information* as well as *risks and opportunities*.

6.1.2.2.2 Background information

The results for the FRQ of *background information* in Table 6-6 underpin that this general company information is a well-established and integral part of corporate annual reports in all three sample countries. All median and mean values of the total and country samples exceed the corresponding values for total FRQ.

FRQ of background information (in % of maximum full disclosure index score)							
Sample	Min.	25% pctl.	Median	Mean	75% pctl.	Max.	Std. Dev.
Total (n=150)	21.2	42.4	48.5	50.4	57.6	81.8	13.3
Brazil (n=50)	21.2	33.3	42.4	42.0	48.5	75.8	11.0
South Africa (n=50)	27.3	42.4	48.5	49.6	57.6	75.8	11.4
Germany (n=50)	33.3	51.5	59.1	59.6	69.7	81.8	11.2
Kruskal-Wallis test: $p < 0.001$							

Table 6-6: FRQ of background information (full disclosure study)

In particular the average *background information* score of the entire sample (50.4%) considerably exceeds the average total FRQ score of 35.7%. Moreover, the standard deviations of the *background information* scores are similar for all three country samples ranging from 11.0% to 11.4%, which indicates a homogenous variability across the countries. However, the Kruskal-Wallis test suggests significant cross-country differences in the FRQ of *background information.*

The untabulated detailed results show that the majority of the companies meet the disclosure items on company structure (66% on average), business activities (59%), industry (67%), and corporate governance (56%). However, German companies have mostly higher disclosure scores, since they do not only describe the relevant facts, but frequently also provide additional **explanations**. For example, 56% of the German companies explain corporate restructurings, whereas only 20% of the Brazilian and 22% of the South African companies provide such explanations.

Furthermore, the German sample's FRQ is considerably higher in the sub category *important business activities* (72%) than in the Brazilian (51%) and South African (54%) samples. In particular, explanations on changes of important business activities (e.g., new products) and the associated impact on the company's result are reasons for the higher scores.

A lack of explanations is also found for all sample companies regarding disclosures on the **economic environment**. Although 85% (72%) of the total sample provide some characteristics of the company's industry (macroeconomic environment), only 49% (17%) explain the potential impact of these characteristics on the company's business activities. Also the level of detail concerning information about **markets and competitors** varies considerably. While almost all sample companies (97%) provide information on the markets they operate in, 28% disclose their market shares and 31% explicitly refer to their main competitors. In particular, only 10% of the South African entities mention competitors in their annual reports. This observation may contradict the idea of integrated reporting, as competitors concern the company's business activities and, thus, should be taken into account when using an integrated reporting approach.

Moreover, the disclosure of **strategy** information is of particular importance to stakeholders. Figure 6-3 illustrates that all companies describe their business models and most companies also name their strategic objectives (e.g., market entries), whereas solely 12% (30%; 34%) of the Brazilian (South African; German) companies provide quantified targets (e.g., targeted market shares). A strategic corporate vision - a picture of the company's future which differs from the current state of the business (in the sense of *where is the company heading to?*)[1088] - is provided by 26% (40%; 64%) of the companies from Brazil (South Africa; Germany). The share of South African companies seems relatively small, since The International <IR> Framework requires integrated reports to identify "*[...] the organization's mission and vision [...]*"[1089]. Although a larger number of South African companies indeed mention the term *vision*, some of them solely provide vague phrases

[1088] Cf. *Henzler* (1992), p. 813.

[1089] Paragraph. 4.5 of The International <IR> Framework.

(e.g. "*our vision is to deliver value to all stakeholders*") and, therefore, do not meet the criterion in the above sense. However, almost 70% of the South African sample companies report on key competencies. This is in line with The International <IR> Framework which explicitly mentions the competencies of the company's employees[1090] and recommends to disclose the "*key elements of the business model*"[1091]. Moreover integrated reports shall describe "*how the organization differentiates itself in the market place*"[1092]. While about half of the South African and German entities inform users of their annual report about their M&A strategies, solely 14% of the Brazilian reports include this information. Moreover, barely any entities reveal which strategic financing scheme they pursue.

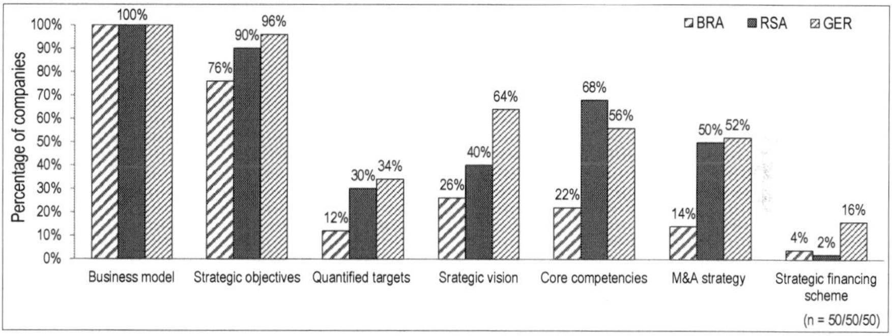

Figure 6-3: Disclosure of strategy information

On the whole, all sample companies provide information on some fundamental *background information* in their annual reports. Although the FRQ of *background information* exceeds total FRQ in all three countries, cross-country differences are also obvious for this reporting category. In line with the above results for strategy disclosures shown in Figure 6-3, the German companies provide a significantly higher FRQ of *background information* than the companies from the two emerging economies.

6.1.2.2.3 Financials

The sample companies' overall FRQ in the category *financials* with a median of 37.7% exceeds the median of the total FRQ (32.0%). One reason might be that several *financials* are commonly disclosed in the annual reports (e.g., explanation of revenue development) or the disclosures are even required by regulation as part of the financial statements (e.g., carrying amount of major assets, such as property, plant and equipment[1093]). The median values of the German (53.6%) and South African (33.1%) samples are on a similar level as the countries' total FRQ scores. Unlike the total FRQ results, however, there are only minor differences in *financials* disclosure quality between the emerging economies Brazil and South Africa (cf. Table 6-7). While the minimum and first quartile values are lower

1090 Cf. paragraph. 4.9 of The International <IR> Framework.
1091 Paragraph. 4.13 of The International <IR> Framework.
1092 Paragraph. 4.16 of The International <IR> Framework.
1093 Cf. IAS 16.73(d).

in Brazil (7.1% and 28.6%) than in South Africa (22.7% and 29.9%), the Brazilian third quartile and maximum values (39.6% and 51.3%) exceed the South African ones (38.3% and 44.2%). Consistent with a lower range of the South African scores, the South African companies provide relatively homogenous results within their country sample resulting in a standard deviation of only 5.5%, which is considerably lower than the standard deviation of Brazil (9.1%) and Germany (9.0%). The FRQ of *financials* differs significantly across the three countries according to the Kruskal-Wallis test.

FRQ of financials (in % of maximum full disclosure index score)							
Sample	Min.	25% pctl.	Median	Mean	75% pctl.	Max.	Std. Dev.
Total (n=150)	7.1	31.2	37.7	40.2	48.7	69.5	12.4
Brazil (n=50)	7.1	28.6	32.8	33.0	39.6	51.3	9.1
South Africa (n=50)	22.7	29.9	33.1	34.1	38.3	44.2	5.5
Germany (n=50)	32.5	47.4	53.6	53.5	61.0	59.5	9.0
Kruskal-Wallis test: $p < 0.001$							

Table 6-7: FRQ of financials (full disclosure study)

While the results show only little variability between the three countries for most *financials* disclosure items (e.g., regarding the description of revenue, profit, liability, equity and liquidity), considerable cross-country differences are found for the sub categories order intake, financial position and the evaluation of the overall economic position. With respect to order intake, Brazil and South Africa reach an average score of 2% and 5%, respectively. Although the score is considerably higher for Germany (22%), the overall quality of disclosures about order intake is very low. Annual report users also have to settle with relatively few information regarding the companies' financing activities. Only 28% (4%; 64%) of the Brazilian (South African; German) entities describe the objectives and principles of their financing management. While 76% of the German companies disclose their weighted average cost of capital (WACC), solely 2% of the Brazilian and 4% of the South African entities reveal this information. An overall evaluation of a company's economic position is provided by 38% (42%; 68%) of the Brazilian (South African; German) companies. However, only 6% (4%; 32%) of the country sample companies disclose an evaluation which reveals the management perspective (management approach).

Remarkable are also the results for the relationship between breakdown of revenue (and profit, respectively), on the one hand, and long-term strategy, on the other. In line with the purpose of integrated reporting, 18% (20%) of the South African companies provide an explanation of these relationships, whereas only 4% (4%) of the Brazilian and 4% (0%) of the German companies provide such information. However, besides this positive effect of the integrated reporting format, integrated reports seem to fall short of comprehensive disclosures on *financials*. Inter alia, the South African reports barely include high quality information regarding the categories overall cost of capital-related information (average score of 3%), hedging instruments (33%), asset breakdown (18%), disclosure of fair values (12%), description of capital structure (36%) and off-balance sheet arrangements (0%). In contrast, all Brazilian companies meet the disclosure index criteria on off-balance sheet arrangements (100%), as the information is required in a separate section of their Reference Forms.[1094] The findings indicate that integrated reports indeed emphasize the integration and connectivity of different aspects, however, neglect some fundamental disclosures in the area of *financials*.

The disclosure index study explicitly distinguishes **qualitative** and **quantitative** descriptions of required disclosure items. Figure 6-4 reveals that the average score of quantitative information is higher than that of qualitative information in all three countries. Considering the nature of *financials*, it is not surprising that companies tend to provide quantitative information rather than qualitative information. Moreover, the gap between the German and the emerging economies' FRQ scores is considerably smaller for quantitative descriptions. An explanation is that many of these quantitative figures are de facto standard disclosures in annual reports or even mandatory by regulation. In contrast to the total FRQ results, the Brazilian scores slightly exceed the South African ones. The reason for this observation might be the aforementioned weaknesses of the South African integrated reports as well as the fact that Brazilian companies have to comply with more mandatory *financials* than South African companies.

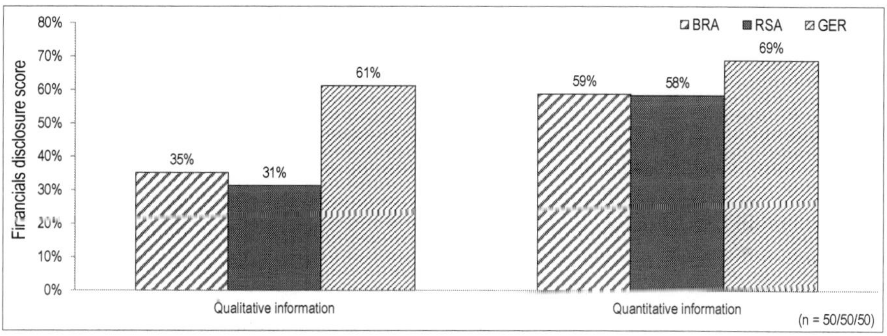

Figure 6-4: Disclosure of qualitative and quantitative information on financials

6.1.2.2.4 Non-financials

As part of *non-financials* disclosures in annual reports, companies provide sensitive information on issues, such as employee, supplier and customer satisfaction as well as on major brands and research & development activities.[1095] Table 6-8 shows that the overall sample's average FRQ in this area (31.3%) is below the mean total FRQ (35.7%). A lower *non-financials* FRQ is also found for every country sample. The country ranking with Brazil showing the lowest and Germany the highest disclosure quality remains unaffected and is significant according to the Kruskal-Wallis test. However, the Brazilian maximum

[1094] Cf. annex 24, no. 10.8 of the CVM Instruction No. 480.

[1095] For an overview of the *non-financials* disclosure index items, cf. Appendix, Table A-1.

value (64.8%) exceeds the South African maximum value (52.3%) considerably, suggesting that Brazilian companies are able to differentiate their annual reports from those of others through high-quality disclosures on *non-financials*. In line with the results for total FRQ and *financials*, the FRQ of *non-financials* varies least among the South African companies with a standard deviation of 11.7%.

FRQ of non-financials (in % of maximum full disclosure index score)							
Sample	Min.	25% pctl.	Median	Mean	75% pctl.	Max.	Std. Dev.
Total (n=150)	5.7	19.3	29.5	31.3	39.8	68.2	15.4
Brazil (n=50)	5.7	12.5	21.0	24.0	31.8	64.8	14.2
South Africa (n=50)	6.8	19.3	25.0	27.8	35.2	52.3	11.7
Germany (n=50)	18.2	27.3	40.3	42.0	53.4	68.2	14.0
Kruskal-Wallis test: p < 0.001							

Table 6-8: FRQ of non-financials (full disclosure study)

In more detail, Figure 6-5 analyzes the customer-related information provided in the annual reports of the sample companies. Although the untabulated average total quality of customer information is on a similar level in Brazil (26%), South Africa (24%) and Germany (28%), the specific reporting contents differ across the country samples. While key customers are described by about 60% of all companies, disclosures on customer satisfaction are relatively scarce. South African entities outperform the other samples regarding descriptions of customer satisfaction (46%), whereas only 2% describe how they measure customer satisfaction (e.g., surveys by independent institutes[1096]).

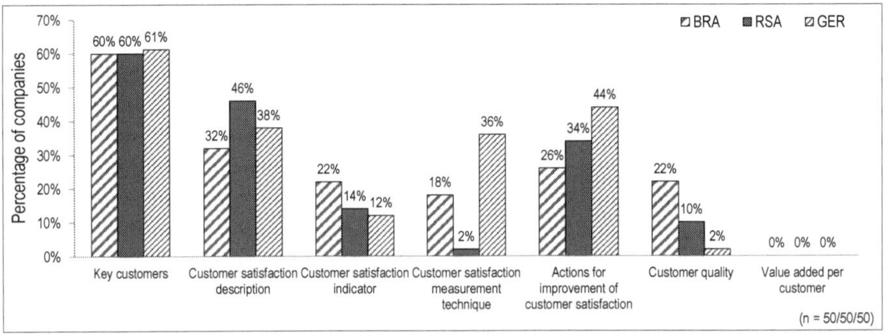

Figure 6-5: Disclosure of customer information

Particularly Brazilian companies disclose quantitative indicators for customer satisfaction (e.g., customer satisfaction score). German entities seem to put more emphasis on the de-

[1096] Cf. *Department of Banking and Finance (University of Zurich)* (2014), p. 7.

scription of the applied measurement technique (36%) and also outperform the other samples' entities concerning the disclosure of concrete actions to improve customer satisfaction (44%). However, only 2% of the German companies actually give insights on the quality of their customers (e.g., through ABC analyses), whereas 22% of the Brazilian companies provide such details. Moreover, none of the sample companies refers to the indicator value added per customer.

Moreover, the majority of the sample companies report on a few fundamental *non-financials*, such as employee fluctuation and trainings, key customers, major brands and the main investments during the financial year. However, there is considerable room for improvement regarding detailed high-quality information, particularly on customer-related topics as well as research and development activities in all three countries. Overall, the results for customer-related disclosures have shown that the focus of the companies' reporting contents differs across countries.

6.1.2.2.5 Sustainability

In line with South Africa's integrated reporting approach, *sustainability* is the only reporting category, where the South African sample (median score of 65.0%) outperforms the German sample (median score of 50.0%). Moreover, Table 6-9 shows that the median for Brazil (17.5%) is considerably lower than for the other countries, suggesting that sustainability information is only of minor importance in Brazilian annual reports. However, Brazilian companies show no homogeneous results for *sustainability* FRQ, as the companies' scores range from 0.0% to 80.0%. The considerable gap between Brazilian median and mean (24.4%) values indicate a right-skewed distribution including outliers with a relatively high *sustainability* FRQ. The Kruskal-Wallis test indicates that the cross-country differences in FRQ of sustainability information are significant.

FRQ of sustainability (in % of maximum full disclosure index score)							
Sample	**Min.**	**25% pctl.**	**Median**	**Mean**	**75% pctl.**	**Max.**	**Std. Dev.**
Total (n=150)	0.0	25.0	47.5	46.6	70.0	95.0	24.7
Brazil (n=50)	0.0	10.0	17.5	24.4	30.0	80.0	20.7
South Africa (n=50)	25.0	50.0	65.0	63.9	75.0	95.0	16.5
Germany (n=50)	15.0	40.0	50.0	51.4	65.0	85.0	18.1
Kruskal-Wallis test: $p < 0.001$							

Table 6-9: FRQ of sustainability information (full disclosure study)

The South African mining company *Royal Baefokeng Platinum* reaches with 17 out of 20 points one of the highest sustainability scores among all companies, however, has only an average total FRQ score. At the same time the company won *EY's Excellence in Integrated*

Reporting Awards 2014 which supports the sustainability focus of integrated reporting.[1097] However, the maximum score of 95% is reached by the companies *Adcock Ingram* and *Exxaro Resources*.

Figure 6-6 reveals how FRQ differs across the three countries regarding the triple bottom line sustainability dimensions. Brazilian disclosures on social aspects (e.g., labor practices and human rights issues) are of higher quality than on the economic and environmental dimensions. While there is only a small difference between South Africa and Germany concerning environmental and social sustainability FRQ, the South African average score for economic sustainability disclosures (66%) exceeds the German score considerably (41%). Reasons for this difference are particularly information on objectives and actions related to economic sustainability which is of higher FRQ in the South African reports.

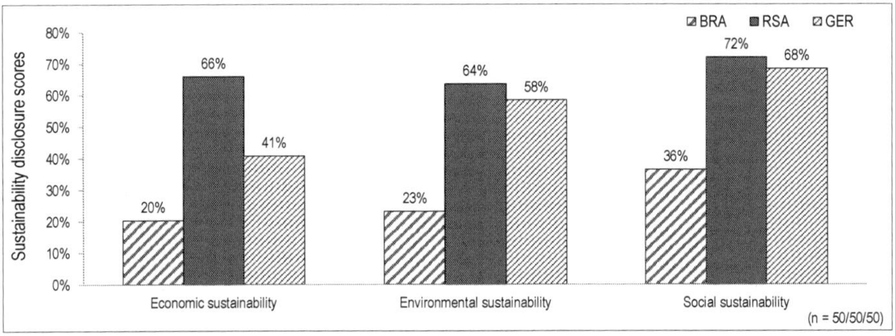

Figure 6-6: FRQ of economic, environmental and social sustainability

Additionally, 48% of the South African companies explain interdependencies among the three sustainability dimensions in contrast to only 14% of the Brazilian and 24% of the German companies. Moreover, the references to other sources of sustainability information about the company (e.g., websites, separate sustainability reports) are provided by 26% (90%; 56%) of the Brazilian (South African; German) sample entities. This seems remarkable, as South African companies already include extensive sustainability disclosures in their annual reports.

6.1.2.2.6 Value based management

While the median and mean FRQ scores are above the corresponding total FRQ scores in South Africa, *value based management* disclosures are below total FRQ in Brazil and Germany, where even companies with a score of 0.0% are found. Further, Table 6-10 shows that the FRQ of *value based management* varies considerably across the three countries (significant according to the Kruskal-Wallis test) and within the (sub) samples ranging from a score of 0.0% to 95.2%. In particular, the standard deviation of 22.0% for the German sample indicates that companies have not agreed on a generally accepted reporting approach regarding this category so far.

[1097] Cf. *EY* (2014), p. 9.

FRQ of value based management (in % of maximum full disclosure index score)							
Sample	Min.	25% pctl.	Median	Mean	75% pctl.	Max.	Std. Dev.
Total (n=150)	0.0	23.8	33.3	35.4	47.6	95.2	20.0
Brazil (n=50)	0.0	14.3	19.0	20.4	28.6	42.9	10.7
South Africa (n=50)	19.0	28.6	33.3	36.4	42.9	71.4	11.5
Germany (n=50)	0.0	38.1	47.6	49.5	66.7	95.2	22.0
Kruskal-Wallis test: $p < 0.001$							

Table 6-10: FRQ of value based management (full disclosure study)

Regarding information on the **management compensation system**, the untabulated average disclosure score of 56% for the total sample suggests a relatively high FRQ. However, the score is considerably higher in South Africa (73%) than in Germany (63%) and Brazil (31%). By contrast, disclosures on **management accounting** activities are poor overall. Figure 6-7 reveals that information on implemented value based management concepts (e.g., value added concepts) is predominantly found in Germany (54%), whereas only 6% of the Brazilian and none of the South African companies provide such information. Moreover, 44% of the German entities calculate value based target figures as part of their value based management concept, although only 42% also provide an explanation of these figures.

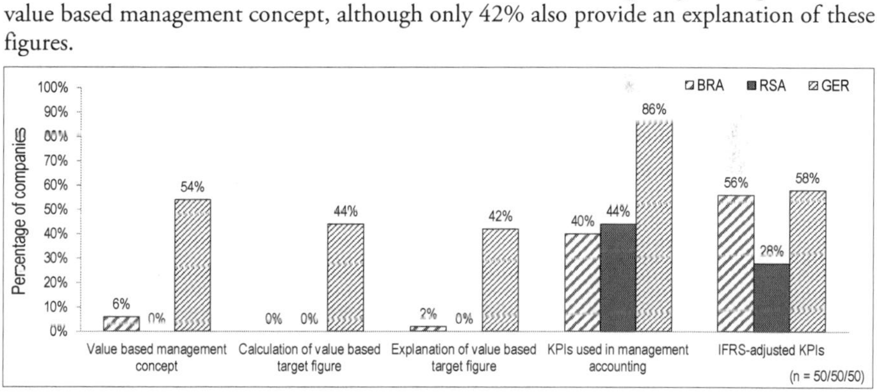

Figure 6-7: Selected disclosures on value based management

While only a few companies refer to an overall value based management concept, 40% (44%; 86%) of the companies in Brazil (South Africa; Germany) name **KPIs** used in management accounting (cf. Figure 6-7). In addition, 56% (28%; 58%) of the Brazilian (South African, German) entities reveal, whether they adjust IFRS figures for management purposes (e.g., as a basis for employee compensation).

6.1.2.2.7 Forward-looking information

Prospective information belongs to the most sensitive information in annual reports and, yet, to the most important figures for investors and analysts as these numbers serve as a main basis for their capital allocation decisions.[1098] For managers, the publication of concrete prospects poses a potential threat, as their personal performance will ultimately be assessed against their predictions. From this perspective, the low overall FRQ level of *forward-looking information* (median score of 15%) seems not surprising. Although *forward-looking* FRQ is below total FRQ in all countries, the gap between Brazil and South Africa with median scores of 5.8.% and 10.8%, on the one hand, and Germany (36.7%), on the other, is very pronounced (cf. Table 6-11). Thus, the median companies in Brazil and South Africa reach lower disclosure scores than the company with the lowest score in Germany (13.3%). According to the Kruskal-Wallis test, the cross-country differences in *forward-looking* FRQ is significant.

FRQ of forward-looking information (in % of maximum full disclosure index score)							
Sample	**Min.**	**25% pctl.**	**Median**	**Mean**	**75% pctl.**	**Max.**	**Std. Dev.**
Total (n=150)	0.0	6.7	15.0	19.7	30.0	68.3	16.8
Brazil (n=50)	0.0	1.7	5.8	8.9	13.3	36.7	8.9
South Africa (n=50)	1.7	6.7	10.8	12.2	18.3	33.3	8.1
Germany (n=50)	13.3	26.7	36.7	37.9	48.3	68.3	14.1
Kruskal-Wallis test: p < 0.001							

Table 6-11: FRQ of forward-looking information (full disclosure study)

In more detail, Figure 6-8 shows, which **operative figures** the sample companies provide forecasts for. While the companies from the two emerging economies provide revenue

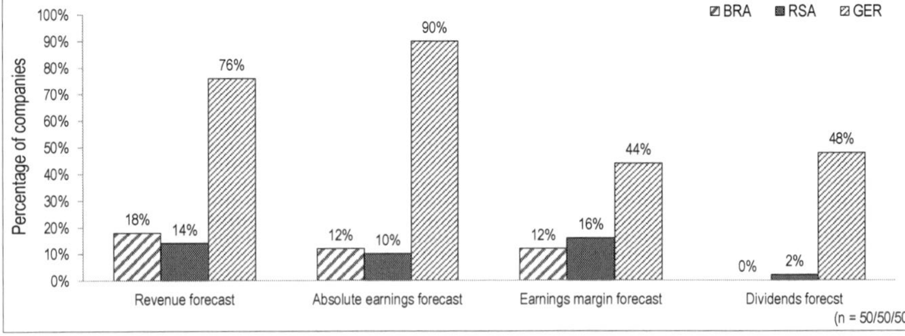

Figure 6-8: Disclosure of forecasts

[1098] Cf. amongst others *Ferling* (1994), p. 60; *Balata/Breton* (2005), p. 12; *Stainbank/Peebles* (2006), p. 72.

forecasts, absolute and relative earnings forecasts on a similar low level, most German companies disclose revenue (76%) and earnings (90%) forecasts and 44% also publish the company's prospective earnings margin. Moreover, about half of the German sample informs the users of the annual report about the prospective dividend payments, whereas hardly any company from Brazil and South Africa disclose this information.

As a company's revenue is one of the most important items to evaluate the entity's future development, investors expect detailed guidance on this figure. Thus, Figure 6-9 illustrates the **accuracy** of the provided revenue forecasts. While in South Africa all disclosed revenue forecasts are of qualitative or comparative nature, 8% of the Brazilian companies provide qualitative or comparative, 2% qualified-comparative and 8% point or interval forecasts. Hence, the revenue forecast accuracy is higher in Brazil than in South Africa. In Germany, not only the percentage of revenue forecasts is considerably higher than in the two emerging economies, but German companies also provide an increased accuracy due to the comprehensive forecast requirements of GAS 20 in Germany. 36% of the German companies provide qualified-comparative forecasts and 34% point or interval forecasts.

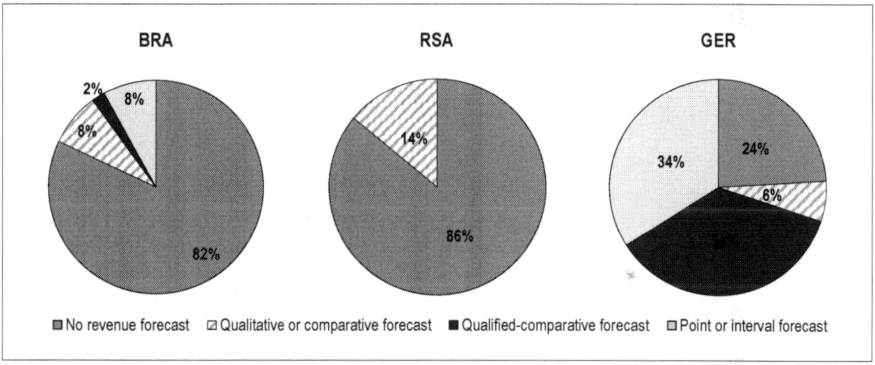

Figure 6-9: Accuracy of revenue forecasts

On the whole, the results provide evidence of a pronounced difference between the FRQ of forward-looking information in the developed Germany and the two emerging economies Brazil and South Africa. Moreover, there is considerable room for improvement in all countries, which might be increasingly demanded by annual report users in light of the importance of forward-looking disclosures.

6.1.2.2.8 Risks and opportunities

Similar to the results for *forward-looking* disclosures, the FRQ of *risks and opportunities* differs considerably between the emerging economies Brazil and South Africa, on the one hand, and Germany, on the other, although the overall disclosure level is substantially higher (cf. Table 6-12). For Brazil and Germany the median *risks and opportunities* FRQ scores (26.7% and 60.8%, respectively) even exceed the countries' total FRQ medians, whereas the median and mean disclosure quality of South African companies is only on the Brazilian level and does not reach the country's total FRQ median and mean scores.

An explanation for the Brazilian minimum score of 15.0% could be the required information on risks by the Brazilian regulation, whereas no such rules exist for South African companies. Thus, the first quartile for South Africa is below the corresponding value for Brazil (21.7%) and the South African minimum score is 0.0%. The highest score in the entire sample is 90.0%, so that there is a large range of *risks and opportunities* FRQ. For Germany, GAS 20 requires several disclosures on *risks and opportunities* explaining the relatively high scores of the German entities. The results suggest that there is neither a consensus regarding an adequate disclosure level within nor across the three countries (significant differences according to the Kruskal-Wallis test).

FRQ of risks and opportunities (in % of maximum full disclosure index score)							
Sample	Min.	25% pctl.	Median	Mean	75% pctl.	Max.	Std. Dev.
Total (n=150)	0.0	25.0	34.2	39.0	55.0	90.0	19.1
Brazil (n=50)	15.0	21.7	26.7	28.0	33.3	43.3	7.7
South Africa (n=50)	0.0	20.0	27.5	28.4	35.0	58.3	12.6
Germany (n=50)	26.7	53.3	60.8	60.7	70.0	90.0	13.2
Kruskal-Wallis test: p < 0.001							

Table 6-12: FRQ of risks and opportunities (full disclosure study)

Figure 6-10 reveals the risk categories, on which the companies provide qualitative information. The results show that a large percentage of companies provide qualitative information on the categories external risks (e.g., macroeconomic risks; environmental risks), industry risks (e.g., market condition risks), performance-related risks and financial risks. Risks related to the company's strategy (e.g., concerning its investment portfolio; investment decisions) are only addressed by 34% (38%; 56%) of the Brazilian (South African; German) entities. Moreover, particularly South African and German companies report on risks arising from personnel issues (e.g., difficulties in recruiting).

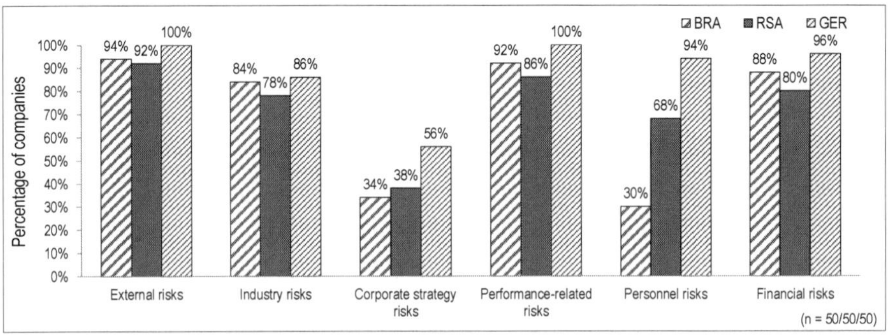

Figure 6-10: Categories of qualitative risk disclosures

Focusing on opportunity disclosures only, the gap between the two emerging economies and Germany is even wider for the FRQ of opportunities than FRQ of risks. While the average disclosure quality for Brazil and South Africa is 1% and 10%, the average German company reaches an opportunities FRQ score of 78%. This reveals that the discussion of opportunities (in the sense of this study) is hardly considered yet in the financial reporting activities of Brazilian and South African companies. In contrast, particularly the national regulation in Germany (section 315 HGB and GAS 20) ensures the reporting of opportunities by German entities. Almost all German sample companies disclose information on, for instance, opportunities arising due to changes in the company's operational environment (96%) and due to the development of the business environment (94%).

Although most sample companies provide a certain level of risk disclosures, the results show a heterogeneous distribution of *risks and opportunities* FRQ both within and across the sample countries.

6.1.2.3 Interim conclusion

Section 6.1.2 sheds light on the financial reporting practices in the sample companies' 2013 annual reports. The formal analysis has shown that **report sizes** vary significantly across Brazil, South Africa and Germany. In particular, the size of the German companies' annual reports exceeds the size of the annual reports of the two emerging economy samples from Brazil and South Africa noticeably. Thus, the formal analysis indicates annual reporting differences between emerging and developed economies.

In addition, the above **content-related** analysis has evaluated the sample companies' total FRQ as well as the FRQ regarding each of the seven reporting categories. Table 6-13 summarizes the FRQ results. It provides evidence of substantial differences in the FRQ of the seven reporting categories. While the total sample provides a relatively high FRQ in the categories *background information* (average score of 50.4%), *sustainability* (46.6%) and *important financials* (40.2%), the FRQ is considerably lower in the categories *important non-financials* (31.3%) and *forward-looking information* (19.7%).

Average FRQ sub score (in % of maximum full disclosure index sub score)				
Reporting category	**Total**	**BRA**	**RSA**	**GER**
Total FRQ	**35.7**	**25.5**	**32.0**	**49.5**
Background information	50.4	42.0	49.6	59.6
Important financials	40.2	33.0	34.1	53.5
Important non-financials	31.3	24.0	27.8	42.0
Sustainability	46.6	24.4	63.9	51.4
Value based management	35.4	20.4	36.4	49.5
Forward-looking information	19.7	8.9	12.2	37.9
Risks and opportunities	39.0	28.0	28.4	60.7
N	150	50	50	50

Table 6-13: Summary of full disclosure index (sub) scores

Furthermore, Table 6-13 shows largely consistent cross-country results, as the German companies provide the highest FRQ in all categories (except for sustainability) and the FRQ of the South African companies exceeds the FRQ of the Brazilian sample in all reporting categories. According to the conducted Kruskal-Wallis tests, the differences in FRQ across the samples from Brazil, South Africa and Germany are not only significant for the total FRQ, but also for the FRQ of all content categories. This is in line with hypothesis H1b.

Regarding some reporting categories, the companies from the two emerging economies tend to provide a similar FRQ, whereas the German entities provide a considerably higher FRQ. For example, the Brazilian and South African disclosure scores are on a similar level in the categories *important financials* and *important non-financials*. In particular, however, the FRQ differences between the two emerging economies and the developed Germany are very pronounced regarding the sensitive reporting categories *forward-looking information* as well as *risks and opportunities*. Hence, the results of this study suggest differences in FRQ between emerging economies and the developed Germany.

After the presentation of the results of the first two FRQ measures (accruals-based proxy and disclosure index measure), the following section is concerned with the findings of the readability study.

6.1.3 Readability of annual reports

Apart from the content-related analysis, also the readability of an annual report determines its quality. Therefore, this study evaluates readability not only in terms of language but also the structure and layout of the annual reports based on the methodology described in section 5.2.3. First, the subjective assessment of three readability indicators is presented. Second, the results of the Fog index and Flesch reading ease (FRE) are shown.

The mean scores of the **readability indicators** *clear cut structure* and *user-friendly use of figures and tables* indicate similar results, as shown in Table 6-14. While the Brazilian values are more than one point below the average score of the total sample, the South African and German evaluations are considerably above the overall mean. There are multiple reasons for this evaluation. In particular, most Brazilian reports follow a relatively simple **structure** with a few main chapters and are strongly oriented towards the elements of financial statements. Important information is frequently provided under unsystematic sub titles, which makes it difficult to find the information. The South African and German reports, by contrast, generally put a more meaningful table of contents in front so that particular information can be found more easily.

The second indicator focuses on the actual **language** used throughout the annual report. Table 6-14 shows the average language evaluation based on the author's impression when reading through the annual reports. In spite of the fact that all reports are generally comprehensible, minor differences in the readability of a textual passage have been noticed due to the used language.

Both the number and the quality of **figures and tables** vary considerably among the Brazilian reports. While some companies provide user-friendly figures and tables, other reports include hardly any or only rudimentary visualizations, which e.g. lack labelling or are formatted inconsistently. The German and South African entities use different visualizations to present information. For example, 96% of the German and 68% of the South African reports include an initial *highlights* page with key figures, whereas none of the Brazilian reports provides such a summary. Similarly, a *financial calendar* (including e.g. the dates of the shareholder meeting or the publication of reports) is not given by any Brazilian entity, but by 94% of the German and 48% of the South African companies. However, the country differences are less pronounced for an illustration comparing a company's *targets, results and outlooks* which is included in 40% of the German, 22% of the South African and 16% of the Brazilian reports. Furthermore, a user-friendly figure of a company's *change in cash* is found in 20% of the German, 16% of the South African and 0% of the Brazilian reports. The untabulated Kruskal-Wallis tests suggest significant differences in readability among the country samples for all three readability indicators ($p < 0.001$).

	Average readability score			
Readability indicator	**Total** (n=150)	**BRA** (n=50)	**RSA** (n=50)	**GER** (n=50)
Clear-cut structure	3.32	2.22	3.68	4.06
Understandable language and style of expression	3.71	3.10	3.86	4.16
User-friendly use of figures and tables	3.23	2.04	3.66	4.00
The table presents the average score of readability indicators based on a Likert scale ranging from 1 ("very poor") to 5 ("very good").				

Table 6-14: Results of readability indicator analysis

Furthermore, the **length** of an **annual report** affects its readability, as the user may encounter increased difficulty to find important information in voluminous reports which can be confusing.[1099] Also *Li* (2008) examines readability on the basis of the length of annual reports arguing that "*[...] longer documents are more deterring and require higher costs of information-processing.*"[1100] The analysis of annual report size in section 6.1.2.1 has shown that the German reports have considerably more pages on average than the reports from the two emerging economy samples suggesting a lower readability.

In addition to the evaluation on the basis of the three rather subjective indicators, the following **semi-objective analysis techniques** are applied to evaluate the language used in the reports.[1101] While the above results are based on the analysis of the entire annual reports, the following figures refer only to the CEO/management's letters to the shareholders in the company's annual reports. Table 6-15 characterizes the language used in these textual passages based on objective observations. The South African companies publish the longest letters with an average of 1,607 words, 66 sentences and 39 numbers. Also the average number of unique words (number of different words used in the passage) is the highest for the South African sample (623). However, the Brazilian entities use more

[1099] Cf. *Li* (2008), p. 222; *Department of Banking and Finance (University of Zurich)* (2014), p. 4.
[1100] *Li* (2008), p. 222.
[1101] For the methodological foundation, cf. section 5.2.3.

words per sentence (26.8) than those in South Africa (24.3) and Germany (20.7). The untabulated Kruskal-Wallis tests reveal that the cross-country differences are significant on the 1% level, except for average number of numbers (significant on the 5% level).

Readability indicator	**Total** (n=150)	**BRA** (n=50)	**RSA** (n=50)	**GER** (n=50)
Average number of words	1,189.3	681.8	1,607.1	1,278.9
Average number of sentences	51.1	25.4	66.1	61.8
Average number of words per sentence	23.3	26.8	24.3	20.7
Average number of unique words	483.5	322.6	622.7	505.1
Average number of numbers	32.9	24.9	38.6	35.3

Table 6-15: Overview of language characteristics

The results of the Fog index analysis (of the CEO/management letters to the shareholders) show relatively low variation (cf. Table 6-16). According to the literature, all median and mean scores indicate a *difficult* (14-18) language. However, the first quartiles of all country samples include entities using an *ideal* (12-14) language; regarding the German distribution, even all entities in the first quartile use an ideal language. On the other end of the distribution, all Brazilian and South African companies in the fourth quartile use a language which is classified as *unreadable*. The study finds the highest standard deviation for Brazil (2.35). Although particularly the readability levels of the Brazilian and South African companies are somewhat similar, the Kruskal-Wallis test indicates significant differences between the three country samples.

Fog index							
Sample	**Min.**	**25% pctl.**	**Median**	**Mean**	**75% pctl.**	**Max.**	**Std. Dev.**
Total (n=150)	10.76	14.30	16.12	16.08	17.74	21.84	2.25
Brazil (n=50)	12.44	15.53	17.27	17.18	19.23	21.84	2.35
South Africa (n=50)	12.80	15.32	16.71	16.59	18.10	19.65	1.78
Germany (n=50)	10.76	13.66	14.33	14.47	15.29	19.20	1.58
Kruskal-Wallis test: p < 0.001							

Table 6-16: Readability results (Fog index)

Also the Flesch reading ease analysis investigates the CEO/management letters to the shareholders as research objects. It is not surprising that the Flesch reading ease results do not differ substantially from those of the Fog index (cf. Table 6-17). They also suggest that the analyzed written passages in the German reports are easier to read than those of the two emerging economies whose average and median scores are on a similar level. However, no annual report reaches a level of 64 which is regarded as *plain English*. According to the Kruskal-Wallis test, the differences in readability across the entities from Brazil, South Africa and Germany are significant.

Flesch reading ease							
Sample	**Min.**	**25% pctl.**	**Median**	**Mean**	**75% pctl.**	**Max.**	**Std. Dev.**
Total (n=150)	16.73	30.08	36.17	37.08	43.60	60.60	9.40
Brazil (n=50)	16.73	27.26	31.31	32.16	36.76	51.66	8.55
South Africa (n=50)	22.49	29.81	33.55	34.81	40.60	52.03	7.05
Germany (n=50)	21.05	40.61	43.81	44.27	50.11	60.60	7.95
Kruskal-Wallis test: p < 0.001							

Table 6-17: Readability results (Flesch reading ease)

Taking into account that a textual passage with a Flesch reading ease score between 30 and 50 is regarded as *difficult,* all of the analyzed annual reports belong to this category. The Brazilian and South African median and mean scores are even close to the category of 0 to 30 points which is labeled *very difficult*. The results are in line with *Courtis* (1995) who finds the readability of annual reports to be difficult or very difficult and argues that

> "*[...] those responsible for narrative sections of the annual report typically are writing corporate messages at a reading level beyond the educational skills of their target audience.*"[1102]

In comparison to other emerging economies the results suggest relatively easy readability provided by Brazilian and South African companies. *Kumar* (2014) finds an average Flesch reading ease score of 14.76 for Indian and 11.74 for Chinese annual reports.[1103] This suggests that there are considerable differences between emerging economies and generalizations are difficult. Also the results of the Fog index analysis indicate easier and, thus, higher FRQ than the results of other research. For a large U.S. sample, *Biddle et al.* (2009), for instance, find an average Fog index of 19.31.[1104] However, the comparability of the results may be limited, as this study's findings are based on the analysis of the CEO/management letters, whereas *Kumar* (2014) and *Biddle et al.* (2009) analyze the entire annual reports as research objects.

1102 *Courtis* (1995), p. 5.
1103 Cf. *Kumar* (2014), p. 14.
1104 Cf. *Biddle et al.* (2009), p. 119.

6.1.4 Comparison of financial reporting quality measures

Subsequent to the analysis of the financial reporting practices in Brazil, South Africa and Germany on the basis of this study's three FRQ measures, this section focuses on the mutual relationships among these three measures. As illustrated in Figure 6-11, the following analysis compares each pair of **FRQ measures**: (1) accruals-based and disclosure index measures, (2) disclosure index and readability measures as well as (3) accruals-based and readability measures. For that purpose, the correlation coefficients between two measures are calculated. Strong positive correlations of FRQ measures may indicate that these measures capture the same aspects of FRQ (as indicated by the overlapping circles in Figure 6-11). Moreover, the correlations are discussed with regard to prior research.

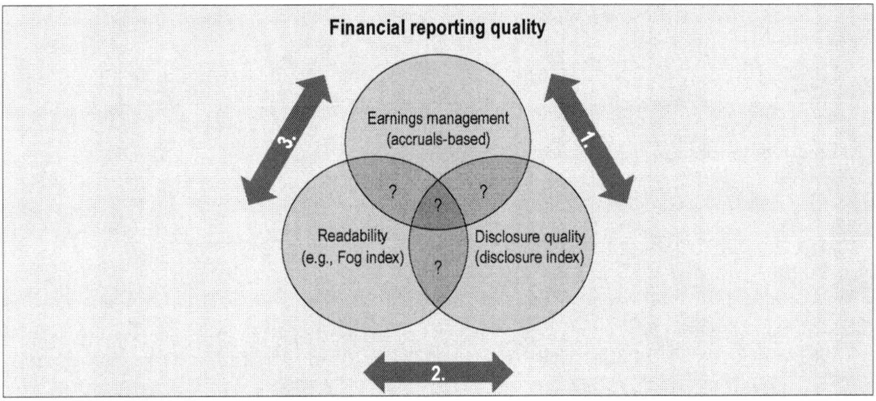

Figure 6-11: Comparison of this study's FRQ measures

First, the results of the **discretionary accruals** and the **disclosure index** are compared. Table 6-18 presents the correlations between the unsigned discretionary accruals (modified-Jones model) proxy and the full disclosure index score. The only statistically significant correlation coefficient is found for the total sample. This correlation coefficient of -0.251 suggests a weak association. However, the total sample regressions do not control for country-fixed effects. Thus, this highly significant correlation coefficient could be driven by country-specific characteristics, particularly as the coefficients for each country sample are not significant.

	FRQ (in % of maximum full disclosure index score)				
	Predicted sign	Total (FRQ_FULL)	Brazil (FRQ_FULL)	South Africa (FRQ_FULL)	Germany (FRQ_FULL)
FRQ_ACCR	-	-0.251 *** (0.002)	-0.234 (0.102)	-0.190 (0.186)	-0.212 (0.140)
N		150	50	50	50

The table presents the Spearman correlation coefficients between the unsigned modified-Jones model proxy (FRQ_ACCR) and the full disclosure index score (FRQ_FULL) per (sub) sample and the p-values in parentheses. *, ** and *** denote significance at the 10%, 5% and 1% level.

Table 6-18: Correlation analysis of discretionary accruals and disclosure index measure

Nevertheless, all correlation coefficients have the predicted negative sign indicating the same direction of the two measures. The negative sign further supports the argumentation that the discretionary accruals and the disclosure index scores measure FRQ consistently, since lower absolute values of discretionary accruals are associated with higher disclosure index scores.

Prior research provides **mixed results** regarding a potential association between earnings management (particularly accruals-based) proxies and direct disclosure measures. In line with this study's result, also *Leuz et al.* (2003), *Bhattacharya et al.* (2003), *Shaw* (2003) as well as *Salewski et al.* (2014) find a negative association between the results of earnings management proxies and disclosure index measures.[1105] However, the correlation coefficients in these studies vary considerably. While *Leuz et al.* (2003) find a relatively strong relationship between their aggregated earnings management proxy and the disclosure scores (correlation coefficient of -0.686),[1106] the results by *Bhattacharya et al.* (2003) show a weaker significant correlation coefficient of -0.404 for the association between the direct disclosure score and earnings aggressiveness as well as only a very weak and not significant relation between disclosure score and earnings smoothing (correlation coefficient of -0.094).[1107] The fact that both studies use considerably larger sample sizes than this investigation could explain differences in significance levels. *Shaw* (2003) finds a significant negative correlation between discretionary accruals and total disclosure quality, which is weaker than this study's finding for the total sample (Pearson correlation coefficient of -0.067).[1108] Also *Salewski et al.* (2014) provide evidence that higher disclosure quality (based on the scores of the *Best Annual Report* (BAR) contest) is associated with higher earnings quality (correlation coefficient of -0.179), arguing that high-quality dislosures lower the room for earnings management.[1109]

On the whole, the negative signs of this study's correlation coefficients are in line with several prior studies. This suggests that the discretionary accruals and the disclosure index measure capture some similar aspects of FRQ in line with the argumentation by *Salewski et al.* (2014). The (very) low and mostly statistically not significant correlation coefficients, however, reveal that there is no economically significant **relation** between the discretionary accruals and disclosure index measures. The results are not altered when using the voluntary disclosure index scores instead of the full disclosure index scores. Based on these findings, discretionary accruals may capture the companies' engagement in earnings management, however, they are not capable of measuring the quality of FRQ in the sense of this study's comprehensive disclosure index.[1110]

Second, the relation between the **readability measures** and the **disclosure index** scores is analyzed. Table 6-19 shows a highly significant relation between the readability indices

[1105] Cf. here and in the following *Bhattacharya et al.* (2003), p. 659; *Leuz et al.* (2003), p. 517.
[1106] Cf. *Leuz et al.* (2003), p. 517.
[1107] Cf. *Bhattacharya et al.* (2003), p. 659.
[1108] Cf. *Shaw* (2003), p. 1046.
[1109] Cf. *Salewski et al.* (2014), p. 31.
[1110] For the quality of different earnings management measures, cf. *Kothari et al.* (2005); *Dechow et al.* (2010).

(both Fog and Flesch reading ease) and the disclosure scores for the total sample. In line with the predicted sign, higher disclosure index scores are associated with greater readability for the total sample. Moreover, the German companies' readability (according to Fog index) is significantly associated with their disclosure index-based total FRQ suggesting the higher the disclosure score of an annual report the easier its readability. The correlation coefficient of -0.280 indicates a weak relation which is significant at the 5% level. In addition, there are no other statistically significant associations on country level. On the whole, the readability measures provide additional insights by capturing a particular part of FRQ. However, their results are not consistent to those of the disclosure index study.

	FRQ (in % of maximum full disclosure index score)				
	Predicted sign	**Total** (FRQ_FULL)	**Brazil** (FRQ_FULL)	**South Africa** (FRQ_FULL)	**Germany** (FRQ_FULL)
FRQ_FOG (Fog index)	-	-0.433 *** (0.000)	0.137 (0.341)	-0.091 (0.528)	-0.280 ** (0.049)
FRQ_FRE (Flesch reading ease)	+	0.424 *** (0.000)	-0.143 (0.324)	-0.047 (0.748)	0.085 (0.560)
N		150	50	50	50

The table presents the Spearman correlation coefficients between Fog index (Flesch reading ease, respectively) and the corresponding full disclosure index FRQ score (FRQ_FULL) per (sub) sample and the p-values in parentheses. *, ** and *** denote significance at the 10%, 5% and 1% level.

Table 6-19: Correlation analysis of readability measures and disclosure index measure

The results of the third comparison between the **readability measures** (Fog and Flesch reading ease) and the unsigned **discretionary accruals** are presented in Table 6-20. Although the correlation coefficients have the predicted signs and are marginally significant for the total sample, there are neither pronounced associations between the measures for the total sample nor for the country samples. The maximum absolute value of a correlation coefficient does not exceed 0.160 (very weak correlation). This result is in line with *Biddle et al.* (2009) who do not find pronounced correlations between their two accruals-based FRQ proxies and the corresponding Fog index scores either (Pearson correlation coefficients of 0.08 and 0.04, respectively).[1111]

	FRQ_ACCR (unsigned discretionary accruals of modified-Jones model proxy)				
	Predicted sign	**Total** (FRQ_FULL)	**Brazil** (FRQ_FULL)	**South Africa** (FRQ_FULL)	**Germany** (FRQ_FULL)
FRQ_FOG (Fog index)	+	0.160 * (0.051)	0.153 (0.290)	-0.041 (0.778)	0.015 ** (0.919)
FRQ_FRE (Flesch reading ease)	-	-0.158 * (0.054)	-0.132 (0.360)	0.023 (0.875)	0.087 (0.546)
N		150	50	50	50

The table presents the Spearman correlation coefficients between Fog index (Flesch reading ease, respectively) and the corresponding unsigned modified-Jones model proxy (FRQ_ACCR) per (sub) sample and the p-values in parentheses. *, ** and *** denote significance at the 10%, 5% and 1% level.

Table 6-20: Correlation analysis of readability measures and discretionary accruals

[1111] Cf. *Biddle et al.* (2009), p. 119.

On the whole, it is not surprising that the three FRQ measures are barely associated with each other considering the different measurement methods and analyzed research objects. While the accruals calculation is based on fundamental financials, the disclosure index study investigates the entire annual report and the readability measures solely the CEO/management letter to the shareholders in the annual report. The results suggest that the three FRQ measures widely capture different aspects of FRQ. In line with this study's understanding of FRQ, therefore, different dimensions should be taken into account when analyzing the abstract notion of FRQ.

6.1.5 Critical evaluation of the results

Investigating the financial reporting practices of the Brazilian, South African and German sample companies, the above sections have presented and compared the results of this study's three measures of FRQ: (1) **accruals-based proxies**, (2) **disclosure index-based content analysis** and (3) **readability measures**. This section discusses the main findings of these FRQ measures critically.

Both of this study's accruals-based **earnings management** proxies indicate that South African companies engage more in earnings management than Brazilian entities. However, the results of the two proxies are not entirely consistent. For instance, the MACCR suggests more earnings management by the German companies than the modified-Jones model. In line with findings in the literature, the multitude of different earnings management proxies do not always provide consistent results. Thus, each proxy has to be interpreted carefully. Overall, the range of the earnings management scores as well as the standard deviations imply that the sample companies tend to engage in earnings management. This inference is supported by *Graham et al.* (2005), who find in an interview-based study that 78% of managers admit earnings management.[1112]

Moreover, the results of the modified-Jones model suggest increased earnings management in the two **emerging economies** Brazil and South Africa compared to Germany. This is in line with assumptions in the literature that there are less favorable financial reporting environments in emerging economies than in developed countries.[1113] The description of the specific environments in Brazil, South Africa and Germany in section 2.3 has indicated that the institutional and cultural environment is indeed more favorable for financial reporting in Germany than in Brazil and South Africa. The finding that German companies engage in less earnings management than the Brazilian and South African ones is further consistent with the general result by *Leuz et al.* (2003) that less earnings management is found in countries "*[...] with relatively dispersed ownership, strong investor protection, and large stock markets [...]*"[1114]. Regarding this study's sample, the aforementioned characteristics tend to be more pronounced for Germany rather than for Brazil and South Africa.[1115]

[1112] Cf. *Graham et al.* (2005), p. 5.
[1113] Cf. sections 2.2.3.
[1114] *Leuz et al.* (2003), p. 525.
[1115] Cf. section 2.3.

The identified difference between earnings management in the two emerging economies, on the one hand, and the developed Germany, on the other hand, is also confirmed by the second FRQ measure, the **disclosure index-based FRQ** measure. Consistent with the findings of the **discretionary accruals proxy** (modified-Jones model), the average total FRQ is higher in Germany (49.5%) than in both emerging economies Brazil (25.5%) and South Africa (32.0%). The fact that the disclosure index-based FRQ is higher in South Africa than in Brazil is further consistent with the mean values of the discretionary accruals, whereas the medians suggest that FRQ (in terms of earnings management) is considerably higher in Brazil than in South Africa.

In line with prior empirical disclosure studies, the disclosure index scores for **total FRQ** suggest considerable room for improvement in all (sub) samples, as none of the average total disclosure scores exceeds 50% of the maximum score. For example, *Francis et al.* (2008) find an average total disclosure score of 46.95% for a U.S. sample in the year 2001,[1116] which is on the same level as this study's result for Germany. The German result is further supported by *Oberdörster* (2009), who measures an average total FRQ for German companies between 43.47% in 1997 and 56.46% in 2005.[1117] Also the relatively poor total FRQ in South Africa is confirmed by the *EY* (2015) study, which criticizes a lack of substance in South African annual reports.[1118]

Regarding **cross-country differences** in **disclosure index-based FRQ** between Brazil, South Africa and Germany the literature review has provided mixed results. While *Cahan et al.* (2005) find a considerably higher FRQ in Brazil (average score of 50) than in Germany (average score of 42),[1119] *Francis et al.* (2005b) confirm this study's finding that FRQ in German annual reports (mean score of 66.42) exceeds the FRQ provided by Brazilian companies (mean score of 55.33).[1120] In contrast to this study's results, however, the South African FRQ (mean score of 76.00) exceeds the German one.

Moreover, the disclosure index-based FRQ varies massively across the different **reporting categories**. While the FRQ for the total sample in the categories *background information* (50.4%), *sustainability* (46.6%), *important financials* (40.2%) as well as *risks and opportunities* (39.0%) exceeds the average total FRQ (35.7%), the reporting areas *value based management* (35.4%), *important non-financials* (31.3%) and *forward-looking information* (19.7%) show below-average disclosure index scores. The results of the U.S. study by *Francis et al.* (2008) for the categories *non-financial measures* (average score of 45.49%) and *projected information* (average score of 33.51%) are similar to this study's German results in the categories **important non-financials** (42.0%) and **forward-looking information** (37.9%), respectively.[1121] Although *Tonkin* (1989) analyzes annual reports from 1986/87, the *non-financial* disclosure score for South Africa (24.7%) is close to this study's corresponding result (27.8%) and is, consistent with this study's finding, lower

[1116] Cf. *Francis et al.* (2008), p. 71.
[1117] Cf. *Oberdörster* (2009), p. 113-115.
[1118] *EY* (2015), p. 15.
[1119] Cf. *Cahan et al.* (2005), p. 82.
[1120] Cf. here and in the following *Francis et al.* (2005b), p. 1133.
[1121] Cf. *Francis et al.* (2008), p. 71.

than for Germany (25.7%).[1122] In contrast to this disclosure index study's total FRQ results, however, *Tonkin* (1989) finds a higher total FRQ for South African (48.5%) than for German (37.5%) companies. On the whole, these comparisons have to be viewed with caution, as prior studies use different measures and samples. Moreover, they have been conducted a considerable time ago.

Furthermore, *Cahan et al.* (2005) support this study's gaps among the **reporting categories' FRQ**. They provide evidence that the FRQ regarding both categories *non-financials* and *prospective information* is relatively low, whereas the FRQ for *background information* is relatively high among all sample companies from 17 countries in the financial year 1999.[1123] In line with these results, *Oberdörster* (2009) finds *prognoses information* to provide the lowest FRQ among all categories of German managements reports in 2005 with a relative score of 30.60%.[1124] Hence, this study's results suggest that disclosures on *non-financials* and *forward-looking information* can still be regarded as problematic, even after a considerable period of time since the aforementioned studies were conducted and in spite of attempts to improve the FRQ in these areas, such as through the Jenkins Report by the *AICPA* (1994), additional management reporting requirements (e.g., GAS 20), integrated reporting developments (e.g., *Kajüter* (2013)) and sustainability reporting focus (e.g., *Global Reporting Initiative* (2013)). Also the recent integrated reporting analysis by *EY* (2015) criticizes that companies put too much emphasis on their past performance instead of providing prospective information in their annual reports.[1125]

Besides *forward-looking information*, a considerable gap in FRQ between the emerging economies Brazil and South Africa, on the one hand, and Germany, on the other, is also found for *risks and opportunities*, whereas such FRQ differences are less pronounced in the categories *background information*, *important financials* and *non-financials* as well as *value based management*. In particular the reporting categories *forward-looking information* as well as *risks and opportunities* are regarded as sensitive and important information to stakeholders.[1126] The national requirements concerning the German management report and established best practices among German annual reports may lead to an increased FRQ in these categories.

Remarkably, the **South African** disclosure scores exceed the Brazilian ones in all reporting categories. Consistent with *Chartered Institute of Management Accountants (CIMA)* (2010), the dominance of South Africa regarding **sustainability** disclosures seems to be boosted by the integrated reporting development in South Africa. It is the only category, where South Africa reaches a higher FRQ than Germany. However, a potential explanation for the considerable difference in *sustainability* scores between South Africa and the other countries is that Brazilian as well as German companies may publish *sustainability* information in separate stand-alone sustainability reports rather than as part of their annual

[1122] Cf. *Tonkin* (1989), p. 48.
[1123] Cf. *Cahan et al.* (2005), p. 80.
[1124] Cf. *Oberdörster* (2009), p. 113.
[1125] Cf. *EY* (2015), p. 15.
[1126] Cf. amongst others *SRI International* (1987), p. 7; *AICPA* (1994), p. 4; *Balata/Breton* (2005), p. 12.

reports.[1127] Moreover, the fact that the performance of sustainability reporting is considerably better than the FRQ of other categories suggests that South African integrated reports run the risk of being regarded as "*traditional annual report with a sustainability report bolted on*"[1128], which would contradict the idea of integrated reports.

Furthermore, the comparison of the full and voluntary disclosure index results reveal that the **Brazilian** companies generally disclose a certain minimum level of required information. In the standardized Reference Forms they report, for example, on employee turnover rate as well as certain risk information. However, the Brazilian companies tend to provide only relatively little or vague additional information on a voluntary basis. Nonetheless, this tendency towards relatively loose elaborations in Brazilian reports simultaneously gives Brazilian companies the opportunity to set their annual reports apart from those of the other entities through disclosing information of above-average FRQ. The fact that the standard deviation of the total disclosure scores is higher in Brazil than in South Africa (despite lower average and median scores) suggests that more outliers seize this opportunity than in South Africa.

Also the **readability** analysis (as third FRQ measure type) indicates considerable differences in reading ease between the annual reports from Brazil, South Africa and Germany. However, the variability of the results within and across the three countries is lower than for the other FRQ measure types. While the median values of the readability measures suggest difficult readability of the annual reports from all three country samples, there are particularly a number of annual reports from Brazil and South Africa, which are classified as *unreadable*. The readability measures show the easiest readability for the annual reports of the German sample. In addition, South African reports are easier to comprehend than Brazilian reports.

In addition to the evaluation of the FRQ measures' individual results, the **comparison of the FRQ measures** has characterized the relationships among the three measurement techniques. Although some (very) weak correlations are found (e.g., between readability and disclosure index-based FRQ for the German sample), the comparison generally suggests that each of the three FRQ measures captures a different dimension of FRQ. In particular, it is found that "*[...] higher disclosure quality is not always synonymous with less earnings management*"[1129] in spite of evidence of pronounced correlations between these measures in prior research.[1130] *Van Beest et al.* (2009) underpin this finding in their evaluation of accruals-based (earnings management) models:

> "*Furthermore, it is only an indirect proxy of earnings quality, excluding non-financial information. Therefore, conclusions concerning the quality of financial reporting information based on accrual models do not provide direct and compre-*

[1127] For the publication of stand-alone sustainability reports in Germany, cf. *Blaesing* (2013).
[1128] *EY* (2015), p. 17.
[1129] *Shaw* (2003), p. 1050.
[1130] Cf. *Bhattacharya et al.* (2003), p. 659; *Leuz et al.* (2003), p. 517.

hensive evidence concerning the quality of financial reporting information and its dimensions of decision usefulness."[1131]

In line with *van Beest et al.* (2009) and other research[1132], this study does not emphasize the companies' earnings management, but indeed attempts to provide evidence of FRQ in terms of overall decision useful information. The disclosure index is regarded as an appropriate approach for that purpose. The comprehensive results of the disclosure index study could not be achieved by the accruals-based proxies. Hence, the disclosure index results are used as the primary FRQ measure in the following determinants and information asymmetries studies. Moreover, this study's hypotheses shall also be tested on the basis of the disclosure index-based measure of FRQ.

Following the above argumentation, the **research hypotheses** H1a and H1b can be assessed as follows: H1a cannot be rejected on the basis of the observed variances and standard deviations within each country sample and is, thus, supported. Significant differences in total FRQ across Brazil, South Africa and Germany (as posited by H1b) have been shown through Kruskal-Wallis significance tests. Although the research hypotheses are tested on the basis of the disclosure index score (as this study's primary FRQ measure), the hypotheses H1a and H1b are also supported on the basis of the other FRQ measures including the accruals-based measures as well as the readability measures. Figure 6-12 summarizes the test results.

H1a	FRQ differs within each of the economies of Brazil, South Africa and Germany.	**Supported**
H1b	FRQ differs across the economies of Brazil, South Africa and Germany.	**Supported**

Figure 6-12: Test results of financial reporting practice hypotheses

The comparison of the three FRQ measures used throughout this study shows that the results of the measures differ. This supports this study's multidimensional understanding of FRQ. Thus, different aspects of FRQ can be investigated. These different dimensions of FRQ allow a detailed description and analysis of the financial reporting practices of the sample companies. Hence, research questions RQ1a and RQ1b have been answered thoroughly.

After describing financial reporting practices on the basis of the results of the applied FRQ measures, the following section identifies potential determinants of this observed FRQ.

1131 *Van Beest et al.* (2009), p. 6-7.

1132 For the limited meaning of earnings management measures for financial reporting contents and, thus, standard setting, cf. also *Healy/Wahlen* (1999), p. 380.

6.2 Determinants of financial reporting quality

After the comparison of the financial reporting practices in Brazil, South Africa and Germany in the previous sections, this section presents the results of the determinants study. First, section 6.2.1 describes the correlations of the independent variables used in the study. Afterwards, the results of both the isolated (section 6.2.2) and simultaneous (section 6.2.3) determinants analyses are presented. Moreover, additional tests examine the sensitivity and robustness of these results (section 6.2.4). Finally, section 6.2.5 provides a critical evaluation of the determinants of FRQ identified in the sample countries.

6.2.1 Correlation analysis of independent variables

Prior to the presentation of the empirical results of the determinant study, this section analyzes the relationships between the **independent variables** of the determinants model. As illustrated in Table 6-21, particularly the **country variables** are significantly correlated with several independent variables. The significant correlations between the country variables and company size, for example, show that the Brazilian entities are the smallest in the sample (-0.441). However, also the South African companies are negatively associated with company size (-0.229). This is in line with the fact that the largest companies are from Germany and a potential German dummy variable, thus, would show a positive correlation coefficient. In line with the evidence of prior research, company size seems to be a central explanatory variable in this study, as it is significantly associated with all other independent variables. The relatively strong relationships to media coverage (0.681) and analyst following (0.626) suggest that both media and analysts are particularly concerned with larger companies. The statistically highly significant positive relationship between the Brazilian country variable and ownership concentration underpins that Brazilian entities tend to be owned by relatively few block holders. The significant negative correlation between the Brazilian dummy variable and company age (-0.386) is consistent with the fact that the Brazilian companies are younger than those from South Africa and Germany in the sample. The existence of young companies may be a typical characteristic in rapidly growing emerging economies.

Furthermore, the Brazilian and South African country variables are significantly negatively associated with the **information environment proxies** (media coverage and analyst following), whereas a German dummy variable would be significantly positively related to these information environment variables. Thus, both media and financial analyst coverage are greater for entities from the developed Germany than for companies from the two emerging economies. The fact that the information environment proxies are strongly correlated with each other (0.645) indicates that both proxies might overlap to some extent. Thus, the regression model of the simultaneous determinants analysis is repeated including only one of the information environment proxies as a sensitivity test. Moreover, the medium and highly significant correlation between company valuation and profitability (0.536) is not surprising, as more profitable entities are generally expected to be of higher value from an investor's perspective. In summary, however, most correlations between the independent variables are (very) weak. Hence, the selection of independent variables seems appropriate to investigate the determinants of the sample companies' FRQ.

	Country_ BRA	Country_ RSA	Company size	Company age	Profitability	Company valuation	Systematic risk	Ownership concentration	Customer basis	Media coverage	Analyst following
Country_BRA											
Country_RSA	-0.500*** (0.000)										
Company size	-0.441*** (0.000)	-0.229*** (0.005)									
Company age	-0.386*** (0.000)	0.124 (0.131)	0.279*** (0.001)								
Profitability	-0.020 (0.809)	0.220*** (0.007)	-0.173** (0.034)	0.153* (0.062)							
Company valuation	-0.202** (0.013)	0.112 (0.174)	0.146* (0.074)	0.096 (0.242)	0.536*** (0.000)						
Systematic risk	-0.076 (0.359)	-0.127 (0.122)	0.326*** (0.000)	-0.025 (0.764)	-0.263*** (0.001)	-0.265*** (0.001)					
Ownership concentration	0.268*** (0.001)	-0.062 (0.448)	-0.236*** (0.004)	-0.300*** (0.000)	-0.044 (0.591)	-0.044 (0.591)	-0.120 (0.142)				
Customer basis	-0.076 (0.354)	-0.019 (0.817)	0.232*** (0.004)	0.013 (0.872)	0.023 (0.784)	0.335*** (0.000)	0.093 (0.260)	-0.053 (0.518)			
Media coverage	-0.439*** (0.000)	-0.293*** (0.000)	0.681*** (0.000)	0.122 (0.136)	-0.224*** (0.006)	-0.049 (0.550)	0.361*** (0.000)	-0.152* (0.064)	0.214*** (0.008)		
Analyst following	-0.241*** (0.003)	-0.519*** (0.000)	0.626*** (0.000)	0.105 (0.201)	-0.132 (0.108)	0.152* (0.063)	0.263*** (0.001)	-0.158* (0.054)	0.195** (0.017)	0.645*** (0.000)	

The table presents the Spearman correlation coefficients with the corresponding p-values in parentheses for the independent variables of the determinant model. *, ** and *** indicate significance at the 10%, 5% and 1% level.

Table 6-21: Correlation analysis of independent variables

6.2.2 Isolated analysis of determinants

6.2.2.1 Introduction

Following the research questions RQ2a and RQ2b, this study aims at investigating what determines FRQ in Brazil, South Africa and Germany as well as how these determinants differ across the three countries. After the previous section has presented the correlations of the independent variables used in the determinants study, the isolated analysis of determinants examines the relation between the determinant variables, on the one hand, and FRQ as measured by the disclosure index study, on the other. The following sections analyze each of the determinants included in the determinants model except for the country variables (country effects), because the descriptive results of the content analysis in section 6.1.2.2 have already shed light on the differences in FRQ across Brazil, South Africa and Germany. These results indicate that the German companies provide a significantly higher total FRQ (average full disclosure score of 49.5%) than the companies from the two emerging economies. The South African entities' total FRQ (32.0%) exceeds the total FRQ of the Brazilian entities (25.5%).

The isolated determinants analysis does not only focus on the empirical results for the total sample, but also compares the results across the three country samples from Brazil, South Africa and Germany. The relationships between the determinants and FRQ are captured through correlation analyses and significance tests. Although the determinant hypotheses are ultimately tested by the simultaneous determinants analysis, the isolated analysis prepares the simultaneous analysis comprehensively and, thereby, allows a better understanding of the investigated determinants.

6.2.2.2 Company size

Numerous studies find company size to be one of the most influential determinants of FRQ.[1133] Due to this importance of company size, Table 6-22 does not only present the association of company size and the total FRQ score, but also its relation to the sub scores of each reporting category. Following prior research, larger companies are found to provide higher FRQ. However, the results reveal that the importance of size is not that obvious in this study's setting.

Consistent with prior determinants studies in developed countries, there is a relatively strong and significant association between company size and total FRQ for the German sample (0.586). Concerning the German companies, also the reporting categories (except for *background information*) show significant relations on a similar level between FRQ and company size. Also the Brazilian correlation coefficient (0.333) suggests a significant association between company size and total FRQ, yet, it is only a weak correlation. The Brazilian companies show relatively strong correlation coefficients between the size and the categories *non-financials* (0.550) as well as sustainability (0.522), which are significant on the 1% level. However, the Brazilian sample shows no significant associations for most reporting categories.

[1133] Cf. section 3.3.

	Company size			
	Total	BRA	RSA	GER
FRQ_full (total score)	**0.650 *** (0.000)**	**0.333 ** (0.018)**	**0.078 (0.592)**	**0.586 *** (0.000)**
FRQ_full (background)	0.480 *** (0.000)	0.350 ** (0.013)	0.131 (0.365)	0.216 (0.132)
FRQ_full (financials)	0.595 *** (0.000)	0.094 (0.518)	0.071 (0.622)	0.598 *** (0.000)
FRQ_full (non-financials)	0.560 *** (0.000)	0.550 *** (0.000)	0.051 (0.727)	0.477 *** (0.001)
FRQ_full (sustainability)	0.371 *** (0.000)	0.522 *** (0.000)	-0.037 (0.797)	0.601 *** (0.000)
FRQ_full (value based)	0.526 *** (0.000)	-0.088 (0.546)	0.230 (0.109)	0.664 *** (0.000)
FRQ_full (forward-looking)	0.561 *** (0.000)	0.132 (0.360)	-0.020 (0.893)	0.304 ** (0.032)
FRQ_full (risks)	0.529 *** (0.000)	-0.043 (0.769)	-0.102 (0.483)	0.458 *** (0.001)
N	150	50	50	50

The table presents the Spearman correlation coefficients between company size (measured by revenues) and the corresponding full disclosure index FRQ score (FRQ_FULL) in each sub sample with p-values in parentheses. *, ** and *** denote significance at the 10%, 5% and 1% level.

Table 6-22: Correlation analysis of company size and FRQ

Concerning the South African sample, a significant relation is neither found for the total FRQ nor for the reporting quality of any sub category. However, using market capitalization as size proxy, the South African companies show a relatively weak correlation coefficient (0.199) between company size and total FRQ, which is significant on the 10% level in a one-tailed test. Moreover, there is a medium correlation between market capitalization and FRQ of *non-financials* (0.416) which is even highly significant.[1134]

Apart from the country perspective, the correlation results for the total sample indicate highly significant associations regarding all reporting categories. However, the results might be driven by country fixed effects. For instance, German companies tend to outperform Brazilian and South African companies regarding both variables company size and FRQ score.

6.2.2.3 Company age

The isolated determinant analysis of company age investigates whether older companies provide a higher FRQ. To examine this association, Table 6-23 presents the correlation analysis of company age and the total score of the full disclosure index study. Although all correlation coefficients suggest a positive association, solely those for the total and the German samples are statistically significant. While the correlation coefficient for the total sample indicates a medium association (0.416), there is a weak correlation for the German

[1134] Cf. Appendix, Table A-8.

sample (0.304). The results further suggest that company age does not play an important role in the reporting decisions of the companies from the two emerging economies.

	Company age			
	Total	BRA	RSA	GER
FRQ_full (total score)	0.416 *** (0.000)	0.206 (0.152)	0.165 (0.253)	0.304 ** (0.032)
N	150	50	50	50

The table presents the Spearman correlation coefficients between company age (measured by years since company's foundation) and the corresponding full disclosure index FRQ score (FRQ_FULL) in each sub sample with p-values in parentheses. *, ** and *** denote significance at the 10%, 5% and 1% level.

Table 6-23: Correlation analysis of company age and FRQ

Thus, a significant association is only found for the country sample with the oldest companies. While the age of the average German sample entity is 84 years, the average age of Brazilian and South African companies is only 35 and 66 years, respectively. Therefore, the relatively young companies in Brazil and South Africa might not have established a comprehensive reporting system over time as the German entities. This may also be a reason for the lower overall FRQ in the two emerging economies.

Analyzing the association of company age and the quality of the individual reporting categories, the Brazilian sample shows only a significant (p = 0.011) relationship for *non-financials* which can be classified as weak (0.357). However, it suggests that particularly older companies may have established accounting systems which capture non-financial information. Similarly, the analysis for South Africa provides solely a marginally significant (p = 0.091) correlation coefficient for the relation between company age and *sustainability* FRQ of 0.242.

For Germany, all FRQ sub scores are positively associated with company age, although three are not statistically significant (*background information*, *non-financials* and *forward-looking information*). The German sample shows the strongest relationship for the category *value based management* (0.411) which suggests that high-quality value based management systems might be implemented over an extended period of time.

6.2.2.4 Profitability

The isolated analysis of determinants finds no significant positive relationship between a company's FRQ and its profitability (cf. Table 6-24). Except for Germany, the correlation coefficients show a negative sign. The finding might indicate that the economic performance of a company does not play a major role in its financial reporting decision process.

Concerning the relation between profitability and the sub categories, it is noticeable that the South African companies' *non-financials* FRQ is positively and significantly (p = 0.041) associated with their profitability, as indicated by the correlation coefficient of 0.290. In line with expectations, thus, more profitable entities from South Africa may be willing to provide information on *non-financials* of higher quality. However, there are no additional correlation coefficients supporting this view. The use of the voluntary disclosure index instead of the full index does not alter the results substantially.

	Profitability			
	Total	BRA	RSA	GER
FRQ_full (total score)	-0.110 (0.182)	-0.004 (0.976)	-0.017 (0.904)	0.142 (0.325)
N	150	50	50	50
The table presents the Spearman correlation coefficients between profitability (measured by return on equity) and the corresponding full disclosure index FRQ score (FRQ_FULL) in each sub sample with p-values in parentheses. *, ** and *** denote significance at the 10%, 5% and 1% level.				

Table 6-24: Correlation analysis of profitability and FRQ

6.2.2.5 Company valuation

As presented in Table 6-25, the correlation analysis does not provide evidence that undervalued companies disclose information of increased FRQ in their annual reports (negative correlation). Only the correlation coefficient for the German sample has a negative sign. However, the relation is neither statistically significant (p = 0.470) nor particularly pronounced with a value of -0.105. For the total sample, the results even show a marginally significant (p = 0.081), however, very weak positive relationship (0.143), which does not change materially when replacing the full disclosure index score by the voluntary disclosure index score resulting in a correlation coefficient of 0.159 (p = 0.052)

	Company valuation			
	Total	BRA	RSA	GER
FRQ_full (total score)	0.143 * (0.081)	0.068 (0.041)	0.162 (0.202)	-0.105 (0.470)
N	150	50	50	50
The table presents the Spearman correlation coefficients between company valuation (measured by price-to-book ratio) and the corresponding full disclosure index FRQ score (FRQ_FULL) in each sub sample with p-values in parentheses. *, ** and *** denote significance at the 10%, 5% and 1% level.				

Table 6-25: Correlation analysis of company valuation and FRQ

The South African results show a medium positive association between the quality of *non-financials* and company valuation (0.531), which is significant on the 1% level (p < 0.001). This relatively pronounced relation suggests that higher valued companies in South Africa tend to provide better non-financial disclosures. The correlation coefficients between company valuation and the FRQ of all reporting categories, except for *background* information, show a negative sign for the German sample. However, none is statistically significant. On the whole, the isolated determinants analysis barely shows pronounced associations between FRQ and company valuation.

6.2.2.6 Systematic company risk

This section investigates whether companies with higher inherent systematic company risks publish disclosures of higher quality in their annual reports. The results in Table 6-26 support this association for the total and German samples. While the correlation coefficient of the total sample suggests a weak relationship (0.243), the German one indicates a medium association (0.413). Both values are highly significant on the 1% level. Although all coefficients have the predicted positive sign, the relation is neither pronounced nor statistically significant for the Brazilian and South African samples.

	Systematic company risk			
	Total	BRA	RSA	GER
FRQ_full (total score)	0.243 *** (0.003)	0.153 (0.289)	0.030 (0.835)	0.413 *** (0.003)
N	150	50	50	50
The table presents the Spearman correlation coefficients between systematic company risk (measured by beta value) and the corresponding full disclosure index FRQ score (FRQ_FULL) in each sub sample with p-values in parentheses. *, ** and *** denote significance at the 10%, 5% and 1% level.				

Table 6-26: Correlation analysis of company risk and FRQ

In addition, the untabulated correlation results show a significant ($p = 0.036$) weak correlation of 0.297 between systematic company risk and the FRQ of *forward-looking information* for the Brazilian sample. The results for the German sample show positive correlation coefficients between systematic company risk and the FRQ of all reporting categories. However, they are not statistically significant for the categories *background information* and *forward-looking information.* The findings indicate that German companies with higher systematic risks tend to provide a higher total FRQ as well as higher qualities regarding most reporting categories in their annual reports.

6.2.2.7 Ownership concentration

According to the isolated determinants analysis, ownership concentration seems to be an important factor for the companies' reporting practices, particularly in Brazil and Germany. The results suggest that companies with a more concentrated ownership structure provide a lower FRQ. Table 6-27 shows highly significant correlation coefficients for the total sample, Brazil and Germany. While the German correlation coefficient of -0.394 is moderately pronounced, the Brazilian coefficient of -0.588 indicates almost a strong relationship between total FRQ and ownership concentration. Although the South African coefficient is not significant, it also has a negative sign.

Concerning the total sample, the correlation analysis further shows weak and medium correlations (between -0.258 and -0.426) for all reporting categories which are statistically significant. Also the result for Brazil is confirmed by similar correlation coefficients for the different reporting categories as for total FRQ (except for *sustainability* with an insignificant coefficient value of 0.040). Also the sub category correlation coefficients for the German sample widely underpin the significant negative relationship between ownership concentration and FRQ. Solely the FRQ of *background information* is positive (0.018) and not statistically significantly (p = 0.903) associated with ownership concentration, whereas the most pronounced relation is found for the category *sustainability* with a value of -0.525 (p < 0.001).

	Ownership concentration			
	Total	BRA	RSA	GER
FRQ_full (total score)	-0.419 *** (0.000)	-0.588 *** (0.000)	-0.162 (0.260)	-0.394 *** (0.005)
N	150	50	50	50

The table presents the Spearman correlation coefficients between ownership concentration (measured by Herfindahl index) and the corresponding full disclosure index FRQ score (FRQ_FULL) in each sub sample with p-values in parentheses. *, ** and *** denote significance at the 10%, 5% and 1% level.

Table 6-27: Correlation analysis of ownership concentration and FRQ

When interpreting these results the ownership structures of the three samples shall be taken into account. Figure 6-13 illustrates the distribution of ownership concentration (based on the Herfindahl index[1135]) in Brazil, South Africa and Germany. The Brazilian ownership concentration is the highest among the three sub samples. The Herfindahl index value of the Brazilian median company (0.120) is more than 2.5 times higher than the corresponding values for South Africa (0.045) and Germany (0.042). This observation is in line with Brazil's history and accounting environment, as Brazilian entities are traditionally owned by powerful families.[1136] The boxplot diagram further reveals that the range of the observed Herfindahl index values is considerably smaller for South Africa than for Germany.

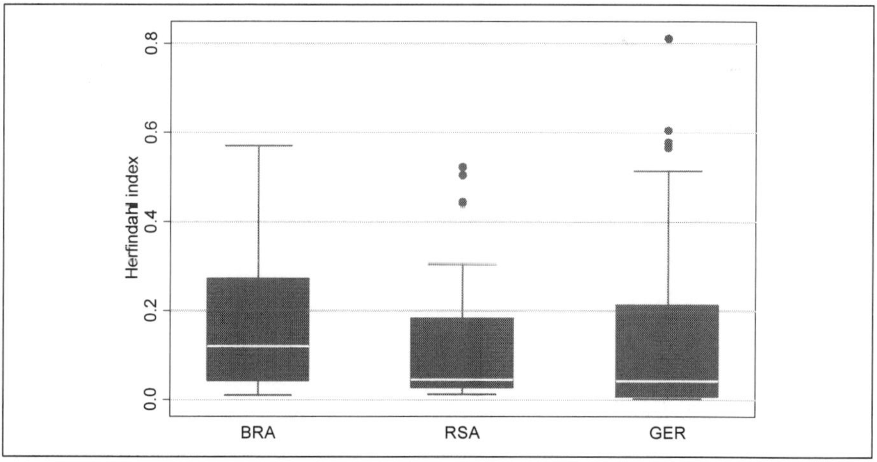

Figure 6-13: Ownership concentration boxplot diagram

[1135] Cf. section 5.3.3.1. For further characteristics of the Herfindahl index, cf. *Rhoades* (1993), p. 188.
[1136] For detailed characteristics of the Brazilian economy, cf. section 2.3.2.

On the whole, not only the negative association between ownership concentration and FRQ is more pronounced for the Brazilian companies compared to the South African and German samples, but also the ownership concentration is considerably higher among the Brazilian entities. Thus, the concentration of ownership might be an important determinant of FRQ particularly in Brazil.

6.2.2.8 Industry

This section examines whether FRQ differs across industries. For example, companies from different industries might focus on different reporting activities. Since industry category is a binary variable and FRQ is measured by a continuous variable, the correlation coefficient concept cannot be applied as for two continuous variables.[1137] Therefore, the non-parametric Kruskal-Wallis test is used instead to investigate the relationship between a company's industry classification and its FRQ. Table 6-28 presents the average full disclosure index scores **(total FRQ)** per industry as a basis for the significance test.

	Total FRQ (in % of maximum full disclosure index score)											
	Total			BRA			RSA			GER		
	N	Mean	Std. Dev.	N	Mean	Std. Dev.	N	Mean	Std. Dev.	N	Mean	Std. Dev.
Consumer	19	33.6	11.7	6	27.7	6.3	8	29.1	4.7	5	47.9	13.6
Manufacturing	34	43.2	13.6	6	26.6	3.1	9	33.3	6.0	19	53.1	8.8
Energy and mining	21	29.0	9.3	12	23.6	6.0	7	33.0	5.7	2	47.1	5.1
Business equipment	4	43.3	9.6	1	33.3	-	-	-	-	3	46.7	8.4
Telecommunication and media	10	41.2	11.9	-	-	-	4	36.8	7.7	6	44.1	13.9
Wholesale and retail	24	31.7	8.7	11	28.1	8.4	10	31.6	5.4	3	45.0	7.1
Healthcare	10	38.0	11.1	1	17.4	-	5	37.0	7.8	4	44.3	9.6
Real estate	10	24.2	6.2	9	23.3	5.7	-	-	-	1	32.8	-
Transport and travel	11	34.0	16.4	3	19.6	6.5	4	25.7	5.3	4	53.0	7.7
Construction	7	41.6	14.8	1	37.5	-	3	28.2	5.6	3	56.2	5.3
Total	150	35.7	12.8	50	25.5	6.8	50	32.0	6.3	50	49.5	10.1
Kruskal-Wallis test	p < 0.001			p = 0.155			p = 0.190			p = 0.307		

Table 6-28: Industry differences of total FRQ

[1137] Cf. *Refaat* (2007), p. 239. For correlations between continuous and binary variables, cf. *Refaat* (2007), p. 239-243.

The industries with the highest average total FRQ are *manufacturing* (43.2%), *business equipment* (41.6%) as well as *telecommunication and media* (41.2%). In contrast, *real estate* (24.2%) and *energy and mining* (29.0%) companies provide the lowest average FRQ.

In addition, Figure 6-14 illustrates the differences in **total FRQ across the industries** (according country samples). While the FRQ of the German entities remains relatively similar throughout the industries, particularly Brazilian companies' total disclosure scores vary considerably. Manufacturing companies provide above average FRQ consistently among the samples from Brazil, South Africa and Germany. In all three country samples, the total FRQ of the *manufacturing* companies is above the countries' average disclosure scores. This trend suggests that *manufacturing* companies might have particular incentives to provide high-quality information in their annual reports.

Interestingly, South African *healthcare* providers reach an average total disclosure score of 37.0% which is above the country's average of 32.0%, whereas the total FRQ of *healthcare* companies in Brazil (17.4%) and Germany (44.3%) is below the countries' means of 35.7% and 49.5%. This might underpin the importance of the *healthcare* industry in South Africa, where *healthcare* entities seem to have incentives to excel in reporting. In contrast, *construction* entities from South Africa provide below average FRQ (28.2%), whereas their Brazilian and German counterparts publish information of increased quality with disclosure scores of 37.5% and 56.2%. Furthermore, the analysis shows a relatively low FRQ for *real estate* companies in Brazil (23.3%) and Germany (32.8%). The FRQ of the *wholesale and retail* industry is above average in Brazil (28.1%) and on average in South Africa (31.6%). In Germany, however, the mean score of 45.0% is below the country's average. The *wholesale and retail* industry plays an important role in the two emerging economies due to the considerable percentage of companies from the industry.

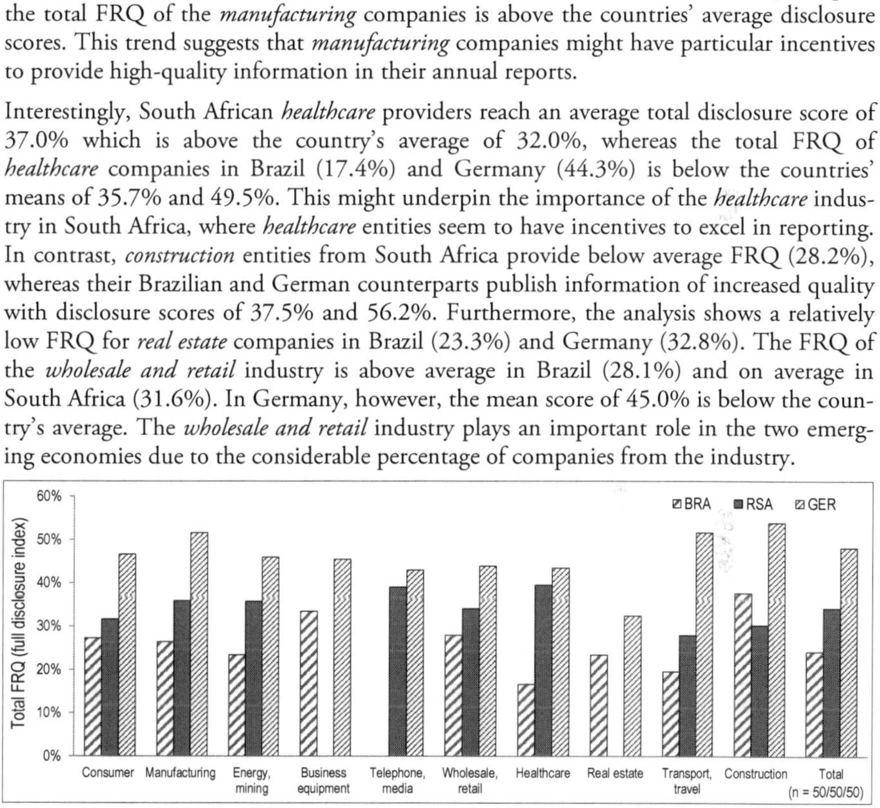

Figure 6-14: Total FRQ per industry

The p-values of the Kruskal-Wallis tests indicate that only the FRQ differences of the total sample ($p < 0.001$) are statistically significant, however, none of the country samples (cf. Table 6-28). After this isolated analysis of total FRQ across the industries of the sample companies, the multivariate regression in section 6.2.3 provides evidence on the relation between industries and total FRQ.

In addition to the investigation of the total FRQ per industry, also the relation between the FRQ of specific reporting and industry classification is analyzed in the following. For instance, *manufacturing* companies provide an increased level of **forward-looking information**. In all three countries their average scores exceed the average *forward-looking* reporting score of the country. In Brazil and Germany also *consumer* companies publish prospective information of above average quality. However, the Kruskal-Wallis test indicates significant differences in *forward-looking* FRQ across industries solely for the total sample ($p < 0.001$).

Moreover, the **sustainability** category shall be examined in more detail. In line with both legitimacy and political cost theory, some industries seem to be more affected by sustainability issues than others. As illustrated in Figure 6-15, companies from the industries *manufacturing* as well as *energy and mining* tend to provide a higher FRQ of *sustainability* information. In all three sample countries the *sustainability* disclosure scores of these industries are on or above their average *sustainability* disclosure scores for all industries. Since both industries can be regarded as environmentally sensitive sectors, particularly the environmental dimension of sustainability appears to be of relevance. In accordance with the theoretical foundation, companies attempt to gain or restore legitimacy through meeting societal reporting expectations.[1138] Further, entities in these industries are particularly exposed to the risk of political costs, e.g. due to social and environmental regulations or inspections by authorities.[1139] They try to avoid such political costs by ensuring transparency through high-quality disclosures on their sustainability-related activities. In contrast, the *sustainability* FRQ of companies from the industries *transport and travel* as well as *wholesale and retail* is below average in all three countries. This indicates that the business activities might be less sensitive regarding sustainability issues in these sectors. On the basis of the Kruskal-Wallis test, *sustainability* FRQ differs significantly across industries for the overall sample ($p < 0.001$), yet, not for the country samples.

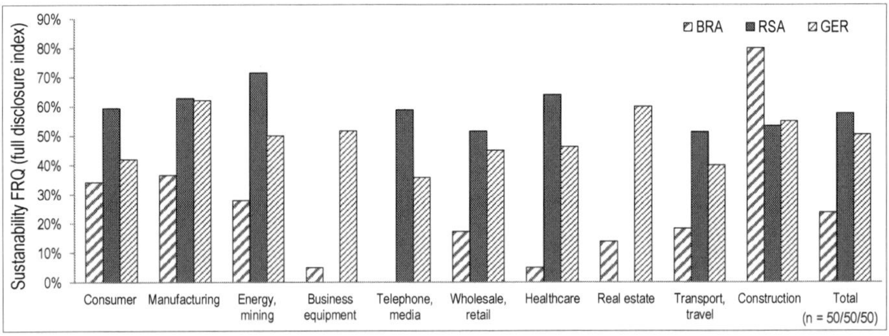

Figure 6-15: Sustainability FRQ per industry

Also the FRQ of important **non-financials** differs across industries. Unlike the disclosure quality of sustainability information, *energy and mining* companies show a lower *non-*

[1138] Cf. section 4.1.5.4.2.

[1139] Cf. section 4.1.5.3.

financials FRQ than the total industry sample in all countries (cf. Figure 6-16). Contrary to the results for total FRQ, the Brazilian companies' *non-financials* FRQ exceeds the FRQ of the South African sample in the industries *consumer, manufacturing, wholesale and retail* as well as *construction* suggesting that there might be stronger incentives for Brazilian entities to provide high-quality information on *non-financials* than for South African companies. This observation is remarkable, since the integrated reporting approach in South Africa generally encourages *non-financials* disclosures. Moreover, the industries *real estate* as well as *transport and travel* show below average *non-financials* FRQ for all country samples. These industry differences for *non-financials* FRQ are not only significant for the total sample ($p < 0.001$), but also for the Brazilian ($p = 0.024$) and South African ($p = 0.004$) samples.

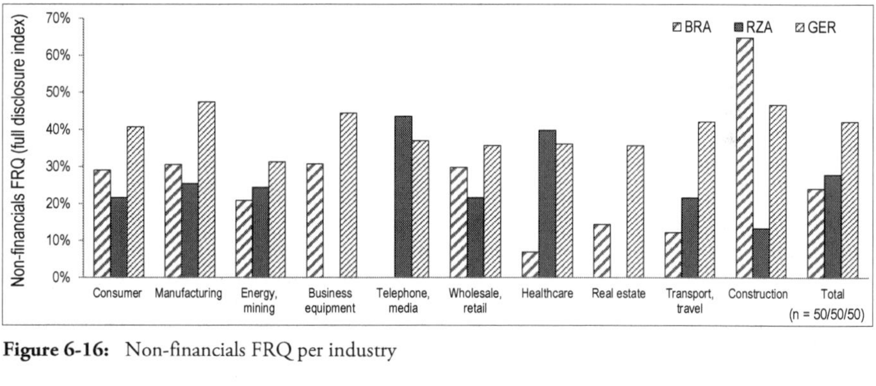

Figure 6-16: Non-financials FRQ per industry

The above analyses have shed light on the differences in FRQ provided in annual reports across industries. While these analyses, yet, cannot control for country effects, the simultaneous analysis of determinants in section 6.2.3 considers country effects in the multivariate regression. Moreover the above analyses of the specific industries suffer from the fact that the results for some industries are based on a small number of companies (small N).

6.2.2.9 Customer basis

The isolated determinants analysis investigates the relation between a company's customer basis and its FRQ. In particular, the study distinguishes between B2C companies which primarily serve end-consumers (more than 50% of revenues are generated by end-consumers) and B2B companies which primarily serve business customers (more than 50% of revenues are generated by business clients). However, distinguishing between B2C and B2B companies is not always trivial (e.g., companies may serve both customer groups) which has to be considered when interpreting the results of this analysis. Table 6-29 provides mixed results. While the Wilcoxon test indicates for the total sample ($p = 0.065$) and the Brazilian sample ($p = 0.002$) that B2C companies have a significantly higher **total FRQ** than B2B companies, the differences are insignificant for the South African and German samples. Unlike Brazilian and South African entities, German B2B companies provide a higher total FRQ (average full disclosure score of 50.5%) than B2C companies (48.8%).

	FRQ (in % of maximum full disclosure index score)											
	Total			BRA			RSA			GER		
	N	Mean	Std. Dev.	N	Mean	Std. Dev.	N	Mean	Std. Dev.	N	Mean	Std. Dev.
B2C customer basis	86	37.3	12.2	26	28.5	5.3	28	32.4	6.6	32	48.8	11.2
B2B customer basis	64	33.4	13.4	24	22.3	6.8	22	31.5	6.2	18	50.5	7.9
Wilcoxon test	p = 0.065			p = 0.002			p = 0.922			p = 0.686		

Table 6-29: Customer basis differences of total FRQ

Using **financials FRQ** instead of total FRQ, the Wilcoxon tests do not show significant differences between B2B and B2C companies. This indicates that companies do not adjust their *financials* disclosures according to their customer basis. In contrast, the customer basis seems to play an important role among the Brazilian and South African companies regarding the reporting of *non-financial* and *sustainability* information. Table 6-30 reveals that B2C companies provide a significantly higher FRQ of *non-financials* information than B2B entities in Brazil ($p < 0.001$) and South Africa ($p = 0.002$), whereas there is no significant difference for the German sample ($p = 0.564$). In Brazil, the B2C companies' average disclosure score of 31.4% is almost twice the mean B2B score of 16.1%. In particular, stakeholder groups other than analysts and investors, such as customers, general public, media, authorities and employees, might have an interest in B2C companies regarding *non-financial* issues (e.g., employee and customer satisfaction as well as important brands and processes).[1140]

	Non-financials FRQ (in % of maximum non-financials disclosure index score)											
	Total			BRA			RSA			GER		
	N	Mean	Std. Dev.	N	Mean	Std. Dev.	N	Mean	Std. Dev.	N	Mean	Std. Dev.
B2C customer basis	86	35.5	13.8	26	31.4	11.6	28	32.6	12.0	32	41.3	15.1
B2B customer basis	64	25.7	15.8	24	16.1	12.6	22	21.7	8.2	18	43.3	12.2
Wilcoxon test	p < 0.001			p < 0.001			p = 0.002			p = 0.564		

Table 6-30: Customer basis differences of non-financials FRQ

Also regarding the FRQ of *sustainability* information the Wilcoxon test shows significant mean differences for the Brazilian ($p = 0.022$) and South African ($p = 0.035$) samples (cf. Table 6-31). While the Brazilian B2C companies, however, publish *sustainability* information of higher quality (29.0%) than the B2B companies (19.4%), the South African mean value is significantly higher for B2B companies (68.0%) than for B2C entities (60.7%). This suggests that the South African B2B companies put more efforts into providing high-quality *sustainability* information than B2C entities. Also for the German

[1140] For the disclosure index items in the category *non-financials*, cf. Appendix, Table A-1.

sample the B2B value (54.7%) exceeds the B2C score (49.5%), although the difference is not significant (p = 0.446). An explanation could be that numerous B2B companies in South Africa and Germany are in sensitive industries regarding sustainability aspects (e.g., mining and chemical industry) and, thus, are expected to publish comprehensive sustainability information to gain societal legitimacy.[1141] In Brazil, B2C companies publish not only a higher quality of *non-financial* information, but also provide a higher *sustainability* FRQ. This result indicates that managers of Brazilian B2C companies attempt to address the sustainability concerns of the stakeholder group of consumers. In comparison to the German and South African companies, however, the *sustainability* FRQ provided by the Brazilian companies is still relatively low.

	Sustainability FRQ (in % of maximum sustainability disclosure index score)											
	Total			BRA			RSA			GER		
	N	Mean	Std. Dev.	N	Mean	Std. Dev.	N	Mean	Std. Dev.	N	Mean	Std. Dev.
B2C customer basis	86	47.0	21.9	26	29.0	21.1	28	60.7	13.9	32	49.5	18.5
B2B customer basis	64	46.0	28.3	24	19.4	19.4	22	68.0	19.0	18	54.7	17.5
Wilcoxon test	p = 0.885			p = 0.022			p = 0.035			p = 0.446		

Table 6-31: Customer basis differences of sustainability FRQ

6.2.2.10 Information environment

The determinants study uses the proxies media coverage and analyst following to investigate the influence of a company's information environment on its FRQ. Table 6-32 and Table 6-33 show the correlation results for **media coverage** and **analyst following**. With values of 0.630 and 0.607 the correlations between both information environment measures and FRQ indicate strong and highly significant correlations for the total sample.

	Media coverage			
	Total	BRA	RSA	GER
FRQ_full (total score)	0.630 *** (0.000)	0.281 ** (0.048)	0.064 (0.659)	0.279 * (0.050)
N	150	50	50	50

The table presents the Spearman correlation coefficients between media coverage and the corresponding full disclosure index FRQ score (FRQ_FULL) in each sub sample with p-values in parentheses. *, ** and *** denote significance at the 10%, 5% and 1% level.

Table 6-32: Correlation analysis of media coverage and FRQ

Regarding the three country samples, however, there is a weak association between total FRQ and media coverage for the Brazilian (0.281) and German (0.279) samples (significant on the 5% and 10% level, respectively). Remarkably, among the Brazilian sub categories only *non-financials* and *sustainability* show a significant positive association between

[1141] Cf. section 4.1.5.4.2.

FRQ and media coverage. Thus, particularly Brazilian companies, which are highly covered by the media, provide high-quality information on *non-financial* and *sustainability* information (e.g., information on customers, social and environmental aspects).

The correlation analysis for analyst following shows even more pronounced positive associations between the information environment and total FRQ on country level. Table 6-33 reveals medium correlations for the South African (0.431) and German (0.508) samples (highly significant on the 1% level). For Brazil, neither the total FRQ nor any sub score is significantly correlated with analyst following. Hence, Brazilian companies' reporting activities seem to be less driven by the extent of their analyst followings.

	Analyst following			
	Total	BRA	RSA	GER
FRQ_full (total score)	0.607 *** (0.000)	0.052 (0.718)	0.431 *** (0.002)	0.508 *** (0.000)
N	150	50	50	50

The table presents the Spearman correlation coefficients between analyst following and the corresponding full disclosure index FRQ score (FRQ_FULL) in each sub sample with p-values in parentheses. *, ** and *** denote significance at the 10%, 5% and 1% level.

Table 6-33: Correlation analysis of analyst following and FRQ

For the South African sample, significant correlation coefficients are found for the categories *background* (0.330), *non-financials* (0.523) and *sustainability* (0.258). This indicates that also financial analysts might indeed require and use *non-financial* information. Except for *background* information, the results for the German sample show significant associations between the FRQ of all reporting categories and analyst following. The correlation coefficients are relatively pronounced with values between 0.247 and 0.568.

6.2.3 Simultaneous analysis of determinants

After the correlation analyses between each determinant and FRQ, this section presents the results of the multivariate regressions which take into account all determinants simultaneously. Following the research questions RQ2a and RQ2b, the determinants study aims at investigating the determinants of FRQ by **testing the hypotheses** H2 to H11. Using the regression model as described in section 5.3.3.2, the results provide evidence on the relation between the identified influencing factors and FRQ and, thereby, test the corresponding determinants hypotheses. To measure and compare country effects, the model uses Brazilian and South African dummy variables which allow comparisons against the benchmark of the developed Germany. Similarly, every industry is represented by a dummy variable, except for business equipment which is used as benchmark industry.

The determinants regressions use this study's **measures of FRQ** as dependent variable. In line with the above isolated determinant analysis, the full disclosure index measure (FRQ_FULL) is this study's main FRQ measure. To examine whether the regression results change when only voluntary disclosures are considered, also the results for the voluntary disclosure index measure (FRQ_VOL) are shown. In addition, these regression results are compared to those for discretionary accruals proxy based on the modified-Jones model

(FRQ_ACCR) and the Fog readability index (FRQ_FOG). Table 6-34 presents the regression results. The coefficients of the accruals-based and Fog index regression results are multiplied by -1 so that positive (negative) values indicate an increase (decrease) in FRQ consistent with the predicted signs. On the whole, all four regression models show highly significant F-statistics ($p < 0.001$) indicating that the models are valid for the entire population and not only for the selected sample. The maximum VIF values raise no concern about multicollinearity in the regressions.

As the **accruals-based earnings management proxy** (FRQ_ACCR) has not been found to measure FRQ in the sense of the full disclosure index (FRQ_FULL),[1142] it is not surprising that its determinants differ from those of the disclosure index measure. The regression results show that company size is positively related to discretionary accruals on a highly significant level ($p < 0.001$). This suggests that larger companies engage less in earnings management and, thus, provide a higher FRQ. In contrast to the other three regressions, the country variable coefficients are not significant suggesting that there are no significant differences in earnings management among Brazil, South Africa and Germany.

This finding contradicts the result of the Kruskal-Wallis test, which has found marginally significant differences between the countries' discretionary accruals.[1143] Moreover, older and more profitable companies are deemed to engage in less earnings management, as the statistically significant coefficients suggest. Regarding economic significance, an increase in company age of 1 year is associated with an increase in accruals-based FRQ of 0.015. The results also show marginally significant industry effects. Companies from the industries *consumer* as well as *wholesale and retail* seem to provide a lower FRQ in comparison to *business equipment*. With an adjusted R^2 of 18.48% the explanatory power of the regression model is considerably lower than the that of the other models. Thus, the determinants solely explain a relatively small fraction of accruals-based FRQ. Additional variables might be necessary to better explain the results of this earnings management measure

The regression results for the **Fog index readability measure** (FRQ_FOG) show significant country effects for both emerging economies Brazil and South Africa. Against the benchmark of Germany, the Fog index of a Brazilian (South African) company increases by 2.053 (1.399) points (with $p = 0.004$ (0.033)) leading to a more difficult readability of its CEO/management letter and, thus, lower FRQ. This is in line with the descriptive results which suggest an easier readability in Germany than in Brazil and South Africa. Regarding the economic significance, however, the suggested Brazilian influence is considerably more pronounced than the South African effect.

This finding is also confirmed by the descriptive results showing that the South African Fog index is lower than the Brazilian one (easier readability of the South African reports). In addition to these country effects, no other determinant is significantly associated with the Fog readability measure and several regression coefficients do not show the predicted sign. In particular, the industry of a company does not seem to be related to its readability score, as none of the industry coefficients is statistically significant.

[1142] Cf. section 6.1.4.

[1143] Cf. section 6.1.1.

Variables	Predicted sign	FRQ_ACCR	FRQ_FOG	FRQ_FULL (Total score)	FRQ_VOL (Total score)
Country_BRA	(-)	0.960 (0.539)	-2.053 *** (-2.689)	-10.321 *** (-4.104)	-11.151 *** (-4.368)
Country_RSA	(-)	-0.345 (-0.196)	-1.399 ** (-1.852)	-7.012 *** (-2.818)	-4.608 ** (-1.824)
Company size	(+)	1.601 *** (4.572)	0.158 (1.054)	1.120 ** (2.264)	1.108 ** (2.205)
Company age	(+)	0.015 * (1.458)	-0.003 (-0.757)	0.032 ** (2.166)	0.033 ** (2.215)
Profitability	(+)	0.001 ** (1.941)	-0.000 (-0.230)	0.001 * (1.491)	0.001 * (1.449)
Company valuation	(-)	-0.068 (-0.695)	0.018 (0.426)	-0.194 * (-1.411)	-0.195 * (-1.399)
Systematic risk	(+)	0.114 (0.120)	0.352 (0.869)	2.046 * (1.532)	1.934 * (1.427)
Ownership concentration	(-)	-2.657 (-1.004)	-1.107 (-0.975)	-12.378 *** (-3.309)	-12.696 *** (-3.344)
Customer basis		-0.206 (-0.214)	-0.344 (-0.834)	-0.127 (-0.094)	0.232 (0.168)
Media coverage		-0.283 (-1.264)	0.129 (1.340)	0.326 (1.033)	0.369 (1.150)
Analyst following		-0.126 (-1.488)	-0.007 (-0.199)	0.375 *** (3.124)	0.382 *** (3.139)
Consumer		-5.054 * (-1.886)	0.215 (0.187)	-4.357 (-1.151)	-4.612 (-1.200)
Manufacturing		-3.751 (-1.491)	0.241 (0.224)	-3.474 (-0.978)	-3.773 (-1.046)
Energy and mining		-4.318 (-1.590)	0.006 (0.005)	-6.635 * (-1.730)	-7.301 * (-1.875)
Telecommunication and media		-4.318 (-1.467)	-0.464 (-0.368)	-0.812 (-0.195)	-0.777 (-0.184)
Wholesale and retail		-4.821 * (-1.811)	-0.179 (-0.157)	-3.585 (-0.953)	-4.198 (-1.100)
Healthcare		-2.524 (-0.890)	0.208 (0.171)	-4.142 (-1.034)	-4.666 (-1.148)
Real estate		-3.874 (-1.343)	0.984 (0.795)	-9.296 ** (-2.281)	-9.862 ** (-2.384)
Transportation		-2.840 (-1.029)	0.150 (0.127)	-6.236 (-1.600)	-7.082 * (-1.790)
Construction		-4.541 (-1.518)	-0.496 (-0.387)	-2.640 (-0.625)	-2.537 (-0.591)
Constant		-20.497 *** (-3.668)	-17.973 *** (-7.501)	20.873 *** (2.644)	16.875 ** (2.110)
N		150	150	150	150
Adj. R^2		18.48 %	23.06 %	74.40 %	75.03 %
F-stat		2.69 ***	3.23 ***	22.66 ***	23.39 ***
Maximum VIF		7.87	7.87	7.87	7.87

The table presents the results of the OLS regressions conducted for the determinant model. As measures for financial reporting quality the regression models use the modified-Jones model discretionary accruals proxy (FRQ_ACCR), the Fog readability index (FRQ_FOG), the full (FRQ_FULL) and voluntary (FRQ_VOL) disclosure index scores. *, ** and *** denote significance at the 10%, 5% and 1% level (one-tailed for coefficients with predicted signs and two-tailed otherwise).

Table 6-34: Regression results for determinants of FRQ

The adjusted R^2 of 23.06% suggests that the model explains FRQ (in terms of readability) only to a small extent which is consistent with the small number of identified determinants influencing the readability of the analyzed textual passages. Overall, the significant determinants of the readability measure seem to differ considerably from the significant determinants of the disclosure index-based FRQ measure. This finding fits to the identified differences between the two measures of FRQ.[1144]

On the basis of the total score of the **full disclosure index** (FRQ_FULL), the regression output provides several statistically significant results. Overall, all regression coefficients show the predicted signs. In particular, country effects are highly significant and economically pronounced. In comparison to the German sample, FRQ decreases by 10.321 points ($p < 0.001$) for a Brazilian company and by 7.012 points ($p = 0.003$) for a South African company. Besides the country variables, also ownership concentration ($p = 0.001$) and analyst following ($p = 0.002$) are associated with FRQ on the 1% significance level. As assumed, there is a negative relationship between ownership concentration and FRQ. Thus, FRQ increases with a more dispersed ownership structure. Analyst following is positively associated with total disclosure quality. Thus, the more analysts capture a company, the higher is its FRQ. The results also present a positive relationship for both company size and company age which are significant on the 5% level. Moreover, marginally significant associations are shown between FRQ and the variables profitability ($p = 0.069$), company valuation ($p = 0.081$) and systematic risk ($p = 0.064$). In line with the hypotheses H5, H6 and H7, thus, more profitable companies, undervalued entities and companies with higher systematic risks tend to provide a higher FRQ. However, the economic significance of these associations is relatively low. Concerning the relation between profitability and FRQ, for instance, an increase in ROE by 1 percentage point is associated with a 0.001 points rise in FRQ. Also industry effects can be observed. The regression coefficients of both industries *energy and mining* (-6.635) and *real estate* (-9.296) indicate that companies from these industries provide a lower FRQ in their annual reports than entities from the *business equipment* industry (as benchmark industry). Significant relationships between other industries and FRQ are not detected. Moreover, the regression model does not find any statistically significant association for the variables customer basis and media coverage. In comparison to the regression models using the accruals-based and quantitative proxies as well as to other determinant studies in the literature, the FRQ_FULL model's explanatory is very high with an adjusted R^2 of 74.40%.

The use of the **voluntary disclosure index** does not alter the results of the full disclosure index substantially. The explanatory power even increases to an adjusted R^2 of 75.03%. However, while the use of the voluntary disclosure index leads to a wider FRQ gap between Brazil and Germany (from -10.321 to -11.151), the gap between South Africa and Germany decreases considerably (from -7.012 to -4.608). This observation is plausible, since the South African companies have to report less disclosure items of the full disclosure index due to financial reporting regulation than the German and Brazilian companies. Hence, there is only a small difference between the South African full and voluntary disclosure scores in accordance with the descriptive results, whereas the Brazilian and

[1144] Cf. section 6.1.4.

German voluntary disclosure scores are substantially lower than the full disclosure scores of these samples. Unlike the FRQ_FULL regression output, the results for the voluntary disclosure index show a marginally significant association between FRQ and the *transportation* industry ($p = 0.076$).

After the description of the main regression results with the total disclosure index (FRQ_FULL) score as FRQ measure, Table 6-35 and Table 6-36 reveal, which influencing factors determine the disclosure quality of the seven **reporting categories**. For this purpose, the total disclosure index score of the FRQ_FULL regression model is replaced by each disclosure index sub score. All other variables remain constant. The predicted signs of the influencing factors are taken from the main regression model. Although most of the regression results are consistent with the above results, some findings differ considerably from those of the total FRQ regression model. This allows a more detailed analysis of the companies' reporting practices regarding the different reporting categories.

With respect to the FRQ of **background information**, cross-country differences are less pronounced than in the total FRQ model. The country variable coefficients suggest that the quality of *background information* decreases by 7.859 percentage points for companies from Brazil ($p = 0.027$) and by 3.146 percentage points for those from South Africa ($p = 0.431$), although only the Brazilian one is statistically significant. Furthermore, the variables profitability, ownership concentration and analyst following are significantly associated with the quality of *background information* in accordance with the predicted signs. While the suggested effects of ownership concentration and analyst following are less pronounced than in the total FRQ results, the results show a stronger effect for profitability. In addition, the regression output presents an untabulated significant coefficient of -11.913 for the transportation industry ($p = 0.058$). However, with an adjusted R^2 of 38.60% the explanatory power of the regression model is considerably lower than that of the main model and the lowest among all sub score regression models.

The regression model with the quality of **financials** information as FRQ measure shows similar results as the total FRQ model and has also a relatively high explanatory power (adjusted R^2 of 66.87%). All variables have the predicted signs and significant relationships are shown for the determinants ownership concentration ($p = 0.002$), analyst following ($p = 0.010$) as well as both country effect variables (both $p < 0.001$). Unlike the country effects in the main determinants model, however, the regression coefficients for Brazil and South Africa are on a similar level suggesting that the *financials* disclosure quality of a Brazilian and South African entity is 10.694 percentage points and 10.916 percentage points lower than for a German entity. Furthermore, the results show a negative association between company valuation and *financials* FRQ, which is significant on the 5% level ($p = 0.011$). Thus, undervalued companies tend to provide a higher quality of *financials* disclosures. The associations between the FRQ measure and both company size ($p = 0.082$) and profitability ($p = 0.059$) are significant on the 10% level, whereas significant industry effects are not found.

With an adjusted R^2 of 48.05% the explanatory power of the **non-financials** regression model is lower than that of the total FRQ model. When comparing to the results of the other sub score regressions, the *non-financials* column in Table 6-35 presents some unique findings. First, it is the only regression model which does not find any significant country effect suggesting that the emerging economy environments in Brazil and South Africa do not affect the quality of reported *non-financials* information. Second, solely this regression model finds a positive association between a company's customer basis and FRQ, which is significant on the 5% level (p = 0.047). The corresponding coefficient posits that the quality of *non-financial* disclosures increases by 4.660 percentage points for companies with end-consumers as customers (B2C). Further, relatively strong relations are found for the variables ownership concentration (p = 0.015) and analyst following (p = 0.004) in line with the main regression results. The regression coefficients of company size, company age and systematic company risk are solely marginally significant on the 10% level. Moreover, the industries *consumer, energy and mining, real estate* as well as *transportation* are significantly associated with the quality of *non-financials* disclosures.

Variables	Predicted sign	FRQ_FULL (Background)	FRQ_FULL (Financials)	FRQ_FULL (Non-financials)	FRQ_FULL (Sustainability)
Country_BRA	(-)	-7.859 ** (-1.952)	-10.694 *** (-3.882)	3.880 (0.902)	-1.118 (-0.177)
Country_RSA	(-)	-3.146 (-0.790)	-10.916 *** (-4.004)	2.562 (0.602)	33.890 *** (5.438)
Company size	(+)	0.319 (0.403)	0.758 * (1.399)	1.330 * (1.572)	3.587 *** (2.894)
Company age	(+)	-0.001 (-0.038)	0.018 (1.152)	0.033 * (1.344)	0.059 * (1.605)
Profitability	(+)	0.002 ** (1.919)	0.001 * (1.577)	0.001 (0.982)	0.001 (1.193)
Company valuation	(-)	-0.102 (-0.465)	-0.353 ** (-2.341)	-0.007 (-0.029)	-0.238 (-0.691)
Systematic risk	(+)	-0.046 (-0.021)	1.106 (0.756)	3.212 * (1.407)	2.476 (0.740)
Ownership concentration	(-)	-9.090 * (-1.518)	-12.798 *** (-3.124)	-14.000 ** (-2.190)	-1.624 (-0.173)
Customer basis		2.469 (1.134)	-1.155 (-0.775)	4.660 ** (2.004)	-1.236 (-0.363)
Media coverage		0.248 (0.491)	0.382 (1.104)	0.581 (1.075)	0.309 (0.390)
Analyst following		0.324 * (1.686)	0.342 ** (2.606)	0.597 *** (2.909)	0.654 ** (2.178)
Constant		46.809 *** (3.704)	31.866 *** (3.685)	3.543 (0.260)	-29.149 (-1.475)
Industry-fixed effects		YES	YES	YES	YES
N		150	150	150	150
Adj. R^2		38.60 %	66.87 %	48.05 %	56.79 %
F-stat		5.68 ***	16.04 ***	7.89 ***	10.79 ***
Maximum VIF		7.87	7.87	7.87	7.87

The table presents the results of the OLS regressions conducted for the determinant model with the full disclosure index sub scores of the categories background information, important financials information, important non-financials information and sustainability information as measures of financial reporting quality. Industry coefficients are not tabulated. *, ** and *** denote significance at the 10%, 5% and 1% level (one-tailed for coefficients with predicted signs and two-tailed otherwise).

Table 6-35: Regression results for determinants of background, financials, non-financials and sustainability FRQ

Also the **sustainability** regression model provides specific results. Consistent with the descriptive results of the disclosure index scores, *sustainability* is the only reporting category, where the FRQ of South African companies increases significantly in comparison to the German sample. The coefficient suggests a strong effect of 33.890 percentage points for entities from the South African reporting environment ($p < 0.001$). However, there is no significant effect shown for the Brazilian setting ($p = 0.859$). In addition, company size ($p = 0.002$) and analyst following ($p = 0.031$) are significantly related to the quality of *sustainability* information. No significant industry associations are observed.

Regarding the FRQ of **value based management** information, Table 6-36 presents a marginally significant negative country effect for Brazil ($p = 0.074$), whereas there is none for the South African variable. In comparison to the main regression model, the results show stronger relationships between the *value based management* disclosure score and the influencing factors company size ($p < 0.001$) and systematic company risk ($p = 0.042$). Moreover, company age ($p = 0.040$) and analyst following ($p = 0.080$) may affect the FRQ of this reporting category. The results discover no significant industry effects.

Using the FRQ of **forward-looking** information as dependent variable, the regression results show strong and highly significant country effects. Against the benchmark of Germany, the disclosure quality decreases by 19.811 percentage points for Brazilian companies ($p < 0.001$) and by 20.462 percentage points for South African ones ($p < 0.001$). Moreover, the results present the most pronounced relationship between ownership concentration and a disclosure quality sub score among all determinant regressions with a coefficient of -19.031 which is significant on the 1% level. This indicates that entities with less concentrated ownership structures provide a significantly higher quality of *forward-looking* disclosures. Further, company age is positively and significantly associated with the FRQ measure ($p = 0.050$). A statistically significant effect is also found for the *real estate* industry ($p = 0.029$).

The last column of Table 6-36 suggests that the associations between the country variables and the FRQ of **risks and opportunities** disclosures are even stronger than their relation to *forward-looking* FRQ. With a regression coefficient of -24.089 ($p < 0.001$) the South African variable is associated with a lower disclosure score than the Brazilian variable with a coefficient of -21.956 ($p < 0.001$) in comparison to Germany. Moreover, particularly the regression coefficient of systematic company risk (4.392) is more pronounced than in the main regression model (total FRQ) and significant on the 5% level ($p = 0.025$). This indicates that companies with higher inherent systematic risks provide a higher quality of information on *risks and opportunities*. Although all variables have the predicted signs, additional significant coefficients are only shown for the determinants company age ($p = 0.020$), ownership concentration ($p = 0.048$) as well as analyst following ($p = 0.024$). Company size is marginally associated with the *risks and opportunities* disclosure score ($p = 0.079$), whereas the results show no significant relation for any industry category.

Variables	Predicted sign	FRQ_FULL (Value based)	FRQ_FULL (Forward)	FRQ_FULL (Risks)
Country_BRA	(-)	-7.673 * (-1.458)	-19.811 *** (-4.952)	-21.956 *** (-5.258)
Country_RSA	(-)	4.915 (0.944)	-20.462 *** (-5.169)	-24.089 *** (-5.830)
Company size	(+)	3.387 *** (3.271)	0.241 (0.306)	1.169 * (1.423)
Company age	(+)	0.054 ** (1.772)	0.038 ** (1.662)	0.050 ** (2.084)
Profitability	(+)	-0.000 (-0.194)	0.000 (0.232)	0.001 (0.865)
Company valuation	(-)	-0.176 (-0.610)	-0.203 (-0.927)	-0.126 (-0.550)
Systematic risk	(+)	4.869 ** (1.742)	1.219 (0.574)	4.392 ** (1.981)
Ownership concentration	(-)	-6.719 (-0.859)	-19.031 *** (-3.199)	-10.403 ** (-1.675)
Customer basis		-4.221 (-1.483)	-0.874 (-0.404)	-2.288 (-1.013)
Media coverage		0.457 (0.691)	0.505 (1.004)	-0.539 (-1.028)
Analyst following		0.444 * (1.768)	0.120 (0.631)	0.455 ** (2.285)
Constant		-26.401 (-1.598)	33.070 *** (2.634)	31.502 ** (2.404)
Industry-fixed effects		YES	YES	YES
N		150	150	150
Adj. R^2		51.77 %	62.16 %	68.02 %
F-stat		9.00 ***	13.24 ***	16.84 ***
Maximum VIF		7.87	7.87	7.87

The table presents the results of the OLS regressions conducted for the determinant model with the full disclosure index sub scores of the categories value based information, forward-looking information and risks and opportunities information as measures of financial reporting quality. *, ** and *** denote significance at the 10%, 5% and 1% level (one-tailed for coefficients with predicted signs and two-tailed otherwise).

Table 6-36: Regression results for determinants of value based, forward-looking and risk FRQ

In addition to the above regression results for the total sample, this study also analyzes the determinants of FRQ within each of the sample countries. This analysis detects, as to what extent the associations of the determinants differ across Brazil, South Africa and Germany in accordance with research question RQ2b. Thus, Table 6-37 presents the results of the **country sample regressions**. In general, the F values of all three regressions are statistically significant, suggesting that the results are valid beyond the sample. However, the F-stat for South Africa is only marginally significant on the 10% level ($p = 0.055$). A reason for the low F value could be the relatively small sample size. Moreover, the explanatory power of the South African determinants model is considerably lower (adj. $R^2 = 23.13\%$) than those of the Brazilian (adj. $R^2 = 45.99\%$) and German (adj. $R^2 = 56.32\%$) models. On the whole, the country-based regression models detect a smaller number of significant determinants than the main regression model on the basis of the total sample. This observation could be explained by the larger number of companies in the total sample. The VIF of the regression for Brazil (11.52) indicates potential multicollinearity of the variables. However, VIF values above 10 are only found for industry variables. The maximum VIF of non-industry variables is 2.55 (customer basis).

The results for **Brazil** show a negative and highly significant relationship between an entity's ownership concentration and its total FRQ (p = 0.003). Moreover, the total FRQ of the Brazilian companies increases significantly with higher media coverage (p = 0.025). Concerning the relation between company valuation and total FRQ the results show a significant negative relation (p = 0.050), which is also consistent with the predicted sign. In line with the findings of the isolated customer basis analysis, the regression results support (based on a one-tailed significance test) that Brazilian B2C companies provide a higher FRQ than B2B companies. Moreover, the untabulated results show this positive association between the B2C customer basis of Brazilian companies and their *non-financials* FRQ (p = 0.020).

Variables	Predicted sign	Brazil (FRQ_FULL)	South Africa (FRQ_FULL)	Germany (FRQ_FULL)
Company size	(+)	0.131 (0.192)	-0.232 (-0.186)	3.770 *** (3.108)
Company age	(+)	-0.017 (-0.523)	0.044 * (1.622)	0.037 * (1.607)
Profitability	(+)	0.030 (1.118)	0.006 (0.515)	0.001 (0.913)
Company valuation	(-)	-0.259 * (-1.693)	0.073 (0.187)	-0.098 (-0.264)
Systematic risk	(+)	-0.275 (-0.109)	-3.086 (-1.166)	1.229 (0.328)
Ownership concentration	(-)	-16.034 *** (-2.928)	-5.726 (-0.747)	-10.639 * (-1.350)
Customer basis		3.478 (1.539)	0.636 (0.217)	-4.440 (-1.650)
Media coverage		1.021 ** (2.356)	-0.180 (-0.412)	0.413 (0.482)
Analyst following		-0.047 (-0.197)	0.489 (1.655)	0.498 ** (2.618)
Constant		30.201 *** (3.004)	37.200 ** (2.436)	-23.615 (-1.500)
Industry-fixed effects		YES	YES	YES
N		50	50	50
Adj. R^2		45.99 %	23.13 %	56.32 %
F-stat		3.45 ***	1.92 *	4.51 ***
Maximum VIF		11.52	7.84	5.61

The table presents the results of the OLS regressions conducted for the determinant model per country sample with the full disclosure index scores (FRQ_FULL) as measure of financial reporting quality. *, ** and *** denote significance at the 10%, 5% and 1% level (one-tailed for coefficients with predicted signs and two-tailed otherwise)..

Table 6-37: Regression results for determinants of FRQ in Brazil, South Africa and Germany

For **South Africa**, the results reveal only a few significant determinants of FRQ, which is consistent with the relatively low explanatory power of the South African regression model. As expected, a significant positive association is found between company age and total

FRQ (p= 0.057). Moreover, the one-tailed test shows that the FRQ of South African annual reports increases significantly with analyst following. Using the FRQ of *non-financials* instead of total FRQ, the regression model identifies a stronger association for analyst following (p = 0.053) and an increased quality of *non-financials* for B2C companies on the basis of a one-tailed test (p = 0.053), which is in line with the findings of the isolated determinant analysis. Furthermore, ownership concentration is negatively and significantly related to the quality of *background information* (p = 0.038) and *financials* (p = 0.089) in South Africa.

For **Germany**, company size is identified as most significant determinant (p = 0.002). In line with the predicted signs, the total FRQ of German companies is also significantly related to analyst following (p = 0.014), company age (p = 0.059) and ownership concentration (p = 0.094). These significant associations are also found for several of the seven reporting categories (German sample). In particular, only the German sample shows a significant relation between the FRQ of *forward-looking information* and company age (p = 0.088). This suggests that the disclosure of *forward-looking information* (which is frequently regarded as particularly sensitive information) is barely affected by the identified determinants. As Table 6-37 reveals, significant relations between total FRQ and the variables profitability, systematic company risk and customer basis are not found in any of the country regressions.

6.2.4 Sensitivity analyses and robustness tests

The determinants study examines the **sensitivity** of the regression results through the use of alternative proxies for both dependent and independent regression variables. In particular, not only the full disclosure index score (FRQ_FULL) is included in the determinants model as proxy of total FRQ, but also the score of the voluntary disclosure index (FRQ_VOL) is applied, which comprises solely voluntary disclosure items. However, the results do not change substantially when using the voluntary disclosure index score so that the main findings remain robust.

Furthermore, the sensitivity analysis investigates how **alternative proxies for company size** affect the results of the multivariate regression. This test seems advisable, since not all of the identified size measures are strongly correlated with each other (cf. section 5.1.2.2). The use of logarithmized market capitalization, logarithmized total assets and number of employees as size measure instead of revenues does not alter the regression results for the total sample substantially. However, the South African regression model provides some differing results using market capitalization as size measure. Contradictory to hypothesis H3, the results show a negative relation between company size and total FRQ, which is marginally significant on the 10% level in a one-tailed test (p = 0.090). Moreover, the South African results show that analyst following is significantly associated with total FRQ (p = 0.015) and the identified marginally significant association of company age is even significant on the 5% level (p = 0.030).

The correlation analysis of the determinant variables has indicated that some of the independent variables are somewhat associated with each other. Consequently, these explanatory variables might impede each other by taking away the other **variable's explanatory**

power. For instance, there is a relatively pronounced correlation between company size and company age. In fact, sensitivity analyses show for the FRQ_FULL model (total FRQ) that the regression coefficient of company size increases from 1.120 to 1.197 (p = 0.018), if company age is excluded from the regression for the total sample. The additional exclusion of the information environment variables media coverage and analyst following even results in an increase of the company size coefficient to 1.570 (p = 0.001). Although there is also a strong correlation between the two information environment variables media coverage and analyst following, the exclusion of one variable does not affect the other variable's explanatory power considerably. Hence, media coverage as well as analyst following seem to measure different aspects of a company's information environment and, therefore, are both included in the determinants model. The sensitivity analysis indicates no substantial effect on the maximum VIF values due to the exclusion of the aforementioned variables.

To test the **robustness** of the main regression results, also the role of **outliers** is analyzed. For this purpose, the study uses *Cook*'s distance method which determines outliers with *Cook's* distances greater than 4/N (with the sample size N).[1145] After discarding 13 outliers, the main regressions are conducted for the reduced sample size. The results of both full (FRQ_FULL) and voluntary (FRQ_VOL) regression models remain largely robust.[1146] However, the marginally significant association between a company's profitability and its total FRQ is not supported by the robustness test. Moreover, the explanatory power of the FRQ_FULL model increases to an adjusted R^2 of 81.29%.

6.2.5 Critical evaluation of the results

After presenting the results of both the isolated analyses of each determinant and the multivariate regression model, this section discusses the identified determinants of FRQ (research question RQ2a) and analyzes how these determinants differ across the three sample countries (research question RQ2b). For this purpose, the results are also contrasted with those of prior research. Since the regression models using the discretionary accruals (FRQ_ACCR) and the Fog readability index (FRQ_FOG) as FRQ measures provide only little evidence on the determinants of these FRQ constructs, this section focuses on the results for the disclosure index measures (FRQ_FULL and FRQ_VOL). As mentioned before, the evaluation of the research hypotheses H2 to H11 is based on the regression results of these disclosure index-based models (with total FRQ as dependent variable).

Country-specific cultural and institutional reporting environments, different stages of financial reporting development as well as stakeholder theory lead to the expectation of **country differences** in FRQ between Brazil, South Africa and Germany. Hypothesis H2a assumes that FRQ of German companies exceeds FRQ of companies from the emerging economies Brazil and South Africa. In addition, hypothesis H2b argues that FRQ is higher in South Africa than in Brazil. Not only the descriptive results show that the average total FRQ of German companies significantly exceeds the average total FRQ of the Brazilian and South African samples, but also the results of the determinants study underpin

[1145] Cf. *Blanchard/Leigh* (2013), p. 10.
[1146] Cf. Appendix, Table A-9.

this finding. The main regression results show that the total FRQ decreases in the Brazilian and South African reporting settings in comparison to the German one. This reduction by about 10 (Brazil) and 7 percentage points (South Africa) according to the FRQ_FULL results is economically significant. As assumed in hypothesis H2b, the suggested negative country effect is more pronounced for Brazil than for South Africa.

The use of the **voluntary** instead of the full **disclosure index** widens the FRQ gap between Brazil and Germany, whereas the gap between South Africa and Germany decreases. The reason for this observation is that the South African voluntary disclosure index barely differs from the full disclosure index so that the FRQ remains on a similar level, whereas in Germany a number of mandatory items are not included in the voluntary index resulting in a decrease in FRQ. In contrast, the non-consideration of the Brazilian mandatory items in the country's voluntary disclosure index has an even stronger effect than in Germany, which leads to a stronger negative country effect compared to Germany. On the whole, however, the regression results of both the full and voluntary disclosure index models support hypotheses H2a and H2b.

Regarding the FRQ of the seven **reporting categories** (full disclosure index), the observed country effects differ. On the one hand, the country coefficients in the regressions for *financials* and *forward-looking information* indicate significant negative effects on a similar level for both Brazil and South Africa. On the other hand, *non-financials* is the only content category, for which the regression results show no significant country effects at all. This finding indicates a particular role of this type of information. The FRQ of *non-financials* does not seem to be driven by a country's reporting environment determining country-specific *non-financials* disclosure practices (e.g., on customer, employee and brand information). This may allow companies to differentiate their annual reports from the reports of other companies particularly through *non-financials* disclosures.

The expected gap between the FRQ in the **developed Germany**, on the one hand, and in the two **emerging economies**, on the other, is most pronounced for the reporting categories *forward-looking information* and *risks and opportunities*, which are regarded as particularly sensitive and important information to stakeholders.[1147] The German management report requirements and tradition regarding these reporting areas as well as established best practices for German annual reports may explain the higher FRQ in Germany. Contradictory to hypothesis H2b, the South African negative associations for both *forward-looking information* and *risks and opportunities* FRQ are even stronger than the Brazilian ones. A reason for this observation might be that Brazilian entities have to report more disclosure items mandatorily, particularly on risk information, than entities in South Africa. The integrated reporting approach in South Africa on comply-or-explain basis, however, does not require these disclosure items on *forward-looking* information and *risks and opportunities* due to regulation. The only reporting category, where the South African sample outperforms the German sample is *sustainability*. This descriptive result is underpinned by the *sustainability* regression model, which finds the only positive and both statistically and economically highly significant country effect for South Africa. The result

[1147] Cf. amongst others *SRI International* (1987), p. 7; *AICPA* (1994), p. 4; *Balata/Breton* (2005), p. 12.

suggests that South Africa's efforts are successful to implement a sustainability dimension into integrated reports.

On the basis of agency and positive accounting theory, hypothesis H3 argues that **company size** is positively associated with FRQ. As assumed, the main regression results show a positive and significant association and, thus, support the hypothesis. The finding is consistent with the literature, which has reached a "*general agreement*"[1148] that there is a positive relationship between a company's size and its FRQ.[1149] However, the association of company size differs across the sample countries. While the isolated determinant analysis has shown that company size is positively and significantly associated with total FRQ in Brazil and Germany, only the German regression model confirms such a significant relationship. This discrepancy between the results for Germany and those for the two emerging economies suggests that company size might play a more important role for reporting in developed countries than in emerging economies. Hence, reporting incentives in emerging economies might not differ considerably between larger and smaller companies. An explanation could be, for example, that larger companies do not expect higher political costs (according to positive accounting theory) than smaller companies. Although most prior determinants studies investigate developed countries, a significant association between company size and FRQ has also been shown for emerging economies.[1150] Moreover, the sample description has illustrated that the volatility of the company size measures is greater for the German companies than for the Brazilian and South African companies.[1151] Consequently, the size effect on FRQ could be more pronounced in Germany than in the two emerging economies. Regarding the different reporting categories, the positive association between company size and the category's disclosure score is particularly pronounced for *sustainability*. Consistent with positive accounting theory, particularly large companies attempt to avoid political costs through the disclosure of sustainability related issues (e.g., addressing environmental authorities).[1152] The results remain robust when alternative proxies for company size (market capitalization, total assets and number of employees) are used in the regressions.

Besides company size, also **company age** is assumed to be positively associated with FRQ (hypothesis H4). Although the isolated determinants analysis indicates a weak relationship between company age and FRQ only for the total and the German sample, the multivariate regressions show significant associations for the total, German and South African samples. Hence, the results suggest that company age determines the quality of financial reporting in South Africa and Germany, however, not in Brazil. The finding appears plausible, since the average Brazilian company (35 years) is considerably younger than its counterparts in South Africa (66 years) and Germany (84 years). The South African and German companies have had more time to establish high-quality reporting systems including

---

[1148] *Dainelli et al.* (2013), p. 271.

[1149] Cf. among others *Leftwich et al.* (1981), p. 57; *Wallace et al.* (1994), p. 41; *Haniffa/Cooke* (2002), p. 342; *Dainelli et al.* (2013), p. 271.

[1150] Cf. e.g. *Haniffa/Cooke* (2002), p. 342.

[1151] Cf. section 5.1.2.2.

[1152] This inference is supported by *Blaesing* (2013), who finds a significant positive relation between company size and quality of sustainability reports for a German sample, cf. *Blaesing* (2013), p. 222.

the set-up of required resources (e.g., trained employees) and the adoption of best-practices. Therefore, company age effects might be more pronounced in these countries. Overall, the main regression results support hypothesis H4. In line with this result, company age is also positively and significantly associated with the disclosure quality of the seven content categories, except for *background information* and *financials*. The relationship is most pronounced for the quality of *sustainability* information. This result is reasonable, as older and, thus, traditional companies might have to put particular efforts into *sustainability* reporting to maintain their reached legitimacy level (legitimacy theory).[1153] Moreover, older companies with highly-developed reporting systems may be more capable of collecting *sustainability* information than younger companies with less developed reporting systems.

Concerning a company's **profitability** as determinant of FRQ, Hypothesis H5 expects more profitable entities to provide a higher FRQ. The assumption is based on both agency and stakeholder theory. While the isolated determinants analysis does not detect a significant correlation for any sub sample, the main regression model supports hypothesis H5, although it finds only a marginally significant association. However, none of the country regression results underpin this finding. Moreover, the regression results for the sub categories show the predicted positive sign, except for *value based management*, but a significant relation is only found between a company's profitability and its quality of *background* information as well as *financials*. As a company's profitability is assessed on the basis of its *financials*, more profitable companies may demonstrate their economic performance by providing high-quality *financials* disclosures. This argument is supported by *Wang et al.* (2008) who also find that a company's profitability particularly influences its *financials* disclosures, rather than other reporting areas.[1154] Also the literature provides mixed results regarding profitability as a determinant of FRQ. While *Bokpin* (2013) and *Dainelli et al.* (2013) provide evidence that more profitable companies provide a higher FRQ, *Ahmed/Courtis* (1999) and *Cahan et al.* (2005) do not find a significant association between profitability and FRQ.[1155] On the whole, the identified relationship is not particularly pronounced so that hypothesis H5 is partially supported.

The expected negative relationship between **company valuation** and FRQ (hypothesis H6) is premised on the assumption that undervalued companies have an incentive to publish high-quality information to signal their actual company value (agency theory). In fact, the results of the main regression model support hypothesis H6, as there is a negative association between company valuation and total FRQ, which is significant on the 10% level. However, the result is only significant for the overall sample and not for any of the three country-level regressions, which is consistent with the results of the isolated determinants analysis. Regarding the regressions for the different reporting categories, all regression coefficients have the predicted signs. However, a significant relation is only found between company valuation and quality of *financials* disclosures. This seems plausible, as investors and financial analysts evaluate companies on the basis of their *financials*. Hence,

[1153] Cf. section 4.1.5.4.2.

[1154] Cf. *Wang et al.* (2008), p. 23.

[1155] Cf. section 3.3.

undervalued entities might publish high-quality *financials* disclosures to encourage investors and financial analysts to revise prior valuations of the company.

According to principal-agent theory, entities with a higher **systematic company risk** might publish annual reports of increased FRQ to reduce agency costs. Thus, hypothesis H7 assumes a positive association between systematic company risk and FRQ. The isolated determinants analysis finds such relations for the total and the German sample. These medium correlations are highly significant. Also the results of the main multivariate regression show a significant association between a company's systematic risk and its total FRQ and, therefore, provide evidence for hypothesis H7. However, the detected relation is solely marginally significant and is not supported by any of the country regression models. In addition, there are significant relations between systematic company risk and FRQ of *non-financials, value based management* and *risks and opportunities.* Remarkably, the most significant positive relationship is found for the *risks and opportunities* category, suggesting that particularly riskier companies tend to provide high-quality risk-related information in their annual reports. This is in line with the underlying theoretical foundation. Companies provide a particularly high FRQ of risk information to avoid costs caused by information asymmetries concerning the entities' relatively high inherent company risks.

On the basis of both agency theory and stakeholder theory, hypothesis H8 expects companies with a low **ownership concentration** to provide increased FRQ. The results of the isolated determinants analysis support the hypothesis, as they show highly significant negative associations between ownership concentration and total FRQ for all samples, except for the South African one. The correlation is particularly pronounced within the Brazilian sample. Consistent with these findings, the multivariate regression results show the most significant regression coefficient (apart from the country coefficients) for ownership concentration. Also prior studies (e.g., *Cohen* (2008)) find ownership concentration to be one of the strongest determinants of FRQ, as companies with a more dispersed ownership structure tend to provide information of higher quality.[1156] The result is further consistent with *La Porta et al.* (1998), who provide general evidence that increased ownership concentration is associated with lower investor protection.[1157] These findings suggest that an entity has less incentive to provide high-quality annual reports, if it is owned by relatively few large block holders. Since such block holders presumably have different sources to obtain information about their company, they are not dependent on annual reports and, therefore, might even be concerned that annual reports could reveal sensitive information, e.g. to competitors. In contrast, in case of a rather dispersed ownership structure, the annual report might be an important source of information for shareholders. The effect is particularly pronounced in Brazil, where ownership is generally more concentrated than in South Africa and Germany as a result of the traditional family businesses in Brazil.[1158] For instance, the median of this study's Herfindahl index for Brazil (0.120) is more than twice the value for South Africa (0.045) and Germany (0.042).[1159] The finding is line

[1156] Cf. *Deegan* (2002), p. 295; *van der Laan Smith et al.* (2005), p. 147; *Cohen* (2008), p. 81.
[1157] Cf. *La Porta et al.* (1998), p. 1113.
[1158] Cf. section 2.3.2.
[1159] For the distribution of the sample companies' ownership concentration, cf. the section 6.2.2.7.

with *Schiehll et al.* (2013) who show that family-controlled companies in Brazil provide a lower quality of disclosures on executive stock options.[1160] The strong relation between ownership concentration and FRQ in Brazil is a central finding, since increased ownership concentration is a typical characteristic of companies in emerging economies.[1161]

On the theoretical basis of agency theory, positive accounting theory and legitimacy theory, hypothesis H9 assumes that FRQ differs across **industries**. However, the investigation of industry effects has shown mixed results. In line with *Cooke* (1991) and *Cahan et al.* (2005),[1162] this study's descriptive results show that companies from the manufacturing industry provide the highest FRQ, even after controlling for country effects. The Kruskal-Wallis test has not identified significant differences in the disclosure scores across the industries, whereas the multivariate regression reveals that some industries are significantly related to total FRQ. However, these results may suffer from a relatively small number of companies in some industries.

When comparing to *business equipment* as a benchmark industry, the regression results show that companies from *energy and mining* as well as *real estate* entities tend to provide a lower FRQ. Using the voluntary disclosure index as FRQ proxy, the results also show a similar effect for *transportation* companies. Therefore, the regression results provide evidence that FRQ differs across industries, as assumed in hypothesis H9, although significant effects are only shown for a few industries. In particular, the regression results do not reveal that companies from sustainability sensitive industries (e.g., *energy and mining*) provide a higher *sustainability* FRQ.

Based on stakeholder theory, hypothesis H10 expects that the companies' FRQ differs according to **customer basis**. In particular, the study distinguishes between companies with end-consumers as customers (B2C) and business-to-business companies (B2B). According to the Wilcoxon test (isolated determinants analysis), there is a significant difference in average total FRQ between B2C and B2B companies for the Brazilian sample. As the main regression results do not show a significant association between customer basis and FRQ, hypothesis H10 is generally not supported. However, the multivariate regression results support the significant association for Brazil in a one-tailed test indicating that B2C entities provide a higher total FRQ than B2B entities.

Moreover, the analysis of the relation between customer basis and the quality of specific reporting areas provides additional insights. While the Wilcoxon test shows no significant differences between B2C and B2B companies for *financials* information in any of the country samples, the FRQ of **non-financials** is significantly higher among B2C companies in Brazil and South Africa, whereas there is no significant difference for Germany. These results further suggest that the lower disclosure environment in Brazil and South Africa allows to detect differences in the companies' reporting decisions depending on their customer bases. Consistently, also the multivariate regression model finds that B2C companies provide a significantly higher reporting quality of *non-financial* information. This is particularly remarkable, as no other reporting category's FRQ is related to custom-

[1160] Cf. *Schiehll et al.* (2013), p. 354.
[1161] Cf. section 2.2.3.2.
[1162] Cf. *Cooke* (1991), p. 174; *Cahan et al.* (2005), p. 83.

er basis on a significant level. The result seems reasonable, since the *non-financials* reporting category encompasses disclosure items which might be particularly relevant to end-consumers of B2C entities, such as information on customers, employees, suppliers as well as important brands.

Finally, the determinants study examines the relationship between a company's **information environment** and its FRQ. According to the undirected hypothesis H11, a company's total FRQ is assumed to be associated with its information environment on the basis of agency theory and legitimacy theory. Two measures are used to operationalize information environment: media coverage and analyst following. However, the results for the two variables differ.

The isolated determinants analysis finds a weak positive relation between **media coverage** and total FRQ for the total, Brazilian and German samples on a significant level. However, the relation is not significant in the main regression model so that hypothesis H11 is not supported. The Brazilian regression model suggests a positive and significant association which is in line with the result of the correlation analysis. The finding indicates that Brazilian companies with higher media coverage publish annual reports of higher FRQ. Regarding the FRQ of the reporting categories, no significant relation is found for media coverage as potential influencing factor.

According to the isolated determinants analysis, there is a medium-strong positive relation between an entity's **analyst following** and its total FRQ for the total, South African and German sample on a significant level. In consistency with this result, also the main regression model identifies such a significant association supporting hypothesis H11. The positive association is also significant for the German and the South African sample on the basis of a one-tailed test. Consequently, analyst following seems to be a major determinant of total FRQ provided in annual reports. This inference is also supported by the reporting categories' regression results. All regressions models, except for the *forward-looking information* regression, find a significant positive relation between analyst following and each category's FRQ. Interestingly, the regression results show the most pronounced relations for the reporting areas *non-financials* and *sustainability*. This could suggest that financial analysts do not only consider financial information as a basis for their evaluations and capital market decisions, but also non-financial information from the reporting categories *non-financials* and *sustainability*. On the whole, the relation between FRQ and information environment (hypothesis H11) is supported by the regression results for analyst following, however, not by the results for media coverage.

Although the above discussion includes the analysis of determinants relevant for the different reporting categories and country sub samples, the main regression models (FRQ_FULL and FRQ VOL) for the full sample are used to evaluate this study's hypotheses and, thereby, provide evidence on the determinants of FRQ (research question RQ2a). Figure 6-17 summarizes the results of the hypotheses testing.

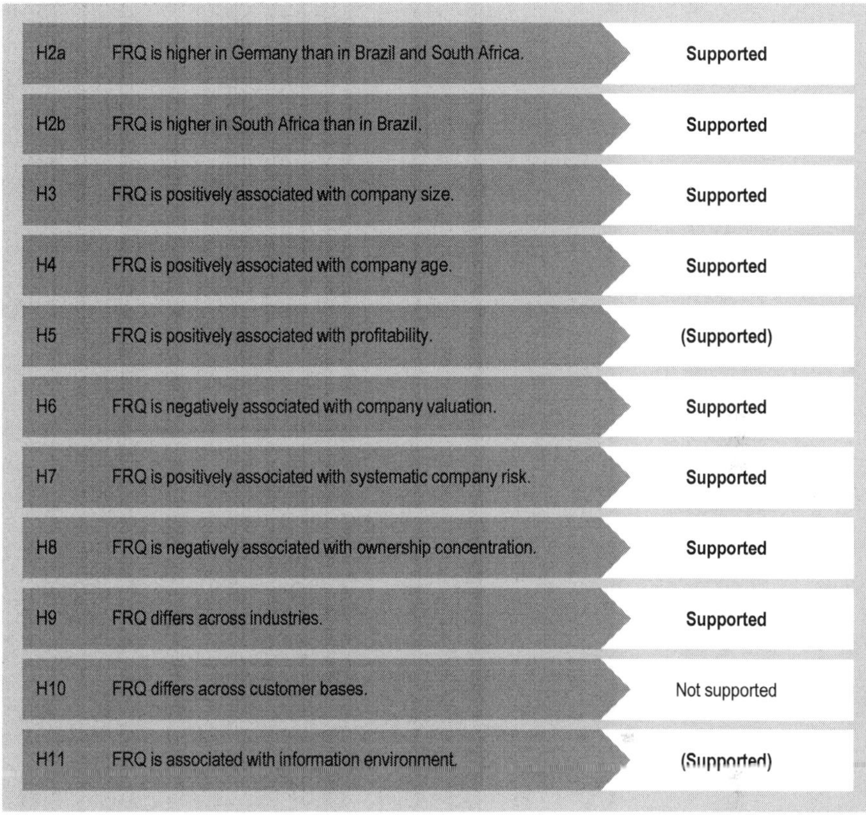

Figure 6-17: Test results of the determinants hypotheses

Furthermore, the determinants study gives several implications. The fact that the identified country effects differ considerably across **Brazil**, **South Africa** and **Germany** provides additional evidence for hypothesis H1b arguing that FRQ is different in each country. This finding also suggests that the reporting environment is unique in each country and transferring the determinants study's results to other country settings might be difficult. With respect to research question 2b, therefore, the importance of the **determinants of FRQ** in Figure 6-17 differs across the three sample countries. Although the theoretical foundation of the determinants remains the same in Brazil, South Africa and Germany, the country-specific financial reporting environments might not only explain general cross-country differences in financial reporting practices, but also affect the manifestation of company-specific determinants in a country.

As mentioned before, the historical and economic development in Brazil has led to a relatively high **ownership concentration** among the country's companies (as well as in other emerging economies[1163]). This seems to be related to the particular role of ownership concentration as a determinant of FRQ in the country. Therefore, ownership concentration may be an important determinant in emerging economies in line with prior studies. Moreover, the results suggest that **company size** is a more pronounced determinant in the developed Germany (in line with numerous developed country studies[1164]) than in the two emerging economies Brazil and South Africa. Assuming that companies are younger in emerging than in developed economies, the results further suggest that **company age** plays a less important role there than in developed countries. This finding is in contrast to prior research. Furthermore, the results of the determinants study indicate differences in FRQ across **customer basis** (particularly regarding disclosure of *non-financial* information) for the Brazilian and South African sample. Thus, the relatively low financial reporting environments in the two emerging economies might allow detecting these reporting incentives. Unlike prior determinants studies in emerging economies, this study does not identify profitability to be an important influencing factor in Brazil or South Africa.

Overall, the analysis sheds light on research question RQ2b and reveals some obvious differences between the two emerging economies and the developed Germany. However, the importance of determinants also differs across emerging economies, as each country has an individual financial reporting environment. These unique country characteristics need to be considered when interpreting the empirical results.

Moreover, the results show that the **explanatory power** of the South African regression model with an adjusted R^2 of 23.13% is about half the value of the Brazilian regression model (45.99%), which is still below the R^2 of the German regression model (56.32%). This generally indicates that FRQ in South Africa is less determined by the investigated determinants than in Brazil and Germany. A reason could be the integrated reporting approach in South Africa requiring companies to use a certain type of annual reports which might be less affected by the investigated determinants (except for company age). Also the comparison of total FRQ across the three sample countries supports this view of relatively homogeneous financial reporting practices in South Africa, as the lowest standard deviation of total FRQ is found for the South African sample, although its average total FRQ is significantly higher than in Brazil.

In comparison to the above disclosure index-based results, the regression models using the discretionary accruals (FRQ_ACCR) and Fog index (FRQ_FOG) measures provide only little evidence. The **discretionary accruals regression** identifies no significant country effects suggesting that earnings management is not affected by country-specific characteristics. The result of the Kruskal-Wallis test finds differences in the three countries' unsigned discretionary accruals which are marginally significant on the 10% level. As most significant determinant, company size is positively associated with the accruals based FRQ proxy. Hence, larger companies are expected to engage less in earnings management than smaller entities. This finding is consistent with the results by *Iatridis* (2012) for Brazilian and South African companies.[1165] The suggested effect of company size on earnings man-

[1163] Cf. section 2.2.3.2.
[1164] Cf. section 3.3.
[1165] *Iatridis* (2012), p. 109.

agement is more significant than on the disclosure index based FRQ. Moreover, the results show that more profitable and older companies engage in significantly more earnings management.

In line with the descriptive results, the **Fog readability** measure of FRQ is significantly associated with the country variables. The FRQ in terms of readability of the CEO/management letters in the Brazilian and South African companies' annual reports decreases considerably when comparing to German annual reports. In line with a better readability provided by the South African companies than Brazilian entities, the suggested country effect is considerably stronger for Brazil than for South Africa. In addition, however, no other significant influencing factors are found.

On the whole, the results show that the use of the disclosure index based FRQ measure allows a more differentiated analysis of the determinants of FRQ than the discretionary accruals proxy and the Fog readability measure.

6.3 Information asymmetries

6.3.1 Introduction

After the previous sections have provided empirical evidence on financial reporting practices in Brazil, South Africa and Germany, assessed by direct and indirect FRQ measures, and have analyzed associated determinants, the following sections present the results of the capital market study. The capital market analysis is concerned with the research questions RQ3a and RQ3b, which deal with the relation between FRQ and information asymmetries in general and, in particular, regarding differences between Brazil, South Africa and Germany. Consistent with economic theory, **information asymmetries** are seen as a component of a company's cost of equity capital. Hence, the investigation contributes to the discussion on the relation between an entity's disclosure level and its cost of capital. Although the study's setting does not allow the identification of **causal effects**, the results show the association between observed information asymmetries and FRQ as measured by this study's disclosure index. The robustness tests of the study use different proxies for information asymmetries and different time windows for assumed capital market reactions. In line with *Gassen* (2014), researchers contribute to the literature by providing descriptions of the investigated relationship as well as inferences based on argumentative reasoning, if causal effects cannot be tested.[1166]

On the basis of the methodological approach described in section 5.3.4, the study uses the **liquidity measures** bid-ask spreads, fraction of zero return days and the *Amihud* (2002) illiquidity measure to capture information asymmetries. In a first step, the descriptive results of these proxies are presented and the correlations between the proxies and FRQ measures are analyzed (section 6.3.2). Although correlation coefficients may indicate relationships between variables, only multivariate regressions are able to provide empirical evidence of associations considering the influence of multiple independent variables. Hence, in a second step, OLS regressions are conducted to examine, whether FRQ is in-

[1166] Cf. *Gassen* (2014), p. 536.

deed negatively associated with information asymmetries, as assumed in hypothesis H12 (section 6.3.3). In addition, the results of the sensitivity analyses and robustness tests show, as to what extent the regression results change, if the sample composition, the proxy variables or the time windows are modified (section 6.3.4). The results and implications of the capital market investigation are critically evaluated in section 6.3.5.

6.3.2 Descriptive statistics and correlation analysis

The literature uses a wide range of different proxies to measure information asymmetries on the basis of a company's liquidity. One of the most used measures is the **bid-ask spreads (BAS)** proxy. It captures the relative spread between daily bid and ask prices on stock exchanges. In line with the other liquidity measures of the study, the BAS measure calculates the mean spreads of the company shares during their financial year 2014, i.e. the period of one year following the balance sheet date used in the disclosure index analysis of the annual reports 2013 which have been subject to the disclosure index analysis.[1167]

The descriptive results in Table 6-38 show relatively low variance between the three sub samples. Nevertheless, the Kruskal-Wallis test finds significant differences between the independent country samples ($p < 0.001$). The statistics do not suggest lower liquidity in the two emerging economies than in Germany. In fact, the mean spread for the South African company shares is even lower than that for the German sample. The Brazilian median (0.38%) and mean values (0.43%) do not differ from the German ones. However, the maximum spread and standard deviation of the shares from Brazil exceed those of the German stocks. Overall, yet, there are no obvious systematic differences in bid-ask spreads during the regarded period between the emerging economies Brazil and South Africa, on the one hand, and Germany as developed country, on the other. This result could imply similar trading environments for market participants at all three capital markets. The fact that solely day-end BAS are available for the sample entities' shares may reduce the volatility and accuracy of the results.

Bid-ask spreads (BAS)							
Sample	**Min.**	**25% pctl.**	**Median**	**Mean**	**75% pctl.**	**Max.**	**Std. Dev.**
Total (n=150)	0.14%	0.27%	0.35%	0.40%	0.44%	1.30%	0.20%
Brazil (n=50)	0.23%	0.31%	0.38%	0.43%	0.43%	1.30%	0.23%
South Africa (n=50)	0.14%	0.22%	0.28%	0.32%	0.36%	1.00%	0.16%
Germany (n=50)	0.21%	0.30%	0.38%	0.43%	0.52%	0.90%	0.17%
Kruskal-Wallis test: p < 0.001							

Table 6-38: Descriptive statistics of bid-ask spreads

[1167] For example, the financial year 2014 for a company with end of fiscal year on 31 March 2014 is the period from 1 April 2014 to 31 March 2015.

According to critics, a problem of the BAS measure is that continuously quoted intraday BAS are difficult to obtain or not available at all,[1168] as it is the case for this study. This supports this study's approach to use different liquidity measures throughout the capital market analysis.

An intuitive proxy is the **fraction of trading days with zero-returns (zeros)** assuming that investors decide not to trade on these days, since transaction costs exceed the value of new, unpriced information.[1169] Thus, the liquidity of a company share declines with increasing values. Table 6-39 summarizes the distribution of the sample companies' fractions of zeros during their financial year 2014. It is not surprising that there are companies without any zero-return days in all three countries, since particularly shares of larger companies are subject to massive daily trading. However, also some companies with a relatively large number of non-trading days are found in the fourth quartiles of the right-skewed distributions for all sub samples. With a median value of 0.40%, the German company shares experience considerably less zeros than stocks in the emerging economies Brazil (median: 3.63%) and South Africa (median: 4.22%). Hence, the liquidity level seems to be higher in Germany than in Brazil and South Africa. This observation is in line with prior reasoning that the financial reporting environments, including equity markets, are less developed in Brazil and South Africa than in Germany. The variance analysis on the basis of a Kruskal-Wallis test shows that the sub samples' results differ significantly ($p < 0.001$) suggesting that country-specific factors are associated with the zeros fractions of companies' shares. *Lesmond* (2005) finds larger fractions of zeros for Brazilian and South African companies,[1170] which could be explained by a larger sample size and lower trading activity during their research period.

Zero return days fractions (zeros)							
Sample	Min.	25% pctl.	Median	Mean	75% pctl.	Max.	Std. Dev.
Total (n=150)	0.00%	0.40%	2.02%	4.42%	5.24%	41.94%	6.72%
Brazil (n=50)	0.00%	2.32%	3.63%	6.58%	6.75%	41.94%	8.63%
South Africa (n=50)	0.00%	1.61%	4.22%	6.31%	9.34%	29.72%	6.09%
Germany (n=50)	0.00%	0.00%	0.40%	0.37%	0.50%	2.38%	0.48%
Kruskal-Wallis test: p < 0.001							

Table 6-39: Descriptive statistics of zero-return days fractions

This study's **Amihud (2002) illiquidity (AIM)** proxy measures the median of the stock's daily absolute return divided by € trading volume for the sample companies during their financial year 2014. Also the AIM proxy's descriptive results in Table 6-40 show statisti-

[1168] Cf. *Lesmond et al.* (1999), p. 1115.
[1169] Cf. *Lesmond et al.* (1999), p. 1115.
[1170] Cf. *Lesmond* (2005), p. 424 and 426.

cally significant differences among the countries' share liquidity (p < 0.001). In line with the zeros results, the German stocks' illiquidity is considerably lower than their Brazilian and South African counterparts. However, this observation is plausible considering the strong variation in the development of equities at stock exchanges in emerging economies. Not only the prices of company shares and market indices vary considerably,[1171] but also large variation in daily returns and trading volumes can be observed. While the zero-return measure, however, shows relatively similar values for Brazil and South Africa, the AIM proxy indicates that company shares from South Africa are less liquid than Brazilian ones. The economic interpretation of the AIM medians is that an additional € 1,000 trade leads to a price impact of € 0.472 (0.047%) in Germany, € 2.418 (0.24%) in Brazil and € 3.603 (0.36%) in South Africa. Moreover, the AIM distributions show that there are outliers in the upper quartile of all country distributions with extraordinary high illiquidity measures. Unlike *Lesmond* (2005), the descriptive results show higher AIM values in South Africa than in Brazil. However, the investigations are hardly comparable in terms of sample size and research period.

Amihud's illiquidity proxy (AIM)							
Sample	**Min.**	**25% pctl.**	**Median**	**Mean**	**75% pctl.**	**Max.**	**Std. Dev.**
Total (n=150)	0.036	0.661	1.519	4.219	3.934	87.718	9.113
Brazil (n=50)	0.648	1.365	2.418	3.639	3.934	18.985	4.141
South Africa (n=50)	0.124	1.363	3.603	8.313	9.450	87.718	14.256
Germany (n=50)	0.036	0.127	0.472	0.693	0.988	4.697	0.826
Kruskal-Wallis test: p < 0.001							

Table 6-40: Descriptive statistics of Amihud's illiquidity proxy

After analyzing the descriptive results of each information asymmetry measure, the following correlation analysis indicates, whether there is a statistically significant relationship between each proxy and FRQ (measured by the full disclosure index). Table 6-41 reveals that all correlation coefficients (except for zero return days for the German sub sample) have the predicted sign. Thus, higher FRQ is associated with lower information asymmetries consistent with economic theory. While the association between zeros and FRQ is relatively strong (-0.598) and highly significant for the total sample, the country sample correlations do not display any significant relationship. The relatively small country samples and country effects are potential reasons for this discrepancy. In contrast, the AIM and BAS measures show consistent correlation coefficients for all sub samples on a significant level (except for the AIM measure for Brazil), which is in line with hypothesis H12.

[1171] For the development of the performance of major stock indices in Brazil, South Africa and Germany, cf. section 2.3.1.

For instance, the relation between BAS and FRQ is particularly pronounced for Germany (-0.596) and Brazil (-0.407).

Liquidity proxy	Predicted sign	Full sample (FRQ_FULL)	Brazil (FRQ_FULL)	South Africa (FRQ_FULL)	Germany (FRQ_FULL)
Bid-ask spread	(-)	-0.174 ** (0.033)	-0.407 *** (0.003)	-0.287 ** (0.043)	-0.596 *** (0.000)
Zero return days	(-)	-0.598 *** (0.000)	-0.130 (0.370)	-0.021 (0.883)	0.044 (0.760)
AIM measure	(-)	-0.593 *** (0.000)	-0.233 (0.103)	-0.344 ** (0.014)	-0.638 *** (0.000)
N		150	50	50	50

The table presents the Spearman correlation coefficients between the full disclosure score (FRQ_FULL) in each sub sample and the corresponding liquidity measures. *, ** and *** denote significance at the 10%, 5% and 1% level.

Table 6-41: Association between FRQ and information asymmetry proxies

On the whole, the correlation analysis indicates a significant negative relationship between FRQ and liquidity, particularly the BAS and AIM measures. However, the liquidity proxies' descriptive statistics have shown some mixed results. Thus, the multivariate regression uses not only the BAS proxy in the main regression model, but also the zeros and AIM as information asymmetry measures in robustness tests. The untabulated correlation coefficients, show a highly significant ($p < 0.001$) Spearman correlation between the BAS and AIM proxy of 0.379, whereas there is neither an economically nor statistically significant ($p = 0.670$) relation between BAS and zeros with a correlation coefficient of 0.035.

6.3.3 Results of multivariate regression analysis

Based on the information asymmetry model introduced in section 5.3.4.2, the multivariate regressions examine whether FRQ is negatively associated with information asymmetries (hypothesis H12). Table 6-42 shows the regression results using BAS of the full financial year 2014 (FY2014) as information asymmetry proxy. The regression model uses different measures for FRQ. In addition to the full disclosure index score (FRQ_FULL), also the voluntary disclosure index score (FRQ_VOL) is included as FRQ measure to investigate the influence of only voluntary disclosures on information asymmetries.

Also the regression results for the basic model without FRQ measure are presented. They are consistent with the application of the model in prior research.[1172] Using the **full disclosure score** as FRQ measure, the results reveal a negative association between BAS and FRQ with a coefficient of -0.545, which is significant at the 5% level. When replacing the full disclosure score with the **voluntary disclosure score** the relationship is even stronger (-0.583) and highly significant at the 1% level. The economic significance of these coefficients is considerable. The interquartile range between the first and third quartile of the full disclosure index scores for the total sample is 0.176 (= 17.6 percentage points), from 26.8% to 44.4%. According to the regression results, an increase in the disclosure score of 17.6 percentage points results in a decrease in BAS of 9.6% (= -0.545 * 0.176).

1172 Cf. *Leuz/Verrecchia* (2000), p. 107.

Variables	Predicted sign	BAS FY2014 (without FRQ)	BAS FY2014 (FRQ_FULL)	BAS FY2014 (FRQ_VOL)
Company size	(-)	-0.188 *** (-9.919)	-0.172 *** (-8.597)	-0.170 *** (-8.510)
Turnover volume	(-)	-0.289 *** (-10.703)	-0.263 *** (-9.063)	-0.260 *** (-8.990)
Volatility	(+)	0.585 *** (7.674)	0.592 *** (7.871)	0.591 *** (7.883)
Share price	(-)	-0.091 *** (-4.133)	-0.088 *** (-4.072)	-0.088 *** (-4.087)
FRQ	(-)		-0.545 ** (-2.254)	-0.583 *** (-2.456)
Country_BRA		-0.718 *** (-11.919)	-0.819 *** (-11.001)	-0.832 *** (-11.062)
Country_RSA		-1.012 *** (-18.160)	-1.066 *** (-17.791)	-1.056 *** (-18.335)
Consumer		-0.197 * (-1.800)	-0.202 * (-1.872)	-0.201 * (-1.874)
Manufacturing		-0.163 (-1.578)	-0.164 (-1.612)	-0.165 (-1.627)
Energy and mining		-0.184 (-1.628)	-0.202 * (-1.814)	-0.206 * (-1.854)
Telecommunication and media		-0.217 * (-1.868)	-0.235 ** (-2.043)	-0.234 ** (-2.046)
Wholesale and retail		-0.215 ** (-2.996)	-0.227 ** (-2.136)	-0.230 ** (-2.165)
Healthcare		-0.243 ** (-2.113)	-0.256 ** (-2.249)	-0.258 ** (-2.278)
Real estate		-0.140 (-1.185)	-0.178 (-1.510)	-0.183 (-1.559)
Transportation		-0.191 * (-1.664)	-0.208 * (-1.828)	-0.212 * (-1.873)
Construction		-0.371 *** (-2.982)	-0.359 *** (-2.930)	-0.357 *** (-2.918)
Constant		0.137 (0.300)	0.217 (0.479)	0.182 (0.406)
N		150	150	150
Adj. R^2		78.61 %	79.25 %	79.39 %
F-stat		37.51 ***	36.45 ***	36.86 ***
Maximum VIF		7.62	7.62	7.62

The table presents the results of the OLS regressions conducted for the bid-ask-spread (BAS) model. In addition to the basic BAS model (without FRQ), FRQ is included as full (FRQ_FULL) or voluntary (FRQ_VOL) disclosure score. *, ** and *** denote significance at the 10%, 5% and 1% level (one-tailed for coefficients with predicted signs and two-tailed otherwise).

Table 6-42: Regression results for BAS information asymmetry model

These findings are in line with hypothesis H12 and provides evidence concerning research question RQ3a. In comparison to the basic information asymmetry model (without FRQ) the inclusion of the disclosure index-based FRQ measures into the model increases its explanatory power from 78.61% to 79.25% and 79.39%, respectively. Thus, FRQ might be an explanatory variable of information asymmetries, yet, raises the regression model's explanatory power only slightly.

The model further considers country- and industry-fixed effects. The country coefficients for Brazil and South Africa indicate a significant negative country effect on BAS against the benchmark of Germany. Thus, BAS decrease for Brazilian and South African companies. Moreover, the coefficients of multiple industry control variables show significant associations between the industry and BAS. In particular, the *construction industry* is negatively related to BAS at the 1% significance level suggesting that construction companies show lower BAS than companies from the reference industry *business equipment* (omitted in the regression). The highly significant F values suggest that the regression results are also valid beyond the study's sample. Moreover, the VIF value of 7.62 does not indicate that the results could be biased due to multicollinearity. On the basis of the above results, a negative relationship between information asymmetries and FRQ is assumed.

Although the above regression results find that FRQ is negatively associated with BAS for the total sample, they do not provide evidence on the relation between FRQ and BAS in the three sample countries (research question RQ3b). To identify such **cross-country differences**, the BAS regression model has to include a term interacting FRQ with the country variables. According to Table 6-43 (FRQ_FULL), the country-specific interaction terms suggest that the negative relation between FRQ and information asymmetries (-0.171) is strengthened considerably in both emerging economies. The relation is stronger in Brazil (-0.887) than in South Africa (-0.551), which is consistent with the results of the correlation analysis. With respect to economic significance, the regression coefficient for Brazil suggests that an increase in FRQ by the aforementioned total sample's interquartile range of 17.6 percentage points leads to an additional reduction in the BAS of 15.6% for the Brazilian companies. After subtracting the regression coefficient for FRQ, the association is -1.058 (= -0.887-0.171) for a Brazilian entity. Consequently, an increase in FRQ by the interquartile range results in a BAS reduction of 18.6%.

The regression results further suggest that the negative relationship between FRQ and information asymmetries is stronger in the emerging economies Brazil and South Africa than in Germany (country dummy variables = 0), as indicated by the negative signs of the regression coefficients. However, the interaction term coefficient is only significant for Brazil and not for the South African sample. An explanation could be the relatively small sample size of 50 companies per country sample. The results do not differ substantially when using the voluntary FRQ measure. Overall, the empirical results suggest cross-country differences which are particularly pronounced between the two emerging economies, on the one hand, and Germany, on the other. Including the interaction terms in the regression model leads to considerably higher VIF values so that the maximum VIF values exceed those of the basic regression model leading to an increased concern about multicollinearity.

Variables	Predicted sign	BAS FY2014 (FRQ_FULL)	BAS FY2014 (FRQ_VOL)
Company size	(-)	-0.181 *** (-8.794)	-0.178 *** (-8.687)
Turnover volume	(-)	-0.260 *** (-8.973)	-0.259 *** (-8.958)
Volatility	(+)	0.561 *** (7.291)	0.562 *** (7.330)
Share price	(-)	-0.091 *** (-4.200)	-0.091 *** (-4.216)
FRQ	(-)	-0.171 (-0.522)	-0.236 (-0.726)
Country_BRA		-0.511 *** (-2.680)	-0.578 *** (-3.471)
FRQ*Country_BRA		-0.887 * (-1.712)	-0.838 * (-1.688)
Country_RSA		-0.835 *** (-3.935)	-0.882 *** (-4.534)
FRQ*Country_RSA		-0.551 (-0.998)	-0.433 (-0.808)
Constant		0.152 (0.336)	0.115 (0.254)
Industry-fixed effects		YES	YES
N		150	150
Adj. R^2		79.42 %	79.53 %
F-stat		32.95 ***	33.15 ***
Maximum VIF		42.61	35.96

The table presents the results of the OLS regressions conducted for the bid-ask-spread (BAS) model including FRQ-country interaction terms. FRQ is measured as full (FRQ_FULL) and voluntary (FRQ_VOL) disclosure score. *, ** and *** denote significance at the 10%, 5% and 1% level (one-tailed for coefficients with predicted signs and two-tailed otherwise).

Table 6-43: Regression results for BAS information asymmetry model (country-FRQ interaction terms)

In addition to the analysis of the relationship between total FRQ (measured by total disclosure index score) and information asymmetries, the following results shed light on the role of the different **reporting areas** with regard to capital market observations. For this purpose, the BAS proxy is regressed on each full disclosure index sub score (as FRQ measure) instead of the full score. The other control variables remain the same as in the above BAS FY2014 model. Table 6-44 shows only the coefficients of the FRQ variables as well as regression characteristics. As the total FRQ measure comprises all reporting sub areas, it is consistent that no sub score coefficient exceeds the above presented total score coefficient of -0.545 (cf. Table 6-42). The results indicate that the FRQ scores of the areas *forward looking information* (-0.433), *important financials* (-0.401), *sustainability* (-0.292) and *important non-financials* (-0.279) are significantly related to the BAS measure, whereas the coefficients for the other reporting categories show no significant associations. This is remarkable, as particularly disclosures on prospective, sustainability as well as non-financial issues are not only seen as sensitive and crucial company information,[1173] but the

[1173] Cf. *AICPA* (1994).

importance of these reporting areas has also been increasingly stressed in the literature over the last few years.[1174] The regression results suggest that high FRQ in these reporting categories may affect the decisions of capital market participants. In contrast, FRQ of the *risks and opportunities* category is not significantly associated with BAS and the absolute value of the regression coefficient (-0.196) is relatively small. An explanation could provide the phenomenon of *cheap talk*. The *cheap talk* approach questions "*[....] how much, if any, information can be credibly disclosed when direct, plain communication is cheap, i.e., costless and non-binding.*"[1175] This study's content analysis has revealed that numerous companies provide information on *risks and opportunities* on a relatively large number of pages in their annual reports. However, these sections frequently comprise standardized formulations which hardly shed light on the companies' actual risks and opportunities. Thus, the decision usefulness of this information is questionable. If users of annual reports, therefore, regard the provided information on *risks and opportunities* as *cheap talk*, they may not consider this information in their capital market decisions.

BAS FY2014 (FRQ_FULL) with:	Predicted sign	Coefficient	N	Adj. R^2	F-stat	Maximum VIF
FRQ_background	(-)	-0.207 (-1.231)	150	76.33 %	30.84 ***	7.61
FRQ_financials	(-)	-0.401 ** (-1.799)	150	76.64 %	33.34 ***	7.62
FRQ_non-financials	(-)	-0.279 ** (-1.865)	150	76.68 %	31.41 ***	7.62
FRQ_sustainability	(-)	-0.292 *** (-2.919)	150	77.51 %	32.89 ***	7.68
FRQ_value based	(-)	-0.010 (-0.082)	150	76.06 %	30.39 ***	7.70
FRQ_forward	(-)	-0.433 *** (-2.656)	150	77.28 %	32.46 ***	7.66
FRQ_risks	(-)	-0.196 (-1.261)	150	76.35 %	30.86 ***	7.61

The table shows selected statistical results of the bid-ask-spread (BAS) model FY2014 (FRQ_FULL) regressions with the disclosure sub scores as FRQ measures. In analogy to the other regressions, country- and industry-fixed effects are included. *, ** and *** denote significance at the 10%, 5% and 1% level (one-tailed).

Table 6 41: Regression results for BAS information asymmetry model (FRQ of reporting categories)

On the whole, the results of the multivariate regressions have found a statistically significant negative association between disclosure index-based FRQ and BAS as proxy for information asymmetries. The relation is also significant for some reporting category sub scores as FRQ measures. Moreover, the results suggest that the negative relationship between total FRQ and information asymmetries is more pronounced in the two emerging economies Brazil and South Africa than in Germany, although not all coefficients are statistically significant. The following section is concerned with the sensitivity and robustness of these results.

1174 Cf. amongst others *Barth* (2009); *Blaesing* (2013); *Kajüter* (2013); *Fink et al.* (2013); *Kajüter* (2014b).
1175 *Dobler* (2008), p. 186.

6.3.4 Sensitivity analyses and robustness tests

The validity of the regression results largely depends on both the proxies used for FRQ and the proxies for information asymmetries. To test the results' sensitivity, the study varies the **FRQ proxies** included in the regressions.[1176] The above multivariate regression models do not only apply the full disclosure index score, but also the voluntary disclosure index score and the sub scores of the disclosure index reporting categories. While the use of the voluntary disclosure index score has not altered the results substantially, the findings for the reporting category scores differ. Significant negative relations between FRQ and information asymmetries are shown for four reporting categories (cf. section 6.3.3).

Moreover, the zeros and AIM **measures of information asymmetries** are used to test whether the results of the BAS model are robust (cf. Table 6-45 and Table 6-46).

Variables	Predicted sign	ZEROS BASIC (FRQ_FULL)	ZEROS BASIC (FRQ_VOL)	ZEROS INTER (FRQ_FULL)	ZEROS INTER (FRQ_VOL)
Company size	(-)	-0.082 (-0.074)	-0.071 (-0.064)	-0.274 (-0.248)	-0.253 (-0.230)
Turnover volume	(-)	-4.872 *** (-3.526)	-4.854 *** (-3.512)	-3.559 ** (-2.293)	-3.704 ** (-2.392)
Volatility	(+)	14.661 *** (3.511)	14.683 *** (3.516)	8.657 ** (2.097)	8.659 ** (2.108)
Share price	(-)	-11.241 *** (-9.544)	-11.237 *** (-9.540)	-11.578 *** (-9.986)	-11.620 *** (-10.046)
FRQ	(-)	7.435 (0.582)	6.843 (0.545)	31.109 (1.767)	32.515 (1.865)
Country_BRA		-19.822 *** (-4.473)	-19.827 *** (-4.448)	18.667 * (1.830)	14.943 * (1.672)
FRQ*Country_BRA				-88.442 *** (-3.184)	-88.193 *** (-3.313)
Country_RSA		-18.564 *** (-4.188)	-18.745 *** (-4.239)	-0.538 (-0.047)	-0.782 (-0.075)
FRQ*Country_RSA				-11.529 (-0.389)	-13.057 (-0.454)
Constant		50.701 * (1.950)	51.269 * (1.977)	50.989 ** (2.103)	50.228 ** (2.081)
Industry-fixed effects		YES	YES	YES	YES
N		150	150	150	150
Adj. R^2		63.24 %	63.53 %	68.24 %	64.08 %
F-stat		15.64 ***	17.12 ***	15.64 ***	15.77 ***
Maximum VIF		7.61	7.61	42.61	35.96
The table presents the results of the OLS regressions conducted for the zero-return days basic models (ZEROS BASIC) and zero-return days models including FRQ-country interaction terms (ZEROS INTER). Financial reporting quality is measured as full (FRQ_FULL) and voluntary (FRQ_VOL) disclosure score. *, ** and *** denote significance at the 10%, 5% and 1% level (one-tailed for coefficients with predicted signs and two-tailed otherwise).					

Table 6-45: Regression results for zeros information asymmetry model

[1176] In line with the argumentation that capital market participants use the contents of the companies' annual reports as basis for their capital market decisions, this model applies the disclosure index based measure of FRQ and does not consider the discretionary accruals and readability measures of FRQ.

For this purpose, the BAS proxy is substituted by the zeros proxy and AIM measure in the main regression model, whereas all control variables remain unchanged. Table 6-45 presents the results of the zeros regression model and the AIM regression results are displayed in Table 6-46. The tables show the basic regression model without the FRQ-country variable interaction terms (BASIC) as well as including these interaction terms (INTER). Moreover, each of these models is calculated for both the full (FRQ_FULL) and voluntary (FRQ_VOL) disclosure index score.

Variables	Predicted sign	AIM BASIC (FRQ_FULL)	AIM BASIC (FRQ_VOL)	AIM INTER (FRQ_FULL)	AIM INTER (FRQ_VOL)
Company size	(-)	-0.526 *** (-13.709)	-0.522 *** (-13.549)	-0.583 *** (-16.803)	-0.574 *** (-16.499)
Turnover volume	(-)	-0.533 *** (-11.201)	-0.528 *** (-11.077)	-0.516 *** (-12.418)	-0.512 *** (-12.274)
Volatility	(+)	0.730 *** (5.076)	0.733 *** (5.084)	0.598 *** (4.659)	0.603 *** (4.676)
Share price	(-)	-0.037 (-0.902)	-0.036 (-0.881)	-0.049 * (-1.375)	-0.050 * (-1.394)
FRQ	(-)	0.427 (0.970)	0.294 (0.679)	2.794 (5.287)	2.629 (4.997)
Country_BRA		-1.138 *** (-7.452)	-1.149 *** (-7.471)	0.404 (1.254)	0.190 (0.668)
FRQ*Country_BRA				-3.905 *** (-4.611)	-3.747 *** (-4.575)
Country_RSA		-0.988 *** (-6.468)	-0.998 *** (-6.542)	1.130 *** (3.141)	0.917 *** (2.732)
FRQ*Country_RSA				-5.440 *** (-6.073)	-5.250 *** (-5.982)
Constant		9.746 *** (10.878)	9.794 *** (10.944)	9.588 *** (12.289)	9.625 *** (12.301)
Industry-fixed effects		YES	YES	YES	YES
N		150	150	150	150
Adj. R^2		84.10 %	84.04 %	87.96 %	87.82 %
F-stat		49.93 ***	49.72 ***	61.05 ***	60.29 ***
Maximum VIF		7.61	7.61	42.61	35.96

The table presents the results of the OLS regressions conducted for the Amihud's illiquidity measure basic models (AIM BASIC) and Amihud's illiquidity measure models including FRQ-country interaction terms (AIM INTER). Financial reporting quality is measured as full (FRQ_FULL) and voluntary (FRQ_VOL) disclosure score. *, ** and *** denote significance at the 10%, 5% and 1% level (one-tailed for coefficients with predicted signs and two-tailed otherwise).

Table 6-46: Regression results for AIM information asymmetry model

In line with the BAS model, the results of the **zeros** and **AIM models** show that all control variables have the predicted sign and are mostly highly significant. In contrast to the results of the BAS model, neither the zeros nor the AIM basic regression model reveals a significant negative relation between FRQ and information asymmetries. The correlation coefficients even suggest positive associations. However, when including the FRQ-country interaction terms, the negative associations between FRQ and both zeros (cf. Table 6-45) and AIM (cf. Table 6-46) are supported for the Brazilian and South African samples. While the zeros model finds only a significant interaction term for Brazil, the AIM model's results also show a significant negative coefficient for the South African interaction term, which even exceeds the coefficient of the Brazilian interaction term in the AIM model. This suggests a more pronounced relation between FRQ and information asymmetries in South Africa than in Brazil. A reason for higher significance levels in other studies could be considerably larger sample sizes.[1177] Both models (zeros and AIM) show that the interaction term coefficients overcompensate the positive regression coefficients of the FRQ variable. This suggests a negative association between FRQ in the two countries and information asymmetries overall. Similar to the BAS model, the inclusion of the interaction terms leads to a considerable increase in maximum VIF indicating a higher risk of multicollinearity.

The results do not differ substantially for the voluntary FRQ measure (FRQ_VOL). On the whole, in spite of some mixed results, the multivariate regressions support a negative relationship between FRQ and information asymmetries, which is more pronounced in the emerging economies Brazil and South Africa than in Germany. This finding is in contrast to the correlation analysis which has suggested a stronger association between FRQ and the liquidity proxies for Germany than for Brazil and South Africa.

In addition, Table 6-47 shows the BAS regression results (FRQ_FULL) considering different **time lags**. Instead of the full financial year 2014 used in the main BAS model, this analysis examines associations in each quarter of the financial year 2014 as time window.

Variables	Predicted sign	BAS FY2014Q1 (FRQ_FULL)	BAS FY2014Q2 (FRQ_FULL)	BAS FY2014Q3 (FRQ_FULL)	BAS FY2014Q4 (FRQ_FULL)
Company size	(-)	-0.209 *** (-8.171)	-0.168 *** (-6.839)	-0.173 *** (-6.492)	-0.188 *** (-6.621)
Turnover volume	(-)	-0.260 *** (-7.610)	-0.266 *** (-7.894)	-0.221 *** (-6.217)	-0.159 *** (-4.025)
Volatility	(+)	0.429 *** (5.367)	0.496 *** (6.620)	0.434 *** (5.206)	0.239 *** (3.131)
Share price	(-)	-0.074 *** (-2.595)	-0.094 *** (-3.573)	-0.128 *** (-4.592)	-0.117 *** (-3.970)
FRQ	(-)	-0.276 (-0.890)	-0.373 * (-1.267)	-0.515 * (-1.590)	-0.757 ** (-2.185)
Constant		-0.581 (-1.049)	-0.394 (-0.751)	-0.053 (-0.098)	-0.154 (-0.235)
Country-fixed effects Industry-fixed effects		YES YES	YES YES	YES YES	YES YES
N		150	150	150	150
Adj. R^2		67.41 %	70.81 %	65.17 %	68.49 %
F-stat		20.26 ***	23.59 ***	18.43 ***	21.24 ***
Maximum VIF		7.70	7.50	7.49	7.50

The table presents the results of the OLS regressions conducted for the bid-ask spreads (BAS) model considering different time lags of the BAS values. The BAS and corresponding independent regression variables for the first (FY2014Q1), second (FY2014Q2), third (FY2014Q3) and fourth (FY2014Q4) quarter 2014 are applied. The full (FRQ_FULL) disclosure score is used as FRQ measure. *, ** and *** denote significance at the 10%, 5% and 1% level (one-tailed for coefficients with predicted signs and two-tailed otherwise).

Table 6-47: Regression results for the bid-ask spreads model with different time lags

[1177] Cf. amongst others *Lesmond* (2005), p. 431-436; *Daske et al.* (2008), p. 1107-1108.

Although the identified negative relationship between FRQ and information asymmetries in the main BAS regression model is consistent with expectations, the finding is based on the assumption that the associated information asymmetry effects occur during the entire financial year 2014. Thus, the study examines the sensibility of this result by using different time lags for capital market reactions.

Table 6-47 shows that the FRQ coefficient is lowest and not significant in the first quarter of FY2014. This finding can be explained by the fact that annual reports are frequently not yet available, as the analysis of the days until annual report publication has shown.[1178] Moreover, the capital market participants may need some time to analyze the information provided in the annual reports to use them as a basis for their capital allocation decisions. In practice, however, some information may reach addressees, particularly large investors, already before the publication of the annual report, e.g. through ad-hoc announcements, conference calls, road shows or personal contacts which can cause immediate stock market reactions. After the first quarter, the results show statistically significant negative associations between FRQ and information asymmetries so that capital market reactions can be assumed. The coefficients increase from the second (-0.373) to the fourth quarter (-0.757) suggesting higher associations between FRQ and information asymmetries in the course of time. The coefficient of the fourth quarter even exceeds that of the full financial year (-0.545) which, however, shows the highest significance level.

On the whole, the study conducts a number of sensitivity tests. The use of the voluntary disclosure score instead of the full score does not alter the results substantially. Although the zeros and AIM regression models do not find a significant negative relation between FRQ and information asymmetries for the basic models, the interaction term regressions suggest a negative association between FRQ and information asymmetries in the emerging economies Brazil and South Africa. Further, the use of different time windows shows that the identified negative relation is particularly pronounced for the fourth quarter, but also for the entire financial year 2014.

6.3.5 Critical evaluation of the results

The literature review has shown that a number of studies investigate the (causal) relationship between the disclosure of information and capital market consequences, particularly cost of equity. However, there is still no general consensus, whether increased disclosure, and increased FRQ, in particular, actually leads to lower cost of equity.[1179] Moreover, most prior studies are conducted in a single-country setting. Mostly researchers investigate companies from large developed countries and particularly U.S.-based studies are widespread. However, *Hail/Leuz* (2006) show that also country-specific factors, such as individual publication requirements, influence the costs of equity.[1180] This study, therefore, contributes to prior research by using a multiple country setting including two emerging economies with less developed capital markets and a **lower disclosure level**[1181]. Hence,

[1178] Cf. section 5.1.4.
[1179] Cf. section 3.4.
[1180] Cf. *Hail/Leuz* (2006), p. 523-524.
[1181] Cf. section 6.1.2.2.1.

the particular sample may allow detecting capital market effects easier than in studies using developed countries. Furthermore, the use of the self-constructed disclosure index allows to capture FRQ more comprehensively than most prior studies.

The descriptive results of the **liquidity measures** zero return days and AIM reveal that the liquidity of stocks in the emerging economies Brazil and South Africa is considerably lower than in Germany. The result is in line with *Lesmond* (2005), who finds low liquidity in a number of emerging markets, which are characterized by high volatility of returns and trading volumes. *Lesmond* (2005) further argues that emerging economies with weaker political and legal institutions have significantly higher liquidity costs than countries with strong political and legal systems.[1182] However, the identification of increased illiquidity in the emerging economies Brazil and South Africa is in line with expectations, as a less developed financial reporting environment is assumed to cause increased information asymmetries and, thus, higher cost of equity capital. Although the descriptive results of the BAS measure show relatively similar bid-ask-spreads across the three countries, the correlation analysis indicates significant negative relationships between BAS-based information asymmetries and FRQ, measured by the full disclosure index score. Also the AIM proxy is significantly related to FRQ according to the correlation analysis. This relationship between FRQ and the information asymmetry proxies is further analyzed on the basis of multivariate regressions which control for additional influencing factors.

Although the study does not isolate a causal effect of FRQ on **information asymmetries**, the regression results provide evidence that a higher level of FRQ (measured by disclosure index score) is associated with lower information asymmetries. The association is not only shown between information asymmetries and total FRQ, but also between information asymmetries and the FRQ of the reporting categories *forward looking information*, *important financials*, *sustainability* and *important non-financials*. Since not all information asymmetry proxies show this relation on a significant level, hypothesis H12 is only partially supported:

Figure 6-18: Test result of information asymmetries hypothesis

The result is in line with the findings of prior studies. For a sample of U.S. manufacturing companies, *Botosan* (1997) shows that greater disclosures in the 1990 annual reports of companies with low analyst following are associated with lower cost of equity.[1183] *Leuz/Verrecchia* (2000) find that German companies, which switched from the German to a reporting regime of increased disclosure level, have lower information asymmetries.[1184] Also *Daske et al.* (2008) investigate the effect of reporting standards change using a sample

[1182] *Lesmond* (2005), p. 411-412.
[1183] Cf. *Botosan* (1997), p. 323.
[1184] Cf. *Leuz/Verrecchia* (2000), p. 91.

of companies from 26 countries and show that the adoption of IFRS is related to lower cost of capital.[1185]

This study's main finding is robust against numerous modifications. Using the voluntary instead of the full disclosure index score, leads to even more pronounced results. This supports the view that particularly voluntary disclosures are able to *make a difference* and affect the decisions of capital market participants. Moreover, the regression is conducted for different time windows, as it is unclear when after the publication of the annual report information capital market reactions occur. Noticeably, the results suggest the strongest effect in the fourth quarter and during the entire 12-month period subsequent to the balance sheet date. Consequently, investors seem to use company information continuously over an extended period of time to make capital allocation decisions, rather than immediately after publication. Moreover, the finding that the association is lower in the first quarter after the balance sheet date is reasonable, as annual report information is barely available yet.

With respect to **cross-country differences**, the interaction terms of the regression models for all three information asymmetry proxies suggest that an increase in FRQ in the emerging economies Brazil and South Africa is associated with a stronger reduction in information asymmetries than in Germany. The finding is in line with the expectation that information asymmetry effects can be better observed in less developed financial reporting environments. Taking into account that the total disclosure index scores are considerably lower in Brazil and South Africa than in Germany, this result is also in line with *Botosan* (1997), *Leuz/Verrecchia* (2000) and *Hail* (2002), who argue that the association between an increased level of disclosure and capital market observations is more pronounced in reporting environments of relatively low disclosure and, thus, easier to detect.[1186]

The empirical results propose that a company's FRQ is associated with the capital market decisions by stock market investors. The capital market investigation **contributes** to the existing, mostly U.S.-based, literature in several ways. It provides evidence on the still controversial discussion about the relationship between company disclosure and information asymmetries by using a unique cross-country emerging economy setting. The fact that the results differ across countries underpins that findings in national studies cannot be transferred to other countries. In particular, the results differ between the emerging economies Brazil and South Africa, on the one hand, and the developed Germany, on the other. Moreover, the use of different proxies for information asymmetries further characterizes and compares the proxies' performances. Future research on emerging economies with unique settings (e.g., exogenous shocks affecting the disclosure environment) may seek to identify causal effects. A larger sample size could further allow the use of additional analysis techniques, such as *propensity score matching*[1187].

[1185] Cf. *Daske et al.* (2008), p. 1085.

[1186] Cf. *Hail* (2002), p. 766.

[1187] Propensity score matching (PSM) estimates treatment effects through matching a treatment group and a control group, which matches observations with the same probability for the treatment, cf. *Dehejia/Wahba* (2002), p. 151.

6.4 Discussion

After the results of the three sub studies have been presented and evaluated separately, this section links and discusses the studies' results from an **integrated perspective**. In line with its research objectives, this study has investigated differences concerning FRQ among the two emerging economies Brazil and South Africa as well as the developed Germany. In addition to differences regarding the actual FRQ provided by companies across the three countries, this study has analyzed differences regarding the determinants of FRQ as well as cross-country differences concerning the relation between FRQ and information asymmetries. This section provides an integrated appraisal of the main results.

FRQ has been identified to be an **abstract and complex notion** which has several dimensions and, thus, can be operationalized by different measures of FRQ. This study applies three FRQ measures: earnings management, disclosure index and readability measure. Although the three measures focus on different aspects of FRQ, their overall results are widely consistent regarding the FRQ provided by the Bra-zilian, South African and German companies. The **discretionary accruals** (modified-Jones model), the **disclosure index scores** (full and voluntary disclosure index) as well as the **readability scores** (Fog index and Flesch reading ease) indicate that the FRQ is higher for the German companies than for those in the Brazilian and South African samples. The measures' results further agree that the FRQ of the South African companies exceeds that of the Brazilian ones.

In more detail, the discretionary accruals-based **earnings management** proxy suggests a higher level of earnings management in the two emerging economies Brazil and South Africa than in Germany. The finding is in line with the literature, which assumes less earnings management in developed countries with a reporting and investor favorable institutional environment (e.g., dispersed ownership structure).[1188] With respect to cultural influences, particularly the relatively pronounced earnings management activities in Brazil are further consistent with *Doupnik* (2008), who argues that strong uncertainty avoidance and collectivism are associated with increased earnings management.[1189]

However, this study's earnings management results are based on the sample countries' mean discretionary accruals. In contrast, the median values suggest more earnings management in South Africa than in Brazil. The results of the second earnings management proxy **magnitude of accruals** (MACCR) partially differ from those of the modified-Jones model. For example, the results suggest that the German companies engage in more earnings management than the South African ones. The literature provides a numerous earnings management proxies. As this study's results and other research show, these measures may differ considerably. Thus, the proxies' results should be interpreted carefully.

The determinants study has only revealed a few associations between the FRQ in the sense of the discretionary accruals and potential influencing factors. The results indicate that larger, older and more profitable companies are significantly related to higher FRQ (less earnings management) in line with theory. However, the regression results particularly do not show significant associations between the country variables (for Brazil and South Afri-

[1188] *Dechow et al.* (2010), p. 378.
[1189] Cf. *Doupnik* (2008), p. 324 and 338.

ca) and FRQ. Thus, the country-specific environments of the sample countries are not suggested to determine the cross-country differences in earnings management shown by the descriptive results. Overall, the explanatory power of the determinants regression model using discretionary accruals as FRQ measure is rather low.

The literature-based **readability measures** Fog index and Flesch-reading ease are used to assess the readability of the CEO/management letters in the sample companies' annual reports. Consistent with the results of existing studies, the overall readability for the total sample has to be interpreted as difficult and possibly even too difficult for some users to comprehend these textual passages. Moreover, both measures indicate an easier readability in Germany than in the two emerging economies. The South African annual reports are still easier to comprehend than the Brazilian ones. These cross-country differences in readability are statistically and economically significant.

In addition, the readability of the companies' entire annual reports has been analyzed on the basis of the three **readability indicators** *structure, language and style of expression* as well as *use of figures and tables*. In line with the results of the Fog index and Flesch reading ease, the results suggest an easier readability for the German annual reports than for those from Brazil and South Africa. The findings are also consistent with the general trend of the main results, as the South African reports' readability exceeds that of the Brazilian annual reports. In particular, German and South African annual reports are found to have a clear-cut structure and include user-friendly figures and tables.

Regarding the determinants of readability, the study provides only little evidence. Using the Fog readability as FRQ measure, the results of the determinants regression model suggest significant associations between the country variables and the readability scores in line with the descriptive results. However, no additional significant relation is found and the model's explanatory power is relatively low.

The self-constructed **disclosure index measure** is the primary FRQ measure of this study. It is applied as part of a content analysis of the sample companies' annual reports for the financial year 2013 (research objects). Although companies face an increasing number of reporting instruments,[1190] the results of the content analysis as well as the findings of the determinants and information asymmetry studies find annual reports to be still a major source of information which includes a multitude of different information types. In particular, the analyzed annual reports provide both qualitative and quantitative information as well as historic and prospective information. Moreover, numerous reporting categories are addressed by the annual reports, including information which is frequently considered as sensitive, such as information on corporate strategy, forecasts as well as risks and opportunities. Also the amount of information indicates the importance of annual reports. In all three sample countries, companies provide more than 100 pages on average. However, the annual reports of the German companies comprise significantly more pages (average of 229 pages) than those of the Brazilian and South African companies.

The results of the disclosure index study show that **total FRQ** of all sample companies can, at most, be regarded as moderate with an average disclosure score of 35.7% of the

[1190] Cf. *Kajüter et al.* (2013), p. 199.

maximum full disclosure score and 32.1% of the maximum voluntary disclosure index score. The voluntary FRQ generally tends to be lower than the full FRQ. This result is not surprising, as the voluntary disclosure index excludes those disclosure items, which are required by regulation. In line with the results of the discretionary accruals and readability measures, the total full disclosure index score is significantly higher for the German annual reports (average of 49.5%) than for the South African (32.0%) and Brazilian ones (25.5%). Consistent with these differences in the countries' FRQ, the determinants study suggests highly significant associations between total FRQ and the **country variables** in the multivariate regression model. Against the benchmark of Germany, the South African setting is suggested to have a negative and the Brazilian setting an even more negative effect on a company's FRQ (assuming a causal relation). Explanations may be found in the **institutional and cultural environments** of the analyzed countries. The cultural characteristics according to *Gray* (1988) have been described as more reporting favorable in Germany and South Africa than in Brazil. In particular, the cultural environment in Germany and South Africa is, at least partly, characterized by transparency as well as optimism, whereas the cultural values for Brazil suggest the most unfavorable reporting environment including the characteristics conservatism and secrecy. These characteristics may again be influenced by the traditionally reciprocity-oriented Brazilian economy, which is dominated by *clans* and *grupos economicos*.[1191]

In addition, the study identifies a number of significant associations between total FRQ and **company-specific determinants**. Besides a company's analyst following, company size and company age, particularly the **ownership concentration** of an entity is significantly related to its total FRQ according to the regression results for the total sample. The negative relation suggests that companies have in fact less incentives to provide high-quality information in their annual reports, if their ownership structure is more concentrated. Large block holders may even have an incentive to impede the reporting of high-quality (particularly sensitive) information to other shareholders as well as to competitors. In contrast to smaller stockholders, large block holders are able to obtain information from other sources than annual reports (e.g., personal contacts). The association is also highly significant in the regression results for the Brazilian sample, which is characterized by a higher ownership concentration than the South African and German samples. A reason for the relatively high ownership concentration in Brazil is the aforementioned reciprocity-dominated economy with the tradition of family-owned businesses.

Moreover, the determinants regressions for the **country samples** provide insights regarding the importance of specific determinants in each of the three countries. While company size and analyst following are significantly associated with total FRQ in the German sample, no such significant relations are found for the companies from Brazil and South Africa. On the one hand, the variations in company size and analyst following are smaller in the two emerging economies and, thus, potential effects are more difficult to detect. On the other hand, company size and analyst following may not pose incentives for high-quality financial reporting in the two emerging economy settings in contrast to the German setting, for example, due to cultural aspects. Unlike the determinants results for the

[1191] Cf. section 2.3.2.

total sample, media coverage is significantly related to total FRQ in the Brazilian sample which suggests that the media play an important role for the Brazilian companies' financial reporting practices.

The total FRQ as measured by this study's full disclosure index is further used in the information asymmetries study. According to economic theory, an increased level of FRQ reduces **information asymmetries** of investors. Therefore, FRQ influences the decisions of capital market participants. The bid-ask-spread regression model finds such a significant negative relationship between disclosure index-based FRQ and information asymmetries. The suggested negative effect of FRQ on information asymmetries is more pronounced in the emerging economies Brazil and South Africa than in Germany. This is in line with findings in the literature and this study's research approach that it is easier to detect information asymmetry effects in a low information environment. The results indicate that FRQ differences across the three countries (as described above) lead to differences in the countries' information asymmetries. In light of the indeed relatively low FRQ (according to this study's FRQ measures) provided by the sample companies from Brazil and South Africa, there is considerable room for improvement. Hence, these companies might be able to raise their FRQ more easily than companies with a higher FRQ and, thereby, reduce information asymmetries. Moreover the investigation of potential time lags shows that the assumed impact of FRQ on information asymmetries seems to be particularly pronounced for the fourth quartile of the financial year after the balance sheet date as well as during this entire financial year. An explanation may be that the capital market participants analyze and use the information provided in the annual reports over a period of time. Thus, assumed capital market effects are not observed immediately after the publication of the annual reports.

The disclosure index analysis further breaks down the total FRQ score into sub scores for different **reporting categories** which are discussed in the following. A relatively high FRQ (total sample) is found for the reporting categories *background information*, *important financials*, *sustainability* and *risks and opportunities*, in comparison to total FRQ, whereas the FRQ in the areas *important non-financials* and, in particular, *forward-looking information* is relatively low. Regarding the categories *risks and opportunities* as well as *forward-looking information*, there are considerable differences in FRQ between the emerging economies Brazil and South Africa, on the one hand, and Germany, on the other. These findings suggest that managers tend to reveal certain information, such as *background information* or *important financials*, rather than more sensitive information, e.g. in the areas *forward-looking information* or *important non-financials*. This inference is in line with prior research.[1192]

Using the FRQ of each reporting category as dependent variable in the determinants regression model provides additional insights. For instance, the results show significant negative relations between the FRQ of **important financials** and company valuation suggesting that particularly undervalued companies provide *financials* information of increased FRQ. Also ownership concentration is related to the FRQ of *financials* on a highly significant level. In addition, the disclosure of information on **important non-financials** seems

[1192] Cf. section 3.2.2.

to differ according to a company's customer basis. The univariate analysis has shown that B2C companies provide a significantly higher *non-financials* FRQ than B2B companies in the Brazilian and South African samples. This finding is supported by the determinants regression model for the total sample using *non-financials FRQ* as dependent variable. The fact that this relation is only observed in the two emerging economies indicates that the relatively low disclosure environment there might allow identifying actual differences in the companies' reporting behavior.

Moreover, **sustainability** is the only reporting category on which South African entities provide a higher FRQ than German companies. Consistent with this finding, the results show a highly significant positive country association for South Africa when using sustainability FRQ in the determinants regression model. This is in line with expectations, since the progressive integrated reporting development in combination with the King III regulation in South Africa put particular emphasis on sustainability issues. The focus on such aspects in South Africa has to be interpreted against the background of the country's historical and political development. The apartheid era and several social problems have led to a sensibilization of social and sustainability topics.[1193] An example is also the dominant position of trade unions in South Africa.

The significant differences in FRQ of **forward-looking information** between German companies and the entities from the two emerging economies is supported by the determinants study which finds highly significant negative associations for the country variables of both Brazil and South Africa. The requirements concerning the German management report are presumably a reason for a higher FRQ of this reporting category in Germany. In addition, ownership concentration is highly negatively associated to FRQ of *forward-looking information*. This suggests that companies with relatively few large block holders do not provide sensitive prospective disclosures of high quality.

The **information asymmetries** study finds for the aforementioned reporting categories, *important non-financials*, *sustainability* and *forward-looking information*, which are frequently characterized as sensitive information (as well as for *important financials*) that FRQ is significantly negatively associated with information asymmetries. Assuming a causal effect of FRQ on information asymmetries, this finding suggests that disclosures in these areas have an influence on capital market decisions, whereas there would be no significant effect for e.g. information on *risks and opportunities*. Thus, investors might use information on these categories for resource allocation decisions. The results of the information asymmetries as well as the other investigations throughout this study have been contrasted with the results of prior research. Since this study's main findings are widely in line with the results of other studies, the applied research methodology is assumed to be **externally valid**. External validity underpins the quality of the conducted empirical research.[1194]

On the whole, the study has applied three measures of FRQ. A **comparison of the FRQ measures** on the basis of correlations has analyzed as to what extent the results of these

[1193] Cf. section 2.3.3.

[1194] Cf. *Blaesing* (2013), p. 259. For external validity, cf. section 5.2.2.2.

measures are consistent. On the one hand, the correlation coefficients mostly have the predicted signs implying that a higher FRQ score of one measure is associated with a higher FRQ score of another measure. On the other hand, the correlations are only (very) weak and a statistically significant relationship on country level is only found for the German sample between the Fog readability index and both full disclosure index and discretionary accruals measure. On the whole, the three measures capture different aspects of FRQ: earnings management, disclosure content and readability, respectively. Hence, overlapping measurement areas among the three measures seem to be small. Furthermore, the use of the accruals-based (modified-Jones model) proxy as well as the Fog readability index as dependent variable in the determinant regression model instead of the disclosure index measure indicates differences between the three complimentary measures of FRQ.

The overall results of the **determinant study** show a number of significant associations between determinants and FRQ which can be explained by this study's theoretical foundation. However, it is questionable whether the **country-specific** financial reporting environment or rather the **company-specific** determinants are the dominant influencing factor for a company's FRQ. This study's results suggest that the country-specific characteristics are dominant. First, the descriptive results have suggested significant cross-country differences in FRQ on the basis of significance tests. Second, the multivariate regression model finds economically pronounced and mostly highly significant associations between disclosure index-based FRQ and the country variables for Brazil and South Africa, whereas the relations between FRQ and the company-specific determinants are mostly less significant. This is underpinned by the determinants regressions for the three country samples which identify only a few associations on lower significance levels. In addition, the country-specific financial reporting environments may also affect the importance of company-specific determinants in a country, as the example of ownership concentration has shown. On the whole, the influence of the country-specific environments is assumed to dominate the influence of company-specific determinants, although also a number of company-specific determinants are regarded as important influencing factors of FRQ.

With respect to research question RQ2b, the company-specific determinants have been found to differ across the three sample countries. Although the underlying theoretical foundation is the same for all companies in Brazil, South Africa and Germany, the manifestation of these determinants may depend on country-specific characteristics and, thus, can be driven by typical characteristics of **emerging economies** (including certain political, cultural and historical developments, relatively weak institutional structures as well as poor accounting education, financial reporting regulation and enforcement)[1195]. Examples for such manifestations in emerging economies have been discussed above: the important role of ownership concentration in the Brazilian sample, the identification of FRQ differences according to customer basis in Brazil and South Africa as well as the observation that company size and analyst following seem to be of minor importance for the financial reporting practices in the two emerging economies. Overall, however, a country's financial reporting environment is unique and, thus, country characteristics may also vary among emerging economies.

[1195] Cf. section 2.3. For accounting characteristics of emerging economies in general, cf. section 2.2.3.

7 Conclusions

7.1 Main findings and implications

Rapidly-growing emerging economies are increasingly gaining in importance for the global economy and, thus, companies from emerging economies have become attractive investment objects over the past years. However, it is questionable as to what extent investors are provided with high-quality information for their capital allocation decisions, in particular, in comparison to the quality of information provided in developed countries. The study has analyzed the abstract notion of **financial reporting quality** (FRQ) in an **emerging economy setting**. For this purpose, the study develops a definition of FRQ and discusses its role as part of the accounting and financial reporting environment on a conceptual level. The conceptual foundation describes measurement techniques how to operationalize FRQ. In addition, the specific characteristics of FRQ in emerging economies are derived.

To analyze FRQ empirically in the emerging economies Brazil and South Africa in contrast to the developed Germany, the study pursues three **research objectives**: (1) description of prevailing financial reporting practices in terms of FRQ; (2) identification of determinants of FRQ; and (3) analysis of information asymmetry effects of FRQ. The study's emerging economy setting is assumed to allow an easier detection of both determinants and capital market associations of FRQ than in a developed country environment. Most prior studies on FRQ have used a U.S. setting.

The empirical investigation applies three **measures** (using different research objects) to capture the FRQ of a sample of 150 listed companies from Brazil, South Africa and Germany: (1) accruals-based earnings management proxies (based on fundamental financials); (2) self-constructed disclosure index (content analysis of annual report); and (3) readability measures (analysis of CEO/management letter and annual report). Although the three measures have been found to capture different aspects of FRQ and are barely correlated, they provide consistent **results**: The average values of the FRQ measures in Figure 7-1 indicate that FRQ differs significantly across the three countries with the highest FRQ in Germany, the second highest in South Africa and the lowest in Brazil.

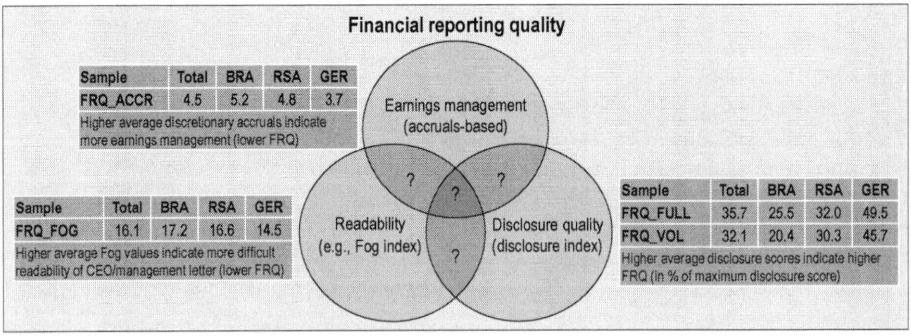

Figure 7-1: Main results of FRQ measures

First, the results of the FRQ measures describe the financial reporting practices of the sample companies and, thereby, shed light on research question RQ1a. Second, these findings allow a comparison of the financial reporting practices across Brazil, South Africa and Germany (research question RQ1b). Overall, the results of all proxies indicate considerable room for improvement in FRQ. The results of the accruals-based modified-Jones model (FRQ_ACCR) suggest that Brazilian companies engage on average in more **earnings management** than South African companies, which still manage earnings more than German companies.

The second FRQ measure is a content analysis of the companies' annual reports 2013 on the basis of a comprehensive **disclosure index**. While the full disclosure index (FRQ_FULL) comprises the entire set of disclosure index items, the voluntary disclosure index (FRQ_VOL) includes only items which would be reported on a voluntary basis. The average scores for both indices reveal that none of the country samples reaches on average at least half of the maximum score. With an average disclosure score for the total sample of 35.7% (FRQ_FULL) and 32.1% (FRQ_VOL), respectively, the FRQ can, at most, be regarded as moderate. The disclosure index scores in Figure 7-1 show a significantly higher FRQ for German companies than for the companies from the emerging economies Brazil and South Africa. The South African disclosure scores further exceed the Brazilian ones.

Moreover, the disclosure index-based FRQ differs across the seven analyzed **reporting categories**. While the FRQ for the total sample is relatively high in the reporting categories *background information, important financials, sustainability* and *risks and opportunities* (compared to total FRQ), the FRQ is relatively low in the areas *important non-financials* and *forward-looking information*. The results of the categories *risks and opportunities* as well as *forward-looking information* differ substantially between Brazil and South Africa, on the one hand, and Germany, on the other. This FRQ gap between the two emerging economies and the developed Germany is considerably lower for the reporting areas *background information* and *important financials*. Consistent with the integrated reporting development in South Africa, the *sustainability* FRQ is relatively high for the South African companies and exceeds the Brazilian and German *sustainability* FRQ. These results are not altered substantially when using the voluntary disclosure index instead of the full disclosure index.

As third FRQ measure in Figure 7-1, the study applies the so-called Fog index (FRQ_FOG) to measure the **readability** of the CEO/management's letters to the shareholder in the annual reports. The results suggest that the analyzed German textual passages are easier to read than South African ones. The readability of the Brazilian passages is most difficult. Overall, the readability results are not satisfying, as the average readability scores of all country samples are interpreted as *difficult* or even *very difficult*. In addition the readability of the entire annual reports has been analyzed on the basis of the three readability indicators *structure, language and style of expression* as well as *use of figures and tables*. The results for all of these readability indicators generally support the results of the Fog index and Flesch reading ease, as the German annual reports are found to be easier to comprehend than the South African and Brazilian annual reports. The latter are the reports with the most difficult readability. In particular, the German and South African annual reports have a considerably better structure than the Brazilian ones and include user-friendly figures and tables. On the whole, the analysis of the three FRQ measures has provided comprehensive insights on the research questions RQ1a and RQ1b.

Regarding the research questions RQ2a and RQ2b, particularly the determinants regression model using the disclosure index measure as dependent variable has identified several potential determinants of FRQ. The results of the **determinants study** show pronounced negative associations between total FRQ and the country variables for Brazil and South Africa on a highly significant level. Assuming a causal relationship, these findings suggest negative country effects for Brazil and South Africa against the benchmark of Germany, which would be in line with the cross-country differences in the disclosure index scores. The negative association is even more pronounced for Brazil. Typical characteristics of emerging economies (e.g., less favorable cultural and institutional environments) are potential reasons for the lower FRQ there.

In addition to the significant country associations, the study has detected several **company-specific determinants** which are assumed to influence the provided FRQ. The results show statistically significant relations between total FRQ (FRQ_FULL), on the one hand, and company size, company age, ownership concentration and analyst following, on the other. Moreover, marginally significant associations are found for profitability, company valuation, and systematic risk. Also a few industries are significantly related to FRQ. Remarkably, undervalued companies provide a particularly high FRQ regarding the category *financials*, which is the information basis for company valuations. Moreover, the positive association between systematic company risk and FRQ is more pronounced for FRQ of *risks and opportunities* instead of total FRQ. Thus, riskier companies provide an increased level of risk information. The use of the voluntary disclosure index measure does not alter the results of the determinants regression substantially. For other FRQ measures than the disclosure index measure, no noticeable results have been found.

Although the theoretical foundation for the company-specific determinants is the same for all three country samples, the manifestation of these determinants differs across the countries (research question RQ2b). With respect to the two **emerging economies**, the role of certain **determinants** could be explained by the countries' characteristic environments. In particular, the significant association between ownership concentration and FRQ in Brazil may be based on the country's political and historical developments (e.g., reciprocity-dominated society) which are typical in multiple emerging economies. Moreover, the aforementioned low reporting environment in emerging economies may explain the identification of FRQ differences according to customer basis for both the Brazilian and South African companies. A company in such an environment might be able to differentiate itself from competitors more easily than in a high reporting environment. The results further suggest that company size and analyst following seem to be of minor importance for the financial reporting practices of the entities from Brazil and South Africa, whereas these determinants are significantly related to FRQ for the German sample.

In spite of multiple significant company-specific determinants, the assumed influence of the country variables (country-specific environments) is suggested to dominate the influence of the company-specific determinants on the basis of the determinants study's results. Overall, the study has not only identified general determinants of FRQ (research question RQ2a), but also discussed as to what extent these determinants differ across Brazil, South Africa and Germany (research question RQ2b).

The capital market study has analyzed whether FRQ is related to **information asymmetries** (research question RQ3a) and has investigated differences between the three sample countries (research question RQ3b). In line with prior research, the study provides evidence for a statistically significant negative relationship between disclosure index-based FRQ (both FRQ_FULL and FRQ_VOL) and information asymmetries (bid-ask-spread model) and, thereby, sheds light on research question RQ3a. The finding is also consistent with the descriptive statistics of both zero return days and AIM measures, which show lower stock liquidity for Brazil and South Africa. This suggests that companies, which provide a higher FRQ, experience lower information asymmetries. Against the benchmark of Germany, the negative relationship between FRQ and information asymmetries is more pronounced in Brazil and South Africa, whereas there are no substantial differences between the two emerging economies (research question RQ3b). Consistent with the literature, thus, information asymmetry effects seem to be easier to detect in low information environments. Considering the relatively low FRQ in Brazil and South Africa, companies might raise their FRQ relatively easily and, thereby, reduce information asymmetries. Furthermore, the results of the capital market study indicate that assumed capital market effects occur particularly in the fourth quarter as well as throughout the entire year subsequent to a company's end of fiscal year suggesting a considerable time lag. In addition, a significant relationship is not only found between information asymmetries and total FRQ, but also for the separate FRQ of the **reporting categories** *financials*, *non-financials*, *sustainability* and *forward-looking information*. Hence, these reporting areas seem to be an important basis for the decisions of capital market participants. Figure 7-2 summarizes the main results of the study.

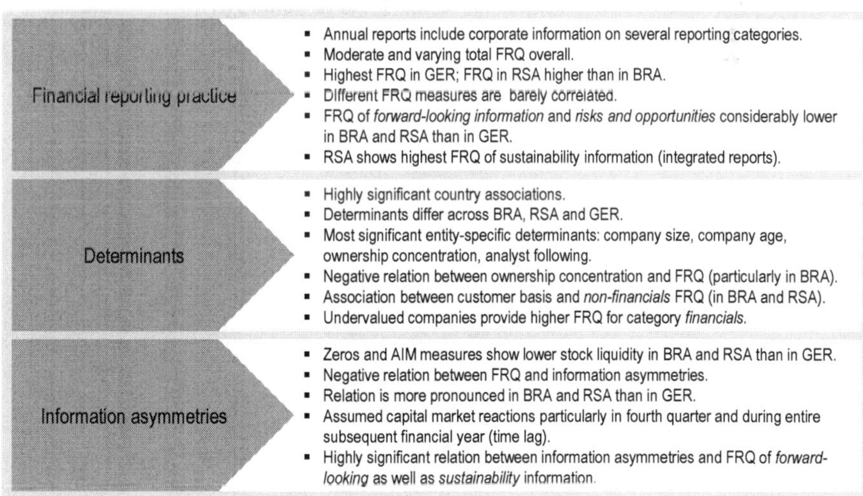

Figure 7-2: Summary of this study's main results

The main results have **implications** for multiple interest groups: preparers of corporate reports (e.g., managers), users of corporate reports (e.g., investors), standard setter and regulating authorities, auditors as well as academics.

A company's management (**preparer of corporate reports**) can use the study's descriptive observations as a benchmark to compare its reporting practice to that of other companies in Brazil, South Africa and Germany. On the basis of the study's results, managers may recognize best practices and starting points to restructure the company's reporting system to improve their FRQ in future. This could also affect the activities of a company's management accounting (e.g., concerning data collection). Moreover, the identified negative relationship between FRQ and information asymmetries implicates that managers may be able to reduce the information asymmetry component of their company's costs of capital through high-quality financial reporting. As this relation has been found to be more pronounced in Brazil and South Africa than in Germany, particularly companies in emerging economies may benefit from increased FRQ. Thus, managements preparing corporate reports are assumed to have incentives for high-quality financial reporting.

With respect to the **addressees of corporate reports**, the considerable variability of FRQ across the three countries may sensitize international investors that the FRQ of information on companies from different countries, particularly emerging economies, may vary considerably. Thus, the comparison of corporate information across countries can be difficult. The results of the determinants study help investors to interpret corporate information. They invite investors in emerging economies to consider factors influencing disclosure incentives.[1196] In particular, the study identifies company-specific as well as country determinants of a company's FRQ in Brazil, South Africa and Germany. For instance, a company's high ownership concentration may raise doubts that the company is willing to provide high FRQ. Consequently, investors may reexamine their investment strategies on the basis of this study's results. Moreover, the analyzed capital market effects have implications for investors and other capital market participants. As FRQ is found to be significantly related to information asymmetries and, thus, may influence discount rates of stock prices, trading strategies could be adjusted on the basis of this study's findings.[1197]

Furthermore, **governmental authorities**, **regulators** and **standard setters** can examine the level of FRQ on the basis of the study's descriptive results. If necessary, they may take measures to improve FRQ. In particular, (international) standard setters should consider that the FRQ of annual reports is heterogeneous across Brazil, South Africa and Germany. The national standard setter in Brazil, for instance, could consider stricter requirements regarding the disclosure of specific information in light of the poor FRQ of some reporting categories. These rules could counterbalance the power of large shareholders due to high ownership concentration.[1198] In general, emerging economies may be willing to adopt (additional) international practices and standards of financial reporting.

Also the results of the earnings management proxies might be of particular interest to standard setting bodies. These proxies describe how earnings management varies across

[1196] Cf. *Schiehll et al.* (2013), p. 355.
[1197] Cf. *Francis et al.* (2004), p. 1007.
[1198] Cf. here and in the following *Schiehll et al.* (2013), p. 355.

the sample countries. Further, the observed integrated reporting practices in South Africa allow the IIRC to assess the success of the integrated reporting approach. Moreover, standard setters (e.g., the IASB) aim at providing financial reporting standards, which ensure decision-useful information for investors. Hence, the results of the information asymmetry study have the implication that standard setters (as well as regulators) are supposed to consider the importance of the reporting categories *non-financials*, *sustainability* and *forward-looking information* in addition to *financials* for the decisions of capital market participants.

The identified financial reporting practices, determinants and information asymmetries are further relevant to **auditors**, since auditors are involved in the financial reporting processes of the companies and, thus, also influence the companies' FRQ.[1199] Auditors ensure a certain quality of disclosures through their auditing activities. Moreover, this study allows auditors to identify reporting areas of relatively poor FRQ. These areas could be subject to additional consulting projects.

With respect to **academics**, the study's results provide links to both researchers and lecturers. Researchers may consider this study's results in several ways to identify future research opportunities. The findings help lecturers in both emerging and developed countries to detect international differences in financial reporting. These topics might be an important teaching focus, as students are the future managers, auditors and standard setters who are supposed to be familiar with up-to-date research on financial reporting in emerging economies. In a globalized economy with rapidly-growing emerging economies, the study's results are also important in developed countries.

7.2 Limitations and outlook

The nature of this empirical study is accompanied by several limitations. In particular, the **generalizability** of the study's results can be questioned. The empirical investigation uses a sample of 150 large listed companies from Brazil, South Africa and Germany and focuses on a single time period (financial year 2013). Hence, results could differ over time as well as for other settings. As the financial reporting environment develops rapidly, as the example of integrated reporting in South Africa underpins, and this study provides only a snapshot of FRQ for the financial year 2013, future research could examine FRQ over multiple years. Such an **intertemporal** analysis of FRQ in emerging economies could help to understand the developments of financial reporting and compare these to the countries' economic developments.

With respect to this study's sample, the results might differ for other samples, particularly, smaller and non-listed companies,[1200] whose financial reporting practices may be influenced by other determinants than those identified in this study. Following the identified role of high ownership concentration in Brazil, also smaller companies are frequently owned by few shareholders so that incentives for high FRQ might be lower than for companies with dispersed ownership concentration.

[1199] Cf. here and in the following *Blaesing* (2013), p. 265-266.

[1200] Cf. *Cooke/Wallace* (1989), p. 57.

Moreover, the study may give the impression that Brazil and South Africa are **representative of emerging economies** in general. However, emerging economies are neither a homogenous group (as shown in section 2.2.1) nor are Brazil and South Africa necessarily representative of the multitude of emerging economies worldwide. Therefore, future research could examine FRQ in an emerging economy setting for a sample of other or additional countries. In particular, a larger sample has advantages over this study's sample. First, a sample with a large number of emerging economies is more representative for emerging economies and, thus, can detect systematic differences compared to developed countries. Second, a large number of countries allows to measure cultural (e.g., specific cultural dimensions by *Hofstede* (1980a)) and institutional effects (e.g., legal systems) on FRQ. However, the disadvantage of such a multi-country study is that a comprehensive content analysis as conducted in this study would be hardly feasible.

Further, the abstract term FRQ is difficult to operationalize. The study applies different indirect as well as direct **measures to capture FRQ**. However, there are other measures, which could provide differing results. The fact that this study's measures have shown consistent results mitigates this concern.

The results of the study largely depend on the **disclosure index** as a basis for the collection of the reporting data. The construction is inevitably affected by a certain degree of subjectivity, particularly concerning the (implicit) weights of the disclosure index items. However, this disclosure index mitigates this concern through the inclusion of a large number of disclosure index items. Such a large number of disclosure index items lowers the impact of the selected weights on the study's results.[1201] Moreover, the disclosure index construction has shown that the weights are largely in line with prior research so that external validity is assumed. Subjectivity during the content analysis is reduced through the definition of specific disclosure items and a generally binary coding scheme (1/0), which leaves only little room for discretion. The disclosure index further analyzes the companies' entire annual reports and does not distinguish between audited and non-audited information, which could be subject to further research. On the whole, the disclosure index allows collecting and evaluating the reported information in a manner which can be verified intersubjectively,[1202] although critics argue that empirical results on the basis of disclosure indices would be found to have only limited generalizability.[1203]

Moreover, the disclosure index focuses on the benefits of information to users of the annual reports, whereas both direct and indirect **costs** of disclosures are not considered. Indirect costs could also arise due to information overload (e.g., in annual reports), which mitigates the usefulness of corporate information.[1204] Thus, investigating the relation between FRQ and these costs could be the subject of future research. This research would contribute to understand cost-benefit considerations by companies, which are the basis for financial reporting decisions.[1205]

[1201] Cf. *Beattie et al.* (2004), p. 210.
[1202] For the criterion of intersubjective verifiability, cf. *Popper* (2005), p. 21-22.
[1203] Cf. *Lerchenmüller* (2012), p. 25.
[1204] Cf. *Schick et al.* (1990), p. 207.
[1205] Cf. *Nienhaus* (2015), p. 208.

With respect to the investigation of the determinants and information asymmetry effects of FRQ, the research design allows detecting statistically significant relationships, but no actual **causal relation** due to **endogeneity problems**. First, *reverse causality* refers to the concern that the direction of a causal effect is the opposite of the assumed direction.[1206] In the determinants study, for instance, it may be unclear whether a company's analyst following influences its FRQ or rather the company's FRQ determines its analyst following. Second, *self-selection* is a concern regarding the information asymmetry investigation.[1207] Companies decide on their own (endogenously) about their FRQ level on the basis of cost-benefit considerations. Thus, the effect of FRQ on information asymmetries might not be isolated, as it might be driven by the endogeneity of FRQ.[1208] Self-selection is further a concern, as Brazilian companies do not have to provide annual reports in English so that non-English reports are excluded from the sample.[1209] Further research could use a larger sample size to control for self-selection through statistical techniques, such as propensity score matching. Third, also *omitted variables* in the regression models could cause endogeneity.[1210] For example, the determinants regression model may have not considered all factors, which determine FRQ. In line with *Gassen* (2014), however, the investigation is able to provide valuable contributions through descriptions and economic reasoning, as a causal setting cannot be created.[1211] This study develops the assumed causal relationships on a large theoretical basis and discusses the results in detail. Future research could use a larger sample as well as a larger number of emerging economies to provide additional evidence on relation between FRQ and information asymmetries in emerging economies. Moreover, researchers could seek a setting with exogenous shocks to investigate actual causal relationships.

Therefore, the limitations of this study offer further research opportunities also with regard to prospective developments. Investors' expectations for emerging economies have been immense, as the following statement by *Salter* (1998) underpins:

> "*In the early 1990s emerging markets seemed to be the answer to investors' prayers.*"[1212]

After years of massive economic growth and minor setbacks, there is a wide consensus that emerging economies still have massive economic potential.[1213] On the basis of forecasts regarding both the economic and demographic development, emerging economies will play an increasingly important role in the **future** global economy. Besides economic

1206 Cf. *Eugster* (2014), p. 17.

1207 Cf. here and in the following *Nikolaev/van Lent* (2005), p. 683; *Eugster* (2014), p. 1.

1208 The identification of an instrumental variable is able to mitigate the self-selection concern. However, no exogenous instrumental variable has been found, which significantly influences FRQ (self-selection decision) and does not influence information aymmetries (dependent variable), cf. *Heckman* (1979), p. 154-157; *Grill* (2011), p. 134.

1209 However, only one company is excluded for that reason.

1210 Cf. *Nikolaev/van Lent* (2005), p. 677.

1211 Cf. *Gassen* (2014), p. 536.

1212 *Salter* (1998), p. 211.

1213 Cf. here and in the following section 2.2.2.

growth, also globalization will draw the attention of international investors, the general public and other players on emerging economies.[1214]

However, a negative impulse on growth in emerging economies could be caused by the Federal Reserve's decision on 16 December 2015 to raise interest rates again.[1215] Brazil and South Africa belong to the so-called *Fragile Five*[1216], which are largely dependent on capital flows in U.S. dollar. Thus, the interest hike might lead to reduced investments and higher costs of capital in the emerging economies. However, the implications on corporate financial reporting are debatable. The situation could create enhanced incentives for companies to provide high-quality information, as this measure could lower information asymmetries and, thereby, attract or keep investors.

Recent global trends comprise particularly **sustainability** issues. An example is the *United Nations* conference on climate change 2015 in Paris. In light of the importance of the topic, all participating countries found a consensus on a global climate agreement. This trend is also noticeable in financial reporting developments. As discussed throughout the study, the South African integrated reporting approach explicitly focuses on sustainability topics. However, the integrated reporting trend is not limited to South Africa. For instance, also the first German companies provide integrated reports (e.g., *BASF*). Moreover, the European Union has issued Directive 2014/95/EU on 22 October 2014, which deals with non-financial reporting. The Directive requires sustainability-related information including, inter alia, environmental matters, social and employee-related matters as well as human rights aspects.[1217]

In line with the results of the information asymmetry study, therefore, information on *sustainability* and *important non-financials* as well as *forward-looking information* (besides *important financials*) seem to be of particular importance in the future. Due to the discussed trends and developments, the financial reporting activities of companies in emerging economies might catch up with those of developed countries. Besides changes in financial reporting on a voluntary basis, it will also be interesting whether regulators in emerging economies will require additional disclosures, which could be subject to discussion on one of the next BRICS summits. Conducting this study in 20 years might not reveal significant differences in the FRQ across Brazil, South Africa and Germany. Referring to the initial quotation of this thesis, the companies' financial reports in emerging economies may today be regarded as blurry *sailing maps*. However, in light of the prospective development in emerging economies, investors call for sharp and detailed *maps*, which can be provided in terms of high-quality financial reports.

1214 Cf. *Rodrigues et al.* (2012), p. 23.

1215 Cf. here and in the following *Morgan Stanley* (2013); *The Wall Street Journal* (2015).

1216 The *Fragile Five* comprise South Africa, Turkey, Brazil, India and Indonesia.

1217 Cf. Directive 2014/95/EU.

Appendix

Table A-1: Disclosure index

A. Background information	
1	Company structure
1.1	Shareholder structure (1/0)
1.2	Subsidiary companies (1/0)
1.3	Corporate restructurings (1/0)
2	Business activities
2.1	Product/service strategy (1/0)
2.2	Business activities [naming] (1/0)
2.3	Business activities [explanation] (1/0)
2.4	Business activities [impact on results] (1/0)
3	Industry
3.1	Industry characteristics [description] (1/0)
3.2	Industry characteristics [impact on business activities] (1/0)
4	Markets & competitors
4.1	Company's markets (1/0)
4.2	Company's market shares (1/0)
4.3	Main competitors (1/0)
5	Macroeconomic factors
5.1	Macroeconomic conditions [naming] (1/0)
5.2	Macroeconomic conditions [impact on company's performance] (1/0)
6	Strategy
6.1	Business model (1/0)
6.2	Strategic objectives [naming] (1/0)
6.3	Strategic objectives [quantifiable target values] (1/0)
6.4	Corporate strategic vision (1/0)
6.5	Core competencies [description] (1/0)
6.6	Core competencies [explanation] (1/0)
6.7	Core competencies [relationship to business activities] (1/0)
6.8	M&A strategy (1/0)
6.9	M&A activities (1/0)
6.10	Strategic financing model/schemes (1/0)
7	Corporate Governance
7.1	Corporate governance policies [description] (1/0)
7.2	Corporate governance policies [explanation] (1/0)
7.3	Management & supervisory board [changes] (1/0)
7.4	Management & supervisory board [procedures/functioning] (1/0)
7.5	Supervision/monitoring systems (1/0)
8	Share price
8.1	Share price development [explanation] (1/0)
8.2	Share price development [illustration] (1/0)

8.3	Price-earnings ratio development (1/0)
8.4	Share price development [compared to benchmark] (1/0)

B. Important financials	
1	Profit situation
1.1	Revenue
1.1.1	Revenue (1/0)
1.1.2	Revenue per segment (1/0)
1.1.3	Revenue [explanation of development] (1/0)
1.1.4	Revenue from core business (1/0)
1.1.5	Relationship between revenue breakdown & long-term strategy (1/0)
1.1.6	Revenue [explanation of actions] (1/0)
1.1.7	Revenue [success of past actions] (1/0)
1.2	Order intake
1.2.1	Order intake (1/0)
1.2.2	Order intake per segment (1/0)
1.2.3	Order intake [explanation of development] (1/0)
1.2.4	Concrete orders/projects (1/0)
1.2.5	Order intake [explanation of actions] (1/0)
1.3	Profit, earnings, dividends
1.3.1	Operating profit (1/0)
1.3.2	Operating profit per segment (1/0)
1.3.3	Non-operating profit (1/0)
1.3.4	Operating profit [explanation of development] (1/0)
1.3.5	Earnings adjustments (1/0)
1.3.6	Interest result (1/0)
1.3.7	Investment result (1/0)
1.3.8	Relationship between profit breakdown & long-term strategy (1/0)
1.3.9	Profit [explanation of actions] (1/0)
1.3.10	Profit [success of past actions] (1/0)
1.3.11	Contribution of associates (1/0)
1.3.12	Dividend proposal (1/0)
1.3.13	Dividend proposal [compared to benchmark] (1/0)
1.3.14	Dividend [impact of corporate events] (1/0)
1.3.15	Undiluted/diluted profit per share (1/0)
1.4	P&L items and profit indicators
1.4.1	Personnel expense (1/0)
1.4.2	Personnel expense per segment (1/0)
1.4.3	Material expense (1/0)
1.4.4	Material expense per segment (1/0)
1.4.5	Depreciation & amortization (1/0)
1.4.6	Depreciation & amortization per segment (1/0)
1.4.7	P&L items [impact of business environment] (1/0)

1.4.8	P&L items [illustration of development] (1/0)
1.4.9	P&L items per segment [illustration of development] (1/0)
1.4.10	Tax expenses (1/0)
1.4.11	EBITDA; EBIT and EBT figures (1/0)
1.4.12	EBITDA; EBIT and EBT figures per segment (1/0)
1.4.13	Profit margins (1/0)
1.4.14	Profit margins per segment (1/0)
1.4.15	P&L ratios (1/0)
2	Assets, liability and equity
2.1	Assets
2.1.1	Assets [structure] (1/0)
2.1.2	Assets [disclosure] (1/0)
2.1.3	Assets [changes] (1/0)
2.1.4	Asset ratios (1/0)
2.1.5	Fair values of tangible/financial assets at amortized cost (1/0)
2.1.6	Fair values of intangible assets at amortized cost (1/0)
2.1.7	M&A activities' impact on balance sheet (1/0)
2.1.8	Off-balance assets/arrangements (1/0)
2.1.9	Changes in equity holdings (1/0)
2.2.	Liability
2.2.1	Total liabilities (1/0)
2.2.2	Pensions provisions (1/0)
2.2.3	Present value of unfunded/funded defined benefit obligations (1/0)
2.3	Equity
2.3.1	Retained earnings (1/0)
2.3.2	Capital reserve (1/0)
2.3.3	Gains & losses directly booked in equity and/or OCI (1/0)
3	Financial position
3.1	Objectives/principles of financing management (1/0)
3.2	Capital structure (1/0)
3.3	Financing sources (1/0)
3.4	Financing analysis
3.4.1	Financing activities (1/0)
3.4.2	Unutilized credit facilities (1/0)
3.4.3	Long-term borrowings (1/0)
3.4.4	Mid-term borrowings (1/0)
3.4.5	Loan terms (1/0)
3.5	Hedging instruments (1/0)
3.6	Cost of capital
3.6.1	Cost of capital [disclosure] (1/0)
3.6.2	Cost of capital [calculation] (1/0)
3.7	Liquidity analysis
3.7.1	Changes in liquidity (1/0)

3.7.2	Extraordinary cash out/in (1/0)
3.7.3	Breakdown of total cash flow (1/0)
3.7.4	Liquidity indicators (1/0)
4	Impact of changes in the accounting regulation (1/0)
5	Overall economic position
5.1	Overall economic position [management's evaluation] (1/0)
5.2	Overall economic position [explanation of management's evaluation] (1/0)
5.3	Overall economic position [management's perspective apparent] (1/0)
5.4	Overall economic position [influence of earnings management] (1/0)

C. Important Non-financials	
1	Human Capital
1.1	Breakdown of employees (1/0)
1.2	Employee fluctuation (1/0)
1.3	Employee satisfaction
1.3.1	Employee satisfaction [description] (1/0)
1.3.2	Employee satisfaction [measurement technique] (1/0)
1.3.3	Employee satisfaction development (1/0)
1.3.4	Employee satisfaction [actions] (1/0)
1.3.5	Company's attractiveness as employer (1/0)
1.4	Employee expertise (1/0)
1.5	Investments in employee education
1.5.1	Investments in employee education [explanation] (1/0)
1.5.2	Investments in employee education [key figures] (1/0)
2	Suppliers & customers
2.1	Suppliers
2.1.1	Suppliers [description] (1/0)
2.1.2	Supplier relationship (1/0)
2.2.	Customers
2.2.1	Customers [description] (1/0)
2.2.2	Customer satisfaction [discussion] (1/0)
2.2.3	Customer satisfaction [indicator] (1/0)
2.2.4	Customer satisfaction [measurement technique] (1/0)
2.2.5	Customer satisfaction [actions] (1/0)
2.2.6	Customer quality (1/0)
2.2.7	Value added per customer (1/0)
3	Processes & important brands
3.1	Processes
3.1.1	Process [changes] (1/0)
3.1.2	Process [measurement technique] (1/0)
3.1.3	Process [actions] (1/0)
3.2	Brands
3.2.1	Brands [naming] (1/0)

3.2.2	Brand positioning (1/0)
3.2.3	New brands/brand repositioning (1/0)
3.2.4	Brand values (1/0)
3.2.5	Communication campaigns for core brands (1/0)
4	Research & Development
4.1	R&D's importance (1/0)
4.2	R&D developments (1/0)
4.3	R&D activities [changes] (1/0)
4.4	R&D areas [breakdown of R&D expenses] (1/0)
4.5	R&D areas [breakdown of R&D employees] (1/0)
4.6	R&D indicators (1/0)
4.7	Development costs [capitalization] (1/0)
4.8	Development costs [amortization] (1/0)
4.9	Development costs [capitalization ratio] (1/0)
4.10	Innovation rate/indicators (1/0)
5	Investments
5.1	Objectives/principles of investment management (1/0)
5.2	Investments (1/0)
5.3	Investments per segment (1/0)
5.4	Investments [actions] (1/0)
5.5	Investments [success of previous actions] (1/0)
5.6	Relationship between investment breakdown & long-term strategy (1/0)
5.7	Investment indicators (1/0)

D. Sustainability information	
1.	General information
1.1	Sustainability framework (1/0)
1.2	Sustainability information [reference to detailed report] (1/0)
1.3	Sustainability strategy (1/0)
2	Economic sustainability
2.1	Economic sustainability [description] (1/0)
2.2	Economic sustainability [explanation] (1/0)
2.3	Economic sustainability [objectives] (1/0)
2.4	Economic sustainability [achievement of formulated objectives] (1/0)
2.5	Economic sustainability [actions] (1/0)
3	Environmental sustainability
3.1	Environmental sustainability [description] (1/0)
3.2	Environmental sustainability [explanation] (1/0)
3.3	Environmental sustainability [objectives] (1/0)
3.4	Environmental sustainability [achievement of formulated objectives] (1/0)
3.5	Environmental sustainability [actions] (1/0)
4	Social sustainability
4.1	Social sustainability [description] (1/0)

4.2	Social sustainability [explanation] (1/0)
4.3	Social sustainability [objectives] (1/0)
4.4	Social sustainability [achievement of formulated objectives] (1/0)
4.5	Social sustainability [actions] (1/0)
5	Interdependencies of three dimensions (1/0)
6	Listings in sustainability indices (1/0)

E. Value based management	
1	Conceptual basis
1.1	Value based management concepts [naming] (1/0)
1.2	Value based management concepts [implementation] (1/0)
1.3	Value based key figure [description] (1/0)
1.4	Value based key figure [explanation] (1/0)
2	Quantifiable data
2.1	Value based key figures [disclosure] (1/0)
2.2	Value based key figures [computation] (1/0)
3	Management compensation system
3.1	Value based compensation (1/0)
3.2	Management compensation system [description] (1/0)
3.3	Management compensation system [underlying philosophy] (1/0)
3.4	Criteria for bonuses & variable compensation (1/0)
3.5	Adjustments in the compensation system (1/0)
3.6	Relationship between company's performance & management compensation (1/0)
3.7	Employee incentive programs (1/0)
3.8	Fixed & variable compensation [executive board] (1/0)
3.9	Fixed & variable compensation [supervisory/non-executive board] (1/0)
4	KPIs used in management accounting
4.1	KPIs used in management accounting [naming] (1/0)
4.2	Adjustments to financial reporting figures [description] (1/0)
4.3	Adjustments to financial reporting figures [explanation] (1/0)
4.4	Business transactions/corporate events [adjusted for] (1/0)
4.5	Other individual adjustments (1/0)
4.6	Reconciliations of adjusted figures (1/0)

F. Forward looking	
1	Operative objectives and forecasts
1.1	Revenues
1.1.1	Qualitative/comparative forecast (1/0)
1.1.2	Qualified-comparative forecast (1/0)
1.1.3	Point forecast/interval forecast (1/0)
1.1.4	Expected revenue [regional/segmental distinctions] (1/0)
1.1.5	Assumptions behind forecast (1/0)
1.1.6	Reference value [previous financial year] (1/0)

1.1.7	Reference value [analyst forecast] (1/0)
1.2	Absolute Earnings
1.2.1	Qualitative/comparative forecast (1/0)
1.2.2	Qualified-comparative forecast (1/0)
1.2.3	Point forecast/interval forecast (1/0)
1.2.4	Expected earnings [regional/segmental distinctions] (1/0)
1.2.5	Assumptions behind forecast (1/0)
1.2.6	Reference value [previous financial year] (1/0)
1.2.7	Reference value [analyst forecast] (1/0)
1.3	Relative earnings margin
1.3.1	Qualitative/comparative forecast (1/0)
1.3.2	Qualified-comparative forecast (1/0)
1.3.3	Point forecast/interval forecast (1/0)
1.3.4	Reference value (1/0)
1.4	Value proposition
1.4.1	Qualitative/comparative forecast (1/0)
1.4.2	Qualified-comparative forecast (1/0)
1.4.3	Point forecast/interval forecast (1/0)
1.4.4	Reference value (1/0)
1.5	Dividends
1.5.1	Qualitative/comparative forecast (1/0)
1.5.2.	Qualified-comparative forecast (1/0)
1.5.3.	Point forecast/interval forecast (1/0)
1.5.4	Reference value (1/0)
2	Financial forecasts
2.1	Other financial forecasts [description] (1/0)
2.2	Other financial forecasts [disclosure of KPIs] (1/0)
2.3	Disclosure of specific KPIs
2.3.1	Capital structure
2.3.1.1	Qualitative/comparative forecast (1/0)
2.3.1.2	Qualified-comparative forecast (1/0)
2.3.1.3	Point forecast/interval forecast (1/0)
2.3.1.4	Reference value (1/0)
2.3.2	Liquidity KPIs
2.3.2.1	Qualitative/comparative forecast (1/0)
2.3.2.2	Qualified-comparative forecast (1/0)
2.3.2.3	Point forecast/interval forecast (1/0)
2.3.2.4	Reference value (1/0)
2.3.3	Financing volume
2.3.3.1	Qualitative/comparative forecast (1/0)
2.3.3.2	Qualified-comparative forecast (1/0)
2.3.3.3	Point forecast/interval forecast (1/0)
2.3.3.4	Reference value (1/0)

3	Strategic & other non-financial objectives
3.1	Long-term strategy [description] (1/0)
3.2	Long-term strategy [disclosure of KPIs] (1/0)
3.3	Planned changes on other non-financial objectives (1/0)
3.4	Planned investments [naming] (1/0)
3.5	Planned investments [explanation] (1/0)
3.6	Planned investments [regional/segmental distinctions] (1/0)
3.7	Future key markets (1/0)
3.8	Future key products (1/0)
3.9	Planned corporate restructurings (1/0)
3.10	Future R&D strategy (1/0)
3.11	Disclosure of specific KPIs
3.11.1	Investment volume
3.11.1.1	Qualitative/comparative forecast (1/0)
3.11.1.2	Qualified-comparative forecast (1/0)
3.11.1.3	Point forecast/interval forecast (1/0)
3.11.1.4	Reference value (1/0)
3.11.2	R&D expenses
3.11.2.1	Qualitative/comparative forecast (1/0)
3.11.2.2	Qualified-comparative forecast (1/0)
3.11.2.3	Point forecast/interval forecast (1/0)
3.11.2.4	Reference value (1/0)
4	Economic trends outside the company
4.1	Prospective overall economic development (1/0)
4.2	Prospective industry/sector development (1/0)

G. Risks and opportunities	
1	General risk tolerance (1/0)
2	Risk management system (1/0)
3	Risk management strategy (1/0)
4	Different risk exposure categories (1/0)
5	Organizational units per risk category (1/0)
6	Reporting of distinctive risks & risk indicators
6.1	External risks (1/0)
6.2	External risks [impact on company] (1/0)
6.3	Industry risks (1/0)
6.4	Industry risks [impact on company] (1/0)
6.5	Corporate strategy risks (1/0)
6.6	Corporate strategy risks [impact on company] (1/0)
6.7	Performance-related risks (1/0)
6.8	Performance-related risks [impact on company] (1/0)
6.9	Personnel risks (1/0)
6.10	Personnel risks [impact on company] (1/0)

6.11	Financial risks
6.11.1	Financial risks (1/0)
6.11.2	Financial risks [actions to overcome] (1/0)
6.11.3	Sensitivity analyses (1/0)
6.11.4	VaR/CFaR indicators (1/0)
6.11.5	Financial risks [impact on company] (1/0)
7	Regular risk reporting to management & supervisory board (1/0)
8	Risk management software (1/0)
9	Risk situation [description by management] (1/0)
10	Risk situation [explanation by management] (1/0)
11	Company rating(s) (1/0)
12	Opportunities
12.1	Opportunity management system (1/0)
12.2	Different opportunity categories (1/0)
12.3	Opportunities [operational environment] (1/0)
12.4	Opportunities [strategy] (1/0)
12.5	Opportunities [business environment] (1/0)

The following items are not considered in the voluntary disclosure indices due to regulation:

Brazil:
A.1.1; A.1.2; A.2.2; A.4.1; B.1.1.2.b; B.1.3.2.b; B.1.3.11; B.1.3.15; B.1.4.5; B.2.1.2; B.2.1.8; B.2.2.1.b; B.2.2.2.b; B.2.2.3; B.2.3.1.b; B.2.3.2.b; B.2.3.3.b; B.3.2.b; B.3.4.3.b; B.3.4.4.b; B.3.5; B.3.7.3.b; B.4; C.1.2.b; C.4.2; C.4.7; C.4.8; C.5.2; E.3.1; E.3.2; E.3.4; E.3.5; G.6.3.a; G.6.11.1; G.6.11.3.

South Africa:
A.1.1; A.1.2; A.7.3; B.1.3.11; B.1.3.15; B.1.4.5; B.2.1.2.b; B.2.2.1.b; B.2.2.2.b; B.2.2.3; B.2.3.1.b; B.2.3.2.b; B.2.3.3.b; B.3.2.b; B.3.5; B.3.7.3.b; C.4.7; C.4.8; G.6.11.1; G.6.11.3.

Germany:
A.1.2; A.3.1; A.5.1; A.5.2; A.7.4; B.1.1.1; B.1.1.2; B.1.1.3; B.1.3.1; B.1.3.4; B.1.3.11; B.1.3.15; B.1.4.5; B.2.1.2.b; B.2.2.1.b; B.2.2.2.b; B.2.2.3; B.2.3.1.b; B.2.3.2.b; B.2.3.3.b; B.3.2.b; B.3.5; B.3.7.1.b; B.3.7.3; B.5.1; B.5.3; C.4.2; C.4.3; C.4.7; C.4.8; E.1.1; E.1.2; E.1.3; E.1.4; E.2.1; E.2.2; E.3.1; E.3.8; G.2; G.3; G.6.11.1; G.6.11.2; G.6.11.3; G.9; G.12.1.

(a=qualitative information; b=quantitative information)

Table A-2: SIC code industry aggregation
Following *French/Fama* (2010).

1 Consumer non-durable (food, tobacco, textiles, apparel, leather, toys) and durables (cars, TVs, furniture)					
0100-0999	2000-2399	2500-2519	2590-2599	2700-2749	2770-2799
3021-3021	3100-3199	3630-3659	3710-3711	3714-3714	3716-3716
3750-3751	3792-3792	3851-3873	3900-3939	3940-3989	3990-3999
2 Manufacturing (machinery, trucks, planes, chemicals, paper, printing)					
2520-2589	2600-2699	2750-2769	2800-2829	2840-2899	2990-3099
3200-3569	3580-3621	3623-3629	3700-3709	3711-3713	3715-3715
3717-3749	3752-3791	3793-3799	3860-3899	9997-9998	
3 Energy and mining (resource extraction, products and utilities)					
1000-1221	1200-1399	1400-1400	2900-2999	4900-4949	
4 Business equipment (computers, software and electronic equipment)					
3570-3579	3622-3622	3660-3692	3694-3711	3810-3839	7370-7372
7373-7373	7374-7374	7375-7375	7376-7376	7377-7377	7378-7378
7379-7379	7391-7391	8730-8734			
5 Telecommunication, television transmission, media					
2711-2790	4800-4899				
6 Wholesale, retail and some services (laundries, repair shops)					
5000-5999	7200-7299	7389-7389	7510-7510	7600-7699	8200-8200
7 Healthcare, medical equipment and drugs manufacturing					
2830-2839	3693-3693	3840-3859	8000-8099		
8 Real Estate					
6500-6552					
9 Transport and travel					
4011-4581	4700-4731	7990-7990			
10 Construction					
1540-1540	1600-1600	2400-2400	3270-3270		

Table A-3: Results of disclosure index study for Brazilian sample

		FRQ (in % of maximum full disclosure index score)							
No.	Company	Background information	Financials	Non-financials	Sustain-ability	Value based mgmt.	Forward-looking information	Risks and opportuni-ties	Total
1	AES TIETE	48	48	27	30	14	13	40	**33**
2	ANHANGUERA	76	42	38	25	33	10	35	**36**
3	B2W DIGITAL	45	42	40	25	29	10	32	**32**
4	BR MALLS	42	44	13	15	38	5	32	**27**
5	BR PROPERTIES	42	49	15	15	43	2	32	**28**
6	CCR RODOVIAS	42	42	15	35	33	3	27	**27**
7	CESP PNB	45	41	30	45	29	0	43	**31**
8	CIA HERING	42	46	39	30	33	25	40	**37**
9	COPASA	27	23	32	45	14	8	18	**22**
10	CYRELA	33	34	13	10	10	5	20	**20**
11	DURATEX	42	32	65	80	33	12	32	**38**
12	ECORODOVIAS	30	30	9	10	14	2	25	**18**
13	ELETROPAULO	27	35	32	20	29	15	32	**28**
14	ENERGIAS BR	55	29	51	80	0	5	22	**31**
15	ENEVA	27	29	9	10	19	0	17	**16**
16	ESTACIO	58	32	43	25	19	13	37	**32**
17	EVEN	42	45	23	35	19	20	27	**31**
18	EZTEC	24	29	13	10	19	0	27	**18**
19	HRT PETROLEO	09	33	9	10	10	7	22	**20**
20	HYPERMARCAS	55	31	31	30	14	10	23	**27**
21	IGUATEMI	42	36	13	15	19	22	27	**26**
22	JBS	52	22	40	65	0	5	25	**26**
23	KROTON	61	45	34	15	29	37	43	**40**
24	LIGHT	45	36	17	30	10	12	15	**24**
25	LOCALIZA	42	45	27	15	33	2	38	**29**
26	LOJAS AMERI-CANAS	36	34	35	30	19	2	23	**25**
27	LOJAS RENNER	48	32	45	5	24	17	32	**30**
28	M DIASBRANCO	48	34	26	10	10	3	18	**23**
29	MARCOPOLO	30	34	19	10	10	18	18	**23**
30	MARFRIG	48	37	24	40	24	27	38	**34**
31	MILLS ON	33	29	8	5	29	8	28	**20**
32	MINERVA	55	31	16	10	19	5	40	**25**
33	MMX MINER	33	28	7	20	24	0	25	**18**

34	MRV	39	35	15	20	24	0	30	23
35	MULTIPLAN	27	24	7	5	5	0	17	13
36	MULTIPLUS	33	19	6	10	5	0	20	13
37	NATURA	52	7	60	80	19	3	20	27
38	ODONTOPREV	30	26	7	5	24	5	25	17
39	PDG REALTY	30	32	19	0	29	10	38	23
40	PRUMO	21	22	13	10	10	2	20	14
41	QGEP	42	32	15	15	19	17	30	25
42	RAIA DROGASIL	58	51	32	15	38	10	33	35
43	RANDON	55	40	32	10	10	25	32	32
44	SMILES	39	16	19	20	14	0	27	17
45	SOUZA CRUZ	42	19	30	50	19	0	23	22
46	SUZANO PAPEL	48	34	13	20	29	12	30	26
47	TAESA	27	19	8	5	24	0	33	15
48	TOTVS	55	35	31	5	38	28	35	33
49	TRACTEBEL	39	31	14	25	14	0	20	20
50	WEG	39	27	28	70	0	10	17	25

Table A-4: Results of disclosure index study for South African sample

		FRQ (in % of maximum full disclosure index score)							
No.	Company	Background information	Financials	Non-financials	Sustain-ability	Value based mgmt.	Forward-looking information	Risks and opportuni-ties	Total
1	ADCOCK INGRAM	64	39	52	95	33	13	42	42
2	AECI	48	36	19	85	33	5	35	32
3	AFN.RAINBOW	48	38	25	85	48	13	58	38
4	ASPEN	70	40	51	80	33	10	28	40
5	ASSORE	48	23	7	50	33	5	35	24
6	AVENG	64	34	17	60	48	12	28	32
7	AVI	48	36	32	70	29	7	30	32
8	BIDVEST GROUP	39	37	23	60	19	10	20	28
9	CLICKS GROUP	58	29	32	45	33	23	13	31
10	EXXARO RESOURCES	48	25	25	95	29	10	20	29
11	FAMOUS BRANDS	58	42	41	30	24	7	23	32
12	GRINDROD	39	37	18	85	29	8	42	32
13	ILLOVO SUGAR	48	29	22	75	33	7	23	28

14	IMPALA PLATINUM	61	43	34	75	33	17	45	**40**
15	INVICTA	45	38	20	25	19	10	28	**27**
16	KUMBA IRON ORE	42	33	33	65	48	18	55	**37**
17	LIFE HEALTHCARE	76	42	50	60	57	18	47	**45**
18	MASSMART	36	30	20	65	29	2	20	**25**
19	MEDICLINIC	48	27	18	55	52	5	28	**27**
20	MONDI	58	33	32	75	43	15	25	**35**
21	MR PRICE GROUP	55	32	48	60	29	17	32	**35**
22	MTN GROUP	64	34	38	50	48	3	17	**32**
23	MURRAY & ROBERTS	48	32	16	75	38	12	28	**30**
24	NAMPAK	55	33	20	65	43	7	37	**31**
25	NASPERS	58	38	52	75	29	12	53	**41**
26	NETCARE	42	33	27	50	38	20	15	**30**
27	NORTHAM PLATINUM	42	38	27	80	43	2	40	**33**
28	OCEANA GROUP	33	23	14	60	29	7	27	**23**
29	OMNIA	55	37	20	80	33	28	20	**36**
30	PICK N PAY STORES	55	41	23	75	24	2	15	**30**
31	PIONEER FOOD GROUP	64	36	25	70	24	7	38	**33**
32	PPC	55	44	36	80	57	33	42	**45**
33	RCL FOODS	52	33	16	50	10	0	27	**27**
34	REMGRO	36	32	25	40	29	5	25	**25**
35	REUNERT	36	30	20	55	43	18	27	**29**
36	ROYAL BAFO-KENG PLATINUM	45	31	19	85	24	18	23	**31**
37	SAPPI	58	44	32	60	62	18	25	**39**
38	SPAR GROUP	55	29	27	70	33	17	23	**32**
39	STEINHOFF	48	36	15	50	29	7	28	**28**
40	SUN INTL.	39	31	25	60	43	18	0	**28**
41	TELKOM SA	67	38	49	75	43	30	52	**46**
42	THE FOSCHINI GROUP	42	31	39	55	43	12	17	**30**
43	TIGER BRANDS	58	42	39	65	24	22	23	**37**
44	TONGAAT-HULETT	45	26	11	75	33	13	5	**25**
45	TRENCOR	27	29	16	35	24	2	13	**19**
46	TRUWORTHS	70	42	39	75	43	33	33	**44**

47	TSOGO SUN	27	27	27	45	33	3	28	**24**
48	VODACOM	33	31	35	50	71	5	15	**29**
49	WILSON BAYLY HOLMES-OVCON	30	29	7	30	43	3	35	**22**
50	WOOLWORTHS	39	31	32	65	43	15	12	**30**

Table A-5: Results of disclosure index study for German sample

		FRQ (in % of maximum full disclosure index score)							
No.	Company	Background information	Financials	Non-financials	Sustain-ability	Value based mgmt.	Forward-looking information	Risks and opportuni-ties	Total
1	ADIDAS	64	64	66	65	57	67	75	**66**
2	AXEL SPRINGER	67	43	25	45	24	30	43	**39**
3	BASF	79	61	61	85	95	52	90	**68**
4	BAYER	70	68	65	85	81	53	73	**67**
5	BEIERSDORF	58	56	42	50	52	25	37	**45**
6	BILFINGER BERGER	73	68	43	40	71	63	58	**61**
7	BMW	58	62	47	50	67	33	80	**54**
8	BRENNTAG	48	47	22	30	48	23	48	**37**
9	CELESIO	64	51	32	30	67	32	62	**46**
10	CONTINENTAL	70	62	36	50	67	33	57	**52**
11	DAIMLER	70	67	66	60	76	47	65	**63**
12	DEUTSCHE LUFTHANSA	61	68	50	60	81	50	70	**61**
13	DEUTSCHE POST	73	64	57	50	62	38	60	**57**
14	DEUTSCHE TELEKOM	76	69	58	60	43	68	77	**66**
15	DEUTSCHE WOHNEN	55	43	23	30	19	20	35	**33**
16	DRAEGERWERK	33	52	47	45	48	52	62	**49**
17	E ON	42	51	36	55	76	45	70	**51**
18	EVONIK INDUSTRIES	58	55	36	65	90	47	57	**54**
19	FIELMANN	45	32	27	25	0	22	43	**29**
20	FRAPORT	61	53	36	25	52	45	77	**50**
21	FRESENIUS	61	55	35	40	43	55	62	**51**
22	FUCHS PETROLUB	45	49	27	45	67	28	38	**41**
23	GEA GROUP	45	57	39	40	48	15	63	**43**
24	HEIDELBERG-CEMENT	55	63	50	70	48	43	80	**57**

25	HENKEL	64	60	48	70	81	45	68	**59**
26	HOCHTIEF	76	60	47	55	52	20	60	**51**
27	HUGO BOSS	61	62	43	45	29	53	77	**55**
28	INFINEON	67	55	64	70	38	48	45	**55**
29	K+S	79	56	36	75	57	48	68	**57**
30	KABEL DEUTSCHLAND	42	37	24	15	33	27	45	**32**
31	LANXESS	52	51	52	80	38	23	63	**48**
32	LINDE	64	54	55	75	52	45	78	**57**
33	MAN	48	52	42	50	48	37	58	**47**
34	MERCK	52	42	38	65	52	37	72	**47**
35	METRO	52	56	53	75	67	23	67	**51**
36	MTU AERO ENGINES	58	46	50	45	43	32	65	**47**
37	OSRAM LICHT	61	49	31	45	38	42	55	**45**
38	PROSIEBEN SAT 1	82	55	60	35	38	45	75	**56**
39	RHOEN-KLINIKUM	58	38	25	35	10	17	27	**30**
40	RWE	55	45	26	45	48	38	58	**44**
41	SIEMENS	52	62	57	75	62	37	67	**56**
42	SKY DEUTSCHLAND	70	42	18	15	24	13	52	**33**
43	SUEDZUCKER	70	52	36	30	10	37	55	**44**
44	SYMRISE	58	41	27	35	33	28	52	**38**
45	TELEFONICA DTL.	55	44	36	45	14	18	52	**37**
46	THYSSENKRUPP	48	53	27	45	81	17	55	**43**
47	TUI	42	49	25	60	52	37	56	**44**
48	UNITED INTERNET	52	45	27	35	19	30	53	**38**
49	VOLKSWAGEN	79	56	68	80	48	48	60	**60**
50	WACKER CHEMIE	64	49	60	70	29	62	70	**57**

Table A-6: Statistics of modified-Jones model regression estimates

	Total	BRA	RSA	GER
Number of observations	949	289	221	439
Mean adj. R^2	5.37%	39.52%	14.19%	6.27%
Discretionary accruals:				
Minimum	-54.6	-78.8	-21.1	-46.0
25% pctl.	-3.7	-3.0	-2.9	-3.7
Mean	0.0	0.0	0.0	0.0
Median	0.7	0.7	0.2	0.4
75% pctl.	4.4	5.1	3.7	4.0
Maximum	47.9	41.3	16.2	49.9
Standard deviation	10.2	12.3	5.8	10.0
The table presents the statistics of the discretionary accruals regression estimates (universe sample).				

Table A-7: Earnings management (signed discretionary accruals)

	Signed discretionary accruals						
Sample	**Min.**	**25% pctl.**	**Median**	**Mean**	**75% pctl.**	**Max.**	**Std. Dev.**
Total (n=150)	-33.4	-2.0	1.0	0.7	3.5	28.1	6.8
Brazil (n=50)	-33.4	-3.9	0.4	-0.3	2.4	28.1	8.5
South Africa (n=50)	-13.7	-1.5	2.1	2.1	4.5	14.1	5.8
Germany (n=50)	-18.9	-1.8	0.3	0.4	2.6	19.4	5.6
Kruskal-Wallis test: p = 0.098							

Table A-8: Correlation analysis of company size (market capitalization) and FRQ (sub) scores

	Predicted sign	Company size (full sample)	Company size (Brazil)	Company size (South Africa)	Company size (Germany)
FRQ_full (total score)	**(+)**	**0.570 *** (0.000)**	**0.084 (0.564)**	**0.199 (0.166)**	**0.593 *** (0.000)**
FRQ_full (background)	(+)	0.458 *** (0.000)	0.236 * (0.099)	0.124 (0.391)	0.290 ** (0.041)
FRQ_full (financials)	(+)	0.514 *** (0.000)	-0.123 (0.395)	0.116 (0.421)	0.594 *** (0.000)
FRQ_full (non-financials)	(+)	0.542 *** (0.000)	0.248 * (0.083)	0.416 *** (0.003)	0.528 *** (0.000)
FRQ_full (sustainability)	(+)	0.278 *** (0.000)	0.267 * (0.061)	0.007 (0.960)	0.527 *** (0.000)
FRQ_full (value based)	(+)	0.450 *** (0.000)	0.016 (0.913)	0.175 (0.223)	0.486 *** (0.000)
FRQ_full (forward-looking)	(+)	0.440 *** (0.000)	-0.197 (0.170)	-0.040 (0.783)	0.360 ** (0.010)
FRQ_full (risks)	(+)	0.511 *** (0.000)	-0.167 (0.246)	0.096 (0.509)	0.471 *** (0.001)
N		150	50	50	50

The table presents the Spearman correlation coefficients between the full disclosure index FRQ score (FRQ_FULL) in each sub sample and the corresponding company size (measured by market capitalization) with p-values in parentheses. *, ** and *** denote significance at the 10%, 5% and 1% level (two-tailed).

Table A-9: Regression results for determinants of FRQ (adjusted for outliers)

Variables	Predicted sign	FRQ_FULL (Total score)	FRQ_VOL (Total score)
Country_BRA	(-)	-9.630 *** (-4.211)	-11.228 *** (-4.80)
Country_RSA	(-)	-5.994 *** (-2.661)	-3.879 ** (-1.683)
Company size	(+)	0.932 ** (2.181)	0.923 ** (2.105)
Company age	(+)	0.029 ** (2.162)	0.028 ** (1.996)
Profitability	(+)	0.001 (0.055)	0.004 (0.344)
Company valuation	(-)	-0.234 * (-1.936)	-0.244 ** (-1.971)
Systematic risk	(+)	1.929 * (1.575)	1.626 * (1.295)
Ownership concentration	(-)	-12.880 *** (-3.915)	-11.183 *** (-3.372)
Customer basis		-0.334 (-0.273)	0.061 (0.048)
Media coverage		0.385 (1.294)	0.533 * (1.743)
Analyst following		0.491 *** (4.556)	0.472 *** (4.280)
Consumer		-5.923 (-1.629)	-6.086 (-1.631)
Manufacturing		-6.609 * (-1.932)	-6.170 * (-1.766)
Energy and mining		-9.426 ** (-2.615)	-9.834 *** (-2.658)
Telecommunication and media		-4.079 (-1.005)	-4.596 (-1.103)
Wholesale and retail		-5.294 (-1.430)	-5.645 (-1.488)
Healthcare		-6.272 (-1.595)	-6.371 (-1.580)
Real estate		-11.340 *** (-2.984)	-11.314 *** (-2.901)
Transportation		-7.108 * (-1.897)	-7.944 ** (-2.065)
Construction		-4.652 (-1.131)	-7.050 (-1.589)
Constant		23.563 *** (3.253)	19.239 ** (2.586)
N		137	137
Adj. R^2		81.29 %	81.62 %
F-stat		30.54 ***	31.19 ***
Maximum VIF		9.53	9.62

The table presents the results of the outlier adjusted (Cook's distance method) OLS regressions conducted for the determinants model. As measures for financial reporting quality the regression models use the full (FRQ_FULL) and voluntary (FRQ_VOL) disclosure index scores. *, ** and *** denote significance at the 10%, 5% and 1% level (one-tailed for coefficients with predicted signs and two-tailed otherwise).

Index of laws, standards and regulations

BBSEE	Broad-Based Socio-Economic Empowerment Charter for the South African Mining Industry, as issued by the Department Mineral Resources of the Republic of South Africa, amended September 2010.
Companies Act No. 71	Companies Act No. 71 of 2008, Republic of South Africa, as amended by Companies Amendment Act 3 of 2011, effective from 1 May 2011, Pretoria and Regulations to the Companies Act No. 71 of 2008, Regulation Gazette No. 9526.
CVM No. 296	CVM Instruction No. 296 of 18 December, 1998.
CVM No. 358	CVM Instruction No. 358 of 3 January, 2002.
CVM No. 457	CVM Instruction No. 457 of 13 July, 2007.
CVM No. 480	CVM Instruction No. 480 of 7 December, 2009.
DCGK	German Corporate Governance Code, Government Commission, as amended on 5 May, 2015.
Directive 2014/95/EU	Directive of the the European Parliament and of the Council of 22 October, 2014 amending Directive 2013/34/EU, in Official Journal of the European Union No. L 330 of 15 November, 2014, p. 1-9.
EC No. 1606/2002	Regulation (EC) No 1606/2002 of the European Parliament and of the Council of 19 July, 2002 on the application of international accounting standards, in Official Journal of the European Union No. L 243 of 11 September, 2002, p. 1-4.
FWB (2015)	Exchange Rules for the Frankfurter Wertpapierbörse (FWB) of 3 December, 2015.
GAS 20	German Accounting Standard (GAS) No. 20 "Group Management Report", adopted by the Accounting Standards Committee of Germany on 2 November 2012, published by the Federal Ministry of Justice on 4 December, 2012.
HGB	Handelsgesetzbuch (German Commercial Code), 58th edition, 2015.
IAS 1	International Accounting Standard (IAS) 1 "Presentation of Financial Statements", IASB, London (2014).
IAS 16	International Accounting Standard (IAS) 16 "Property, Plant and Equipment", IASB, London (2014).
IAS 33	International Accounting Standard (IAS) 33 "Earnings Per Share", IASB, London (2003).

IAS 38	International Accounting Standard (IAS) 38 “Intangible Assets”, IASB, London (2014).
IASB (2010a)	The Conceptual Framework for Financial Reporting, London (2010).
IASB (2010b)	IFRS Practice Statement Management Commentary – A Framework for Presentation, London (2010).
IIRC (2013)	The International <IR> Framework, issued by the International Integrated Reporting Council (IIRC), 2013, available at: http://integratedreporting.org/, last revised 09/03/2016.
JSE (2015)	JSE Listing Requirements, Johannesburg (2015).
King Code	King Code of Governance for South Africa 2009, The Institute of Directors in Southern Africa and the King Committee on governance, Johannesburg (2009).
Law 4595/64	Brazilian Law 4595 of 12 December, 1964 – National Financial System.
Mineral Act 2002	Mineral and Petroleum Resources Development Act 2002, as issued by the Republic of South Africa.
Securities Trading Act	German Securities Trading Act as published in the announcement of 9 September, 1998 (Federal Law Gazette I, p. 2708), last amended by Article 3 G of the Act of 10 May, 2016 (Federal Law Gazette I, p. 1142, 1148).

References

A

Abd-Elsalam, O. H./Weetman, P. (2003): Introducing international accounting standards to an emerging capital market: relative familiarity and language effect in Egypt, in: Journal of International Accounting, Auditing and Taxation, 12 (1), p. 63-84.

AbuGhazaleh, N. M./Qasim, A./Roberts, C. (2012): The determinants of web-based investor relations activities by companies operating in emerging economies: the case of Jordan, in: The Journal of Applied Business Research, 28 (2), p. 209-226.

Acharya, A. (2014): Constructing a Security Community in Southeast Asia: ASEAN and the Problem of Regional Order, 3rd edition, Abingdon (2014).

Ackermann, F./Eden, C. (2011): Strategic Management of Stakeholders: Theory and Practice, in: Long Range Planning, 44 (3), p. 179-196.

Adams, J./Pendlebury, D./Stembridge, B. (2013): Building bricks – Exploring the global research and innovation impact of Brazil, Russia, India, China and South Korea (2013), available at: http://sciencewatch.com, last revised 09/03/2016.

Adhikari, A./Wang, S. Z. (1995): Accounting for China, in: Management Accounting, 76(10), p. 27-33.

Ahmed, K./Courtis, J. K. (1999): Associations between corporate characteristics and disclosure levels in annual reports: a meta-analysis, in: The British Accounting Review, 31 (1), p. 35-61.

Ahmed, K./Nicholls, D. (1994): The Impact of Non-financial Company Characteristics on Mandatory Disclosure Compliance in Developing Countries: The Case of Bangladesh, in: The International Journal of Accounting, 29, p. 62-77.

AICPA (ed.) (1994): Improving Business Reporting – A Customer Focus, available at: http://www.aicpa.org, last revised 09/03/2016.

Ajinkya, B./Bhojraj, S./Sengupta, P. (2005): The Association between Outside Directors, Institutional Investors and the Properties of Management Earnings Forecasts, in: Journal of Accounting Research, 43 (3), p. 343-376.

Akerlof, G. A. (1970): The Market for "Lemons": Quality Uncertainty and the Market Mechanism, in: The Quarterly Journal of Economics, 84 (3), p. 488-500.

Akisik, O. (2011): The Efficient Management of Shareholder Value and Stakeholder Theory: An Analysis of Emerging Market Economies, in: Devi, S. S./Hooper, K. (eds.): Accounting in Asia – Research in Emerging Economies, Volume 11, Bingley (2011), p. 155-182.

Al Mamun, A./Rafique Yasser, Q./Ashikur Rahman, M. (2013): A Discussion of the Suitability of Only One vs More than One Theory for Depicting Corporate Governance, in: Modern Economy, 4 (1), p. 37-48.

Albu, N./Albu, C. N./Gîrbină, M. M. (2012): Educating accounting students in an emerging economy – An analysis of the importance of stereotypes in teaching IFRS, in: International Journal of Academic Research, 4 (3), p. 51-57.

Ali, A./Hwang, L.-S. (2000): Country-specific factors related to financial reporting and the value relevance of accounting data, in: Journal of Accounting Research, 38 (1), p. 1-21.

Ali, M. J./Ahmed, K./Henry, D. (2004): Disclosure compliance with national accounting standards by listed companies in South Asia, in: Accounting and Business Research, 34 (3), p. 183-199.

Al-Najjar, B./Abed, S. (2014): The association between disclosure of forward-looking information and corporate governance mechanisms – Evidence from the UK before the financial crisis period, in: Managerial Auditing Journal, 29 (7), p. 578-595.

Alon, I./Lattemann, C./Fetscherin, M./Li, S./Schneider, A.-M. (2010): Usage of public corporate communications of social responsibility in Brazil, Russia, India and China (BRIC), in: International Journal of Emerging Markets, 5 (1), p. 6-22.

Amihud, Y. (2002): Illiquidity and stock returns: cross-section and time-series effects, in: Journal of Financial Markets, 5 (1), p. 31-56.

Anderson, C. W. (1999): Financial contracting under extreme uncertainty: an analysis of Brazilian corporate debentures, in: Journal of Financial Economics, 51 (1), p. 45-84.

Ashforth, B. E./Gibbs, B. W. (1990): The double-edge of organizational legitimation, in: Organization science, 1 (2), p. 177-194.

Atteslander, P. (2010): Methoden der empirischen Sozialforschung, 13th edition, Berlin (2010).

Auer, B./Rottmann, H. (2015): Statistik und Ökonometrie für Wirtschaftswissenschaftler – Eine anwendungsorientierte Einführung, 3rd edition, Wiesbaden (2015).

Aveng (ed.) (2014): Integrated Report 2014, Johannesburg (2014).

B

Backhaus, K./Erichson, B./Plinke, W./Weiber, R. (2016): Multivariate Analysemethoden – Eine anwendungsorientierte Einführung, 14th edition, Berlin (2016).

Baetge, J./Glaum, M./Grothe, A./Oberdörster, T. (2010): Lohnt sich „gute Berichterstattung" am Kapitalmarkt? – Die Qualität der Konzernanhänge und -lageberichte deutscher Unternehmen und Gewinnschätzungen von Analysten, in: Zeitschrift für Betriebswirtschaft, 80 (3), p. 65-104.

Baetge, J./Kirchhoff, K. R. (1997): Der Geschäftsbericht – Die Visitenkarte des Unternehmens – Bedeutung, Inhalt, Sprache, Design, Servicefunktion, Praxisbeispiele, Wien (1997).

Baetge, J./Kirsch, H.-J./Thiele, S. (2014): Bilanzen, 13th edition, Düsseldorf (2014).

Baetge, J./May, M./Oberdörster, T. (2012): Der Geschäftsbericht – alles andere als die Visitenkarte des Unternehmens, in: Everling, O./Schaub, P./Stephan, R. (eds.): Transparenzrating. Wege zur effizienten Analyse und Bewertung der Rechnungslegung von Unternehmen, Wiesbaden (2012), p. 59-73.

Baird, J. E./Zelin, R. C. (2000): The effects of information ordering on in-vestor perceptions: An experiment utilizing presidents' letters, in: Journal of Fi-nancial and strategic Decisions, 13 (3), p. 71–80.

Balakrishnan, K./Billings, M. B./Kelly, B./Ljungqvist, A. (2014): Shaping liquidity: On the causal effects of voluntary disclosure, in: The Journal of Finance, 69 (5), p. 2237-2278.

Balata, P./Breton, G. (2005): Narratives vs numbers in the annual report: are they giving the same message to the investors?, in: Review of Accounting and Finance, 4 (2), p. 5-25.

Ball, R./Brown, P. (1968): An empirical evaluation of accounting income numbers, in: Journal of Accounting Research, 6 (2), p. 159-178.

Ball, R./Kothari, S. P./Robin, A. (2000): The effect of international institutional factors on properties of accounting earnings, in: Journal of Accounting and Economics, 29 (1), p. 1-51.

Ball, R./Robin, A./Wu, J. S. (2003): Incentives versus standards: properties of accounting income in four East Asian countries, in: Journal of Accounting and Economics, 36 (1), p. 235-270.

Ball, R./Shivakumar, L. (2005): Earnings quality in UK private firms: comparative loss recognition timeliness, in: Journal of Accounting and Economics, 39 (1), p. 83-128.

Barley, S. R./Tolbert, P. S. (1997): Institutionalization and Structuration: Studying the Links between Action and Institution, in: Organization Studies, 18 (1), p. 93-117.

Barrett, M. E. (1976): Financial Reporting Practices: Disclosure and Comprehensiveness in an International Setting, in: Journal of Accounting Research, 14 (1), p. 10.

Barry, C. B./Brown, S. J. (1985): Differential information and security market equilibrium, in: Journal of Financial and Quantitative Analysis, 20 (04), p. 407-422.

Barth, D. (2009): Prognoseberichterstattung. Praxis, Determinanten und Kapitalmarktwirkungen bei deutschen börsennotierten Unternehmen, Frankfurt am Main (2009).

Barth, M. E./Landsman, W. R./Lang, M. H. (2008): International accounting standards and accounting quality, in: Journal of Accounting Research, 46 (3), p. 467–498.

Bartlett, S. A./Chandler, R. A. (1997): The corporate report and the private shareholder: Lee and Tweedie twenty years on, in: The British Accounting Review, 29 (3), p. 245–261.

Basu, S. (1997): The conservatism principle and the asymmetric timeliness of earnings, in: Journal of Accounting and Economics, 24 (1), p. 3–37.

Be One South Africa (ed.) (2015): Why B-BBEE?, available at: http://bee.b1sa.co.za, last revised 09/03/2016.

Beattie, V./McInnes, B./Fearnley, S. (2004): A methodology for analysing and evaluating narratives in annual reports: a comprehensive descriptive profile and metrics for disclosure quality attributes, in: Accounting Forum, 28 (3), p. 205–236.

Beattie, V./Thomson, S. J. (2007): Lifting the lid on the use of content analysis to investigate intellectual capital disclosures, in: Accounting Forum, 31 (2), p. 129-163.

Beaver, W. H./McNichols, M. F./Nelson, K. K. (2007): An Alternative Interpretation of the Discontinuity in Earnings Distributions, in: Review of Accounting Studies, 12 (4), p. 525-556.

Becker, A./Messner, M. (2005): After the Scandals: A German-Speaking Perspective on Management Accounting Research and Education, in: European Accounting Review, 14 (2), p. 417–427.

Becker, C. (2012): Einfluss der räumlichen Markenherkunft auf das Markenimage – Kausalanalytische Untersuchung am Beispiel Indiens, Wiesbaden (2012).

Bekaert, G./Harvey, C. R. (2002): Research in emerging markets finance: looking to the future, in: Emerging Markets Review, 3 (4), p. 429-448.

Bekaert, G./Harvey, C. R./Lundblad, C. (2007): Liquidity and Expected Returns: Lessons from Emerging Markets, in: The Review of Financial Studies, 20 (6), p. 1783-1831.

Benham, A./Benham, L. (1998): Property rights in transition economies: A commentary on what economists know, in: Transforming Post-Communist Political Economies, p. 35-60.

Berelson, B. (1971): Content Analysis in Communication Research, New York (1971).

Beretta, S./Bozzolan, S. (2004): A framework for the analysis of firm risk communication, in: The International Journal of Accounting, 39 (3), p. 265-288.

Beretta, S./Bozzolan, S. (2008): Quality versus Quantity: The Case of Forward-Looking Disclosure, in: Journal of Accounting, Auditing & Finance, 23 (3), p. 333–375.

Bertrand, M./Mullainathan, S. (2000): Do CEOs set their own pay? The ones without principals do (Working paper), available at: http://www.nber.org, last revised 09/03/2016.

Beyer, A./Cohen, D. A./Lys, T. Z./Walther, B. R. (2010): The financial reporting environment: Review of the recent literature, in: Journal of Accounting and Economics, 50 (2), p. 296-343.

Bhattacharya, N./Ecker, F./Olsson, P. M./Schipper, K. (2012): Direct and mediated associations among earnings quality, information asymmetry, and the cost of equity, in: The Accounting Review, 87 (2), p. 449-482.

Bhattacharya, U./Daouk, H. (2002): The world price of insider trading, in: The Journal of Finance, 57 (1), p. 75-108.

Bhattacharya, U./Daouk, H./Welker, M. (2003): The world price of earnings opacity, in: The Accounting Review, 78 (3), p. 641-678.

Bhattacharyya, A. K./Raychaudhuri, A./Rao, S. V. (2005): Economic Consequences of 'Regulation on Corporate Governance': Evidence from India, available at: http://papers.ssrn.com, last revised 09/03/2016.

Bhimani, A. (2005): International comparative management accounting, in: Garrett, I./Cooper, C. L./Argyris, C./Starbuck, W. H. (eds.): The Blackwell encyclopedia of management, Malden (2005), p. 250-255.

Biddle, G. C./Hilary, G./Verdi, R. S. (2009): How does financial reporting quality relate to investment efficiency?, in: Journal of Accounting and Economics, 48 (2), p. 112-131.

Bieling, H.-J. (2014): Die BRIC(S) in der globalen politischen Ökonomie: Weltordnungspolitische Perspektiven der Europäischen Union, in: Nölke, A./May, C./Claar, S. (eds.): Die großen Schwellenländer. Ursachen und Folgen ihres Aufstiegs in der Weltwirtschaft, Wiesbaden (2014), p. 377-394.

BILANZ (ed.) (2015): Das ist „der beste Geschäftsbericht" 2015, available at: http://www.bilanz-magazin.de, last revised 09/03/2016.

Bird, A. (1998): Philosophy of science, London (1998).

Blaesing, D. (2013): Nachhaltigkeitsberichterstattung in Deutschland und den USA – Berichtspraxis, Determinanten und Eigenkapitalkostenwirkungen, Frankfurt am Main (2013).

Blanchard, O. J./Leigh, D. (2013): Growth Forecast Errors and Fiscal Multipliers. Edited by IMF, available at: https://www.imf.org, last revised 09/03/2016.

BM&FBOVESPA (ed.) (2014): Brazil 100 Index (IBrX 100) Methodology, available at: http://www.bmfbovespa.com.br, last revised 09/03/2016.

BM&FBOVESPA (ed.) (2015): Indices, available at: http://www.bmfbovespa.com.br, last revised 09/03/2016.

Bodnar, G. M./Gebhardt, G. (1999): Derivatives Usage in Risk Management by US and German Non-Financial Firms: A Comparative Survey, in: Journal of International Financial Management & Accounting, 10 (3), p. 153-187.

Bokpin, G. A. (2013): Determinants and value relevance of corporate disclosure: Evidence from the emerging capital market of Ghana, in: Journal of Applied Accounting Research, 14 (2), p. 127-146.

Borker, D. R. (2012): Accounting, culture, and emerging economies: IFRS in the BRIC countries, in: Journal of Business & Economics Research (JBER), 10 (5), p. 313-324.

Borker, D. R. (2013): Accounting And Cultural Values: IFRS In 3G Economies, in: International Business & Economics Research Journal (IBER), 12 (6), p. 671-686.

Bösch, M. (2013): Finanzwirtschaft: Investition, Finanzierung, Finanzmärkte und Steuerung, 2nd edition, München (2013).

Botosan, C. A. (1997): Disclosure Level and the Cost of Equity Capital, in: The Accounting Review, 72 (3), p. 323-349.

Botosan, C. A. (2004): Discussion of a framework for the analysis of firm risk communication, in: The International Journal of Accounting, 39 (3), p. 289-295.

Botosan, C. A. (2006): Disclosure and the cost of capital: what do we know?, in: Accounting and Business Research, 36 (Supplement), p. 31-40.

Botosan, C. A./Plumlee, M. A. (2002): A Re-Examination of Disclosure Level and the Expected Cost of Equity Capital, in: Journal of Accounting Research, 40 (1), p. 21-40.

Bowen, R. M./Rajgopal, S./Venkatachalam, M. (2008): Accounting Discretion, Corporate Governance, and Firm Performance, in: Contemporary Accounting Research, 25 (2), p. 351-405.

Brose, P. (1984): Konzeption, Varianten und Perspektiven der Kontingenztheorie, in: Journal für Betriebswirtschaft, 34 (5), p. 230-243.

Brosius, F. (2011): SPSS 19, Heidelberg (2011).

Brown, P./Preiato, J./Tarca, A. (2014): Measuring Country Differences in Enforcement of Accounting Standards: An Audit and Enforcement Proxy, in: Journal of Business Finance & Accounting, 41 (1/2), p. 1–52.

Burgstahler, D./Dichev, I. (1997): Earnings management to avoid earnings decreases and losses, in: Journal of Accounting and Economics, 24 (1), p. 99-126.

Bushman, R. M./Piotroski, J. D./Smith, A. J. (2011): Capital allocation and timely accounting recognition of economic losses, in: Journal of Business Finance & Accounting, 38 (1-2), p. 1-33.

Bushman, R. M./Smith, A. J. (2001): Financial accounting information and corporate governance, in: Journal of Accounting and Economics, 32 (1), p. 237-333.

Bushman, R. M./Smith, A. J. (2003): Transparency, financial accounting information, and corporate governance, in: Financial Accounting Information, and Corporate Governance. Economic Policy Review, 9 (1), p. 65-87.

Buzby, S. L. (1974): Selected items of information and their disclosure in annual reports, in: Accounting Review, 49 (3), p. 423-435.

Buzby, S. L. (1975): Company Size, Listed Versus Unlisted Stocks, and the Extent of Financial Disclosure, in: Journal of Accounting Research, 13 (1), p. 16.

C

Cahan, S. F. (2014): Earnings management and auditing, in: Hay, D./Knechel, W. R./Willekens, M. (eds.): The Routledge Companion to Auditing, Abingdon (2014), p. 119-129.

Cahan, S. F./Rahman, A./Perera, H. (2005): Global Diversification and Corporate Disclosure, in: Journal of International Accounting Research, 4 (1), p. 73-93.

Capaul, C./Rowley, I./Sharpe, W. F. (1993): International Value and Growth Stock Returns, in: Financial Analysts Journal, 49 (1), p. 27-36.

Carlisle, H. M. (1973): Situational management: a contingency approach to leadership, New York (1973).

Carvalho, L. N./Salotti, B. M. (2013): Adoption of IFRS in Brazil and the Consequences to Accounting Education, in: Issues in Accounting Education, 28 (2), p. 235-242.

Cerf, A. R. (1961): Corporate reporting and investment decisions, Berkeley (1961).

Chambers, R. J. (1993): Positive accounting theory and the PA cult, in: Abacus, 29 (1), p. 1-26.

Chan, M. C./Watson, J./Woodliff, D. (2014): Corporate Governance Quality and CSR Disclosures, in: Journal of Business Ethics, 125 (1), p. 59-73.

Chaney, P. K./Jeter, D. C./Lewis, C. M. (1988): The use of accruals in income smoothing: a permanent earnings hypothesis, in: Advances in Quantitative Analysis of Finance and Accounting, 6, p. 103-135.

Chartered Institute of Management Accountants (CIMA) (ed.) (2010): Sustainability in emerging markets – Lessons from South Africa, available at: http://www.cimaglobal.com, last revised 09/03/2016.

Chartered Secretaries Southern Africa (ed.) (2015): Integrated Reporting Awards, available at: http://www.chartsec.co.za, last revised 09/03/2016.

Chen, F./Hope, O.-K./Li, Q./Wang, X. (2011): Financial reporting quality and investment efficiency of private firms in emerging markets, in: The Accounting Review, 86 (4), p. 1255-1288.

Chen, H./Tang, Q./Jiang, Y./Lin, Z. (2010): The role of international financial reporting standards in accounting quality: Evidence from the European Union, in: Journal of International Financial Management & Accounting, 21 (3), p. 220-278.

Chen, J. J./Cheng, X./Gong, S. X./Tan, Y. (2014): Do higher value firms voluntarily disclose more information? Evidence from China, in: The British Accounting Review, 46 (1), p. 18-32.

Chen, S./Chen, X./Cheng, Q. (2008): Do family firms provide more or less voluntary disclosure?, in: Journal of Accounting Research, 46 (3), p. 499-536.

Chenhall, R. H./Juchau, R. (1977): Investor information needs – an Australian study, in: Accounting and Business Research, 7 (26), p. 111-119.

Child, J. (1981): Culture, contingency and capitalism in the cross-national study of organizations, in: Research in Organizational Behavior, 3 (3), p. 303-356.

Choi, F. D./Meek, G. K. (2011): International accounting, 7th edition, Upper Saddle River (2011).

Christie, A. A./Zimmerman, J. L. (1994): Efficient and Opportunistic Choices of Accounting Procedures: Corporate Control Contests, in: The Accounting Review, 69 (4), p. 539-566.

Christodoulou, D./Sarafidis, V. (2008): The Econometrics of Estimating Unexpected Accruals, available at: http://nzae.katipo.co.nz, last revised 09/03/2016.

Chu, C. I./Chatterjee, B./Brown, A. (2012): The current status of greenhouse gas reporting by Chinese companies – A test of legitimacy theory, in: Managerial Auditing Journal, 28 (2), p. 114–139.

Claar, S. (2014): Handelspolitik als Entwicklungsmotor in Südafrika, in: Nölke, A./May, C./Claar, S. (eds.): Die großen Schwellenländer. Ursachen und Folgen ihres Aufstiegs in der Weltwirtschaft, Wiesbaden (2014), p. 193-208.

Clarkson, M. B. E. (1995): A Stakeholder Framework for Analyzing and Evaluating Corporate Social Performance, in: The Academy of Management Review, 20 (1), p. 92-117.

Cleff, T. (2015): Deskriptive Statistik und moderne Datenanalyse – Eine computergestützte Einführung mit Excel, PASW (SPSS) und STATA, 3rd edition, Wiesbaden (2015).

Coenenberg, A. G./Haller, A. (1993): Externe Rechnungslegung, in: Hauschildt, J./Grün, O. (eds.): Ergebnisse empirischer betriebswirtschaftlicher Forschung: Zu einer Realtheorie der Unternehmung. Festschrift für Eberhard Witte, Stuttgart (1993), p. 557-599.

Coenenberg, A. G./Haller, A./Marten, K.-U. (1999): Accounting education for professionals in Germany – current state and new challenges, in: Journal of Accounting Education, 17 (4), p. 367–390.

Coetzee, S. A./Schmulian, A. (2012): A Critical Analysis of the Pedagogical Approach Employed in an Introductory Course to IFRS, in: Issues in Accounting Education, 27 (1), p. 83–100.

Coetzee, S. A./Schmulian, A. (2013): The Effect of IFRS Adoption on Financial Reporting Pedagogy in South Africa, in: Issues in Accounting Education, 28 (2), p. 243-251.

Cohen, D. A. (2008): Does information risk really matter? An analysis of the determinants and economic consequences of financial reporting quality, in: Asia-Pacific Journal of Accounting & Economics, 15 (2), p. 69-90.

Cohen, J./Krishnamoorthy, G./Wright, A. (2004): The corporate governance mosaic and financial reporting quality, in: Journal of Accounting Literature, 23 (1), p. 87-152.

Cooke, T. E. (1991): An assessment of voluntary disclosure in the annual reports of Japanese corporations, in: The International Journal of Accounting, 26 (3), p. 174-189.

Cooke, T. E./Wallace, R. S. O. (1989): Global surveys of corporate disclosure practices and audit firms: a review essay, in: Accounting and business research, 20 (77), p. 47-57.

Cooke, T. E./Wallace, R. S. O. (1990): Financial disclosure regulation and its environment: A review and further analysis, in: Journal of Accounting and Public Policy, 9 (2), p. 79-110.

Copeland, R. M. (1968): Income Smoothing, in: Journal of Accounting Research, 6, p. 101-116.

Core, J. E./Guay, W. R./Verdi, R. (2008): Is accruals quality a priced risk factor?, in: Journal of Accounting and Economics, 46 (1), p. 2-22.

Corsetti, G./Pesenti, P./Roubini, N. (1999): Paper tigers?: A model of the Asian crisis, in: European Economic Review, 43 (7), p. 1211-1236.

Courtis, J. K. (1995): Readability of annual reports: Western versus Asian evidence, in: Accounting, Auditing & Accountability Journal, 8 (2), p. 4-17.

Courtis, J. K. (1998): Annual report readability variability: tests of the obfuscation hypothesis, in: Accounting, Auditing & Accountability Journal, 11 (4), p. 459-472.

Coy, D./Tower, G./Dixon, K. (1993): Quantifying the quality of tertiary education annual reports, in: Accounting & Finance, 33 (2), p. 121-130.

CVM (ed.) (2015): Regulation of Interest, available at: http://www.cvm.gov.br, last revised 09/03/2016.

D

da Costa, R. T. (1993): Preface., in: Tertuliano, F. A./Pessoa Jr., I./Aguiar, João Francisco de/Ayoub, R./Tracanella, R./Rioli, V. A. (eds.): Full disclosure. Como aperfeiçoar o relacionamento das empresas abertas com o mercado de capitais, São Paulo (1993), p. 11-13.

Dahl, S. (2004): Intercultural Research: The Current State of Knowledge – Middlesex University Discussion Paper No. 26, available at: http://papers.ssrn.com, last revised 09/03/2016.

Dahrendorf, R. (2010): Homo Sociologicus, 17th edition, Wiesbaden (2010).

Dainelli, F./Bini, L./Giunta, F. (2013): Signaling strategies in annual reports: Evidence from the disclosure of performance indicators, in: Advances in Accounting, 29 (2), p. 267-277.

Daske, H./Gebhardt, G. (2006): International financial reporting standards and experts' perceptions of disclosure quality, in: Abacus, 42 (3-4), p. 461-498.

Daske, H./Hail, L./Leuz, C./Verdi, R. (2008): Mandatory IFRS reporting around the world: Early evidence on the economic consequences, in: Journal of Accounting Research, 46 (5), p. 1085-1142.

de Lima, V. S./de Lima, G. A. S. F./de Carvalho, L. N. G./Lima, I. S. (2010): Toward IFRS: Economic Consequences of Accounting Convergence in an Emerging Economy, in: Research in Accounting in Emerging Economies (10), p. 251-295.

Dechow, P./Ge, W./Schrand, C. (2010): Understanding earnings quality: A review of the proxies, their determinants and their consequences, in: Journal of Accounting and Economics, 50 (2), p. 344-401.

Dechow, P. M./Dichev, I. D. (2002): The quality of accruals and earnings: The role of accrual estimation errors, in: The Accounting Review, 77 (Supplement), p. 35-59.

Dechow, P. M./Richardson, S. A./Tuna, I. (2003): Why Are Earnings Kinky? An Examination of the Earnings Management Explanation, in: Review of Accounting Studies, 8 (2-3), p. 355-384.

Dechow, P. M./Sloan, R. G./Sweeney, A. P. (1995): Detecting Earnings Management, in: The Accounting Review, 70 (2), p. 193-225.

Deegan, C. (2000): Financial accounting theory, Sydney (2000).

Deegan, C. (2002): The legitimising effect of social and environmental disclosures – a theoretical foundation, in: Accounting, Auditing & Accountability Journal, 15 (3), p. 282-311.

Deegan, C./Rankin, M./Tobin, J. (2002): An examination of the corporate social and environmental disclosures of BHP from 1983-1997: A test of legitimacy theory, in: Accounting, Auditing & Accountability Journal, 15 (3), p. 312-343.

Deegan, C./Rankin, M./Voght, P. (2000): Firms' disclosure reactions to major social incidents: Australian evidence, in: Accounting Forum, 24 (1), p. 101-130.

Deegan, C. M./Unerman, J. (2011): Financial accounting theory, 2nd European edition, Maidenhead (2011).

Dehejia, R. H./Wahba, S. (2002): Propensity Score-Matching Methods for Nonexperimental Causal Studies, in: Review of Economics and Statistics, 84 (1), p. 151-161.

Deloitte (ed.) (2012): Doing Business in Brazil – New tastes for opportunities in financial industry, available at: https://www2.deloitte.com/, last revised 09/03/2016.

Demski, J. S. (1988): Positive accounting theory: A review, in: Accounting, Organizations and Society, 13 (6), p. 623-629.

Department of Banking and Finance (University of Zurich) (ed.) (2014): Kriterienkatalog: Value Reporting, available at: http://www.bf.uzh.ch, last revised 09/03/2016.

Deutsch-Brasilianische Industrie- und Handelskammer (ed.) (2012): Brasilien Aktuell (Dezember 2012) – Brasilien – Im globalen Rennen um mehr Wettbewerbsfähigkeit, available at: http://www.ahkbrasilien.com.br, last revised 09/03/2016.

Deutsche Börse AG (ed.) (2014): Guide to the Equity Indices of Deutsche Börse AG, available at: http://www.dax-indices.com, last revised 09/03/2016.

Dharan, B. G. (1987): The effect of sales and collection disclosures on cash flow forecasting and income smoothing, in: Contemporary Accounting Research, 3 (2), p. 445-459.

Diamond, D. W./Verrecchia, R. E. (1991): Disclosure, liquidity, and the cost of capital, in: The Journal of Finance, 46 (4), p. 1325-1359.

DiMaggio, P. J./Powell, W. W. (1983): The iron cage revisited: institutional isomorphism and collective rationality in organizational fields, in: American Sociological Review, 48 (2), p. 147-160.

Ding, Y./Jeanjean, T./Stolowy, H. (2005): Why do national GAAP differ from IAS? The role of culture, in: The International Journal of Accounting, 40 (4), p. 325–350.

Dobler, M. (2008): Incentives for risk reporting – A discretionary disclosure and cheap talk approach, in: The International Journal of Accounting, 43 (2), p. 184–206.

Doidge, C./Andrew Karolyi, G./Stulz, R. M. (2007): Why do countries matter so much for corporate governance?, in: Journal of Financial Economics, 86 (1), p. 1-39.

Donaldson, L. (1999): The Normal Science of Structural Contingency Theory, in: Clegg, S. R./Hardy, C. (eds.): Handbook of organization studies. Theory & method, Thousand Oaks, London (1999), p. 51-70.

Donaldson, T./Preston, L. E. (1995): The Stakeholder Theory of the Corporation: Concepts, Evidence, and Implications, in: The Academy of Management Review, 20 (1), p. 65-91.

Doupnik, T. S. (2008): Influence of culture on earnings management: A note, in: Abacus, 44 (3), p. 317-340.

Doupnik, T. S./Salter, S. B. (1995): External environment, culture, and accounting practices: A preliminary test of a general model of international accounting development, in: The International Journal of Accounting, 30 (3), p. 189-207.

Dowling, J./Pfeffer, J. (1975): Organizational Legitimacy: Social Values and Organizational Behavior, in: The Pacific Sociological Review, 18 (1), p. 122-136.

Dugger, W. (1990): The new institutionalism: new but not institutionalist, in: Journal of Economic Issues, p. 423–431.

E

Ecker, F./Francis, J./Kim, I./Olsson, P. M./Schipper, K. (2006): A returns-based representation of earnings quality, in: The Accounting Review, 81 (4), p. 749-780.

Eggertsson, T. (1997): Rethinking the Theory of Economic Policy: Some Implications of the New Institutionalism, in: Nelson, J. M./Tilly, C./Walker, L. (eds.): Transforming post-Communist political economies, Washington (1997), p. 61-79.

Elbannan, M. A. (2011): Accounting and Stock Market Effects of International Accounting Standards Adoption in an Emerging Economy, in: Review of Quantitative Finance and Accounting, 36 (2), p. 207-245.

Elbannan, M. A./Elbannan, M. A. (2014): Corporate Governance and Accounting Performance: A Balanced Scorecard Approach, in: Accounting and Finance Research, 3 (2), p. 60-76.

Elliott, R. K./Jacobson, P. D. (1995): The Jenkins Committee Report: What If They're Right?, in: The Journal of Corporate Accounting and Finance (3), p. 77-86.

Elston, J. A./Goldberg, L. G. (2003): Executive compensation and agency costs in Germany, in: Journal of Banking & Finance, 27 (7), p. 1391-1410.

Encyclopædia Britannica Online (ed.) (2015): Institutionalism, available at: http://www.britannica.com, last revised 09/03/2016.

Epps, R. W./Guthrie, C. P. (2010): Sarbanes-Oxley 404 material weaknesses and discretionary accruals, in: Accounting Forum, 34 (2), p. 67-75.

Epstein, M. J./Palepu, K. G. (1999): What Financial Analysts Want, in: Strategic Finance, 80 (10), p. 48-57.

Erlei, M./Leschke, M./Sauerland, D. (2007): Neue Institutionenökonomik, Stuttgart (2007).

Ernstberger, J./Vogler, O. (2008): Analyzing the German accounting triad — "Accounting Premium" for IAS/IFRS and U.S. GAAP vis-à-vis German GAAP?, in: The International Journal of Accounting, 43 (4), p. 339-386.

Errunza, V. R. (1983): Emerging Markets: A New Opportunity for Improving Global Portfolio Performance, in: Financial Analysts Journal, 39 (5), p. 51-58.

Ertugrul, M./Qiu, J./Wan, C. (2015): Financial report readability, tone ambiguity, and the cost of borrowing, available at: http://papers.ssrn.com, last revised 09/03/2016.

Estrin, S./Prevezer, M. (2011): The role of informal institutions in corporate governance: Brazil, Russia, India, and China compared, in: Asia Pacific Journal of Management, 28 (1), p. 41-67.

Eugster, F. (2014): Endogeneity and the Dynamics of Voluntary Disclosure Quality: Is There Really an Effect on the Cost of Equity Capital? (Working Paper), available at: http://papers.ssrn.com, last revised 09/03/2016.

Ewert, R./Wagenhofer, A. (2014): Interne Unternehmensrechnung, 8th edition, Berlin, Heidelberg (2014).

Ewert, R./Wagenhofer, A. (2011): Earnings Quality Metrics and What They Measure, available at: http://papers.ssrn.com, last revised 09/03/2016.

EY (ed.) (2011): Doing business in Brazil, available at: http://www.ey.com, last revised 09/03/2016.

EY (ed.) (2014): EY's Excellence in Integrated Reporting Awards 2014 – A survey of integrated reports from South Africa's top 100 JSE-listed companies and top 10 state-owned companies, available at: http://www.ey.com, last revised 09/03/2016.

EY (ed.) (2015): EY's Excellence in Integrated Reporting Awards 2015 – A survey of integrated reports of South Africa's top 100 JSE-listed companies, available at: http://www.ey.com, last revised 09/03/2016.

Ezzamel, M./Xiao, J. Z. (2011): Accounting in transitional and emerging market economies, in: European Accounting Review, 20 (4), p. 625-637.

F

Fama, E. F./French, K. R. (1992): The Cross-Section of Expected Stock Returns, in: Journal of Finance, 47 (2), p. 427-465.

Faulkender, M./Petersen, M. A. (2006): Does the source of capital affect capital structure?, in: Review of Financial Studies, 19 (1), p. 45-79.

Ferling, R. L. (1994): Final Jenkins Committee Report Debuts at Symposium, in: Financial Executive, 10 (6), p. 60-61.

Fifield, S. G./Lonie, A. A./Power, D. M. (1998): A Review of Research into Emerging Stock Markets, in: Economic Issues, 3 (1), p. 1-36.

Fifth BRICS Summit (ed.) (2013): About BRICS, available at: http://www.brics5.co.za, last revised 09/03/2016.

Filiz, A. (2013): The company secretary within the corporate governance framework, St. Gallen (2013).

Fink, C./Kajüter, P./Winkeljohann, N. (2013): Lageberichterstattung – HGB, DRS und IFRS Practice Statement Management Commentary, Stuttgart (2013).

Firth, M. (1979): The Impact of Size, Stock Market Listing, and Auditors on Voluntary Disclosure in Corporate Annual Reports, in: Accounting and Business Research, 9 (36), p. 273-280.

Flesch, R. (1948): A new readability yardstick, in: Journal of Applied Psychology, 32 (3), p. 221-233.

Foucault, T./Pagano, M./Röell, A. (2013): Market Liquidity – Theory, evidence, and policy, Oxford (2013).

Francis, J./LaFond, R./Olsson, P. M./Schipper, K. (2005a): The market pricing of accruals quality, in: Journal of Accounting and Economics, 39 (2), p. 295-327.

Francis, J./LaFond, R./Olsson, P. M./Schipper, K. (2004): Costs of equity and earnings attributes, in: The Accounting Review, 79 (4), p. 967-1010.

Francis, J./Nanda, D./Olsson, P. M. (2008): Voluntary Disclosure, Earnings Quality, and Cost of Capital, in: Journal of Accounting Research, 46 (1), p. 53-99.

Francis, J. R./Khurana, I. K./Pereira, R. (2005b): Disclosure incentives and effects on cost of capital around the world, in: The Accounting Review, 80 (4), p. 1125-1162.

Frankel, R./Li, X. (2004): Characteristics of a firm's information environment and the information asymmetry between insiders and outsiders, in: Journal of Accounting and Economics, 37 (2), p. 229-259.

Freeman, R. E. (1984): Strategic Management – A Stakeholder Approach, Boston (1984).

Freeman, R. E./Harrison, J. S./Wicks, A. C./Parmar, B. L./de Colle, S. (2010): Stakeholder theory: The state of the art, Cambridge et al. (2010).

Freiberg, J. (2013): Qualitative Berichtspflichten für alle Unternehmen? – Pro, in: PiR, 9 (2), p. 59.

Fremgen, J. M. (1963): Book Review – Corporate Reporting and Investment Decisions. by Alan Robert Cerf, in: The Journal of Business, 36 (4), p. 465-467.

French, K. R./Fama, E. F. (2010): Detail for 10 Industry Portfolios, available at: http://mba.tuck.dartmouth.edu, last revised 09/03/2016.

Friend, C. (2015): Internet Encyclopedia of Philosophy – Social Contract Theory, available at: http://www.iep.utm.edu, last revised 09/03/2016.

FTSE (ed.) (2015a): FTSE Factsheet 30 November 2015 – FTSE/JSE All-Share Index, available at: http://www.ftse.com/, last revised 09/03/2016.

FTSE (ed.) (2015b): Ground Rules for the FTSE/JSE Africa Index Series, available at: https://www.jse.co.za, last revised 09/03/2016.

Fülbier, R. U. (2004): Wissenschaftstheorie und Betriebswirtschaftslehre, in: Wirtschaftswissenschaftliches Studium, 33 (5), p. 266-271.

Fülbier, R. U. (2005): Wissenschaftstheorie und Betriebswirtschaftslehre, in: Horsch, A./Meinhövel, H./Paul, S. (eds.): Institutionenökonomie und Betriebswirtschaftslehre, München (2005), p. 15-29.

Fülbier, R. U./Klein, M. (2013): Financial Accounting and Reporting in Germany: A Case Study on German Accounting Tradition and Experiences with the IFRS Adoption (Working Paper), available at: http://econstor.eu, last revised 09/03/2016.

Füss, R. (2004): Emerging Markets im internationalen Portfoliomanagement – Entwicklungsstand, Integrationsgrad und Rendite-Risiko-Verhalten von Aktienmärkten in Schwellenländern, Bad Soden (2004).

G

Gande, A. (1997): American Depositary Receipts: Overview and Literature Survey, in: Financial Markets, Institutions & Instruments, 6 (5), p. 61-83.

Gassen, J. (2007): Empirische Rechnungslegungsforschung, in: Köhler, R./Küpper, H.-U./Pfingsten A. (eds.): Handwörterbuch der Betriebswirtschaft, 6th edition, Stuttgart (2007).

Gassen, J. (2014): Causal inference in empirical archival financial accounting research, in: Accounting, Organizations and Society, 39 (7), p. 535-544.

Gazdar, K. (2014): Schönheit oder Substanz? Über die Sinnhaftigkeit von Reporting-Rankings, in: Fifka, M. S. (ed.): CSR und Reporting. Nachhaltigkeits- und CSR-Berichterstattung verstehen und erfolgreich umsetzen, Berlin (2014), p. 125-131.

Giersch, H./Paqué, K.-H./Schmieding, H. (1994): The fading miracle – Four decades of market economy in Germany, Cambridge (1994).

Global Reporting Initiative (ed.) (2013): G4 Sustainability Reporting Guidelines, available at: https://www.globalreporting.org, last revised 09/03/2016.

Glosten, L. R./Milgrom, P. R. (1985): Bid, ask and transaction prices in a specialist market with heterogeneously informed traders, in: Journal of Financial Economics, 14 (1), p. 71-100.

Göbel, E. (2002): Neue Institutionenökonomik – Konzeption und betriebswirtschaftliche Anwendungen, Stuttgart (2002).

Goetzmann, W. N./Jorion, P. (1999): Re-emerging markets, in: Journal of Financial and Quantitative Analysis, 34 (1), p. 1-32.

Goncharov, I. (2005): Earnings Management and Its Determinants: Closing Gaps in Empirical Accounting Research, Frankfurt am Main (2005).

Goyenko, R. Y./Holden, C. W./Trzcinka, C. A. (2009): Do liquidity measures measure liquidity?, in: Journal of financial economics, 92 (2), p. 153-181.

Graham, J. R./Harvey, C. R./Rajgopal, S. (2005): The economic implications of corporate financial reporting, in: Journal of Accounting and Economics, 40 (1-3), p. 3-73.

Grant Thornton (ed.) (2010): The Bottomline – South Africa leads the way for global auditing and reporting standards, available at: http://www.gt.co.za, last revised 09/03/2016.

Graser, S. (2011): Realwirtschaftliche und finanzwirtschaftliche Internationalisierung – Die besondere Relevanz für Emerging Market Multinationals, Wiesbaden (2011).

Gray, S. J. (1988): Towards a theory of cultural influence on the development of accounting systems internationally, in: Abacus, 24 (1), p. 1-15.

Gregoire, T. G./Driver, B. L. (1987): Analysis of ordinal data to detect population differences, in: Psychological Bulletin, 101 (1), p. 159-165.

Grill, P. (2011): Die Bedeutung strategisch wertvoller Ressourcen für erfolgreiche Mergers & Acquisitions-Entscheidungen, Wiesbaden (2011).

Grochla, E. (1978): Einführung in die Organisationstheorie, Stuttgart (1978).

Grootings, P. (1986): Technology and work: a topic for East-West comparison?, in: Grootings, P. (ed.): Technology and Work. East-West comparison, London (1986), p. 275-301.

Güleş, N. (2014): Way ahead – South Africa's pioneering introduction of integrated reporting has had far-reaching consequences, in: Accounting and Business Magazine (International edition), 17 (3), p. 26-28.

Gup, B. (2005): Capital Markets, Globalization, and Economic Development, New York (2005).

H

Hail, L. (2002): The impact of voluntary corporate disclosures on the ex-ante cost of capital for Swiss firms, in: European Accounting Review, 11 (4), p. 741-773.

Hail, L./Leuz, C. (2006): International Differences in the Cost of Equity Capital: Do Legal Institutions and Securities Regulation Matter?, in: Journal of Accounting Research, 44 (3), p. 485-531.

Hail, L./Leuz, C. (2009): Cost of capital effects and changes in growth expectations around U.S. cross-listings, in: Journal of financial economics, 93 (3), p. 428-454.

Haller, A. (1988): Positive Accounting Theory, in: Die Betriebswirtschaft, 48 (3), p. 398-399.

Haller, A. (1994): Positive Accounting Theory – Die Erforschung der Beweggründe bilanzpolitischen Verhaltens, in: Die Betriebswirtschaft: DBW, 54, p. 597-612.

Haller, A. (2002): Financial accounting developments in the European Union: past events and future prospects, in: European Accounting Review, 11 (1), p. 153-190.

Halpern, P. J. (2000): Systemic perspectives on corporate governance systems, in: Cohen, S. S./Boyd, G. (eds.): Corporate governance and globalization: Long range planning issues, Cheltenham (2000), p. 1-58.

Hammond, T./Clayton, B. M./Arnold, P. J. (2012): An "unofficial" history of race relations in the South African accounting industry, 1968–2000: Perspectives of South Africa's first black chartered accountants, in: Critical perspectives on accounting, 23 (4–5), p. 332–350.

Han, J. C./Wang, S.-w. (1998): Political costs and earnings management of oil companies during the 1990 Persian Gulf crisis, in: Accounting Review, 73 (1), p. 103-117.

Haniffa, R. M./Cooke, T. E. (2002): Culture, corporate governance and disclosure in Malaysian corporations, in: Abacus, 38 (3), p. 317-349.

Hannan, M. T./Freeman, J. (1977): The population ecology of organizations, in: American Journal of Sociology, 82 (5), p. 929-964.

Hantrais, L. (1999): Contextualization in cross-national comparative research, in: International Journal of Social Research Methodology, 2 (2), p. 93-108.

Hantrais, L. (2009): International Comparative Research: Theory, Methods and Practice, Houndmills (2009).

Harvey, C. R. (1995): The Risk Exposure of Emerging Equity Markets, in: The World Bank Economic Review, 9 (1), p. 19-50.

Hasnas, J. (1998): The Normative Theories of Business Ethics: A Guide for the Perplexed, in: Business Ethics Quarterly, 8 (1), p. 19.

Hassan, O./Marston, C. (2010): Disclosure measurement in the empirical accounting literature: A review article (Working Paper), available at: http://www.hw.ac.uk, last revised 09/03/2016.

Hasse, R./Krücken, G. (2005): Neo-Institutionalismus, 2nd edition, Bielefeld (2005).

Healy, P. M./Hutton, A. P./Palepu, K. G. (1999): Stock Performance and Intermediation Changes Surrounding Sustained Increases in Disclosure, in: Contemporary Accounting Research, 16 (3), p. 485-520.

Healy, P. M./Palepu, K. G. (2001): Information asymmetry, corporate disclosure, and the capital markets: A review of the empirical disclosure literature, in: Journal of Accounting and Economics, 31 (1), p. 405-440.

Healy, P. M./Wahlen, J. M. (1999): A Review of the Earnings Management Literature and Its Implications for Standard Setting, in: Accounting Horizons, 13 (4), p. 365-383.

Heckman, J. J. (1979): Sample Selection Bias as a Specification Error, in: Econometrica, 47 (1), p. 153-161.

Hellriegel, D./Slocum, J. W. (1976): Organizational behavior: contingency views, Saint Paul (1976).

Henzler, H. A. (1992): Vision und Führung, in: Hahn, D./Taylor, B. (eds.): Strategische Unternehmungsplanung – strategische Unternehmungsführung. Stand und Entwicklungstendenzen, 6th edition, Heidelberg (1992), p. 811-824.

Heumann, R. (2005): Value reporting in IFRS-Abschlüssen und Lageberichten, Düsseldorf (2005).

Hills, M. (2002): Kluckhohn and Strodtbeck's Values Orientation Theory. (Online Readings in Psychology and Culture), 4 (4), available at: http://scholarworks.gvsu.edu, last revised 09/03/2016.

Hofbauer, E. (2011): Kapitalkosten bei der Unternehmensbewertung in den Emerging Markets Europas, Wiesbaden (2011).

Hoffman, M. (2012): Integrated Reporting in practice: The South African story, available at: https://www.kpmg.com, last revised 09/03/2016.

Hofstede, G. (1980a): Culture's Consequences: International Differences in Work Related Values, Newbury Park (1980).

Hofstede, G. (1980b): Motivation, leadership, and organization: Do American theories apply abroad?, in: Organizational Dynamics, 9 (1), p. 42-63.

Hofstede, G. (1984): Cultural dimensions in management and planning, in: Asia Pacific Journal of Management, 1 (2), p. 81-99.

Hofstede, G. (2001): Culture's consequences: comparing values, behaviors, institutions, and organizations across nations, 2nd edition, Thousand Oaks (2001).

Hofstede, G./Hofstede, G. J./Minkov, M. (2010): Cultures and Organizations – Software of the Mind, 3rd edition, New York (2010).

Holsti, O. R. (1969): Content analysis for the social sciences and humanities, Reading et al. (1969).

Holthausen, R. W. (2003): Testing the relative power of accounting standards versus incentives and other institutional features to influence the outcome of financial reporting in an international setting, in: Journal of Accounting and Economics, 36 (1-3), p. 271–283.

Hooghiemstra, R. (2010): Letters to the shareholders: A content analysis comparison of letters written by CEOs in the United States and Japan, in: The International Journal of Accounting, 45 (3), p. 275–300.

Hope, O.-K. (2003): Firm-level Disclosures and the Relative Roles of Culture and Legal Origin, in: Journal of International Financial Management & Accounting, 14 (3), p. 218-248.

Hoskisson, R. E./Eden, L./Lau, C. M./Wright, M. (2000): Strategy in emerging economies, in: Academy of Management Journal, 43 (3), p. 249-267.

Hossain, M./Perera, M. H./Rahman, A. R. (1995): Voluntary disclosure in the annual reports of New Zealand companies, in: Journal of International Financial Management & Accounting, 6 (1), p. 69-87.

Hribar, P./Collins, D. W. (2002): Errors in Estimating Accruals: Implications for Empirical Research, in: Journal of Accounting Research, 40 (1), p. 105-134.

Hribar, P./Kravet, T./Wilson, R. (2014): A new measure of accounting quality, in: Review of Accounting Studies, 19 (1), p. 506-538.

Hughes, J. S./Liu, J./Liu, J. (2007): Information asymmetry, diversification, and cost of capital, in: The Accounting Review, 82 (3), p. 705-729.

I

IASB (ed.) (2010): Memorandum of Understanding among the International Standards Board (IASB), the Brazilian Federal Council of Accounting (CFC), and the Brazilian Accounting Pronouncements Committee (CPC), available at: http://www.ifrs.org, last revised 09/03/2016.

Iatridis, G. E. (2012): Audit quality in common-law and code-law emerging markets: Evidence on earnings conservatism, agency costs and cost of equity, in: Emerging Markets Review, 13 (2), p. 101-117.

IBSA Dialogue Forum (ed.) (2015): About IBSA – Introduction, available at: http://www.ibsa-trilateral.org, last revised 10/03/2016.

IFRS Foundation (ed.) (2013a): IFRS application around the world – jurisdiction profile: Brazil, available at: http://www.ifrs.org, last revised 09/03/2016.

IFRS Foundation (ed.) (2013b): IFRS application around the world – jurisdictional profile: South Africa, available at: http://www.ifrs.org, last revised 09/03/2016.

IMF (ed.) (2014): World Economic Outlook Database – October 2014 edition, available at: https://www.imf.org, last revised 09/03/2016.

IMF (ed.) (2015a): How does the WEO categorize advanced versus emerging market and developing economies?, available at: https://www.imf.org, last revised 09/03/2016.

IMF (ed.) (2015b): Detailed assessment of implementation on the IOSCO objectives and principles of securities regulation, available at: https://www.imf.org, last revised 09/03/2016.

IMF (ed.) (2015c): World Economic Outlook – Update, available at: http://www.imf.org, last revised 09/03/2016.

IMF (ed.) (2015d): World economic outlook, April 2015 – Uneven Growth, Washington (2015).

Inchausti, B. G. (1997): The influence of company characteristics and accounting regulation on information disclosed by Spanish firms, in: European Accounting Review, 6 (1), p. 45-68.

Integrated Reporting Committee of South Africa (ed.) (2014): Preparing an integrated report – A starter's guide, available at: http://www.integratedreportingsa.org, last revised 09/03/2016.

International Finance Corporation (ed.) (2015): IFC's Sustainability Framework, available at: http://www.ifc.org, last revised 09/03/2016.

Ioannou, I./Serafeim, G. (2014): The Consequences of Mandatory Corporate Sustainability Reporting: Evidence from Four Countries – Working Paper, available at: http://www.hbs.edu, last revised 09/03/2016.

J

Janovsky, J./Khashabian, B./Pilarek, D./Pulg, C. (2011): Marktexpansion in Schwellenländern – Mit Service-Innovationen zum Geschäftserfolg, Wiesbaden (2011).

Jeanjean, T./Stolowy, H. (2008): Do accounting standards matter? An exploratory analysis of earnings management before and after IFRS adoption, in: Journal of Accounting and Public Policy, 27 (6), p. 480-494.

Jenner, T. (2001): Zur Verwendung des Kontingenzansatzes in der betriebswirtschaftlichen Forschung, in: Das Wirtschaftsstudium, 30 (1), p. 79-84.

Jensen, M. C./Meckling, W. H. (1976): Theory of the firm: Managerial behavior, agency costs and ownership structure, in: Journal of Financial Economics, 3 (4), p. 305-360.

Jiang, H./Habib, A. (2009): The impact of different types of ownership concentration on annual report voluntary disclosures in New Zealand, in: Accounting Research Journal, 22 (3), p. 275-304.

Johannesburg Stock Exchange (ed.) (2004): Guide to Calculation Methods for the FTSE/JSE Africa Index Series, available at: https://www.jse.co.za, last revised 10/03/2016.

Johannesburg Stock Exchange (ed.) (2015): JSE Overview, available at: https://www.jse.co.za, last revised 09/03/2016.

Jonas, G. J./Blanchet, J. (2000): Assessing Quality of Financial Reporting, in: Accounting Horizons, 14 (3), p. 353-363.

Jones, J. J. (1991): Earnings Management During Import Relief Investigations, in: Journal of Accounting Research, 29 (2), p. 193-228.

K

Kajüter, P. (2011): Wertorientierte Performancemessung, in: Busse von Colbe, W./Coenenberg, A. G./Kajüter, P./Linnhoff, U./Pellens, B. (eds.): Betriebswirtschaft für Führungskräfte. Eine Einführung für Ingenieure, Naturwissenschaftler, Juristen und Geisteswissenschaftler, 4th edition, Stuttgart (2011), p. 452-470.

Kajüter, P. (2013): Aktuelle Entwicklungen in der Unternehmensberichterstattung. Konzernlagebericht nach DRS 20 – Management Commentary – Integrated Reporting, in: Freidank, C.-C./Velte, P. (eds.): Unternehmenssteuerung im Umbruch. Internationale Reformen in Reporting und Corporate Governance, Berlin (2013), p. 119-153.

Kajüter, P. (2014a): Das Rahmenkonzept des IIRC zum Integrated Reporting – Revolution in der Unternehmensberichterstattung?, in: Deutsches Steuerrecht, 52 (5), p. 222-225.

Kajüter, P. (2014b): Nachhaltigkeitsberichterstattung nach den G4-Leitlinien der GRI, in: Die Wirtschaftsprüfung, 67 (12), p. 599-607.

Kajüter, P./Blaesing, D./Hannen, S. (2013): "Connectivity of information" as a key principle of integrated reporting, in: IRZ, 8 (5), p. 199–205.

Kajüter, P./Nienhaus, M./Mohrschladt, H. (2015): Chancen- und Risikoberichterstattung nach DRS 20 – Berichtspraxis und Anwendungserfahrungen bei DAX- und MDAX-Unternehmen, in: Die Wirtschaftsprüfung, 68 (11), p. 514–525.

Kamarudin, K. A./Wan Ismail, W. A. (2014): Earnings Quality Construct and Measures in Empirical Accounting Studies, available at: http://www.researchgate.net, last revised 09/03/2016.

Kanagaretnam, K./Lobo, G. J./Yang, D.-H. (2004): Joint Tests of Signaling and Income Smoothing through Bank Loan Loss Provisions, in: Contemporary Accounting Research, 21 (4), p. 843–884.

Karamanou, I./Vafeas, N. (2005): The Association between Corporate Boards, Audit Committees, and Management Earnings Forecasts: An Empirical Analysis, in: Journal of Accounting Research, 43 (3), p. 453–486.

Kassarjian, H. H. (1977): Content Analysis in Consumer Research, in: The Journal of Consumer Research, 4 (1), p. 8–18.

Kast, F. E./Rosenzweig, J. E. (1972): General systems theory: Applications for organization and management, in: Academy of Management Journal, 15 (4), p. 447-465.

Kent, P./Routledge, J./Stewart, J. (2010): Innate and discretionary accruals quality and corporate governance, in: Accounting & Finance, 50 (1), p. 171-195.

Kent, P./Zunker, T. (2013): Attaining legitimacy by employee information in annual reportsnull, in: Accounting, Auditing & Accountability Journal, 26 (7), p. 1072–1106.

Keukeleire, S./Mattlin, M./Hooijmaaijers, B./Behr, T./Jokela, J./Wigell, M./Kononenko, V. (2011): The EU Foreign Policy towards the BRICS and Other Emerging Powers: Objectives and Strategies, available at: http://dseu.lboro.ac.uk, last revised 09/03/2016.

Khor, A. K. (2003): Social contract theory, legitimacy theory and corporate social and environmental disclosure policies: constructing a theoretical framework – Nottingham University Business School, Nottingham (2003).

Kim, J./Mahoney, J. T. (2005): Property rights theory, transaction costs theory, and agency theory: an organizational economics approach to strategic management, in: Managerial and Decision Economics, 26 (4), p. 223-242.

Kluckhohn, F. R./Strodtbeck, F. L. (1961): Variations in value orientations, Evanston (1961).

Knutson, P. H. (1993): Financial Reporting in the 1990s and Beyond: A Position Paper, Charlottesville (1993).

Kornmeier, M. (2007): Wissenschaftstheorie und wissenschaftliches Arbeiten – Eine Einführung für Wirtschaftswissenschaftler, Heidelberg (2007).

Kosiol, E. (1964): Betriebswirtschaftslehre und Unternehmensforschung – Eine Untersuchung ihrer Standorte und Beziehungen auf wissenschaftstheoretischer Grundlage, in: Zeitschrift für Betriebswirtschaft, 34 (5), p. 743-762.

Kostyuk, A. (2003): Board practices: an international review, in: Corporate Ownership and Control, 1 (1), p. 102 111.

Kothari, S. P./Leone, A. J./Wasley, C. E. (2005): Performance matched discretionary accrual measures, in: Journal of Accounting and Economics, 39 (1), p. 163-197.

KPMG (ed.) (2013): Accounting News – Aktuelles zur Rechnungslegung nach HGB und IFRS, available at: http://www.kpmg.com, last revised 09/03/2016.

Krippendorff, K. (2013): Content Analysis – An Introduction to Its Methodology, 3rd edition, Newbury Park (2013).

Krishnamurti, C./Šević, A./Šević, Ž. (2005): Voluntary disclosure, transparency, and market quality: Evidence from emerging market ADRs, in: Journal of Multinational Financial Management, 15 (4-5), p. 435-454.

Kromrey, H. (2009): Empirische Sozialforschung – Modelle und Methoden der standardisierten Datenerhebung und Datenauswertung, 12th edition, Stuttgart (2009).

Kruskal, W. H./Wallis, W. A. (1952): Use of Ranks in One-Criterion Variance Analysis, in: Journal of the American Statistical Association, 47 (260), p. 583-621.

Kumar, G. (2014): Determinants of Readability of Financial Reports of U.S.-Listed Asian Companies, in: Asian Journal of Finance & Accounting, 6 (2), p. 1-18.

Küting, K./Weber, C.-P. (2012): Der Konzernabschluss – Praxis der Konzernrechnungslegung nach HGB und IFRS, 13th edition, Stuttgart (2012).

L

La Porta, R./Lopez-de-Silanes, F./Shleifer, A./Vishny, R. (1997): Legal determinants of external finance, in: Journal of Finance, 52 (3), p. 1131-1150.

La Porta, R./López-de-Silanes, F./Shleifer, A./Vishny, R. (1998): Law and Finance, in: Journal of Political Economy, 106 (6), p. 1113-1155.

La Porta, R./Lopez-de-Silanes, F./Shleifer, A./Vishny, R. (2000): Investor protection and corporate governance, in: Journal of Financial Economics, 58 (1), p. 3-27.

Lambert, R./Leuz, C./Verrecchia, R. E. (2007): Accounting information, disclosure, and the cost of capital, in: Journal of Accounting Research, 45 (2), p. 385-420.

Lambert, R./Leuz, C./Verrecchia, R. E. (2012): Information asymmetry, information precision, and the cost of capital, in: Review of Finance, 16 (1), p. 1-29.

Lane, C. (1989): Management and labour in Europe – The industrial enterprise in Germany, Britain and France, Aldershot (1989).

Lang, M./Lundholm, R. (1993): Cross-Sectional Determinants of Analyst Ratings of Corporate Disclosures, in: Journal of Accounting Research, 31 (2), p. 246-271.

Leftwich, R. W./Watts, R. L./Zimmerman, J. L. (1981): Voluntary Corporate Disclosure: The Case of Interim Reporting, in: Journal of Accounting Research, 19 (Supplement), p. 50–77.

Lerchenmüller, J. (2012): Measurement, determinants and consequences of forward-looking reporting disclosure, Vallendar (2012).

Lesmond, D. A. (2005): Liquidity of emerging markets, in: Journal of Financial Economics, 77 (2), p. 411-452.

Lesmond, D. A./Ogden, J. P./Trzcinka, C. A. (1999): A New Estimate of Transaction Costs, in: The Review of Financial Studies, 12 (5), p. 1113-1141.

Lessambo, F. I. (2014): The International Corporate Governance System: Audit Roles and Board Oversight, Houndmills (2014).

Leuz, C./Nanda, D./Wysocki, P. D. (2003): Earnings management and investor protection: an international comparison, in: Journal of Financial Economics, 69 (3), p. 505-527.

Leuz, C./Oberholzer-Gee, F. (2006): Political relationships, global financing, and corporate transparency: Evidence from Indonesia, in: Journal of Financial Economics, 81 (2), p. 411-439.

Leuz, C./Verrecchia, R. E. (2000): The economic consequences of increased disclosure, in: Journal of Accounting Research, 38 (Supplement), p. 91-124.

Levitt, A. (2012): Understanding The Risk In The BRICs, available at: http://www.investopedia.com, last revised 09/03/2016.

Li, F. (2008): Annual report readability, current earnings, and earnings persistence, in: Economic Consequences of Alternative Accounting Standards and Regulation, 45 (2–3), p. 221-247.

Lindahl, F./Schadewitz, H. (2013): Are Legal Families Related to Financial Reporting Quality?, in: Abacus: A Journal of Accounting, Finance and Business Studies, 49 (2), p. 242-267.

Lindblom, C. K. (1994): The implications of organizational legitimacy for corporate social performance and disclosure – Critical perspectives on accounting conference, New York (Volume 120), in: Gray, R./Bebbington, J./Gray, S. (eds.): Social and environmental accounting. Volume 2: Developing the field, London (2010), p. 51-63.

Lingnau, V. (1995): Kritischer Rationalismus und Betriebswirtschaftslehre, in: Wirtschaftswissenschaftliches Studium, 24 (3), p. 124-129.

Liu, C./Yao, L. J./Hu, N./Liu, L. (2011): The impact of IFRS on accounting quality in a regulated market: An empirical study of China, in: Journal of Accounting, Auditing & Finance, 26 (4), p. 659-676.

Lockhart, J. (1983): Early Latin America: A History of Colonial Spanish America and Brazil, Cambridge (1983).

Lopes, A. B. (2011): Teaching IFRS in Brazil: News from the front, in: Accounting Education, 20 (4), p. 339-347.

Lopes, A. B./de Alencar, R. C. (2010): Disclosure and cost of equity capital in emerging markets: The Brazilian case, in: The International Journal of Accounting, 45 (4), p. 443-464.

Lopes, A. B./Walker, M. (2012): Asset revaluations, future firm performance and firm-level corporate governance arrangements: New evidence from Brazil, in: The British Accounting Review, 44 (2), p. 53-67.

Lopes, R. B./Tukamoto, Y./Galdi, F. C. (2007): Earnings management and cross listing in Brazil, available at: http://citeseerx.ist.psu.edu, last revised 09/03/2016.

Loughran, T./McDonald, B. (2014): Measuring Readability in Financial Disclosures, in: The Journal of Finance, 69 (4), p. 1643-1671.

Lundholm, R. J./Rogo, R./Zhang, J. L. (2014): Restoring the Tower of Babel: How Foreign Firms Communicate with U.S. Investors, in: Accounting Review, 89 (4), p. 1453-1485.

M

Ma, T. (2012): Financial Reporting Quality and Information Asymmetry: Evidence from the Chinese Stock Market, available at: http://www.nber.org, last revised 09/03/2016.

Machado, M. A./Macedo, M. A./Machado, M. R. (2015): Analysis of the Relevance of Information Content of the Value Added Statement in the Brazilian Capital Markets, in: Revista Contabilidade & Finanças, 26 (67), p. 57-69.

Mäki, U. (2008): Economics, in: Psillos, S./Curd, M. (eds.): The Routledge companion to philosophy of science, London, New York (2008), p. 543-554.

Mankiw, N. G./Shapiro, M. D. (1984): Risk and return: Consumption versus market beta – Working Paper No. 1399, available at: http://sa.shufe.edu.cn, last revised 09/03/2016.

Marston, C. (1986): Financial reporting in India, London, Dover (1986).

Marston, C./Polei, A. (2004): Corporate reporting on the Internet by German companies, in: International Journal of Accounting Information Systems, 5 (3), p. 285–311.

Marston, C. L./Shrives, P. J. (1991): The use of disclosure indices in accounting research: a review article, in: The British Accounting Review, 23 (3), p. 195-210.

Maurer, T. J./Pierce, H. R. (1998): A comparison of Likert scale and traditional measures of self-efficacy, in: Journal of Applied Psychology, 83 (2), p. 324-329.

Maurice, M./Sorge, A./Warner, M. (1980): Societal differences in organizing manufacturing units: A comparison of France, West Germany, and Great Britain, in: Organization Studies, 1 (1), p. 59-86.

May, C. (2014): Die Kultur des Kapitalismus in Brasilien, Indien und China, in: Nölke, A./May, C./Claar, S. (eds.): Die großen Schwellenländer. Ursachen und Folgen ihres Aufstiegs in der Weltwirtschaft, Wiesbaden (2014), p. 85-99.

McGee, R. W./Preobragenskaya, G. G. (2005): Accounting and Financial System Reform in a Transition Economy: A Case Study of Russia: A Case Study of Russia, Boston (2005).

McNichols, M./Wilson, G. P. (1988): Evidence of Earnings Management from the Provision for Bad Debts, in: Journal of Accounting Research, 26 (Supplement), p. 1–31.

McNichols, M. F./Stubben, S. R. (2008): Does earnings management affect firms' investment decisions?, in: The Accounting Review, 83 (6), p. 1571-1603.

Meinhövel, H. (2005): Grundlagen der Principal-Agent Theorie, in: Horsch, A./Meinhövel, H./Paul, S. (eds.): Institutionenökonomie und Betriebswirtschaftslehre, München (2005), p. 65-80.

Meran, J. (1979): Individualismus oder Kollektivismus?, in: Zeitschrift für allgemeine Wissenschaftstheorie, 10 (1), p. 35-53.

MerComm (ed.) (2015): ARC Awards International XXIX – Judging Procedures, available at: http://www.mercommawards.com, last revised 09/03/2016.

Merten, K. (1995): Inhaltsanalyse – Einführung in Theorie, Methode und Praxis, 2nd edition, Opladen (1995).

Meyer, H. (2010): Aktuelle Entwicklungen des Enforcement in Deutschland, in: IRZ, 5 (4), p. 153–158.

Meyer, K. (2009): Industry specialization and discretionary accruals for Big 4 and non-Big 4 auditors, available at: http://diginole.lib.fsu.edu, last revised 09/03/2016.

Milne, M. J. (2002): Positive accounting theory, political costs and social disclosure analyses: A critical look, in: Critical Perspectives on Accounting, 13 (3), p. 369-395.

Milne, M. J./Adler, R. W. (1999): Exploring the reliability of social and environmental disclosures content analysis, in: Accounting, Auditing & Accountability Journal, 12 (2), p. 237-256.

Morgan, G. (2006): Images of Organization, Williston (2006).

Morgan Stanley (ed.) (2013): Tales from the Emerging World, available at: https://www.morganstanley.com, last revised 09/03/2016.

Morris, R. D. (1987): Signalling, Agency Theory and Accounting Policy Choice, in: Accounting & Business Research, 18 (69), p. 47-56.

Moxter, A. (1976): Fundamentalgrundsätze ordnungsmäßiger Rechenschaft, in: Baetge, J./Moxter, A./Schneider, D. (eds.): Bilanzfragen. Festschrift zum 65. Geburtstag von Ulrich Leffson, Düsseldorf (1976), p. 87–100.

MSCI (ed.) (2015): MSCI Emerging Markets Index (USD), available at: https://www.msci.com, last revised 09/03/2016.

Müller-Armack, A. (1976): Wirtschaftsordnung und Wirtschaftspolitik: Studien und Konzepte zur sozialen Marktwirtschaft und zur Europäischen Integration, 2nd. edition, Bern (1976).

Mulyaningsih, T. (2014): Banking competition and its relationship with banking stability: Evidence from Indonesia 1980-2010 – Dissertation, available at: http://www.canberra.edu.au, last revised 09/03/2016.

Muresan, S. S. (2014): Social Market Economy: The Case of Germany, Heidelberg (2014).

N

Nel, E. (2001): Local Economic Development: A Review and Assessment of its Current Status in South Africa, in: Urban Studies, 38 (7), p. 1003–1024.

Neuendorf, K. A. (2002): The content analysis guidebook, Thousand Oaks (2002).

Newson, M./Deegan, C. (2002): Global expectations and their association with corporate social disclosure practices in Australia, Singapore, and South Korea, in: The International Journal of Accounting, 37 (2), p. 183-213.

Nienhaus, M. (2015): Segment Reporting under IFRS 8 – Reporting Practice and Economic Consequences, Frankfurt am Main (2015).

Nikolaev, V./van Lent, L. (2005): The endogeneity bias in the relation between cost-of-debt capital and corporate disclosure policy, in: European Accounting Review, 14 (4), p. 677-724.

Nobes, C. (1998): Towards a general model of the reasons for international differences in financial reporting, in: Abacus, 34 (2), p. 162-187.

Nobes, C. (2012): Causes and examples of international differences, in: Nobes, C./Parker, R. H. (eds.): Comparative international accounting, 12th edition, Harlow et al. (2012), p. 27-54.

Nobes, C. (2014): International classification of financial reporting, 3rd edition, London (2014).

Nölke, A./May, C./Claar, S. (2014): Ursachen und Folgen des Aufstiegs der großen Schwellenländer in der Weltwirtschaft: Perspektiven der Politikwissenschaft, in: Nölke, A./May, C./Claar, S. (eds.): Die großen Schwellenländer. Ursachen und Folgen ihres Aufstiegs in der Weltwirtschaft, Wiesbaden (2014), p. 9-18.

Nölke, A./Vliegenthart, A. (2009): Enlarging the varieties of capitalism: The emergence of dependent market economies in East Central Europe, in: World Politics, 61 (4), p. 670-702.

Nurmi, H. (2006): Models of Political Economy, Abingdon (2006).

O

O'Neill, J./Wilson, D./Purushothaman, R./Stupnytska, A. (2005): How Solid are the BRICs? – Global Economics Paper No: 134. Goldman Sachs, available at: https://portal.gs.com, last revised 09/03/2016.

Oberdörster, T. (2009): Finanzberichterstattung und Prognosefehler von Finanzanalysten, Wiesbaden (2009).

O'Donovan, G. (2002): Environmental disclosures in the annual report: Extending the applicability and predictive power of legitimacy theory, in: Accounting, Auditing & Accountability Journal, 15 (3), p. 344-371.

OECD (ed.) (2011): Special Focus: Inequality in Emerging Economies (EEs), available at: http://www.oecd.org, last revised 09/03/2016.

OECD (ed.) (2014): Germany: Keeping the Edge – Competitiveness for Inclusive Growth, Paris (2014).

OECD (ed.) (2015): Members and partners, available at: http://www.oecd.org, last revised 09/03/2016.

O'Neill, J. (2001): Building Better Global Economic BRICs. Global Economics Paper No: 66, available at: http://www.goldmansachs.com, last revised 09/03/2016.

Opp, K.-D./Schmidt, P. (1976): Einführung in die Mehrvariablenanalyse: Grundlagen der Formulierung und Prüfung komplexer sozialwissenschaftlicher Aussagen, Reinbek (1976).

Orij, R. (2010): Corporate social disclosures in the context of national cultures and stakeholder theory, in: Accounting, Auditing & Accountability Journal, 23 (7), p. 868-889.

Otley, D. T. (1980): The contingency theory of management accounting: achievement and prognosis, in: Accounting, Organizations and Society, 5 (4), p. 413-428.

Owusu-Ansah, S. (1998): The Impact of Corporate Attributes on the Extent of Mandatory Disclosure and Reporting by Listed Companies in Zimbabwe, in: The International Journal of Accounting, 33 (5), p. 605-631.

P

Paisley, W. J. (1969): Studying Style as Deviation from Encoding Norms, in: Gerbner, G./Holsti, O. R./Krippendorff, K./Paisley, W. J./Stone, P. J. (eds.): The Analysis of Communication Content: Developments in Scientific Theories and Computer Techniques, New York (1969), p. 133-146.

Parry, M. J./Groves, R. E. (1990): Does training more accountants raise the standards of accounting in Third World Countries? A study of Bangladesh, in: Research in Third World Accounting, 1, p. 117-140.

Patten, D. M. (1992): Intra-industry environmental disclosures in response to the Alaskan oil spill: a note on legitimacy theory, in: Accounting, Organizations and Society, 17 (5), p. 471-475.

Pava, M. L./Krausz, J. (1997): Criteria for evaluating the legitimacy of corporate social responsibility, in: Journal of Business Ethics, 16 (3), p. 337-347.

Pellens, B./Fülbier, R. U./Gassen, J./Sellhorn, T. (2014): Internationale Rechnungslegung. IFRS 1 bis 13, IAS 1 bis 41, IFRIC-Interpretationen, Standardentwürfe; mit Beispielen, Aufgaben und Fallstudie, 9th edition, Stuttgart (2014).

Peng, S./van der Laan Smith, J. (2010): Chinese GAAP and IFRS: An analysis of the convergence process, in: Journal of International Accounting, Auditing and Taxation, 19 (1), p. 16-34.

Penman, S. H./Zhang, X.-J. (2002): Accounting Conservatism, the Quality of Earnings, and Stock Returns, in: The Accounting Review, 77 (2), p. 237–264.

Perera, M. H. (1989): Towards a framework to analyze the impact of culture on accounting, in: The International Journal of Accounting, 24 (1), p. 42-56.

Picot, A. (1991): Ökonomische Theorien der Organisation – Ein Überblick über neuere Ansätze und deren betriebswirtschaftliches Anwendungspotential, in: Ordelheide, D./Rudolph, B./Büsselmann, E. (eds.): Betriebswirtschaftslehre und Ökonomische Theorie, Stuttgart (1991), p. 143-170.

Pilz, G. (2008): Emerging Markets: Geld anlegen in Schwellenländern, München (2008).

Polishchuk, L. (1997): Missed Markets: Implications for Economic Behavior and Institutional Change, in: Nelson, J. M./Tilly, C./Walker, L. (eds.): Transforming post-Communist political economies, Washington, D.C. (1997), p. 80-101.

Popper, K. R. (1957): Philosophy of Science – A Personal Report, in: Mace, C. A. (ed.): British Philosophy in the Mid-Century, a Cambridge Symposium, London (1957), p. 155-189.

Popper, K. R. (2005): Logik der Forschung, 11th edition, Tübingen (2005).

Pospeschill, M. (2006): Statistische Methoden – Strukturen, Grundlagen, Anwendungen in Psychologie und Sozialwissenschaften, München (2006).

Pounder, B. (2013): Measuring Accounting Quality, in: Strategic Finance, 95 (5), p. 18-20.

Pratt, J. W./Zeckhauser, R. J. (1985): Principals and Agents: An Overview, in: Pratt, J. W./Zeckhauser, R. J. (eds.): Principals and Agents: The Structure of Business, Boston (1985), p. 1-35.

Prigge, C. (2006): Konzernlageberichterstattung vor dem Hintergrund einer Bilanzierung nach IFRS, Düsseldorf (2006).

PwC (ed.) (2014): IFRS adoption by country, available at: http://www.pwc.com, last revised 09/03/2016.

PwC (ed.) (2015a): IFRS in India – Mandatory applicability, available at: http://www.pwc.in, last revised 09/03/2016.

PwC (ed.) (2015b): The World in 2050 – Will the shift in global economic power continue?, available at: www.pwc.co.uk, last revised 09/03/2016.

R

Radebaugh, L. H./Gray, S. J./Black, E. L. (2006): International accounting and multinational enterprises, 6th edition, New York (2006).

Raffée, H. (1993): Gegenstand, Methoden und Konzepte der Betriebswirtschaftslehre, in: Bitz, M./Egner, H./Domsch, M./Dellmann, K./Baetge, J. (eds.): Vahlens Kompendium der Betriebswirtschaftslehre 1, 3rd edition, München (1993), p. 1-46.

Raffée, H./Abel, B. (1979): Einführung – Aufgaben und aktuelle Tendenzen der Wissenschaftstheorie in den Wirtschaftswissenschaften, in: Raffée, H./Abel, B. (eds.): Wissenschaftstheoretische Grundfragen der Wirtschaftswissenschaften, München (1979), p. 1-10.

Rajagopalan, N./Zhang, Y. (2008): Corporate governance reforms in China and India: Challenges and opportunities, in: Business Horizons, 51 (1), p. 55-64.

Ramanathan, K. V. (1976): Toward a Theory of Corporate Social Accounting, in: The Accounting Review, 21 (3), p. 516-528.

Refaat, M. (2007): Data Preparation for Data Mining Using SAS, Amsterdam (2007).

Regierungskommission Deutscher Corporate Governance Kodex (ed.) (2015): Deutscher Corporate Governance Kodex, available at: http://www.dcgk.de, last revised 09/03/2016.

Reisloh, C. (2011): Influence of national culture on IFRS practice – An empirical study in France, Germany and the United Kingdom, Frankfurt am Main (2011).

Rhoades, S. A. (1993): The Herfindahl-Hirschman Index, in: Federal Reserve Bulletin 79 (3), p. 188-189.

Robb, Sean W. G./Single, L. E./Zarzeski, M. T. (2001): Nonfinancial disclosures across Anglo-American countries, in: Journal of International Accounting, Auditing and Taxation, 10 (1), p. 71-83.

Rodrigues, L. L./Schmidt, P./dos Santos, J. L./Fonseca, P. C. D. (2011): A research note on accounting in Brazil in the context of political, economic and social transformations, 1860-1964, in: Accounting History, 16 (1), p. 111-123.

Rodrigues, L. L./Schmidt, P./dos Santos, J.L. (2012): The origins of modern accounting in Brazil: Influences leading to the adoption of IFRS, in: Research in Accounting Regulation, 24 (1), p. 15-24.

Rokeach, M. (1979): Understanding human values: Individual and societal, New York (1979).

Rosefielde, S. (2007): The Russian Economy: From Lenin to Putin, Malden (2007).

Rössler, P. (2010): Inhaltsanalyse, Konstanz (2010).

S

Salewski, M./Teuteberg, T./Zülch, H. (2014): Short-Term and Long-Term Effects of IFRS Adoption on Disclosure Quality and Earnings Management, available at: http://papers.ssrn.com, last revised 09/03/2016.

Salter, S. B. (1998): Corporate Financial Disclosure in Emerging Markets: Does Economic Development Matter?, in: The International Journal of Accounting, 33 (2), p. 211-234.

Salzman, J. (2003): Methodological Choices Encountered in the Construction of Composite Indices of Economic and Social Well-Being. Edited by Centre for the Study of Living Standards, available at: http://www.csls.ca, last revised 09/03/2016.

Santema, S./van de Rijt, J. (2001): Strategy disclosure in Dutch annual reports, in: European Management Journal, 19 (1), p. 101-108.

Santos, E. S./Ponte, V. M. R./Mapurunga, P. V. R. (2014): Mandatory IFRS Adoption in Brazil (2010): Index of Compliance with Disclosure Requirements and Explanatory Factors of Firms Reporting, in: Revista Contabilidade & Finanças, 25 (65), p. 161-176.

Saucke, M. (2015): Full IFRS and IFRS for SMEs adoption by private firms. Empirical evidence on country level, Frankfurt am Main et al. (2015).

Saudagaran, S. M./Diga, J. G. (1998): Accounting harmonization in ASEAN: Benefits, models and policy issues, in: Journal of International Accounting, Auditing and Taxation, 7 (1), p. 21-45.

Schewe, G. (2015): Unternehmensverfassung. Corporate Governance im Spannungsfeld von Leitung, Kontrolle und Interessenvertretung, 3rd edition, Berlin (2015).

Schick, A. G./Gordon, L. A./Haka, S. (1990): Information overload: A temporal approach, in: Accounting, Organizations and Society, 15 (3), p. 199-220.

Schiehll, E./Terra, P. S./Victor, F. G. (2013): Determinants of voluntary executive stock option disclosure in Brazil, in: Journal of Management & Governance, 17 (2), p. 331–361.

Schipper, K. (1989): Commentary on Earnings Management, in: Accounting Horizons, 3 (4), p. 91-102.

Schipper, K./Vincent, L. (2003): Earnings Quality, in: Accounting Horizons, 17 (Supplement), p. 97-110.

Schmalz, S./Ebenau, M. (2014): Brasilien, Indien und China – Unterschiedliche Transformationspfade in der Krise, in: Nölke, A./May, C./Claar, S. (eds.): Die großen Schwellenländer. Ursachen und Folgen ihres Aufstiegs in der Weltwirtschaft, Wiesbaden (2014), p. 44-59.

Schmid, M./Maurer, A. (2003): Institution und Handeln, in: Schmid, M./Maurer, A. (eds.): Ökonomischer und soziologischer Institutionalismus. Interdisziplinäre Beiträge und Perspektiven der Institutionentheorie und -analyse, Marburg (2003), p. 9-46.

Schmidt, J. (1997): Eigentum und Strategisches Management: Eine systemtheoretische Perspektive für die mittelständische Familienunternehmung – Teil 1: Grundlagenforschung, Wiesbaden (1997).

Schneider, B. R. (2009): Hierarchical market economies and varieties of capitalism in Latin America, in: Journal of Latin American Studies, 41 (3), p. 553-575.

Schwartz, S. H. (1992): Universals in the Content and Structure of Values: Theoretical Advances and Empirical Tests in 20 Cultures, in: Zanna, M. P. (ed.): Advances in Experimental Social Psychology, San Diego (1992), p. 1-65.

Schweitzer, M. (1978): Wissenschaftsziele und Auffassungen in der Betriebswirtschaftslehre – Eine Einführung, in: Schweitzer, M. (ed.): Auffassungen und Wissenschaftsziele der Betriebswirtschaftslehre, Darmstadt (1978), p. 1-14.

Scott, W. R. (2014): Institutions and Organizations. Ideas, Interests & Identities, 4th edition, Los Angeles et al. (2014).

SEC (ed.) (2013): Accessing the U.S. Capital Markets – A Brief Overview for Foreign Private Issuers, available at: http://www.sec.gov, last revised 09/03/2016.

Senge, K. (2006): Zum Begriff der Institution im Neo-Institutionalismus, in: Senge, K./Hellmann, K.-U. (eds.): Einführung in den Neo-Institutionalismus. Mit einem Beitrag von W. Richard Scott, Wiesbaden (2006), p. 35–47.

Sengupta, P. (1998): Corporate disclosure quality and the cost of debt, in: Accounting Review, 73 (4), p. 459-474.

Shaw, K. W. (2003): Corporate disclosure quality, earnings smoothing, and earnings' timeliness, in: Journal of Business Research, 56 (12), p. 1043-1050.

Shaw, R. (2000): Shareholder value or stakeholder value? That is the question, in: Schuster, L. (ed.): Shareholder value management in banks, Basingstoke, New York (2000), p. 36-51.

Shleifer, A./Vishny, R. W. (1986): Large Shareholders and Corporate Control, in: Journal of Political Economy, 94 (3), p. 461-488.

Shocker, A. D./Sethi, S. P. (1973): An Approach to Incorporating Societal Preferences in Developing Corporate Action Strategies, in: California Management Review, 15 (4), p. 97-105.

Singhvi, S. S./Desai, H. B. (1971): An Empirical Analysis of the Quality of Corporate Financial Disclosure, in: The Accounting Review, 46 (1), p. 129-138.

Smith, J./Haniffa, R./Fairbrass, J. (2011): A conceptual framework for investigating 'capture' in corporate sustainability reporting assurance, in: Journal of Business Ethics, 99 (3), p. 425-439.

Sorge, A. (1991): Strategic Fit and the Societal Effect: Interpreting Cross-National Comparisons of Technology, Organization and Human Resources, in: Organization Studies, 12 (2), p. 161-190.

Sorge, A. (1996): Societal effects in Cross-National Organization Studies – Conceptualizing Diversity in actors and systems, in: Whitley, R./Kristensen, P. H. (eds.): The changing European firm: Limits to convergence, London, New York (1996), p. 67-86.

SRI International (ed.) (1987): Investor Information Needs and the Annual Report, Morristown (1987).

Stainbank, L./Peebles, C. (2006): The usefulness of corporate annual reports in South Africa: perceptions of preparers and users, in: Meditari Accountancy Research, 14 (1), p. 69-80.

Steinbach, K. D./Tang, R. Y. W. (2014): IFRS Convergence: Learning from Mexico, Brazil, and Argentina, in: Journal of Corporate Accounting & Finance, 25 (3), p. 31-41.

Stephen, M. D. (2013): Pivotal rising powers India, Brazil, South Africa and contestation in global governance – Dissertation, Berlin (2013).

Sterling, R. R. (1990): Positive accounting: An assessment, in: Abacus, 26 (2), p. 97-135.

Stinchcombe, A. L. (1959): Bureaucratic and craft administration of production: A comparative study, in: Administrative Science Quarterly, 4 (2), p. 168-187.

Stoll, H. R. (2000): Friction, in: The Journal of Finance, 55 (4), p. 1479-1514.

Stolowy, H./Lebas, M. J./Ding, Y. (2013): Financial accounting and reporting – A global perspective, 4th edition, Andover (2013).

Stoney, C./Winstanley, D. (2001): Stakeholding: Confusion or Utopia? Mapping the Conceptual Terrain, in: Journal of Management Studies, 38 (5), p. 603-626.

Stubben, S. R. (2010): Discretionary revenues as a measure of earnings management, in: The Accounting Review, 85 (2), p. 695-717.

Stuenkel, O. (2014): Emerging Powers and Status: The Case of the First BRICs Summit, in: Asian Perspective, 38 (1), p. 89-109.

Subramaniam, N. (2006): Agency theory and accounting research: an overview of some conceptual and empirical issues, in: Hoque, Z. (ed.): Methodological issues in accounting research. Theories, methods and issues, London (2006).

Suchman, M. C. (1995): Managing legitimacy: Strategic and institutional approaches, in: Academy of Management Review, 20 (3), p. 571-610.

Sun, C. (2013): The possible application of international accounting standards in China, Dissertation, University of Birmingham (2013).

Sweeney, P. (1994): Polishing the Tarnised Image of Investor Relations Executives, in: The New York Times (03.04.1994).

T

Tang, Q. (2008): How to Measure Financial Reporting Quality Internationally? (Conference Paper), AFAANZ, Sydney, 2008, available at: http://arrow.uws.edu.au, last revised 09/03/2016.

Tang, Q./Chen, H./Lin, Z. (2012): How to Measure Country level Financial Reporting Quality? (Working Paper), available at: http://papers.ssrn.com, last revised 09/03/2016.

The Economist (ed.) (2006): A question of definition. (September 16th), available at: http://www.economist.com, last revised 09/03/2016.

The Wall Street Journal (ed.) (2015): Fed Rate Move Compounds Fears in Emerging Markets – Worries linger about debt and economic weakness, available at: http://www.wsj.com, last revised 09/03/2016.

The World Bank (ed.) (2005): Report on the observance of standards and codes (ROSC) – Brazil, available at: http://www.worldbank.org/ifa/rosc_aa_bra.pdf, last revised 09/03/2016.

The World Bank (ed.) (2011): Global Development Horizons 2011—Multipolarity: The New Global Economy, available at: http://econ.worldbank.org, last revised 09/03/2016.

The World Bank (ed.) (2014): 2014 World Bank Income Classifications: Kyrgyz Republic Becomes Lower Middle Income Country, available at: http://www.worldbank.org, last revised 09/03/2016.

The World Bank (ed.) (2015a): Global Economic Prospects – Having Fiscal Space and Using It, available at: https://www.worldbank.org, last revised 09/03/2016.

The World Bank (ed.) (2015b): Why use GNI per capita to classify economies into income groupings?, available at: https://datahelpdesk.worldbank.org, last revised 09/03/2016.

Thompson, J. D. (1967): Organizations in action – Social science bases of administrative theory, New York (1967).

Tomlinson, B. R. (2013): The economy of modern India – From 1860 to the twenty-first century, 2nd edition, Cambridge (2013).

Tonkin, D. (1989): World survey of published accounts: an analysis of 200 annual reports from the world's leading companies, London (1989).

Torres, S. (1999): A culturally-relevant theoretical framework for the study of successful ageing, in: Ageing & Society, 19 (1), p. 33-51.

Tosi, H./Aldag, R./Storey, R. (1973): On the measurement of the environment: An assessment of the Lawrence and Lorsch environmental uncertainty subscale, in: Administrative Science Quarterly, 18 (1), p. 27-36.

Tucker, J. W./Zarowin, P. A. (2006): Does Income Smoothing Improve Earnings Informativeness?, in: Accounting Review, 81 (1), p. 251-270.

Turner, L. E. (2000): Charting a Course for High Quality Financial Reporting – Speech by SEC Staff at the European FASB-SEC Financial Reporting Conference Frankfurt, Germany, available at: http://www.sec.gov, last revised 09/03/2016.

U

U.S. Small Business Administration (ed.) (2015): The Leader in SIC and NAICS Codes, available at: https://www.sba.gov, last revised 09/03/2016.

Udy Jr, Stanley H (1959): "Bureaucracy" and "Rationality" in Weber's Organization Theory: An Empirical Study, in: American Sociological Review, 24 (6), p. 791-795.

Ullmann, A. A. (1985): Data in Search of a Theory: A Critical Examination of the Relationships among Social Performance, Social Disclosure, and Economic Performance of U. S. Firms, in: The Academy of Management Review, 10 (3), p. 540-557.

Ulrich, B. (1993): Kontingenztheorie und autopoietische Systemtheorie der Organisation: ein evaluativer Vergleich zweier organisationstheoretischer Ansätze unter besonderer Berücksichtigung der Organisations-Umwelt-Beziehung, Innsbruck (1993).

Ulrich, P./Hill, W. (1976): Wissenschaftstheoretische Grundlagen der Betriebswirtschaftslehre (Teil II), in: Wirtschaftswissenschaftliches Studium, 5 (8), p. 345-350.

Unerman, J. (2000): Methodological issues-reflections on quantification in corporate social reporting content analysis, in: Accounting, Auditing & Accountability Journal, 13 (5), p. 667-681.

United Nations (ed.) (2007): International accounting and reporting issues – 2006 Review, Geneva (2007).

United Nations (ed.) (2013a): Composition of macro geographical (continental) regions, geographical sub-regions, and selected economic and other groupings, available at: http://unstats.un.org, last revised 09/03/2016.

United Nations (ed.) (2013b): World Population Prospects: The 2012 Revision – Volume I: Comprehensive Tables, available at: http://esa.un.org, last revised 09/03/2016.

United Nations (ed.) (2015): The Ten Principles of the UN Global Compact, available at: https://www.unglobalcompact.org, last revised 09/03/2016.

United Nations Development Programme (ed.) (2014): Human Development Report 2014 – Sustaining Human Progress – Reducing Vulnerabilities and Building Resilience, New York (2014).

University of Münster (Research Team Baetge) (ed.) (2015): Die Checklisten für den Wettbewerb „Der beste Geschäftsbericht", available at: http://www.wiwi.uni-muenster.de, last revised 09/03/2016.

V

Vale (ed.) (2015): Investors – CVM annual report, available at: http://www.vale.com, last revised 09/03/2016.

van Beest, F./Braam, G./Boelens, S. (2009): Quality of Financial Reporting: measuring qualitative characteristics, Working Paper 09-108, available at: http://www.ru.nl, last revised 09/03/2016.

van der Laan Smith, J./Adhikari, A./Tondkar, R. H. (2005): Exploring differences in social disclosures internationally: A stakeholder perspective, in: Journal of Accounting and Public Policy, 24 (2), p. 123-151.

van der Merwe, N./McChlery, S./Visser, S. S. (2014): Balancing academic and professional pedagogies: a comparative study of two accounting departments in South Africa and the UK, in: Teaching in Higher Education, 19 (3), p. 276–288.

van der Steen, M. P. (2006): Human agency in management accounting change – A cognitive approach to institutional theory, Groningen (2006).

van Schalkwyk, L. (2013): The insider view: South Africa, in: Financial Management September 2013, p. 18–19.

Verdi, R. S. (2006): Financial Reporting Quality and Investment Efficiency, available at: http://papers.ssrn.com, last revised 09/03/2016.

Verrecchia, R. E. (1983): Discretionary disclosure, in: Journal of Accounting and Economics, 5, p. 179-194.

Verrecchia, R. E. (2001): Essays on disclosure, in: Journal of Accounting and Economics, 32 (1), p. 97-180.

von Auer, L. (2013): Ökonometrie – Eine Einführung, 6th edition, Berlin (2013).

W

Wagenhofer, A./Ewert, R. (2015): Externe Unternehmensrechnung, 3rd edition, Berlin (2015).

Wallace, R. S. O./Naser, K./Mora, A. (1994): The relationship between the comprehensiveness of corporate annual reports and firm characteristics in Spain, in: Accounting and Business Research, 25 (97), p. 41-53.

Wanderley, L. S. O./Lucian, R./Farache, F./de Sousa Filho, J. M. (2008): CSR Information Disclosure on the Web: A Context-Based Approach Analysing the Influence of Country of Origin and Industry Sector, in: Journal of Business Ethics, 82 (2), p. 369-378.

Wang, K./Sewon, O./Claiborne, M. C. (2008): Determinants and consequences of voluntary disclosure in an emerging market: Evidence from China, in: Journal of International Accounting, Auditing and Taxation, 17 (1), p. 14-30.

Watts, R. L. (1995): Developments in positive accounting theory – Introduction, in: Jones, S./Romano, C./Ratnatunga, J. (eds.): Accounting theory. A Contemporary Review, Sydney, London (1995), p. 297-353.

Watts, R. L./Zimmerman, J. L. (1978): Towards a positive theory of the determination of accounting standards, in: Accounting Review, 53 (1), p. 112-134.

Watts, R. L./Zimmerman, J. L. (1986): Positive accounting theory, London (1986).

Watts, R. L./Zimmerman, J. L. (1990): Positive accounting theory: a ten year perspective, in: Accounting Review, 65 (1), p. 131-156.

Weale, A. (2013): Democratic Justice and the Social Contract, New York (2013).

Weiner, A. B. (1980): Reproduction: A replacement for reciprocity, in: American Ethnologist, 7 (1), p. 71-85.

Weinlich, S./Fues, T. (2014): Aufstrebende Schwellenmächte in den Vereinten Nationen, in: Nölke, A./May, C./Claar, S. (eds.): Die großen Schwellenländer. Ursachen und Folgen ihres Aufstiegs in der Weltwirtschaft, Wiesbaden (2014), p. 299-316.

White, G. E. (1970): Discretionary Accounting Decisions and Income Normalization, in: Journal of Accounting Research, 8 (2), p. 260-273.

White, H. (1980): A Heteroskedasticity-Consistent Covariance Matrix Estimator and a Direct Test for Heteroskedasticity, in: Econometrica, 48 (4), p. 817-838.

Wien, A./Franzke, N. (2014): Unternehmenskultur – Zielorientierte Unternehmensethik als entscheidender Erfolgsfaktor, Wiesbaden (2014).

Williamson, O. E. (1975): Markets and Hierarchies: Analysis and Antitrust Implications, New York (1975).

Williamson, O. E. (2000): The new institutional economics: taking stock, looking ahead, in: Journal of Economic Literature, 38 (3), p. 595-613.

Wilson, D./Purushothaman, R. (2003): Dreaming with BRICs: The Path to 2050, Global Economics Paper No: 99, available at: http://www.goldmansachs.com, last revised 09/03/2016.

Wöhe, G./Döring, U. (2013): Einführung in die Allgemeine Betriebswirtschaftslehre, 25th edition, München (2013).

Wolf, J. (2013): Organisation, Management, Unternehmensführung: Theorien, Praxisbeispiele und Kritik, 5th edition, Wiesbaden (2013).

Woodward, J. (1958): Management and technology, London (1958).

World Federation of Exchanges (ed.) (2015): Datasets, available at: https://www.quandl.com, last revised 09/03/2016.

World Heritage Encyclopedia (ed.) (2014a): Emerging market, available at: http://www.worldheritage.org, last revised 09/03/2016.

World Heritage Encyclopedia (ed.) (2014b): Emerging nation, available at: http://www.worldheritage.org, last revised 09/03/2016.

Wysocki, P. (2008): Assessing earnings and accruals quality: U.S. and international evidence (Working Paper), available at: https://www.researchgate.net, last revised 09/03/2016.

Y

Young, M. N./Peng, M. W./Ahlstrom, D./Bruton, G. D./Jiang, Y. (2008): Corporate governance in emerging economies: A review of the principal–principal perspective, in: Journal of Management Studies, 45 (1), p. 196-220.

Z

Zimmermann, E. (1972): Das Experiment in den Sozialwissenschaften, Stuttgart (1972).

Zucker, L. G. (1977): The Role of Institutionalization in Cultural Persistence, in: American Sociological Review, 42 (5), p. 726-743.

Münsteraner Schriften zur Internationalen Unternehmensrechnung

Herausgegeben von Peter Kajüter

Band 1 Daniela Barth: Prognoseberichterstattung. Praxis, Determinanten und Kapitalmarktwirkungen bei deutschen börsennotierten Unternehmen. 2009.

Band 2 Tobias Dickmann: Controllingintegration nach M&A-Transaktionen. Eine empirische Analyse. 2010.

Band 3 Simon Esser: Produktorientiertes Kostenmanagement in der chemischen Industrie. Eine empirische Analyse. 2011.

Band 4 Christian Reisloh: Influence of National Culture on IFRS Practice. An Empirical Study in France, Germany and the United Kingdom. 2011.

Band 5 Matthias Moeschler: Cost Accounting in Germany and Japan. A Comparative Analysis. 2012.

Band 6 Martin Merschdorf: Der Management Approach in der IFRS-Rechnungslegung. Implikationen für Unternehmen und Investoren. 2012.

Band 7 Kristian Bachert: Fair Value Accounting. Implications for Users of Financial Statements. 2012.

Band 8 Daniel Blaesing: Nachhaltigkeitsberichterstattung in Deutschland und den USA. Berichtspraxis, Determinanten und Eigenkapitalkostenwirkungen. 2013.

Band 9 Christina Voets: Kulturelle Einflüsse auf die Anwendung des Impairment-Tests nach IAS 36. Eine experimentelle Untersuchung in Asien und Europa. 2013.

Band 10 Thomas Poplat: Foreign Investments in BRIC Countries. Empirical Evidence from Multinational Corporations. 2014.

Band 11 Moritz Schröder: Cost Accounting in Anglophone Subsidiaries. Empirical Evidence from Germany. 2014.

Band 12 Maximilian Saucke: Full IFRS and IFRS for SMEs Adoption by Private Firms. Empirical Evidence on Country Level. 2015.

Band 13 Martin Nienhaus: Segment Reporting under IFRS 8. Reporting Practice and Economic Consequences. 2015.

Band 14 Gregor Hagemann: Financial Reporting Quality in Emerging Economies. Empirical Evidence from Brazil and South Africa. 2017.

www.peterlang.com